Counterfactual Romanticism

Manchester University Press

Series editors: Anna Barton, Andrew Smith

Editorial board: David Amigoni, Isobel Armstrong, Philip Holden, Jerome McGann, Joanne Wilkes, Julia M. Wright

Interventions: Rethinking the Nineteenth Century seeks to make a significant intervention into the critical narratives that dominate conventional and established understandings of nineteenth-century literature. Informed by the latest developments in criticism and theory the series provides a focus for how texts from the long nineteenth century, and more recent adaptations of them, revitalise our knowledge of and engagement with the period. It explores the radical possibilities offered by new methods, unexplored contexts and neglected authors and texts to re-map the literary-cultural landscape of the period and rigorously re-imagine its geographical and historical parameters. The series includes monographs, edited collections, and scholarly sourcebooks.

Already published

Spain in the nineteenth century: New essays on experiences of culture and society
Andrew Ginger and Geraldine Lawless

Creating character: Theories of nature and nurture in Victorian sensation fiction
Helena Ifill

Margaret Harkness: Writing social engagement 1880–1921   Flore Janssen and Lisa C. Robertson (eds)

Richard Marsh, popular fiction and literary culture, 1890–1915: Re-reading the fin de siècle   Victoria Margree, Daniel Orrells and Minna Vuohelainen (eds)

Charlotte Brontë: Legacies and afterlives   Amber K. Regis and Deborah Wynne (eds)

The Great Exhibition, 1851: A sourcebook   Jonathon Shears (ed.)

Interventions: Rethinking the nineteenth century   Andrew Smith and Anna Barton (eds)

Counterfactual Romanticism

Edited by Damian Walford Davies

Manchester University Press

Copyright © Manchester University Press 2019

While copyright in the volume as a whole is vested in Manchester University Press, copyright in individual chapters belongs to their respective authors, and no chapter may be reproduced wholly or in part without the express permission in writing of both author and publisher.

Published by Manchester University Press
Oxford Road, Manchester M13 9PL
www.manchesteruniversitypress.co.uk

British Library Cataloguing-in-Publication Data is available

ISBN 978 1 7849 9141 8 hardback
ISBN 978 1 5261 7183 2 paperback

First published by Manchester University Press in hardback 2019

This edition first published 2023

The publisher has no responsibility for the persistence or accuracy of URLs for any external or third-party internet websites referred to in this book, and does not guarantee that any content on such websites is, or will remain, accurate or appropriate.

Typeset by Servis Filmsetting Ltd, Stockport, Cheshire

Contents

List of illustrations		*page* vii
Notes on contributors		viii
Acknowledgements		xii
	Introduction: Counterfactual Romanticism *Damian Walford Davies*	1
1	'The object as in itself it really is not': Counterfactual Romanticism and the aesthetics of contingency *Anne C. McCarthy*	33
2	Door-to-door and across-the-counter factuals: history as fashion, furniture, fraud, forgery, folklore and fiction in the Romantic onset of modernity *Gary Kelly*	52
3	The possibilists: Romantic-era literary forgery and British alternative pasts *Mary-Ann Constantine*	79
4	Sophia Lee's *The Recess* and the epistemology of the counterfactual *Tilottama Rajan*	107
5	Lord Byron reads *The Prelude* *Kenneth R. Johnston*	129
6	Counterfactual obstetrics: Mary Wollstonecraft's *Frankenstein* *Damian Walford Davies*	155

Contents

7	John Thelwall: a counterfactual ghost story *Judith Thompson*	202
8	Counterfactual speculations in late Romanticism: Scott, Banim, Galt and Mitford *Angela Esterhammer*	232
9	Piratical counterfactual, piratical counterfictional: from Misson to melodrama *Manushag N. Powell*	251
10	Romanticism and the (counterfactual) Chinese awakening *Peter J. Kitson*	277
11	Counterfactual and future Romanticisms: the academy and the canon *Edward Larrissy*	300
	Index	317

Illustrations

0.1 William Blake, *The Marriage of Heaven and Hell* (1790–93), Plate 10; © Fitzwilliam Museum, Cambridge. *page* 3
6.1 Mary Wollstonecraft, *L'Estrange; Or, The Modern Menoetius. An Irish Tale* (London: Joseph Johnson, 1799). 166
6.2 Jan van Riemsdyk, dissection of a retroverted gravid uterus (five months pregnant), red chalk on paper; preparatory drawing for William Hunter, *Anatomia Uteri Humani Gravidi/Anatomy of the Human Gravid Uterus* (1774), table XXVI, figure 1; Archives and Special Collections, University of Glasgow Library. 174
6.3 Isaac Cruikshank, *A Man-Mid-Wife*, frontispiece to John Blunt [Samuel William Fores], *Man-midwifery Dissected; Or, The Obstetric Family Instructor, for the Use of Married Couples and Single Adults of Both Sexes* (London: S. W. Fores, 1793); Wellcome Collection. 179
6.4 Henry Fuseli, *Theodore Meets in the Wood the Spectre of His Ancestor Guido Cavalcanti* (*c*.1783), oil on canvas, 276 cm × 317 cm; National Museum of Western Art, Tokyo. 180
6.5 Training mannequins ('birthing phantoms') of the kind used by Angélique Marguerite le Boursier du Coudray (*c*.1712–94) in France and, in England, by William Smellie; Musée Flaubert et d'Histoire de la Médecine, CHU de Rouen, France. 185

Notes on contributors

Mary-Ann Constantine is Reader at the University of Wales Centre for Advanced Welsh and Celtic Studies. She works on the literature and history of Romantic-period Wales and Brittany, and has a particular interest in travel writing and in the cultural politics of the 1790s. With Dafydd Johnston, she was General Editor of the ten-volume series, *Wales and the French Revolution* (2012–15; University of Wales Press). Other publications include *The Truth Against the World: Iolo Morganwg and Romantic Forgery* (University of Wales Press, 2007) and (jointly edited with Nigel Leask), *Enlightenment Travel and British Identities: Thomas Pennant's Tours in Scotland and Wales* (Anthem Press, 2017). She is currently working on a book about the Welsh Tour, 1760–1820.

Angela Esterhammer is Principal of Victoria College and Professor of English at the University of Toronto. She is the author of *Creating States: Studies in the Performative Language of John Milton and William Blake* (University of Toronto Press, 1994); *The Romantic Performative: Language and Action in British and German Romanticism* (Stanford University Press, 2000); and *Romanticism and Improvisation, 1750–1850* (Cambridge University Press, 2008). Other publications include the edited and co-edited volumes *Romantic Poetry* (John Benjamins, 2002); *Spheres of Action: Speech and Performance in Romantic Culture* (University of Toronto Press, 2009); and *Romanticism, Rousseau, Switzerland: New Prospects* (Palgrave, 2015). Her current research project – 'Print and Performance in the Late-Romantic Information Age: Speculation, Improvisation, Identity' – examines the interrelations of print culture, theatre, periodicals and fiction during the 1820s. She is General Editor of the *Edinburgh Edition of the Works of John Galt*.

Notes on contributors

Kenneth R. Johnston is Ruth N. Halls Professor of Literature Emeritus at Indiana University – Bloomington, where he was chair of the Department of English. He is the author of *Wordsworth and 'The Recluse'* (Yale University Press, 1984); *The Hidden Wordsworth* (W. W. Norton, 1998); and *Unusual Suspects: Pitt's Reign of Alarm and the Lost Generation of the 1790s* (Oxford University Press, 2013). He has co-edited *The Age of William Wordsworth: Critical Essays on the Romantic Tradition* (Rutgers University Press, 1988) and *Romantic Revolutions* (Indiana University Press, 1990). He has received distinguished scholar awards from the American Conference on Romanticism and the Keats-Shelley Association. His work has been supported by the Guggenheim Foundation, the National Endowment for the Humanities, the Fulbright Commission and the Mellon and Lilly foundations. He has taught at Bucharest, Colorado and Georgetown universities, and has been a fellow of the Institute for the Humanities (Edinburgh).

Gary Kelly is Distinguished University Professor at the University of Alberta, Canada, where he currently teaches Research Methods, Long-eighteenth-century Atlantic Archipelago Studies, History of the Book, and Comparative Literature. He was Canada Research Chair and Director of the CRC Digital Humanities Studio at the University of Alberta, 2001–7. He is General Editor of the ongoing *Oxford History of Popular Print Culture* and author and editor of books on and of the long-eighteenth-century anglophone Atlantic world, especially the novel and women's writing. Current projects include 'Sixpenny Romanticism' and a 'History of Modern Fun'.

Peter J. Kitson is Professor of English in the School of Literature, Drama and Creative Writing at the University of East Anglia, where he specialises in research into the long eighteenth century and the literature of the Romantic period. His books on the subject include *Literature, Science and Exploration in the Romantic Era: Bodies of Knowledge* (Cambridge University Press, 2004), *Romantic Literature, Race, and Colonial Encounter, 1760–1840* (Palgrave, 2007) and *Forging Romantic China: Sino-British Cultural Encounters, 1760–1840* (Cambridge University Press, 2013). He has edited three multi-volume editions of writings concerning slavery and travel in the period. His most recent co-edited collection of essays (with Robert Markley), *Writing China: Essays on the Amherst Embassy (1816) and Sino-British Cultural Relations*, was published by D. S. Brewer in 2016. He was elected chair and then president of the English Association, of which he is an honorary fellow.

Edward Larrissy is Emeritus Professor in the School of Arts, English and Languages at Queen's University, Belfast, where he is affiliated to the Seamus Heaney Centre for Poetry. He is the author, among other books, of *Blake and Modern Literature* (Palgrave, 2006) and *The Blind and Blindness in Literature of the Romantic Period* (Edinburgh University Press, 2007). He is the editor, among other works, of *Romanticism and Postmodernism* (Cambridge University Press, 1999); *W.B. Yeats: The Major Works* (Oxford University Press, 2001); and *The Cambridge Companion to British Poetry, 1945–2010* (2016). He is a member of the Royal Irish Academy.

Anne C. McCarthy is Assistant Professor of English at Penn State University. She is the author of *Awful Parenthesis: Suspension and the Sublime in Romantic and Victorian Poetry* (University of Toronto Press, 2018) and co-editor of *Romanticism and Speculative Realism* (Bloomsbury, 2019). Her article, 'Reading the Red Bull Sublime' (*PMLA*, 2017), was the recipient of the Best Essay Prize from the Keats-Shelley Association of America. Her essays have also appeared in *Victorian Poetry*, *Studies in Romanticism* and numerous other venues. She is a founding editor of the Keats Letters Project (keatslettersproject.com).

Manushag N. Powell is Associate Professor and university faculty scholar at Purdue University. She is the author of *Performing Authorship in Eighteenth-century English Periodicals* (Bucknell University Press, 2012) and co-author, with Frederick Burwick, of *British Pirates in Print and Performance* (Palgrave, 2015). Her essays have appeared in *SEL: Studies in English Literature*; *JEMCS*; *Tulsa Studies in Women's Literature*; *Literature Compass*; and *Eighteenth-century Studies*. With Jennie Batchelor, she co-edited the anthology *Women's Periodicals and Print Culture in Britain, 1690–1820s* (Edinburgh University Press, 2018) and she is preparing an edition of Daniel Defoe's *Captain Singleton* for Broadview Press (2019).

Tilottama Rajan is Canada Research Chair and Distinguished University Professor at the University of Western Ontario, where she was also Director of the Centre for Theory and Criticism. She is the author of over a hundred articles on Romantic literature and/or philosophy and contemporary theory. She has published four books, including *Dark Interpreter: The Discourse of Romanticism* (Cornell University Press, 1980); *Deconstruction and the Remainders of Phenomenology* (Stanford University Press, 2002); and *Romantic Narrative: Shelley, Hays, Godwin, Wollstonecraft* (Johns Hopkins University Press, 2010). She has also edited seven collections and scholarly editions, most recently Godwin's *Mandeville* (Broadview, 2015). She is currently working on encyclopedic (dis)organisations of knowledge from German Idealism to deconstruction, with a particular emphasis on the pressure that the life sciences bring to bear on philosophy, and also on the eighteenth-century physiological theorist, John Hunter.

Judith Thompson is Carnegie Professor of English in the joint faculty of the University of Kings College and Dalhousie University in Halifax, Canada. The leading authority on the Romantic-era radical and polymath John Thelwall, she is the author of numerous books and articles including *John Thelwall in the Wordsworth Circle: The Silenced Partner* (Palgrave, 2012), and has edited or co-edited several volumes by or about Thelwall, including a digital archive of his *Words and Work* (wordsandwork.johnthelwall.org). She is currently writing John Thelwall's biography.

Damian Walford Davies is Professor of English and Pro Vice-Chancellor (College of Arts, Humanities and Social Sciences) at Cardiff University. His most recent publications – on Keats's negotiation of contemporary conceptions of the disease that killed him, and on Coleridge's *The Rime of the Ancient Mariner* as shipwreck trauma narrative – have focused on Romantic pathologies. An edited volume reassessing the work of Roald Dahl – *Roald Dahl: Wales of the Unexpected* – was published by University of Wales Press in 2016. He is currently co-editing a volume entitled *Romantic Cartographies* for Cambridge University Press. He is General Editor of the forthcoming *Oxford Literary History of Wales* and is editing *The Misfortunes of Elphin* for the *Cambridge Edition of the Novels of Thomas Love Peacock*. His most recent volumes of poetry are *Docklands* (2019), *Judas* (2015) and *Witch* (2012), all published by Seren. He is a fellow of the Learned Society of Wales.

Acknowledgements

I wish to thank the contributors for supporting this collection, and Anna Barton and Andrew Smith, as Series Editors, for including the volume in the *Interventions: Rethinking the Nineteenth Century* series. Thanks are also due to Mark Llewellyn, Richard Marggraf Turley and Manchester University Press's two readers for their valuable suggestions.

Damian Walford Davies
Cardiff University

Introduction: Counterfactual Romanticism

Damian Walford Davies

The Counterfactual Angel

Walter Benjamin's great, final crisis-document of early 1940, the twenty numbered paragraphs comprising his 'Theses on the Philosophy of History', offers a cryptic critique of historicism, specifically of the determinism, continuum mentality and narrative of progress articulated by Marxist historical materialism. The document's most creative and conceptually troubling moment is the ekphrastic angelology provided in the ninth thesis, in which Benjamin famously offers an interpretation of Paul Klee's watercolour, *Angelus Novus* (1920), which he had owned since 1921. In subdued browns, yellows and auburn tones, Klee's childlike drawing depicts a long-faced, winged figure with scroll-like tresses and large eyes in an indeterminate attitude of flight and/or fright. Benjamin sees the figure disposed 'as though he is about to move away from something he is fixedly contemplating'; 'This', he continues, 'is how one pictures the angel of history'. He proceeds to historicise this seemingly ahistorical, impossible figure, in the process temporalising and spatialising the position of the reader/viewer:

> His face is turned toward the past. Where we perceive a chain of events, he sees one single catastrophe which keeps piling wreckage upon wreckage and hurls it in front of his feet. The angel would like to stay, awaken the dead, and make whole what has been smashed.[1]

However, the angelic figure seems incapable of resisting a 'storm' that 'is blowing from Paradise'; his wings are useless, and the tempest 'propels him into the future to which his back is turned, while the pile of debris before him grows skywards'. This ninth thesis concludes: 'This storm is what we call progress.'² The image, and Benjamin's personal and philosophical inhabitation of it, have been subject to much discussion. Commentators have focused on what appears to be Benjamin's thwarted messianism at this juncture of Nazi terror, captured in the baffled angel's desire for a disruptive intervention that would call time on the cataclysmic amassing of wreckage on wreckage – an appeal, as Alan Wall sees it, redemptively 'to fracture the continuum into consciousness' and adopt a new relation and agency vis-à-vis the past and future.³ Describing Klee's image, mediated through Benjamin, as 'an icon of the left', Otto Karl Werckmeister notes:

> It has seemed to hold out an elusive formula for making sense of the senseless, for reversing the irreversible, while being subject to a kind of ideological brooding all the more protracted the less promising the outlook for political practice appears to be. Through the stream of its exegesis, Benjamin's suggestive visual allegory has become a meditative image – an *Andachtsbild* – for a dissident mentality vacillating between historical abstraction and political projection, between despondency and defiance, between challenge and retreat.⁴

The interruption of process prompted by the angel's resurrectionary hunger; the new relation with time and the sense of agency this would imply; an acknowledgement of the 'horror' of what Benjamin in thesis VII sees as the 'triumphal procession' of 'cultural treasures' that are contingent debris rather than a chain of historically *necessary* (in all senses) relics, entailed to us; the defamiliarisation of what in thesis VIII is described as the 'historical norm'; the dissatisfaction with what is found piled randomly before one's feet; the rejection of teleology (itself a theodicy); and the desire no longer to fetishise 'enslaved ancestors' (whose eventual victory is naively assumed) but rather to action, now, the ideal of emancipated heirs – these (and not some all-solving apocalypse founded on quietism) seem to be what is striven for in the teeth of that hegemonic wind that ultimately blows the angel, and history itself, back and unseeing into its own future.⁵

There is, however, another angel – an *Angelus Redivivus*, one might say, who has always been with us as Romanticists. It is one of Blake's angels – very much like a devil – represented in Plate 10 of *The Marriage of Heaven and Hell* (1790–93; see Figure 0.1) beneath the final nine 'Proverbs of Hell'. This, I propose, is our own icon, the Counterfactual Angel. He is engaged in the work of prompting a radically defamiliarised relation to history and its relics and 'exploding' the 'continuum of

Introduction

0.1 William Blake, *The Marriage of Heaven and Hell* (1790–93), Plate 10

history'. He does so by foregrounding the historical accidents that we regard as linear entailments and by revealing the contingency that creates, and continues to shadow, the objects we fetishise as teleologically received (even if – or perhaps especially when – we 'discover' them in the archive).[6] Never merely frivolous, and a hater of fake news, he is busy troubling ideas of continuity, lineage and inheritance in both historical and literary-historical spheres. His project is to reveal the plenitude of a field to which Romanticism – despite (because of) its governing historicist orthodoxy – has insufficiently attended: that which did not happen. He inhabits a quantum universe (a version of Blakean Eternity, similarly opposed to an Urizenic philosophy/historiography of the Five Senses) in which *what ifs*, *might-have-beens* and *but fors* energise, clarify and render spectral the world we inhabit and the history we live.

Blake's revisionary demonology gives us (in the Fitzwilliam Museum copy) an image of a kneeling, verdigris-toned, crimson-winged male, flanked by two female figures, both of whom are writing. An unfurled scroll – history's supposed record, I suggest, rendered deviously serpent-like in form – is open before him; he points questioningly to a particular detail. The red-gowned figure to his right – whose work the angel-devil is challenging – is hunched over conventional historicist work. Her very form is monolithic. The angel has already emancipated the other figure, on his left – the creative-critical counterfactual historiographer, for whom history is not a flat surface or continuum (witness the shape the historical 'archive' takes in front of her) but rather a more complex field of scrolled foldings (indeed, like the tresses of Klee's angel). She leans over in the hope of being witness to the moment at which her red-gowned fellow historiographer's consciousness of history is exploded, her relation to the past (which she seems at present to be diligently 'receiving', not remaking) is reconfigured. Blake has disposed the already-liberated figure in such a way as to mirror the openness and receptivity of the angel-devil; hope for a similar transformative vision for the red-gowned figure is suggested in the cactus-like growth next to her, which – through crabbed and defensive – at least echoes the form of the angel-devil's wings.

I see our Counterfactual Angel pointing to an incident in the record that need not necessarily have been so, that might have been otherwise, that occurred and was inherited only through a process of historical contingency and whose form and significance remain conditioned and shadowed by what did not come to pass. He is identifying the multiple potentialities of history's field that flank and ghost (and thus ironise and relativise) the relics (cultural, literary, historical) that the red-gowned writer still insists on receiving as necessary entailments, determined for us by a conception of (literary) history as a chain. Such a view of history is one of the 'strait roads' referred to in Blake's proverb. The angel is pointing out how 'crooked' all history's roads actually are, and does so under another of the Proverbs of Hell that is now to be read ironically: 'Truth can never be told so as to be understood, and not be believ'd'.

This image of Romanticism's Counterfactual Angel illustrates the effects and affordances of the creative-critical counterfactual literary historiography that this present volume performs. These can be identified as the following: a hypersensitivity and openness to contingency, alterity and variability, and a scepticism regarding the dogma of causality; a humility born of the realisation that the inevitability of the literary history we have inherited is illusory; the salutary uncertainty that proceeds from an awareness that we are misled by our hubris-inspiring position at the latest point of literary reception, to which we mistakenly assume all texts and interpretation have tended; uncanny doubleness; possibility-hood; the multiverse of the material; quantum observation; dissident anachronism; the ironic and spectral; the frisson of a restitutive historical imagination; an acute consciousness of the constructedness of our various Romanticisms; and a dissatisfaction with things-as-they-are (in that talismanic Godwinian phrase).

A fool sees not the same literary history that a wise man sees.

Counterfactual heuristic, counterfactual imagination

Catherine Gallagher has recently charted the genealogy of the 'counterfactual imagination' – 'a certain kind of historical speculation' – across disciplines, genres and 'diverse set of venues'.[7] For Gallagher, the counterfactual is defined as a discourse 'premised on a counterfactual-historical hypothesis [–] an explicit or implicit past-tense, hypothetical, conditional conjecture pursued when the antecedent condition is known to be contrary to fact'.[8] A number of insights concerning the use, value and genetics of counterfactual thinking in history and fiction emerge from her case-study-driven map of related modalities of the counterfactual imagination. The latter range from seventeenth- and early-eighteenth-century anti-determinist philosophico-theological speculation to critical military history, legal theory and nineteenth- and twentieth-century narrative forms of 'alternate history' (to which numerous modes of speculative fiction belong) and to which, as Karen Hellekson reminds us, those other terms, 'allohistory' and 'uchronia', are related.[9] 'Counterfactual thought experiments in narrating history' in a military context reveal knowledge that will be of service in 'future planning'; today, Gallagher notes, counterfactual analysis 'tend[s] to cluster in areas where historical data might inform current policy debates', and it therefore becomes a Janus-faced 'instrument for shaping history' and for mapping out what Hellekson terms 'fictive futures'.[10]

What one might call the counterfactual moment or prompt – known in critical counterfactual speculation as the 'nexus event' – is identified as emerging when deterministic models of history – fatalism, predestination, providentialism, necessitarianism, philosophical optimism, teleological histories (Whig, Marxist) and *narrative* itself as a shaping principle – are questioned, and when human agency, responsibility, probability and the consequentiality of different causes are subject to scrutiny.[11] Further, Gallagher finds the counterfactual moment to be located 'at a juncture … recognized to have been both crucial and underdetermined' – in other words, a nodal point of uncertainty or paradox where that which seems naturally bequeathed rears up in all its contingency and relativism.[12] Battles (Waterloo as Wellington's 'damn close-run thing') or wars are, of course, prime examples of such a moment, and moment of consciousness. This volume contends that the genesis and reception of literary texts – seemingly far less dramatic a phenomenon – should be seen in the same light. Gallagher also explores the affordances of the 'story-generating energy of historical counterfactuals' – the fundamentally creative narrative-spinning stimulus of the 'what if?' moment (though it should be noted that Gallagher's discussion of counterfactual thinking implicitly accepts that its value depends on the plausibility, allowability and probability – all contested categories – of the divergent scenario envisaged). Her analysis of fictions relating to the American Civil War and the Second World War yield the insight that the counterfactual imagination has been used as a politicised, reparative tool in which history's perceived injustices are remedied. She has elsewhere referred to such a move as an act of 'undoing' that offers 'an enlarged sense of temporal possibility correlating with a newly activist, even interventionist, relation to our collective past'.[13]

Gallagher also offers a kind of phenomenology or psychology of the counterfactual imagination, remarking that the mode 'helps satisfy our desire to quicken and vivify historical entities, to make them seem not only solid and substantial but also suspenseful and unsettled'.[14] This is particularly insightful, attuned to our residual dissenting instinct to test received pieties, disembalm them, experience them for ourselves and invest them with potential energy rather than with the weight of history. What the counterfactual imagination valorises, Gallagher argues, almost as an aside, is 'the vitality of the permanently unfinished' (an apt paradox) – history, in other words, as negotiable fragment and accident, to which the creative-critical imagination is asked to respond with a historical version of Keats's negative capability and with a relish for what Gallagher has described as 'the contingency effect'.[15]

Mark Salber Phillips has also discussed counterfactualism's 'compensatory' narratives, which offer 'consolations not present in history itself'.[16]

Introduction

Equally, of course, the counterfactual imagination has posited more catastrophic outcomes, and a number of commentators have acknowledged the 'susceptibility' of counterfactuals – like any other discourse or research tool – to revisionary political agendas across the ideological spectrum (as Jeremy Black remarks: 'It is all too easy to transform the "what if?" into "If only"').[17] Counterfacutal history, for example, has often been seen as alt-right 'retrospective wishful thinking'.[18]

Counterfactual reasoning, as Philip E. Tetlock and Aaron Belkin note, 'is unavoidable in any field – history, the social sciences (particularly econometrics/cliometrics) – in which researchers want to draw cause–effect conclusions' and 'advance our causal understanding' of events, 'but cannot perform controlled experiments'.[19] Is a hypothesis concerning the significance of a particular cause and historical crux or turning point convincing? To find out, deploy a counterfactual scenario to test the causal concatenation by imagining otherwise. Richard Ned Lebow reminds us that such counterfactual simulations are also a routine evaluative tool in the physical and biological sciences, in which 'researchers routinely use them to develop and evaluate non-linear models'.[20] Far from clouding our historical sight and insight, thinking counterfactually – 'retrospective scenario generation' – can function as a useful safeguard against the 'creeping determinism' of what Tetlock and Belkin call 'certainty of hindsight'.[21] Analysing the logic of plausibility and possibility in the narratives that history and the social sciences construct, Geoffrey Hawthorn similarly asks us not 'cognitively to foreclose' the past.[22] Admittedly, this calls for a mental swerve or 'undoing' that may seem – in an age of so-called 'alternative facts' and bogus counterknowledge (something different entirely) – to require being of the devil's party.[23] But the devil is of course an angel; conceiving how things might easily have been otherwise becomes 'a means of preventing the world that did occur from blocking our view of the worlds that might well have occurred if some antecedent condition had taken a different value'.[24] Again, our position at the culmination of what seems to be a progressive march of progress, knowledge and causality is the very thing that calls for a 'debiasing effect' that is the result of having sensitised ourselves to 'the causes and contingency of the world' and its complex 'relations of entailment'.[25] Such is the power of the tendency to regard what *did* happen as *the only thing that could have happened*, that a number of commentators – alive as they also are to 'the susceptibility of the genre to political agendas' – have emphasised the value of 'high-imaginative-content counterfactuals' that ramify the nexus event into the realm of second- and third-order counterfactuals

7

and even into the world of 'miracle' counterfactuals, as a way of bringing home to us 'the complex interplay between change and necessity in shaping world history'.[26] Steven Weber acknowledges the liberalising and interrogatory value of imagining otherwise: 'Counterfactuals can … be used to open minds, to raise tough questions about what we think we know'; Mark Turner sees the counterfactual mentality as the product of a fundamentally yoking, non-compartmentalising mechanism termed 'cognitive blending'.[27] Both Lebow and Niall Ferguson valuably emphasise how customary (actually) 'imagin[ing] alternative scenarios' is in 'human mental life'.[28]

Uncanny doubleness is at the heart of the counterfactual imagination and method. Every statement of causality reveals the presence of a counterfactual other. As Hawthorn states, 'the force of an explanation turns on the counterfactual which it implies', and counterfactual imagining 'promises that kind of understanding … which comes from locating an actual in a space of possibles, showing "the connections it would have to other non-actual things"'.[29] There is an energising spectrality to embrace here in the form of a history (still) thronged and indeed conditioned by that which did not happen – a Romanticism, also, whose forms are the *product* of what did not come to pass. Thus 'historical causation' – which issues in literary lives and literary texts as well as in disastrous cavalry charges on the French left flank at Waterloo – gains what Stephen M. Best terms 'a structure of internal difference' through the 'imputation' of a counterfactual, by which past events are relativised, supplemented, creatively estranged, radically contextualised in a field that historicism has yet fully to grasp, and instructively intuited as the *possibilities or imponderables* they once were for the contemporaries who first experienced them.[30] What counterfactuals explode are 'fictions of radical presentness'.[31] A counterfactual, in Mark Salber Phillips's formulation, 'serves as a comment on its double'; this opens up the possibility of historical and literary critique through the affordances of parody and irony – tools that throw the contours of the 'original' into sharper relief.[32]

A radical counterfactual Romanticism – as heuristic and research tool – would concern itself not only with the ways in which Romantic-period thinkers and imaginative writers occupied themselves with thinking otherwise but also with extending to the practice of *literary* historiography a concept developed by Gary Saul Morson: 'sideshadowing'. Coined by obvious analogy to 'foreshadowing', 'sideshadowing', in Morson's model, 'conveys the sense that actual events might just as well not have happened' and that 'in an open universe, the illusion is inevitability itself …

what exists need not have existed'.³³ Morson asks us to hone a peripheral vision – what one might call a sensitivity to penumbras – in which 'the ghostly presence of might-have-beens or might-bes' can be detected and their consequent pressures on the 'received' object or event (or text) calibrated: 'In this way, the hypothetical shows through the actual and so achieves its own shadowy kind of existence in the text.'³⁴ What such a vision reveals is that multiple 'temporalities' contend 'for each moment of actuality'; plural texts jostle – clamour – for recognition in a quantum canon whose extent offers a challenge to New Historicist concepts of 'context' and which raises questions similar to those that have occupied New Historicists as they question how 'context' should be defined and delimited. I suggest that the result of acknowledging such a literary multiverse (predicated on the insight that the 'actual is ... just another possibility that somehow came to pass') would be a refreshing ironisation and delegitimisation of that which we assume we have inherited, a new purchase on 'history' and an expansion of horizons whose effects would be as transformative as those of feminism and New Historicism have been in their recuperative reconstruction of the Romantic canon.³⁵ Morson's is the most succinct formulation of the hubris our historical position and governing conceptions of (literary) history – nuanced as they have been by Romantic New Historicism – engender:

> When a sequence of events seems so coherent as to be necessary, we are usually deceived by our own presence at the sequence's culmination. The mirage is not other possibilities but the necessity of the actual one. Sideshadowing therefore induces a kind of temporally based humility ... [A] field is mistakenly reduced to a point, and, over time, a succession of fields is reduced to a line. Sideshadowing restores the field.³⁶

While Morson regards parody as '*an unwelcome* [or 'unwanted'] sideshadow', I argue that the extension of his concept of sideshadowing to literary history has the potential to bring into focus a field of 'parodic' shadow-texts whose shapes might very effectively serve to contextualise and highlight the circumstances of the surviving text's own genesis and transmission.³⁷

It is important to note that in the academic and professional disciplines in which it is – in a range of ways – deployed, and in most of the theoretical literature defending its value, counterfactualism labours under 'methodological constraint[s]'.³⁸ In 1961, E. H. Carr famously dismissed counterfactual speculation in historiography as a 'Dodgsonian mode' – a case of frivolously playing 'parlour-games with might-have-beens'.³⁹ This is an allegation usually pinned on the genre of the speculative essay as showcased in J. C. Squire's *If It Had Happened Otherwise* (1931), whose subtitle – *Lapses Into Imaginary History* – constructs counterfactualism as solecistic postlapsarian play (sin?) even as the volume itself innovatively exposes conventional academic historiography as the creative act it is by allowing the reader, for example, to construct a counterfactual scenario 'through a series of cuttings from [counterfactual] historical texts'.[40] The spectre (angel–devil) of fast-and-loose fiction is never far away, and so, as already noted, counterfactualism's respectability is usually predicated on canons of plausibility. 'Imagination' is regularly proscribed.[41] (Witness Catherine Gallagher's need to characterise her study of the rich affordances of counterfactuals as 'a non-partisan consideration'.)[42] Lebow adduces some of the more 'surgical' limitations imposed on counterfactual practice, such as the insistence that counterfactuals be grounded in 'a system of statistical contingency for which we have reasonable evidence' or within 'a general deductive theory with clear microfoundational scope conditions'.[43] But, as Lebow remarks, 'Surgical counterfactuals are no more realistic than surgical air strikes.' Quoting Steven Weber, he emphasises that such supposed circumspection merely generates counterfactuals 'close to the margins of existing theories'; that it 'presupposes that we know what "minimal" [change] really means'; and that adherence to what is known as the 'minimal-rewrite rule' radically underestimates the 'multiple consequences' of the smallest temporal inflection, which may give rise to complex 'second-order counterfactuals'.[44]

In his unnecessarily laboured introduction to the edited collection, *Virtual History: Alternatives and Counterfactuals* (1997), Niall Ferguson, though recognising what H. A. L. Fisher called 'the play of the contingent and the unforeseen', insisted that the counterfactuals 'we need to construct' must be 'simulations based on calculations about the relative probability of plausible outcomes in a chaotic world (hence "virtual history")'.[45] The tension between the wishful scientism of the core claim and the implications of the concept held in brackets at the end of the sentence – virtuality, with all that that implies concerning our access to the past and historiography's (self-deluding) faith in its ability to find a core 'grammar of events' (Louis Mink's phrase) from the 'causal matrix of history' – is palpable.[46] Further, there is a deathliness and philosophical dubiousness to an additional limitation that Ferguson imposes in the guise of robust principle: '*We should consider as plausible or probable only those alternatives which we can show on the basis of contemporary evidence that contemporaries actually considered.*'[47] This is to fetishise – and assume the retrievability of – the past's own partial knowledge; further, it closes down our relation to the past and actually falls prey to a form of the very anachronism it seeks to reject. A more philosophically robust understanding would self-consciously embrace counterfactuals as tools that return us to the very state of *unknowing, possibility, anxiety* and *hope* within which 'contemporaries' recognised they could not understand their chaotic world.

Although Lebow ultimately valorises the importance of plausibility, his emphasis is valuably on the mutually dependent nature of the categories of knowledge at stake: 'Every good counterfactual thus rests on multiple factuals, just as every factual rests on counterfactual assumptions'.[48] It is Lebow who also enjoins us to 'worry less about the uncertainty of counterfactual experimentation and think more about its mind-opening implications'. In doing so, he underscores the value of 'miracle' counterfactuals – those which, unlike 'easily imagined variations', beggar historical belief or go well beyond the accepted limits of statistical contingency to reveal the theoretical/analytical 'utility of considering alternative worlds'.[49] In the same vein, Steven Weber urges us to use counterfactuals as 'idea generators'.[50] Tetlock and Belkin formulate the purpose of counterfactual experimentation in startlingly Blakean terms, underscoring its ability as a provocation that helps us 'mentally ... undo' that to which we are inured (the very canonicity, one might say, of 'history'), unpick the iron matrix of relations we have persuaded ourselves we have no agency to inflect, and unfossilise literary works.[51]

Towards (back to) a counterfactual Romanticism

As I note in Chapter 6 of this volume, from the early 1980s, Romantic New Historicism flirted with the counterfactual without admitting so and without recognising that liaison in quite those terms. New Historicism's eclectic invocation (or construction) of broad historical 'context' – in which a too-well-known text (paradigmatically a Romantic lyric) would suddenly appear revivified, defamiliarised, evasive and itself uncannily counterfeit and counterfactual – actually displayed the core credentials of the counterfactual imagination. New Historicism's summoned 'context' revealed a parallel or multi-stor(e)y universe of 'alternatives'. These included the dialogic ontology of a text that is never merely 'itself' but which rather speaks to, speaks with, ventriloquises and is ventriloquised by countless other utterances; the troubling socio-political relations *not* treated in the manifest poem or subtly encoded in the text; and within those relations, the multiple ghost-forms that the poem-as-received *might have* (and, as implied in the more aggressive modalities of New Historicism, *should have*) taken.

What is the result of Marjorie Levinson's 1986 revisionist reading of Wordsworth's 'Tintern Abbey' other than a counterfactual poem?[52] Such was the resourcefulness with which deconstructionist historicism brought such multiverses (*multi-verses*) into view as a 'field' that relativised and ironised texts, and such was the freedom it exercised in resisting the delimitation of 'context', that one might appropriately speak of the New Historicist Imagination. As a method, New Historicism had a critical head and a creative heart, and should properly be viewed as one of the literary-critical heirs of the Romantic-period stocktaking of the 'porous boundaries' between history and fiction, data and discourse, information and narrative – boundaries at which the counterfactual imagination is always called into play.[53] Seeking a more affective, empathetic engagement with a 'history' they recognised as surviving only in ossified fragments, William Godwin (in 'Of History and Romance (1797)) and writer-historiographers such as Charlotte Smith, invested in what Greg Kucich calls 'feminized sympathetic historicism', recognised historical narratives as what Hayden White terms 'figurative characterizations of the events they purport to represent and explain'.[54] For Godwin and Smith, the very irretrievability of a lived past prompted the need for new affective strategies of engagement and animating dialogue with history that amounted to a new subjectivism. What such strategies opened up was a new context for historical inquiry: the past's own affective field.

A decade ago, at the end of the introduction to a collection of essays that reflected on the inheritance of Romantic New Historicism (which has shown no signs of being supplanted as a methodological orthodoxy in Romantic Studies in the intervening years), I called for a counterfactual turn that would represent not so much a break with New Historicism as an innovative development of it. If counterfactual speculation imagines history otherwise, why might it not imagine *literary* history – that related 'causal path' – otherwise also?[55] I remarked in that 2009 introduction that, to date, 'no sustained attempt' had been made 'to extend counterfactualism into the spheres of literary studies and literary history'.[56] I found this surprising, given the promise the counterfactual heuristic offers as a means of estranging literary history and individual texts, simultaneously relativising and confirming the significance of individual authors, involving us in the so-called 'Romantic Ideology' while at the same time 'guaranteeing a sceptical distantiation', and affording us a metaperspective on the political partisanship and psychological biases of our critical allegiances. Indulging in rhetoric that is – one hopes – to be forgiven in the final sentence of an introduction, I called Romantic counterfactualism 'a literary-critical version of Romantic dissidence – resistant, then as now, to the tyranny of "things as they are"'.[57]

Like the 'infernal method' of Blake's actual printing technique (involving 'corrosives', 'which in Hell are salutary and medicinal'), bringing counterfactualism into our understanding of and engagement with Romanticism holds out the possibility of 'melting … away' the 'apparent surfaces' of (literary) history, and 'displaying the infinite which was hid'.[58] The exhortation seriously to embrace a counterfactual turn in Romantic Studies has recently been answered by Alex Broadhead, who calls for a cross-fertilisation of 'critical counterfactual historiography' and the counterfactual energies and strategies of various works of fictionalised 'alternate history' in which Romantic authors themselves figure, from Nathaniel Hawthorne's 'P.'s Correspondence' (1845) to Susanna Clarke's *Jonathan Strange and Mr Norrell* (2004):

> Alternate history … might be employed to conjure and to interrogate the necessarily fragmentary structures and symbolic subtexts of the stories we tell about Romanticism.[59]

Broadhead regards his chosen examples of alternate history – in which famous Romantic lives and Romantic-period histories are transformed, fractured and estranged – as performing fundamentally creative-critical work that contests the ways in which those lives and histories are constructed in the likewise narrativised, and thus necessarily fictionalised and implicitly counterfactualised, professional academic discourse of Romantic Studies.

It might be remarked, however, that Hawthorne's well-known story of 1845, which Gallagher calls 'a proto-alternate-history', can be read as a warning against such a move.[60] The story's central consciousness is 'P.', an inmate of a New England asylum, incarcerated in a 'little whitewashed, iron-grated room'. The story takes the form of an example of one of his letters – dated 'London, February 29, 1845' (1845, by the way, was *not* a leap year) – addressed to the story's frame 'editor', who describes his friend's mental illness as 'not so much a delusion, as a partly wilful and partly involuntarily sport of the imagination'.[61] His friend inhabits a 'world of moonshine' and 'misty excursions' – a London populated by Romantic authors living counterfactual (extended or unbroken) lives. It is significant that the editor remarks that 'P.' 'had always a hankering after a literary reputation'. Thus, in one of the first major examples of alternate history, Romantic counterfactualism is configured as *pathology*, as fictional imposition, wilful play. An emphasis on the pathological continues in the very physiology of the surviving Romantics whom 'P.' encounters. We read of his encounter with a reformed Byron, who now 'combines the most rigid tenets of Methodism with the ultra-doctrines of the Puseyites', is 'overladen with his own flesh', and whose hand is 'so puffed out with alien substance' that 'P.' can scarcely believe he has 'touched the hand that wrote Childe Harold'.[62] This 'hobgoblin' Byron is not, it seems, himself; the plenitude of possibilities on which the counterfactual imagination is predicated seems to be figured in Hawthorne's text as a killing corpulence. Byron is busy expurgating and amending his past work in the light of his 'present creed of taste, morals, politics and religion' (Romantic revision, here, as a form of counterfactualism); as 'P.' pointedly remarks: 'Positively, he no longer understands his own poetry.' Thus in what one might see as Hawthorne's allegory of an alternate Romantic literary historiography, the counterfactual is the source of an *interpretative* pathology that leads only to a lack of 'understanding'.

We learn that 'P.' also encounters a living Robert Burns as a 'hearty old man' who is not 'embalmed in biography' (that is, dead and wrapped archivally in the winding sheets of critical interpretation and partial biographical narrative). This counterfactual Burns may be alive; however, he has become insect-like, with a 'cricketty suit of liveliness', and the sounds he emits are mere cackles and coughs. Walter Scott is not dead, but 'vegetat[ing] at Abbotsford, dictating to an 'imaginary amanuensis'; Napoleon, suffering from post-traumatic stress disorder, takes chaperoned walks in Pall Mall, 'buried beneath his own mortality'; Keats is alive but has published nothing for decades, and is chronically coughing arterial blood (not so much the famous 'death-warrant' as the curse of lifelong haemorrhage); Mrs Siddons and John Kemble are 'decrepit' and 'broken-down'; while the actor-manager Charles Matthews is 'hideous', his features 'paralysed' by a stroke.[63] Taken together, these meetings amount to a gerontological hell imagined by 'disordered reason'; Hawthorne's very experiment in counterfactual Romantic literary history yields monitory results.

And yet – always historicising – we should remind ourselves that to call for such a counterfactual swerve, for Romantic Studies to be done 'otherwise', is both to argue for a return to the period's own conditions and to refresh and extend already articulated critical insights and methods. As noted, a counterfactual turn gives us a clearer sense of the genetics

Introduction

of New Historicism, and is only the latest in a series of epistemological, phenomenological and disciplinary 'crises' that valuably – if at first disconcertingly – reconfigure our relationship to our (literary) past. As Nicholas Roe notes, '"speculate" was … a buzz word of the 1790s'.[64] Were not the very objects of our study – Romantic-period authors and thinkers – themselves counterfactualists, committedly speculative but also bewildered, who recognised, and were disorientated by, the ways in which the fields of their pasts and their futures were sideshadowed by the oppositional-ironic 'data' of the counterfactual? Certainly, in its revolutionary moments, the Romantic aesthetic was acutely, if complexly, alive to possibility-hood, to the conditional of the quantum field in a period of revolutionary upheaval, social instability, apocalyptic expectation and total war. Romanticism's willingness to entertain the contingent and possible against the dogmatically determinist was, of course, always a struggle.

Thomas Pfau's reading of contemporaries' experience of 'early romantic history (1789–98)' and the Napoleonic era as one of 'paranoia' followed by 'trauma' has already offered us a glimpse into the way in which the period was processed – first agitatedly as an 'entropic psychosocial world' from which 'the concept of causation ha[d] materially disappeared except as an all-consuming, retroactive fantasy about the hidden coherence of acts and outcomes' and then as a universe rendered alien and uncanny.[65] It was Coleridge in 'Fears in Solitude' (1798) who – in this entropic world – identified as the mark of an unthinking, unimaginative, deceived, vitiated and vicious nation-at-war an inability and unwillingness to 'speculate' on 'contingency':

> … we have lov'd
> To swell the war-whoop, passionate for war!
> Alas! for ages ignorant of all
> It's ghastlier workings (famine or blue plague,
> Battle, or siege, or flight thro' wintry snows)
> We, this whole people, have been clamorous
> For war and bloodshed, animating sports,
> The which we pay for, as a thing to talk of,
> Spectators and not combatants! no guess
> Anticipative of a wrong unfelt,
> No speculation on contingency,
> However dim and vague, too vague and dim
> To yield a justifying cause …[66]

Such ethical 'speculation' – alive both to the algorithms and to the accidents of events – is an act of the dissenting imagination that clarifies the link between causes and horrific effects, assigns agency and reveals responsibility, and refuses to accept both the 'ghastlier workings' of things as they are and the position of passive and unfeeling spectator.

To be sure, strategies related to the counterfactual imagination have already been identified in the work of Romantic-period authors. In Chapter 1 of this book, Anne C. McCarthy emphasises that William Galperin's analyses of strategies of Romantic 'counterhegemony' in Jane Austen's work have revealed an author who is 'ever alert to possibilities that animate an ostensibly predictable and patriarchal society' – a writer who sees 'missed opportunit[ies]', 'what never happened' and that which has been 'missed or bypassed' as a conditioning 'lingering materiality' in the world actually inherited. Such shadowing allows us to see how troublingly indeterminate the generic dynamics of Austen's romances are.[67] A 'horizon of plenitude' and 'an ever pressing anteriority' – never left behind as done-with or exorcised – trouble each iteration of Austen's present. Galperin notes that the field of the missed, lost, 'unfulfilled' and 'unrecuperable' is 'unwritable'; however, its trace is emphatically the shaping 'other' of 'what the narrative aggressively promotes'. As Galperin summarises, '"what really happened" doubles alternately and retrospectively as "what never happened"'; '"what" happens in Austen's novels finds an accompaniment in what *also* happens only under a condition of somehow not happening'.[68] In short, the counterfactual is the very condition of Austen's irony. In her chapter, McCarthy valuably goes on to emphasise that Galperin's reading of Austen has a parallel in Andrew H. Miller's discussion of a modality of the counterfactual imagination in Dickens's work that he terms 'optative historiography' (following Stuart Hampshire).[69] The 'optative' involves reflecting on the newness, the 'singularity', of one's identity precisely by acknowledging its relation to other lives one is *not* living. Grammatically, the optative mood ('having the function of expressing [a] wish or desire') shades into the imperative and subjunctive; this is blurred territory in which desire and regret straddle past, present and future. Lives unlived – as in the relational, conditioning, substitutive play of language itself – become the ground of the life one *is* living.

Christopher M. Bundock has recently asked us to think differently and counterintuitively about the purpose and temporal dynamics of the prophetic mode during revolutionary upheaval, 'when history, as the narrative synthesis of events, lost its capacity for producing complete accounts' and when 'subjects encounter[ed] several parallel yet discordant historical times, at the same time'.[70] Prophecy, for Bundock, is a product

Introduction

of the experience of 'this kind of historical multiplicity'; as a discourse of subjectivity-in-crisis, prophecy 'is most important for Romantic revolutionaries not when it maps the future but when it disencumbers the future from the weight of the past and from attempts to entail the future to the past through prediction'.[71] Dissatisfaction with things-as-they-are and with the 'empirical histories' that claim to map the past *for* the future – in short, an 'anxiety surrounding the very notion of being historical' – prompts Romantic prophecy to articulate not 'the future of the past', but rather 'unprethinkable futures'. It is a modality, actually, of counterfactual thought – an imaginative agent that dispenses with 'predictive exigencies', exploding the subject's experience of history into fragments and imagining that which is 'radically unpredictable' and 'radically unexpected' – indeed, 'strictly *impossible* given the prevailing frame of social, intellectual, and political life'.[72] Counterfactualism, by the same token, is a mode of dissident anachronism, a historicised counter- or para-historicism.

In his study of the uses to which 'Romantic ethics' can be put as critique (including the discipline of literary criticism itself) and practical policy, Jerome Christensen boldly claims that we can be 'educated by the Romantics' in the business of both 'living' and 'making a living'.[73] Christensen pits the Romantic mindset against that of the 'historicist'; while the latter is 'dead set on decoding the iron logic of past events', the former 'fully credits the possibility of accidents and readies [itself] to take advantage of swerves and lapses from the norm as opportunities for change'. Christensen offers further broad statements relevant to the theory and practice of Romantic counterfactualism as I have been developing them in this introduction: 'Romantic idealism involves a principled frustration with the way things have turned out and a deliberate impatience to turn them right'; 'Romanticism is primordially and persistently open to unforeseen consequences, one of which is Romantic criticism … which is a species of the poetic imagination.'[74] Unashamedly embraced here is an essentialism and immersion in Romanticism's own discourses that is only partially offset by the openness to contingency and disruption. Indeed, being saturated in the Romantic Ideology seems a necessary part of the plan: 'This undertaking will involve a blurring of the distinction between Romantic and Romanticist that has been the pride of the practitioners of ideology critique.'[75] What Christensen calls for is a 'conspiracy' between the Romantics and 'posthistorical' Romanticists – a collaborative project of ongoing mutual and social critique in the service of political agency in the present, for the future. The modes of critical

Romantic counterfactualism this volume recommends both enable and question that aim.

Performing Counterfactual Romanticism

Introducing contingency as a necessary and revealing condition both of Romanticism and of our critical and affective relationship with it, the eleven chapters in *Counterfactual Romanticism* analyse, demonstrate and – given counterfactualism's inherently creative-critical nature – *perform* Romantic counterfactualism in multiple modalities: as object of inquiry, as multiform critical method and as broader mindset. Its presiding spirit is the angel–devil we encountered earlier. One of the book's central aims is to showcase the affordances of a counterfactual heuristic, variously deployed, for historicist, creative-critical, biographical and philosophical-theoretical modalities of literary history and literary criticism.

Counterfactual Romanticism begins from the premise that there was nothing *inexorable* about the period we study and likewise nothing *inevitable* about the shapes taken by our ongoing construction of it. The volume offers counterfactualism – as concept and method – both as a way of closely connecting with the events, lives and imaginative writing of the period and as a tool of critical distance and estrangement. It reveals the period's own investment in such strategies and thus the Romantic genetics of the swerve, aligning the tools available to us as critics in the academy with the imaginative resources deployed by those whose works we study. The counterfactual methods profiled here share nothing with the toxic 'post-truth' culture of fact-refutation institutionalised by the present White House administration, which is a mode of denial and flight, not of creative speculation and analytical inquiry.[76] Indeed, a counterfactual Romanticism offers a robust critique of, and defence against, such sophistry.

Extending the closet-counterfactual insights of William Galperin (on Austen) and Andrew Miller (on the optative mode) into the realms of personal identity and our relation to literary texts, Anne C. McCarthy argues for an engagement with a 'counterfactual sublime' that is profoundly ethical in its effects. Firmly establishing the Romantic credentials of such a move, her chapter makes a Wildean case for the need to see 'the object as in itself it really is not' – literary texts and periods included. Such an act – aligned, as McCarthy notes, with strategies of 'reparative reading' – would declare the object vitally unowned by us, defamiliarised as part of a 'weird' layered temporality whose relations are governed by

Introduction

an 'aesthetics of contingency'. McCarthy's insight that the counterfactual sensibility relies less on a gesture actively staged – the active imagining of an otherwise – than on the realisation that one's own present is already shadowed by multiple, 'dissonant' possibilities is key to her argument concerning the conditioning counterfactuality of our lived lives. Implicit in her concluding call for a counterfactual 'intervention' that is 'no longer indebted to notions of primacy, influence or period' is the potentially transformative effect of the counterfactual heuristic on the Romantic curriculum – an issue taken up in various forms in subsequent chapters, most explicitly the last.

What emerges from Gary Kelly's detailed portrait of 'the unfolding commercial, political and cultural embodiment and variegation of the narrativised assemblage of national historical fact' from the mid-eighteenth century onwards is historiography's fundamental rhetoricity. The chapter is cued to the volume's central theme in its emphasis on the commerciality, marketisation, revisability, updatability, popularisation, bowdlerisation, partisanship, gendered inflections, generic hybridity and portability of the array of 'national' histories that circulated during the period – Rapin-Tindal, Hume, Smollett, Hume–Smollett and crossbreed versions from a host of 'bogus authors' and copyright-holders in mid- and low-market publishing firms. All were engaged in the curation – for different audiences – of conceptions of 'modernity' and 'cultural citizenship' that were defined against the very 'history' they were constructing. As Kelly notes, this corpus of texts, which assembled various pasts in the service of the present under the sign of 'authentic history', represented 'a body of national historical factuals' that 'counter[ed] and contradict[ed]' one another and which conditioned the emergence of the 'historified fiction' of the novel. Kelly shows how the 'history' of these historiographies is best understood as that which, adaptably, claimed various kinds of 'credit' as it fulfilled an array of public and personal needs for its 'makers and users'.

It is the credit afforded to forged pasts and texts that occupies Mary-Ann Constantine in Chapter 3 as she conceptualises the relation between eighteenth-century forgery and counterfactualism. In the hands of James Macpherson, Thomas Chatterton and Edward Williams ('Iolo Morganwg'), forgery becomes a modality of counterfactualism's investment in *possibilism*. Locating forgery in spaces of loss – epistemological, material, topographical, cultural, political – and in 'unmapped' territories of recuperative 'possibilities', Constantine reveals the counterfactual dynamics and frissons of forged literary and historical documents that enfolded 'plausible alternative versions of the past' into a localised present in the service of nation-building and the construction of national literary histories. Examples of archival loss cited by Constantine dramatically bring home the 'permanently oscillatory state' in which certain possibly forged documents will forever remain. The case of Edward Williams, whose vast 'counterfactual world' became accepted history and literary history in the nineteenth century (to be fully debunked only in the early twentieth century), prompts Constantine's insight that a *'making true'* (an institutionalised acceptance) of forged worlds results in the counterfactual becoming merely 'counterfeit' and 'fake'.

Counterfactualism's uncanny enfoldings, already adumbrated by Constantine, are central to Chapter 4. Tilottama Rajan's discussion of the epistemological 'folds' of the actual and the virtual in Sophia Lee's early alternate history novel of sixteenth-century Scotland and England, *The Recess: Or, A Tale of Other Times* (1783–85), forges a conception of counterfactualism's very form and ontology that yields a theory of narrative and of history. The novel's core space – the underground labyrinth of the 'Recess' itself, connected to the world above – becomes a spatial figure of the novel's very method (and implied alternate historiography) as Lee 'exposes' romance to history, thus allowing 'an upsurge of the possible within the real' that makes 'virtually present' roads not taken (we recall Galperin's reading of Austen). Rajan employs Deleuze to help conceptualise the novel's bewildering doublings and twinnings, its uncanny returns and resemblances, potential-filled recessiveness and interplay of historical and fictional personages (many with the same names). These render history's 'facts' 'exchangeable', 'depthless', phantasmic – a collection of 'intensities', not successive patterns; a 'narratology', not a 'geneaology'. The novel presents a universe in which there are no 'unique selves', only the paradox of relational difference – the very ground, as argued earlier in this introduction, of counterfactualism's own ghosting of the 'real'.

Chapters 5 and 6, invested to differing degrees in the 'plausible', explore the consequences for literary history – and, crucially, for our own relationship with Romanticism – of counterfactual scenarios. First, Kenneth R. Johnston dares to imagine Wordsworth's *Prelude* published 'not long after he first finished it (May 1805)' as a platform from which to envision the effects on younger writers of the poem's radical 'self-creation mode'. To put it differently and recuperatively (a key element of counterfactualism's affective politics, as noted), what Johnston explores are the models that contemporaries were denied as a consequence of

Introduction

Wordsworth's reticence to publish his autobiographical epic at that point. Johnston's focus is the impactfulness of *The Prelude*'s models on Byron; what emerges is an uncanny Wordsworth, an actively 'Romantic' (rather than Victorian) *Prelude*, and a defamiliarised-and-yet-true-to-his-historical-self Byron (interestingly *contra* Hawthorne). Suggesting convincing political reasons why *The Prelude* was not published around 1805, Johnston can be seen to approach 'non-publication' itself as one of those spaces of loss-and-possibility identified by Constantine. It is denial and detriment that are emphasised; as he does in *Unusual Suspects: Pitt's Reign of Alarm and the Lost Generation of the 1790s* (2013), Johnston speaks of the 'cost' of that missed opportunity, that resonant lacuna. Envisaging a 19-year-old Byron reviewing Wordsworth's poem, Johnston is careful to emphasise how challenging and at first unsympathetic certain aspects of *The Prelude* would have been for Byron, as well as the forms in which he might have assimilated and inflected the multiple stylistic, generic and structural models that Wordsworth's poem offered. As the chapter moves to its conclusion, we witness Wordsworth and Byron becoming each other's avatar.

In creative-critical mode, my own chapter presents a second-order 'miracle' counterfactual, as I construct a literary-critical universe in which Mary Wollstonecraft does not die of puerperal sepsis in childbed in September 1797 (as might well have been the case, given the contingencies in play) but goes on to write a version of her daughter's novel, *Frankenstein, avant la lettre*. I offer a psychologisation of our complex critical relation to (and disillusionment with) that which is entailed to us by literary history by seeking a self-aware purchase on the affective as well as analytical itches that prompt such an experiment. In retrojecting (a version of) *Frankenstein* to the late 1790s – where it becomes, in Wollstonecraft's hands, a novel of the Irish Rebellion of summer 1798 – and in reanimating an energisingly 'zombie' Wollstonecraft, I aim to challenge the pious stratifications of literary historiography; bring into focus the swirling economy of literary genres and 'disjecta-membra' sources from which literary productions emerge at times of personal and political trauma; retrieve elements of Wollstonecraft's own identity in relation to which she remained curiously unforthcoming; and ultimately deliver us into a renewed, defamiliarised relation to the *Frankenstein* we (think we) have. Throughout – as is true in each chapter of *Counterfactual Romanticism* – the uncanny figures prominently. My own contribution, brought to birth within the frame of what I term a critical obstetrics, enacts that uncanniness by inhabiting and ventriloquising Wollstonecraft's counterfactual novel of 1799. I ask the reader to consider how far such a breach of critical protocol, such apparent trespassing on the past and such co-authorship *really* are from our seemingly more orthodox New Historicist engagements with 'received' literary history.

It is also in creative-critical mode that Judith Thompson's chapter begins (and ends) – a move that again prompts a debate as to the quantum and nature of the imaginative investment informing all critical and theoretical engagements with the literary past. Counterfactualism's spectral territory is highlighted by Thompson's subtitle reference to the genre on which her intervention is self-consciously modelled: the ghost story (spliced with the detective story). As she prepares to write 'the first full modern biography' of the political theorist, poet and 'acquitted felon', John Thelwall, Thompson's *entente* with counterfactual speculation is prompted by her frustration with the archive's gaps, fissures and fragments, and by her fascination with Thelwall's own self-conscious acts of indirection and ventriloquism in a body of transgressive poetry ('seductive allegories') that emerged from a complex, taboo-haunted family drama in 1816. In a bold move as biographer, Thompson proposes to embrace 'counterfactual literary techniques' – here signalling a method characterised by an openness to 'creative intuition' and a willingness to work both within and at a critical distance from fictional frames and Thelwallian genres – to investigate 'the extent to which an unknown life may be reconstructed'. In Thompson's analysis, a species of 'Thelwallian counterfactualism' is identified in textual aporiae, ellipses, 'conditional syntax' and the poetry's multi-vocal (and possibly multi-author) 'theatrical ventriloquism' – all of which vex 'biographical reading'. Testing the limits of 'counterfactual conjecture', Thompson argues, allows access to such possibility-rich, pregnant spaces.

Angela Esterhammer identifies 1824 as a 'crux in the history of factual and counterfactual writing' – a juncture at which Walter Scott, John Banim, John Galt and Mary Russell Mitford simultaneously opt for a counterfactual turn ('*not* by accident') that produces 'varieties of the counterfactual' at a moment of 'rampant speculation' in the wider economic sphere. Esterhammer instructively brings together a historical novel that allows the fictional and the historical uncannily to interact (Scott's *Redgauntlet*), a 'quirky hybrid' of fact and time-travel 'speculative fantasy' (Banim's *Revelations of the Dead-Alive*), a compilation of literary extracts framed by a domestic, spousal dialogue (Galt's *The Bachelor's Wife*) and prose sketches that blend 'documentation' and 'idealisation' (Mitford's *Our Village*). She reveals how a portfolio of 'soft' counterfactual strategies – ranging from Scott's historical swerves to 'speculation about the future', ontologically impossible interactions and geographies both actual and symbolic – yields teasing metaperspectives on, and ironic allegories and critiques of, contemporary commercial literary production, reading practices, historiography and literary history.

Conceptualising the layered forms in which the figure of the pirate was entailed to the Romantic-period stage and novel, Manushag N. Powell offers a case study in the accretive, multi-genre energies of counterfactual speculation and what she terms 'counterfictional' experimentation. She contends that pirate histories offer a particularly rich demonstration of processes of adaptation and speculation-driven laminations of fact, fiction, counter-fact and counter-fiction, with the latter two operating in 'upward' (valorising) and 'downward' (demonising) modalities. The entertaining hybridities of John Cartwright Cross's pirate melodrama, *Black Beard; Or, The Captive Princess*, which had its successful premiere in 1798, are traced back to the ur-pirate history, *A General History of the Robberies and Murders of the Most Notorious Pyrates* (1724–28). Powell sees in this latter work the interpenetration of history and fiction and the complex coalescing and desynonymisation of individuals, their histories and their values, not as a generic quirk or mere narrative frisson, but rather as a profound thought experiment and 'intellectual act' by the volume's author (whose true identity remains the subject of debate). At stake in the *History* (and in all subsequent representations of pirates) are a series of radical possibilities, including that of a 'republican' pirate colony founded on 'revolutionary principles of liberty' that would be 'less out of place in 1789 than in the 1720s'. The interplay between fact and fiction, however, allows the author of the *History* to entertain such a possibility only ultimately to contain and neutralise it by 'pushing it more firmly into the realm of fiction' and returning the narrative to history.

Peter J. Kitson imagines the counterfactual at scale in Chapter 10, by exploring the contours of an all-pervasive China-centric strand of Romantic Orientalism – a Romantic Sinology – that never was. Part of the counterfactual experiment involves seeking to account for why China, as both 'topos' and 'culture', failed to make as profound a mark on Romantic-period writing as one might have expected, given the pervasive influence of chinoiserie and various cultural and political engagements that promised a significant 'Chinese moment' in British life in the mid-eighteenth century. Kitson's large-scale counterfactual, which rejects inevitability and imagines a way back out of what was a 'cultural dead end' in the period, characteristically involves the defamiliarisation of individual authors and structures. Thus we comport ourselves anew to a Thomas Percy who was *not* diverted from his (actual) 'China project' into the 'medieval English ballad tradition'; a Horace Walpole who writes a novel of thirteenth-century China as an allegory of the contemporary English political system; and a Strawberry Hill of 'pagodas and Chinese temples'. At the chapter's mid-point, Kitson seamlessly layers the counterfactual into his historicised literary criticism, artfully interpellating the reader into the counterfactual universe by means of indiscernible hinges between factual and speculative formulations, only to brave the breaking of the spell through alienation effects that have as much to do with the subtleties of critical tone and sentence structure as with the nature of the counterfactual claims made. Later in the chapter, Kitson marks the counterfactual turn more explicitly, only for its subtle embeddedness to return towards the end, by which time a new literary history has been mapped out, eastwards. Kitson's chapter is a wily example of the counterfactual method's provocative but genuinely exploratory ironies, whose doubleness is here experienced as a troubling defamiliarisation of the past and of our reading present. The return to the 'actual' at the end of the chapter carries the force of a repression of the Chinese counterfactual that parallels the evasions, repressions and forgettings that Kitson sees as characterising Romanticism's own vexed relation to the East.

We round back in the volume's final chapter, by Edward Larrissy, to explore further some of the issues broached in the first concerning counterfactualism in the classroom and the value-laden process of canon-formation. Having been reminded again of our 'over-confidence about what might constitute the factual', we are witness to the forging of an alternative Romantic canon-curriculum in the face of the very difficulty Larrissy sees in imagining such an entity at the present time. What emerges – in the form of a 'core' course in a counterfactualised academy – is something akin 'to what exists already', but different enough to render the latter uncanny and questionable. The chapter channels the spirit both of a conformist Blakean angel and of our counterfactual devil, promoting to the new core course writers who are already the subject of 'current trends' and whose works are aligned with 'themes that animate contemporary investigation', while also admitting semi-disruptive wildcards that serve both to globalise and to centralise/localise Romanticism and which prophesy the end of some of those fashionable 'current trends'. Larrissy's method is maieutic and polemical; that is, it has the effect of drawing out the reader's own views concerning who should be the beneficiaries of the new–old canon, as Larrissy outlines with semi-ironic insouciance the contours of a curriculum whose (new–old) gaps, elisions and repressions clamour for (re-)admission. Looking to the future rather than to the present or past, Larrissy then forecasts the shape of the Romantic curriculum in English literature departments in which the influence of the values, methods and forms of creative writing and creative-critical practice are becoming increasingly significant. Prophesied here is a canon that looks very much like that of a past we thought we had outgrown, but one that is to be theorised according to a radically different set of principles and investments.

I return to the disposition of figures in Plate 10 of Blake's *The Marriage of Heaven and Hell*, in which I identified the central figure as the Counterfactual Angel and presiding genius of the methods analysed and performed in this volume. What he is exploring with the red-gowned figure, whose slablike form suggests a fundamental unreceptiveness to his prompts, are the modalities of the counterfactual imagination as practised by the contributors to *Counterfactual Romanticism*. And what I imagine the red-gowned woman's freer companion – with her excited look – is about to say is this: if, as Marjorie Levinson puts it, our literary history and our criticism are 'an *effect* of the past which we study', let us (dear sister) embrace and swerve that ideology by further exploring the ways in which the past that we study can be disruptively reencountered as an *effect* of our criticism.[77]

Notes

1 Walter Benjamin, *Illuminations*, trans. Hannah Arendt (London: Fontana, 1992), p. 249.
2 *Ibid.*
3 Alan Wall, 'Reflections on Walter Benjamin – 8', *The Fortnightly Review*, 18 December 2015; http://fortnightlyreview.co.uk/2015/12/reflections-benjamin-8/ (accessed 31 January 2018).
4 Otto Karl Werckmeister, *Icons of the Left: Benjamin and Eisenstein, Picasso and Kafka after the Fall of Communism* (Chicago: University of Chicago Press, 1999), pp. 11–12.
5 Benjamin, *Illuminations*, pp. 248, 249, 252.
6 *Ibid.*, p. 253.
7 Catherine Gallagher, *Telling It Like It Wasn't: The Counterfactual Imagination in History and Fiction* (Chicago: University of Chicago Press, 2018), p. 1. Richard J. Evans offers another valuable survey of counterfactual speculation in *Altered Pasts: Counterfactuals in History* (Waltham, MA: Brandeis University Press), pp. 1–30.

8 *Ibid.*, p. 2.
9 Karen Hellekson, *The Alternate History: Refiguring Historical Time* (Kent, OH: Kent State University Press, 2001), p. 3.
10 Gallagher, *Telling It Like It Wasn't*, pp. 5, 6; Hellekson, *The Alternate History*, p. 4.
11 Hellekson, *The Alternate History*, p. 5.
12 Gallagher, *Telling It Like It Wasn't*, p. 2.
13 See Catherine Gallagher, 'Undoing', in Karen Newman, Jay Clayton and Marianne Hirsch (eds), *Time and the Literary* (New York: Routledge, 2002), pp. 11–29.
14 *Ibid.*, p. 11.
15 *Ibid.*, p. 21.
16 Mark Salber Phillips, *On Historical Distance* (New Haven, CT: Yale University Press, 2013), p. 231.
17 Philip E. Tetlock and Geoffrey Parker, 'Why We Can't Live Without Them and How We Must Learn to Live With Them', in Philip E. Tetlock, Richard Ned Lebow and Geoffrey Parker (eds), *Unmaking the West: 'What-If?' Scenarios That Rewrite World History* (Ann Arbor, MI: University of Michigan Press, 2006), p. 37n.; Jeremy Black, *What If? Counterfactuals and the Problem of History* (London: The Social Affairs Unit, 2008), p. 5.
18 The phrase is that of Niall Ferguson, who has himself been accused of such appropriation; Niall Ferguson (ed.), *Virtual History: Alternatives and Counterfactuals* (London: Papermac, 1997), p. 11. See also, for example, Evans, *Altered Pasts*, *passim*.
19 Philip E. Tetlock and Aaron Belkin, 'Counterfactual Thought Experiments in World Politics', in Philip E. Tetlock and Aaron Belkin (eds), *Counterfactual Thought Experiments in World Politics: Logical, Methodological, and Psychological Perspectives* (Princeton, NJ: Princeton University Press, 1996), pp. 5, 6.
20 Richard Ned Lebow, 'What's So Different About a Counterfactual?', *World Politics*, 52:4 (July 2000), 550.
21 Tetlock and Belkin, 'Counterfactual Thought Experiments', p. 15.
22 Geoffrey Hawthorn, *Plausible Worlds: Possibility and Understanding in History and the Social Sciences* (Cambridge: Cambridge University Press, 1991), p. 17.
23 Tetlock and Belkin, 'Counterfactual Thought Experiments', p. 5; Black, *What If? Counterfactuals and the Problem of History*, p. 6.
24 Tetlock and Belkin, 'Counterfactual Thought Experiments', p. 15.
25 Richard Ned Lebow, *Forbidden Fruit: Counterfactuals and International Relations* (Princeton, NJ: Princeton University Press, 2010), p. 6; Stephen

Introduction

L. Morgan and Christopher Winship, *Counterfactuals and Causal Inference: Methods and Principles for Social Research*, 2nd edn (Cambridge: Cambridge University Press, 2014), p. 5n.
26 Lebow, 'What's So Different About a Counterfactual?', 566; Tetlock and Parker, 'Why We Can't Live Without Them', pp. 37n., 36.
27 Steven Weber, 'Counterfactuals Past and Future', in Tetlock and Belkin (eds), *Counterfactual Thought Experiments in World Politics*, p. 268; and Mark Turner, 'Conceptual Blending and Counterfactual Argument in the Social and Behavioural Sciences', in the same volume, p. 291.
28 Lebow, *Forbidden Fruit*, p. 29; Ferguson (ed.), *Virtual History*, p. 3.
29 Hawthorn, *Plausible Worlds*, p. 17.
30 Stephen M. Best, *The Fugitive's Properties: Law and the Poetics of Possession* (Chicago: University of Chicago Press), p. 254.
31 *Ibid.*
32 Phillips, *On Historical Distance*, p. 221.
33 Gary Saul Morson, 'Sideshadowing and Tempics', *New Literary History*, 29:4 (Autumn 1998), 601. See also Gary Saul Morson, *Narrative and Freedom: The Shadows of Time* (New Haven, CT: Yale University Press, 1994).
34 Morson, 'Sideshadowing and Tempics', 601.
35 *Ibid.*, 602.
36 *Ibid.*, 601–2.
37 See Morson, *Narrative and Freedom*, pp. 151–2.
38 Ferguson (ed.), *Virtual History*, p. 87.
39 E. H. Carr, *What is History?* (London: Penguin, 1990 [1961]), p. 97.
40 Hellekson, *The Alternate History*, p. 15, and see Hawthorn, *Plausible Worlds*, pp. 5–6.
41 See for example Martin Bunzl, 'Counterfactual History: A User's Guide', *The American Historical Review*, 109:3 (June 2004), 857–8.
42 Gallagher, *Telling It Like It Wasn't*, p. 9.
43 See Lebow, 'What's So Different About a Counterfactual?', 575–7. For less surgical parameters, see Tetlock and Belkin's portfolio of conditions: 'Counterfactual Thought Experiments in World Politics', pp. 17–18.
44 Lebow, 'What's So Different About a Counterfactual?', 577, 578; Tetlock and Belkin, 'Counterfactual Thought Experiments in World Politics', p. 18.
45 Ferguson (ed.), *Virtual History*, pp. 46, 85. For other collections that bring together speculations on the nature and consequences of the historical 'otherwise', see Andrew Roberts (ed.), *What Might Have Been? Leading Historians on Twelve What Ifs of History* (London: Weidenfeld & Nicolson, 2004), and Robert Cowley (ed.), *What If? The World's*

Foremost Military Historians Imagine What Might Have Been (London: Macmillan, 2000).
46 Quoted in Ferguson (ed.), *Virtual History*, p. 64; Tetlock and Belkin, 'Counterfactual Thought Experiments in World Politics', p. 8.
47 Ferguson (ed.), *Virtual History*, p. 86 (italics in the original).
48 Lebow, 'What's So Different About a Counterfactual?', 556.
49 *Ibid.*; Tetlock and Belkin, 'Counterfactual Thought Experiments in World Politics', p. 8.
50 Weber, 'Counterfactuals Past and Future', p. 268.
51 Tetlock and Belkin, 'Counterfactual Thought Experiments in World Politics', p. 5.
52 See Marjorie Levinson, *Wordsworth's Great Period Poems: Four Essays* (Cambridge: Cambridge University Press, 1986), pp. 14–57.
53 Porscha Fermanis and John Regan, 'Introduction', in Fermanis and Regan (eds), *Rethinking British Romantic History, 1770–1845* (Oxford: Oxford University Press, 2014), p. 1.
54 Greg Kucich, 'The History Girls: Charlotte Smith's *History of England* and the Politics of Women's Educational History', in Fermanis and Regan (eds), *Rethinking British Romantic History*, pp. 45, 46, 48; Hayden White, *Tropics of Discourse: Essays in Cultural Criticism* (Baltimore, MD: Johns Hopkins University Press, 1978), p. 94.
55 See Lebow, 'What's So Different About a Counterfactual?', 578.
56 See Damian Walford Davies, 'Introduction: Reflections on an Orthodoxy', in Damian Walford Davies (ed.), *Romanticism, History, Historicism: Essays on an Orthodoxy* (New York: Routledge, 2009), pp. 9–12.
57 *Ibid.*, p. 12.
58 W. H. Stevenson, *Blake: The Complete Poems*, 3rd edn (London: Routledge, 2014), p. 120.
59 Alex Broadhead, 'The Romantics in Alternate History from Hawthorne to Clarke: Generic Edges and the Counterfactual Turn', *Romanticism*, 24:2 (June 2018), 214.
60 See Gallagher, *Telling It Like It Wasn't*, pp. 77–80.
61 Nathaniel Hawthorne, 'P.'s Correspondence', in William Charvat *et al.* (eds), *The Centenary Edition of the Works of Nathaniel Hawthorne, Volume 10: Mosses from an Old Manse* (Columbus, OH: Ohio State University Press, 1974), p. 361.
62 *Ibid.*, pp. 363, 364.
63 See *ibid.*, pp. 367–70, 374–6, 377–8.
64 Nicholas Roe, *Fiery Heart: The First Life of Leigh Hunt* (London: Pimlico, 2005), p. 41.

65 See Thomas Pfau, *Romantic Moods: Paranoia, Trauma and Melancholy, 1790–1840* (Baltimore, MD: Johns Hopkins University Press, 2005), pp. 20–1 and *passim*.
66 S. T. Coleridge, *Fears in Solitude, To Which are Added, France, An Ode; and Frost at Midnight* (London: Joseph Johnson, 1798), p. 5.
67 William Galperin, *The Historical Austen* (Philadelphia, PA: University of Pennsylvania Press, 2003), p. 93; Galperin, '"Describing What Never Happened": Jane Austen and the History of Missed Opportunities', *ELH*, 73:2 (Summer 2006), 355, 356.
68 Galperin, 'Describing What Never Happened', 356, 363, 378.
69 See Andrew H. Miller, *The Burdens of Perfection: On Ethics and Reading in Nineteenth-century British Literature* (Ithaca, NY: Cornell University Press, 2008), pp. 191–217.
70 Christopher M. Bundock, *Romantic Prophecy and the Resistance to Historicism* (Toronto, ON: Toronto University Press, 2016), p. 8.
71 *Ibid.*, p. 7.
72 *Ibid.*, pp. 123, 147.
73 Jerome Christensen, *Romanticism at the End of History* (Baltimore, MD: Johns Hopkins University Press, 2000), p. 1.
74 *Ibid.*, p. 2.
75 *Ibid.*, p. 1.
76 See Ed Pilkington, '"Truth Isn't Truth": Giuliani Trumps "Alternative Facts" with New Orwellian Outburst', *Guardian*, 19 August 2018, www.theguardian.com/us-news/2018/aug/19/truth-isnt-truth-rudy-giuliani-trump-alternative-facts-orwellian (accessed 20 August 2018).
77 Marjorie Levinson, 'The New Historicism: Back to the Future', in Marjorie Levinson, Marilyn Butler, Jerome McGann and Paul Hamilton, *Rethinking Historicism: Critical Readings in Romantic History* (Oxford: Basil Blackwell, 1989), p. 21.

Works cited

Primary texts

Benjamin, Walter, *Illuminations*, trans. Hannah Arendt (London: Fontana, 1992)
Coleridge, S. T., *Fears in Solitude, To Which are Added, France, An Ode; and Frost at Midnight* (London: Joseph Johnson, 1798)
Stevenson, W. H. (ed.), *Blake: The Complete Poems*, 3rd edn (London: Routledge, 2014)

Secondary texts

Best, Stephen M., *The Fugitive's Properties: Law and the Poetics of Possession* (Chicago: University of Chicago Press)

Black, Jeremy, *What If? Counterfactuals and the Problem of History* (London: The Social Affairs Unit, 2008)

Broadhead, Alex, 'The Romantics in Alternate History from Hawthorne to Clarke: Generic Edges and the Counterfactual Turn', *Romanticism*, 24:2 (June 2018), 203–15

Bundock, Christopher M., *Romantic Prophecy and the Resistance to Historicism* (Toronto, ON: Toronto University Press, 2016)

Bunzl, Martin, 'Counterfactual History: A User's Guide', *The American Historical Review*, 109:3 (June 2004), 845–58

Carr, E. H., *What is History?* (London: Penguin, 1990 [1961])

Christensen, Jerome, *Romanticism at the End of History* (Baltimore, MD: Johns Hopkins University Press, 2000)

Cowley, Robert (ed.), *What If? The World's Foremost Military Historians Imagine What Might Have Been* (London: Macmillan, 2000)

Evans, Richard J., *Altered Pasts: Counterfactuals in History* (Waltham, MA: Brandeis University Press)

Ferguson, Niall (ed.), *Virtual History: Alternatives and Counterfactuals* (London: Papermac, 1997)

Fermanis, Porscha and John Regan, 'Introduction', in Porscha Fermanis and John Regan (eds), *Rethinking British Romantic History, 1770–1845* (Oxford: Oxford University Press, 2014), pp. 1–31

Gallagher, Catherine: *Telling It Like It Wasn't: The Counterfactual Imagination in History and Fiction* (Chicago: University of Chicago Press, 2018)

Gallagher, Catherine, 'Undoing', in Karen Newman, Jay Clayton and Marianne Hirsch (eds), *Time and the Literary* (New York: Routledge, 2002), pp. 11–29

Galperin, William, '"Describing What Never Happened": Jane Austen and the History of Missed Opportunities', *ELH*, 73:2 (Summer 2006), 355–82

Galperin, William, *The Historical Austen* (Philadelphia, PA: University of Pennsylvania Press, 2003)

Hawthorn, Geoffrey, *Plausible Worlds: Possibility and Understanding in History and the Social Sciences* (Cambridge: Cambridge University Press, 1991)

Hawthorne, Nathaniel, 'P.'s Correspondence', in William Charvat *et al.* (eds), *The Centenary Edition of the Works of Nathaniel Hawthorne, Volume*

10: Mosses from an Old Manse (Columbus, OH: Ohio State University Press, 1974), pp. 361–80

Hellekson, Karen, *The Alternate History: Refiguring Historical Time* (Kent, OH: Kent State University Press, 2001)

Kucich, Greg, 'The History Girls: Charlotte Smith's *History of England* and the Politics of Women's Educational History', in Porscha Fermanis and John Regan (eds), *Rethinking British Romantic History, 1770–1845* (Oxford: Oxford University Press, 2014), pp. 35–53

Lebow, Richard Ned, *Forbidden Fruit: Counterfactuals and International Relations* (Princeton, NJ: Princeton University Press, 2010)

Lebow, Richard Ned, 'What's So Different About a Counterfactual?', *World Politics*, 52:4 (July 2000), 550–85

Levinson, Marjorie, 'The New Historicism: Back to the Future', in Marjorie Levinson, Marilyn Butler, Jerome McGann and Paul Hamilton, *Rethinking Historicism: Critical Readings in Romantic History* (Oxford: Basil Blackwell, 1989), pp. 18–63

Levinson, Marjorie, *Wordsworth's Great Period Poems: Four Essays* (Cambridge: Cambridge University Press, 1986)

Miller, Andrew H., *The Burdens of Perfection: On Ethics and Reading in Nineteenth-century British Literature* (Ithaca, NY: Cornell University Press, 2008)

Morgan, Stephen L. and Christopher Winship, *Counterfactuals and Causal Inference: Methods and Principles for Social Research*, 2nd edn (Cambridge: Cambridge University Press, 2014)

Morson, Gary Saul, *Narrative and Freedom: The Shadows of Time* (New Haven, CT: Yale University Press, 1994)

Morson, Gary Saul, 'Sideshadowing and Tempics', *New Literary History*, 29:4 (Autumn 1998), 599–624

Pfau, Thomas, *Romantic Moods: Paranoia, Trauma and Melancholy, 1790–1840* (Baltimore, MD: Johns Hopkins University Press, 2005)

Phillips, Mark Salber, *On Historical Distance* (New Haven, CT: Yale University Press, 2013)

Pilkington, Ed, '"Truth Isn't Truth": Giuliani Trumps "Alternative Facts" with New Orwellian Outburst', www.theguardian.com/us-news/2018/aug/19/truth-isnt-truth-rudy-giuliani-trump-alternative-facts-orwellian

Roberts, Andrew (ed.), *What Might Have Been? Leading Historians on Twelve What Ifs of History* (London: Weidenfeld & Nicolson, 2004)

Roe, Nicholas: *Fiery Heart: The First Life of Leigh Hunt* (London: Pimlico, 2005)

Tetlock, Philip E. and Aaron Belkin, 'Counterfactual Thought Experiments in World Politics', in Philip E. Tetlock and Aaron Belkin (eds), *Counterfactual Thought Experiments in World Politics: Logical, Methodological, and Psychological Perspectives* (Princeton, NJ: Princeton University Press, 1996), pp. 1–38

Tetlock, Philip E. and Geoffrey Parker, 'Why We Can't Live Without Them and How We Must Learn to Live With Them', in Philip E. Tetlock, Richard Ned Lebow and Geoffrey Parker (eds), *Unmaking the West: 'What-If?' Scenarios That Rewrite World History* (Ann Arbor, MI: University of Michigan Press, 2006), pp. 14–44

Turner, Mark, 'Conceptual Blending and Counterfactual Argument in the Social and Behavioural Sciences', in Philip E. Tetlock and Aaron Belkin (eds), *Counterfactual Thought Experiments in World Politics: Logical, Methodological, and Psychological Perspectives* (Princeton, NJ: Princeton University Press, 1996), pp. 291–5

Walford Davies, Damian, 'Introduction: Reflections on an Orthodoxy', in Damian Walford Davies (ed.), *Romanticism, History, Historicism: Essays on an Orthodoxy* (New York: Routledge, 2009), pp. 1–13

Wall, Alan, 'Reflections on Walter Benjamin – 8', *The Fortnightly Review*, 18 December 2015, http://fortnightlyreview.co.uk/2015/12/reflections-benjamin-8/

Weber, Steven, 'Counterfactuals Past and Future', in Philip E. Tetlock and Aaron Belkin (eds), *Counterfactual Thought Experiments in World Politics: Logical, Methodological, and Psychological Perspectives* (Princeton, NJ: Princeton University Press, 1996), pp. 268–88

Werckmeister, Otto Karl, *Icons of the Left: Benjamin and Eisenstein, Picasso and Kafka after the Fall of Communism* (Chicago: University of Chicago Press, 1999)

White, Hayden, *Tropics of Discourse: Essays in Cultural Criticism* (Baltimore, MD: Johns Hopkins University Press, 1978)

1

'The object as in itself it really is not': Counterfactual Romanticism and the aesthetics of contingency

Anne C. McCarthy

The one duty we owe to history is to rewrite it.

(Oscar Wilde)[1]

Counterfactual methodologies ask us to confront the reality of contingency, prompting us to reconsider the status of a past often assumed to have been inevitable. In doing so, the counterfactual recasts the present and the future as sites of radical possibility where basic assumptions about identity are undone through the recognition of their own facticity. Asking 'what if?' is a kind of lingering, a provocatively untimely activity in the face of an urgent, totalising now. Imagining what might have been and what still could be, the counterfactual mode seeks futurity's shadows on the surfaces of the present. It brings history home in order to reveal the *unheimlich*.[2] It is by now a critical commonplace to note the nineteenth century's burgeoning awareness of epistemological uncertainty, fuelled by the French Revolution, the Napoleonic Wars, debates over reform and so on. Around the same time, the influence of the Higher Criticism went beyond religious circles to ask new questions about the stability of the historical past. Emerging from the crucible of a late-eighteenth- and nineteenth-century culture, a counterfactual Romanticism provokes a fundamental inquiry into the relationship between identity and contingency. At what point does an object – personal and collective history, a literary text, 'Romanticism' itself – cease to be what it is? Beginning at the point where 'the rest is history', Counterfactual Romanticism asks how we can be so sure that the past is over, or that the future has not already begun.

Counterfactual Romanticism

This chapter theorises the aesthetics of contingency that emerge from the conjunction of the counterfactual and the Romantic. Broadly construed, Romanticism, as Eric Hayot writes, is 'world-creating' in that it 'restores to world the idea of its being a work; and if the world is a work, then it has been (and can be) made'. 'Romantic works', he continues, 'thus make visible the world's *contingency*'.[3] Participating in what Jerome Christensen calls 'a conspiracy against the given', Counterfactual Romanticism 'fully credits the possibility of accidents and readies [itself] to take advantage of swerves or lapses from the norm as opportunities for change'. 'Romantic idealism', he goes on, 'involves a principled frustration with the way things have turned out and a deliberate impatience to turn them right.'[4] A specifically counterfactual Romanticism discloses the contingency of the past, but also that of the present and future. Its critical aesthetics are those of Oscar Wilde. To see – as Wilde suggests – 'the object as in itself it really is not' is deliberately to return to a creative Romanticism, just as Matthew Arnold's proclamation that the work of the critic is 'to see the object as in itself it really is' had been a rejection of the same.[5] Wilde's declaration of aesthetic independence possesses a profoundly ethical dimension. It declares that the object, broadly understood, is determined neither by the intention of its creator nor by its manifestation or reception at a given moment; it contains unrealised possibilities and unseen attributes, and its parts are neither more nor less real than the whole. To 'see the object as in itself it really is not' is to be conscious that the object is not exhausted by its appearance for us – an argument that has been made more recently by object-oriented philosophers who envision a 'weird realism' where things (and ideas and people) interact through aesthetic projections in contingent and sometimes unexpected ways.

Plunging deliberately into the abyss of what never happened, the counterfactual imagination lodges its protest against the inexorable – a 'Romantic' gesture if ever there was one. Thomas Pfau characterises literature as resistance to 'the vexing determinacy of history as it reproduces itself in often rigid and irrational languages and beliefs'. Literature, he argues, 'does not simply imagine some dreamworld but aims to recover a knowledge occluded by the specious, indeed irrational, fixity and coherence of so-called actual history'.[6] It is possible to detect in this statement something similar to Wilde's contempt for the 'careless habits of accuracy' and 'morbid and unhealthy faculty of truth-telling' displayed by so many of his contemporaries.[7] Both Pfau and Wilde are, in a sense, opening a space for aesthetic modes of knowing that resist the ways that 'so-called actual history' obscures its own contingency. The implied warning is the same: beware of those who claim to have grasped the object as in itself it really is, for they may have a hidden agenda in excluding the object as in itself it really is not. In this view, Romantic thought (practised by both Romantic-period writers and scholars of Romanticism) is nothing less than a world-creating endeavour that moves beyond the given – or, at least, maintains a sceptical orientation towards the kinds of claims that make a virtue out of necessity and construct retrospective, ideologically charged teleologies for what came into being as contingent.

Arguably the best evidence for the Romantic spirit of counterfactual thinking is the way that self-described 'straight' historians talk about this 'once-unwanted bastard child of their profession'.[8] Counterfactual speculation acknowledges itself to be a by-product of causal argumentation; alternat(iv)e histories are nonetheless suspect for being 'merely an act of imagination, and unconstrained imagination at that' – a pastime that needs to be reined in by 'laws, rationality, and causal analysis'.[9] Counterfactual history is viewed as being both subjective and 'inherently presentist' in that it 'explores the past less for its own sake than to utilize it instrumentally to comment upon the present' – as if other forms of historical thinking are free from such uses or do not also 'necessarily reflec[t] [their] authors' hopes and fears'.[10] In the introduction to his anthology of counterfactual historical experiments, which are mostly to do with the outcomes of military and political decisions, Niall Ferguson defends the approach by limiting its speculative scope to '*only those alternatives which we can show on the basis of contemporary* [archival] *evidence that contemporaries actually considered*'.[11] I am not so much of a disciplinary chauvinist that I am unable to appreciate the concerns and evidentiary standards that affect the profession of history or the utility (and even the responsibility) of maintaining a separation between evidence-based fact and conjecture when it comes to matters of the past. If counterfactuals are going to function as 'a necessary antidote to determinism', as Ferguson claims, they need some standard of plausibility – otherwise, they risk falling into irresponsible speculations that do nothing to enhance a reader's sense of the past.[12]

But Counterfactual Romanticism, as distinct from the traditional historian's controlled foray into the margins of the past as it really was, reintroduces hope and fear into historical thinking. Against the practice of a 'straight' history that limits the range of imagination and seeks to keep affect out of the archive, Counterfactual Romanticism, as I consider it here, is a profoundly disruptive, 'queer' process. Aligned with the practices of reparative reading, Counterfactual Romanticism abandons what Eve Kosofsky Sedgwick calls the 'dogged, defensive narrative stiffness of a paranoid temporality' (or, for that matter, Pfau's specious fixities) in favour of attention to 'a heartbeat of contingency' within and beyond the archive of recorded history.[13] Letting go of attachments to necessity, inevitability and paranoia, the reparative, Romantically oriented reader 'has room to realize that the future may be different from the present, [and that] it is also possible for her to entertain such profoundly painful, profoundly relieving, ethically crucial possibilities as that the past, in turn, could have happened differently from the way it actually did'.[14] To suspend the notion of a fixed, unchangeable past is to open oneself at once to the sublime terror of an utterly contingent world that could become otherwise at any moment and to the sublime relief – even joy – of the possibilities of a new world that will not simply replicate itself in lockstep with the same. Such practices do not constitute an escape from the world as it is, a rejection of the historical or the political, but rather a potentially more profound, non-totalising, sense of the way the world may be engaged to bring about change that remains both proximate to and unimaginable in the present moment. In the aesthetics of contingency, transcendence is imagined not as a freedom *from* external conditions (nor as the mastery of those conditions) but as a freedom *within* those conditions – a sublime whose *telos* is not reason but contingency, the undoing or suspension of *telos*. The counterfactual sublime provides access to the essentially ungovernable and ungoverning operations of contingency; it shows us not only what is, but also what could have been, illuminating for a moment the infinite regress of ungraspable causality.

Believing that we have a more or less firm grasp on where we are and how we got here, we tend to push the workings of contingency, in a given moment, to the edge of our emotional landscape. The weather could change, or the particularities of a daily schedule, but our own identities and the basic constitution of life as we know it will still be there. Until, suddenly, they are not. 'Man's yesterday may ne'er be like his morrow; / Nought may endure but Mutability.'[15] The last two lines of Percy Bysshe Shelley's lyric, 'Mutability', encapsulate the aesthetics of contingency in deceptively simple form. On an abstract level, it is relatively easy to assent to the nebulous thought of a distant future that will differ from an equally different past, leaving a more or less stable present in the middle. The more things change, the more they stay the same. *Que sera, sera*. But there is also a more literal dimension to this statement that turns out to be much more challenging to contemplate. The poem asks its reader to assent to the surprisingly frightening proposition that Wednesday is – or at least could be – radically different, even unrecognisable, from Monday. It brings contingency into the now, revealing the movements of change that are no longer safely housed in a past somehow disconnected from us.

One of Shelley's strengths, of course, is that he is able to imagine both the way that contingency operates on an intensely personal scale as well as the slow movements of geological time. It is within these incommensurable yet overlapping time schemes that Mary Wollstonecraft Shelley redeploys 'Mutability' – which had first appeared in the *Alastor* collection of 1816 – at a key moment in *Frankenstein*. Just before he confronts his 'hideous progeny' on the Alpine heights of Chamouni – a moment both unexpected and utterly determined – Victor Frankenstein climbs the glacier of Montanvert on a rainy day, pausing to seek the elevation of his spirits in the contemplation of nature:

> I looked on the valley beneath; vast mists were rising from the rivers which ran through it, and curling in thick wreaths around the opposite mountains, whose summits were hid in the uniform clouds, while rain poured from the dark sky, and added to the melancholy impression I received from objects around me. Alas! why does man boast of sensibilities superior to those apparent in the brute; it only renders them more necessary beings. If our impulses were confined to hunger, thirst, and desire, we might be nearly free; but now we are moved by every wind that blows, and a chance word or scene that that word may convey to us.
>
> We rest; a dream has power to poison sleep.
>   We rise; one wand'ring thought pollutes the day.
> We feel, conceive, or reason; laugh, or weep,
>   Embrace fond woe, or cast our cares away;
> It is the same: for, be it joy or sorrow,
>   The path of its departure still is free.
> Man's yesterday may ne'er be like his morrow;
>   Nought may endure but mutability![16]

The complaint seems a familiar one: despite our best efforts to focus on higher things, human beings are the playthings of chance and easy prey to their own divided nature. Victor Frankenstein doubly evades his own responsibility by breaking off his personal thoughts in favour of a quotation that, understood as a conventional statement about the constancy of change – with the implication of human helplessness before it – displaces and obscures the central role he has played in his, and his family's, misfortunes as well as the fact that his actions stem from a desire to control and manage contingency.

The poetic double vision of Percy's poem thus breaks into the plotted world of Mary's novel, turning a moment of suspense into one of suspension set against the paradigmatically sublime location of the Alps. (This is, of course, also the setting for 'Mont Blanc'.) Victor fails to achieve the sublime transcendence such scenes are supposed to guarantee. His insight is essentially a set of excuses. Not only does he not rise above his worries; he is about to become even more entangled in the dire consequences of his past actions. The human mind experiences states of unrest, happiness and sadness, but is never wholly identified with any one of those states. In the context of the novel, that is, the poem is invoked to emphasise an adversarial relation between nature and the mind. But the poem itself belies such conventionality, presenting a view that is both attentive to the instability of a personal identity crossed by conflicting emotions and willing to understand that such instability is to some extent constitutive of identity itself. In short, 'Mutability' constructs personal identity as open and contingent – a view that necessarily conflicts with the novel's plotting of the same. The poem invites its readers to maintain a certain scepticism about the coherence of the world by seeing it both as it is and as it is not. In the context of *Frankenstein*, however, the citation of 'Mutability' also marks an elegiac foreclosure of possibility, the abandonment of changes that can no longer occur and decisions that cannot be made differently – that is, the object as in itself it really is not, glimpsed only in its passing beyond the threshold of the actual. On a more material plane, Mary's citation of this version of 'Mutability' in *Frankenstein* temporarily arrests its circulation. The poem does not appear in the *Posthumous Poems* she edited in 1824; a previously unpublished lyric from 1821 takes its place under the same title – an exchange that makes 'Nought may endure but Mutability' an uncannily literal and performative utterance.[17]

Few of these details constitute alternative history as it is usually understood. Nevertheless, I contend that these gestures and speculations participate in a broader Romantic orientation towards the counterfactual that depends less on the actual staging of alternatives than on the acknowledgement that those alternatives exist as something other than idle dreams or fantasies. The Shelleyan affirmation that 'Man's yesterday may ne'er be like his morrow' intimates futures that respond to dissonant, even hidden, elements of the present – a present that is itself rendered more unknowable, less stable, less absolute by this realisation. 'We cannot ever apprehend the totality of the networks that organize us', Caroline Levine has observed.[18] Form gives a shape to experience, but also, as Levine argues, enables a single element of that experience to become much larger than it first appears. What Levine calls the 'networked plot' of the Victorian realist novel 'hints at immeasurable durations and extensions that lie beyond its own considerable reach. The vastness of *Bleak House* affords not individual agency, not the primacy of families, and not the wholeness of the nation, but a kind of narratively networked sublime'.[19] The seemingly simple attempt to account for one's present circumstances – whether in the context of a sweeping nineteenth-century novel or a particular historical moment – loses itself in a potentially infinite recursion of causes, contingencies, confrontations and obscured connections. The counterfactual – arguably more than other postures of thought – draws attention to the element of calculation that underlies any definition of reality. Never simply given, reality is always at least partly a side-effect or symptom of the decisions that go into the ordering of experience (in both literature and history) – decisions that render some things essential and others contingent.[20]

As a statement about the constitution of reality, Shelley's 'Nought may endure but Mutability' bears a striking similarity to a definition offered by the twentieth-century science-fiction writer (and counterfactual historian) Philip K. Dick: 'Reality is that which, when you stop believing in it, doesn't go away.'[21] Like Shelley's paradox about the persistence of change, Dick offers what is basically a negative epistemology: the first step in deciding whether something is real is believing that it is not – or, at the very least, cutting oneself off from the usual sorts of empirical proofs of its existence. As a result, it becomes possible, even necessary, to understand reality largely as a formal proposition that remains curiously resistant to the determining of content.

Whatever its philosophical merits, this statement does seem to have a certain practical appeal. Most of us operate on a day-to-day basis with the assumption that other people (not to mention animals, objects and so on) have real existences even when we are not perceiving them; in doing so, we grant to the external world at least some measure of solidity that does not depend on our having access to it. Indeed, this is one of the central aesthetic practices of realism – one of the things it does to make its worlds seem real. These narratives, as Hayot observes, are characterised by a high level of 'completeness' – that is, they produce worlds that do not depend on the single perspective of an individual character and in which all characters are understood to be living more or less continuous offstage lives. Intriguingly, he notes that the 'continued existence of imaginary objects beyond their immediate apprehension by a living audience' is a quality that the realist novel shares with online virtual worlds – games that don't end when an individual player stops playing. 'History in such worlds', Hayot explains, 'is not a function of the attention of any single player, nor is it necessarily the function of the combined attention of all players'; rather, 'it results from the arrangement of the game-space's most basic ludic structure, which mimics the real world by disconnecting narrative and descriptive viability from any single or collective act of perception'.[22] Reality – at least as far as realism is concerned – is the sound of the tree that falls in the forest when no one is there to hear it; it is the world that continues when no one is looking or even, necessarily, believing in it.

We can detect a similar counterfactually constituted reality in William Galperin's reading of the first sentence of *Pride and Prejudice*: 'It is a truth universally acknowledged, that a single man in possession of a good fortune, must be in want of a wife.'[23] Of this famous opening line, Galperin comments:

> The mere fact that this truth must also be universally acknowledged, that it cannot stand alone without the continuous prop of opinion, custom, and fantasy, raises another possibility, which all the weight of coercion and probability cannot suppress. This of course would be a condition wherein women no longer need or want to be married and where men, accordingly, are no longer obligated, much less entitled, to rescue them … [T]he prospect of things being otherwise, however far this may be from the 'truth', is surprisingly close at hand.[24]

The 'must' of Austen's narrator, Galperin argues, draws attention to the affective resources that are marshalled to ensure that this 'truth' remains an object of universal approbation and teleological pursuit, even as it also registers the existence, however evanescent, of alternative possibilities that haunt the edges of the real. Thus, if this famous declaration does not fully dismantle the structures that it briefly illuminates, it nonetheless raises the question of whether this particular 'truth' would, in the absence of universal acknowledgement, be able to persist on its own. Galperin's broader argument here has to do with the way in which Austen, whom he calls 'an historian of a dense and inscrutable present', uses the resources of the everyday to convey a 'sense of the past [that] is less an endorsement of precedent, or a subscription to the empirical logic of probability, than an orientation that inclines toward romanticism in the way the past, as an index of what was also possible, operates alternately if all too briefly as a site of opportunity'.[25] Austen's Romanticism, that is, operates most effectively in the affective and aesthetic register of the ordinary, where the missed opportunities generated by the momentum of plot seem to

The aesthetics of contingency

linger as a trace of what never was, of possibilities recognised only in their foreclosure but palpably felt nonetheless.

Austen's Romanticism is also manifestly a counterfactual one. Granted, the 'what if' questions in her work tend to be muted (or posed indirectly, as in the 'truth universally acknowledged'). The most fully realised speculations tend to come to fruition in the end: Elizabeth Bennet finds out what it is like to be mistress of Pemberley; Anne Elliot no longer has to wonder what she missed with Captain Wentworth. However, Austen's counterfactually Romantic method mobilises the affective energies of the missed opportunity against the belief in an unshakeable, inevitable past, as well as against the ideologically and narratively constructed perception of an inevitable present worth preserving.[26] Drawing attention to the traces of alternatives that remain unpursued in *Mansfield Park*, Galperin observes that 'what the missed opportunity exposes is the winner-take-all logic that drives the narrative in the very image of the imperium it serves. On the losing side of a culture war, in other words, in which both the narrative and its heroine are impressed, are possibilities that time and progress have to a large degree vanquished.'[27] If Austen's characters frequently mistake the artifices that regulate experience for experience itself – that is, if they allow a 'truth universally acknowledged' to become a truth, full stop – Austen's narratives remain open to the potential of counterfactual revision, even if that potential is registered only as a distant flicker.

Andrew Miller's theorisation of the 'optative' mode in nineteenth-century literature represents a somewhat broader (though more explicit) version of the Austenian missed opportunity. Optative reflection 'conceives of one's singularity – the sense that one has this particular life to live and no other – by contrasting it with lives one is not living'.[28] If future-oriented moral perfectionism is, in Miller's view, the overarching *telos* of much mid-nineteenth-century writing, the retrospective optative mode opens up a crucial space for exploring – in ways that can be both ethically productive and entirely self-indulgent – the contours of other pasts and other presents. This 'counterfictional' process is, Miller argues, 'a structural feature of nineteenth-century realistic prose. As realism proposes to give us fictions about how things really were, a space naturally opens up within that mode to tell us how things might have been but were not.'[29] These moments of reflection may come to constitute fully fledged alternative histories that open into (counter-)fictional space, but they may also remain more abstract, revealing the 'peculiar contingency of modern experience' by calling up the 'continuing but dreamlike presence' of lives that remain unled and roads not taken.[30] Obviously, there is a limit to how much counterfactual speculation a realist novel can take before it becomes something else. Yet it seems to me that we could rightly think of this 'lateral prodigality' of the realist novel as the mark of an enabling 'Romanticism' – a resistance to what is, an ethical inclination to honour the experiences that are not necessarily our own – that persists within the world-affirming genre of realism.

Both Galperin and Miller reveal the ways in which counterfactual Romanticism operates within and against the determinist impulses of plot. What might it mean, however, to apply Miller's insight that we are defined as much by what we are not as by what we are to the literary text? That is, when does a literary text – the literary object – stop being itself and become something else? This question has been asked on a much more encompassing scale by philosophers associated with object-oriented ontology. This school of speculative philosophy proposes that 'objects have an essence that is profoundly withdrawn. Even when objects appear to touch one another physically, they are withdrawn from one another ontologically.'[31] This essential withdrawnness of all objects – call it the reality that remains when you stop believing in (i.e. perceiving) it – instantiates a structural, constitutive 'rift' between the object and its appearance that extends even to the object's appearance to itself. So, in a sense, the object of object-oriented ontology is constitutively contradictory, 'a weird entity withdrawn from access, yet somehow manifest'.[32]

In a 2012 article, object-oriented philosopher Graham Harman proposes a '*counter*method' of literary criticism that sets out to consider a text neither as the sum of its various parts nor as an object whose meaning is exhausted by its cultural and historical context. Rather, he says, 'we should focus specifically on how it resists such dissolution'.[33] He goes on to make a series of suggestions as to what this might look like in practice:

> Instead of just writing about *Moby-Dick*, why not try shortening it to various degrees in order to discover the point at which it ceases to sound like *Moby-Dick*? Why not imagine it lengthened even further, or told by a third-person narrator rather than by Ishmael, or involving a cruise in the opposite direction around the globe? Why not consider a scenario under which *Pride and Prejudice* were set in upscale Parisian neighborhoods rather than rural England – could such a text plausibly still be *Pride and Prejudice*? Why not imagine that a letter by Shelley was actually written by Nietzsche, and consider the resulting consequences and *lack* of consequences?[34]

The 'modifications' that Harman suggests are at least superficially counterfactual, but the countermethod ends up looking a lot like more familiar forms of adaptation. Replace *Pride and Prejudice* with *Emma*, and 'upscale Parisian neighborhoods' with 'Beverly Hills in the 1990s', and the result would look like the movie *Clueless*. On the other hand, of course, most of us don't consider *Emma* and *Clueless* to be interchangeable. Even the film adaptations that cleave more closely to period detail are not identical to the novel itself; at the same time, we know almost instinctively that, for most purposes, the Penguin and Oxford editions are both *Emma*. All of this seems self-evident, but Harman – and, for that matter, the last two centuries of debate over copyright law – reminds us that such distinctions may not be so straightforward.

Most of us are at least dimly aware that certain literary texts have fuzzy boundaries – for example, how a reader's recollection of *Lyrical Ballads* might turn out, on reflection, to be a monstrous hybrid of the best-known poems of the 1798 edition together with elements of the 1800 and 1802 prefaces. Manuscript scholars and book historians have long been able to speculate about the ways that certain texts bear within them the traces of authorial decision and even hesitation, codifying variant readings and alternative endings. To a large degree, however, the textual object is allowed to be blurrier than it first appears, which is why professors of Romantic literature are able to have passionate discussions about the relative merits of the 1818 and 1831 texts of *Frankenstein* (along with the virtues of a given scholarly edition) in an undergraduate survey course but would be less likely to argue that one of these editions is simply 'not *Frankenstein*'.

Yet, in suggesting the types of alterations that could be made to the works of Austen or Melville without causing the dissolution of the literary object, Harman assumes that there is critical consensus on what *Moby-Dick* 'sounds like' – a consensus that can be separated from the materiality of the text itself. This comes close to seeming like a return to a mystified transcendence, what Claire Colebrook describes as an 'ongoing sameness' possible '*if and only if* we think of an immaterial or ideal object that remains the same through time regardless of inscription'.[35] In other words, 'Lines Written A Few Miles Above Tintern Abbey' is still 'Lines Written A Few Miles Above Tintern Abbey', whether one encounters it in a crumbling copy of the 1798 *Lyrical Ballads* or the latest version of the *Norton Anthology of British Literature* – until it isn't. Many of the details that Harman dismisses as more or less irrelevant to the essence of a given literary text are in fact, as Colebrook argues, part of the materiality – in Paul de Man's sense – of literary reading itself:

> It would be unscientific to attend to the binding, colours, penmanship and erasures of a mathematical manuscript, but even though we can read *The Prelude* or *The Four Zoas* in a reprinted poetry anthology, the material object can always open up new relations, rendering what we thought to be merely material and irrelevant into a part that ... opens an entirely divergent whole.[36]

In much the same way that Galperin argues for the Austenian everyday as the site of contingency and possibility, the counterfactual capabilities of the literary text arise from its materiality – not simply the materiality of a manuscript or first edition, but the materiality of the signifier itself. Today's irrelevant detail could be tomorrow's key to all mythologies.

Literary objects, then, have the potential to offer a privileged example of the consequences of object-oriented philosophy's concept of the rift between projection and appearance. The rift, as Timothy Morton argues, is 'disturbing' because 'it's undecidable. We can't specify "where" or "when" the rift "is". The rift forces us to confront an illusion-like reality ... Appearances (relations between objects) are deceptive: they are aesthetic.'[37] Relations, interactions and even causality belong, Morton writes, to the realm of the aesthetic, because they involve qualities that are projected 'in front of' the object, which itself remains ontologically prior to its relations and not reducible to them. In other words, the uniqueness of the object consists in what withdraws from all possible relations, even of the self to itself. Given that this 'rift between appearance and essence' obtains '*within the object itself*', Morton argues that 'We should accept some kind of paraconsistent, possibly dialetheic logic that allows things to be what they seem, and not what they seem, simultaneously.'[38] As he points out, this type of logic has long been operative in literary studies. In fact, it might not be too much of an overstatement to posit that most literary criticism is a kind of counterfactual process to the extent that it engages in the work of weighing intention against accident, tracing the contingent as well as the deliberate and considering the implications of alternatives. At the same time, it also produces new objects, themselves obscurely marked by what they are not.

It can, of course, be difficult to contemplate the contingencies of the identities that we hold most dear. This is why the optative moments to which Miller refers are often affectively overwrought: 'the supervening emotions – whether happy or unhappy – may themselves be motivated by a desire to cover and obscure the deeper and more disturbing ontological or metaphysical experience of contingency'.[39] Indeed, until this point, I have used 'Counterfactual Romanticism' as a heuristic that accords to the second term a protected and stable status. However intimately linked to the counterfactual, 'Romanticism' slips under the radar of revisionist thinking, enabling the celebration of contingency while remaining immune to it. Yet, few forms are as contingently organised or as inviting to counterfactual speculation as literary periods – a point that Paul Saint-Amour makes in a humorous counterfactual re-imagining of the configurations of Victorian and modernist literature. What if, he asks, the young Queen Victoria had been assassinated in 1840, setting off 'sixty years' worth of contentious regencies, short undistinguished reigns, and agonistic successions'?[40] And furthermore, what if that 'dog's breakfast of regents and unremarkable monarchs' had been redeemed by a George V who was only a distant relation of Victoria, and who ruled 'steadily and as a moral exemplar, from 1901 to 1965'?[41] Had this been the case, it would be much less likely that literary historians or others would speak in terms of a 'Victorian' era; in this counterfactual scenario, the literature of the nineteenth century is studied under the generic and aesthetic rubric of 'realism' – a term that implies something more deliberate than mere historical convenience. Modernism, by contrast, corresponds to a counterfactual 'Georgian' literature.

In essence, then, Saint-Amour destabilises many of the assumptions that Modernism makes about Victorianism – and vice versa – by offering an alternative history of the nineteenth and twentieth centuries. His reversal exposes the contingency of the forms that organise scholarly practice and offers a humorous reminder that such forms are not simple reflections of historical and aesthetic realities. They are, however, highly influential, and Saint-Amour ends his counterfactual experiment by considering the affective dimension of scholarly affiliation: 'If you study realism and realists, you are neither a *realism-ist* or a *realist-ist*; you're a *realist*, and consequently any neurotic identification or other transferential relationship you may have to the field is underscored, or even solicited, by the terms of your scholarly self-reference. You are invited to think that you are what you study, that field is a byword for ontology.'[42] The barriers to rethinking periodisation are generally considered to be institutional (how we organise the curricular and departmental structure at university level, how hiring works), but Saint-Amour identifies something that hits rather closer to home, something that makes history a lot more personal.

We are what we read, and this appears to be doubly true of Romanticists. Against the encroachments of the long nineteenth and long eighteenth centuries, Romanticism struggles for a space apart, a way of being neither the origin of one period nor the *telos* of another.[43] I am sympathetic to Hayot's contention that an attachment to 'such notions as originality, novelty, progress' effectively limits the kinds of questions we can ask, particularly on a global scale. So long as linear forms and 'being first' remain the privileged organising principles, 'we are', Hayot writes, 'essentially doomed by the fact that Haroldo de Campos read James Joyce, and not the other way around, to tell a progressive history of aesthetic innovation in which the contributions of the non-West remain supplemental, or constitute thematic appendixes to form'.[44] These are the necessary concessions we make when we understand history as continuous and progressive. Recovering a sense of historical and temporal contingency could have the effect of loosening the lockstep of primacy and influence and according a central place to the non-Western subject of literary cultivation.[45] This isn't the only solution, of course, but it does constitute a possible future of Counterfactual Romanticism, where Romanticism is understood as something other than a historical container. Not all notions of discontinuity are themselves counterfactual (nor does every counterfactual experiment presuppose discontinuity), but there is no doubt that the ability to imagine a past shot through with gaps and missed opportunities enhances, in turn, the thinking of a contingent present characterised by conflicting temporalities and forms – which, in turn, is ripe for a counterfactual intervention no longer indebted to notions of primacy, influence or period. Asking 'what if' is only the initiatory gesture of a broader aesthetics of contingency.

Notes

1 Josephine M. Guy (ed.), *The Complete Works of Oscar Wilde, Vol 4: Criticism: Historical Criticism, Intentions, The Soul of Man* (Oxford: Oxford University Press, 2007), p. 147.
2 See William Galperin's description of Jane Austen's *Pride and Prejudice* as possessing an 'uncanny dynamic' in which 'a world of possibility shadows the probable and representable world'; *The Historical Austen* (Philadelphia, PA: University of Pennsylvania Press, 2003), p. 126.
3 Eric Hayot, *On Literary Worlds* (New York: Oxford University Press, 2012), pp. 128, 129 (emphasis in original).
4 Jerome Christensen, *Romanticism at the End of History* (Baltimore, MD: Johns Hopkins University Press, 2000), p. 2.
5 Guy (ed.), *Criticism*, p. 159; Matthew Arnold, 'The Function of Criticism at the Present Time,' in R. H. Super (ed.), *The Complete Prose Works of*

Matthew Arnold, Volume 3: Lectures and Essays in Criticism (Ann Arbor, MI: University of Michigan Press, 1962), p. 258.
6 Thomas Pfau, *Romantic Moods: Paranoia, Trauma, and Melancholy, 1790–1840* (Baltimore, MD: Johns Hopkins University Press, 2005), p. 25.
7 Guy (ed.), *Criticism*, p. 77.
8 Gavriel Rosenfeld, 'Why Do We Ask "What If?": Reflections on the Function of Alternate History', *History and Theory*, 41:4 (December 2002), 91.
9 Martin Bunzl, 'Counterfactual History: A User's Guide', *The American Historical Review*, 109:3 (June 2004), 845.
10 Rosenfeld, 'Why Do We Ask "What If?"', 93.
11 Niall Ferguson, 'Introduction: Towards a "Chaotic" Theory of the Past', in Niall Ferguson (ed.), *Virtual History: Alternatives and Counterfactuals* (New York: Basic Books, 1997), p. 86 (italics in the original).
12 *Ibid.*, p. 89.
13 Eve Kosofsky Sedgwick, *Touching Feeling: Affect, Pedagogy, Performance* (Durham, NC: Duke University Press, 2003), p. 147.
14 *Ibid.*, p. 146.
15 Percy Bysshe Shelley, 'Mutability'; Donald H. Reiman and Neil Fraistat (eds), *Shelley's Poetry and Prose*, 2nd edn (New York: W.W. Norton, 2008), pp. 91–2.
16 Mary Shelley, *Frankenstein*, ed. D. L. Macdonald and Kathleen Scherf, 3rd edn (Peterborough, ON: Broadview Press, 2012), pp. 116–17. I have reproduced the spelling and punctuation of 'Mutability' as it appears here, even though it differs slightly from the text in Reiman and Fraistat.
17 I discuss this convergence at greater length in *Awful Parenthesis: Suspension and the Sublime in Romantic and Victorian Poetry* (Toronto, ON: University of Toronto Press, 2018), pp. 110–14.
18 Caroline Levine, *Forms: Whole, Rhythm, Hierarchy, Network* (Princeton, NJ: Princeton University Press, 2015), p. 129.
19 *Ibid.*, p. 130.
20 Kenneth R. Johnston makes this point with particular clarity in the introduction to *Unusual Suspects*, a book that sets out to take some account of the personal and historical losses incurred by the political repressions of 1790s Britain and, in so doing, reconsider historical assumptions about Romanticism and revolution. The members of this 'lost generation' are, Johnston explains, 'writers and intellectuals of the time, who were not usually activists in the cause of reform, nor, for the most part, direct victims of the state machinery of repression'. They are, rather, 'bystanding sympathetic fellow-travellers for reform who did not expect to get into

trouble for their liberal sympathies, but did, big time'; *Unusual Suspects: Pitt's Reign of Alarm and the Lost Generation of the 1790s* (Oxford: Oxford University Press, 2013), p. 12. Though not a work of alternative history as it is generally understood, *Unusual Suspects* is, unquestionably, a critical act informed by what I am calling Counterfactual Romanticism.
21 Philip K. Dick, 'How to Build a Universe that Doesn't Fall Apart Two Days Later', in Lawrence Sutin (ed.), *The Shifting Realities of Philip K. Dick: Selected Literary and Philosophical Writings* (New York: Pantheon Books, 1995), p. 261.
22 Hayot, *On Literary Worlds*, p. 65.
23 Jane Austen, *Pride and Prejudice*, 3rd edn, ed. Donald Gray (New York: W. W. Norton, 2001), p. 3.
24 Galperin, *The Historical Austen*, p. 126.
25 *Ibid.*, p. 23; William Galperin, 'Describing What Never Happened: Jane Austen and the History of Missed Opportunities', *ELH*, 73:2 (Summer 2006), 363.
26 Galperin identifies the resistance to inevitability in Austen's depiction of the 'everyday' as that which is 'at variance with plot, both in its temporal movement forward and as a vehicle of both ideology and regulation'; 'Describing What Never Happened', 361.
27 *Ibid.*, 366.
28 Andrew Miller, *The Burdens of Perfection: On Ethics and Reading in Nineteenth-century British Literature* (Ithaca, NY: Cornell University Press, 2008), pp. 191–2.
29 *Ibid.*, p. 196.
30 *Ibid.*, pp. 194, 195.
31 Timothy Morton, 'An Object-oriented Defense of Poetry', *New Literary History*, 43:2 (Spring 2012), 207.
32 *Ibid.*, 208.
33 Graham Harman, 'The Well-wrought Broken Hammer: Object-oriented Literary Criticism', *New Literary History*, 43:2 (Spring 2012), 200. Emphasis in original.
34 *Ibid.*, 202. Emphasis in original.
35 Claire Colebrook, 'Not Kant, Not Now: Another Sublime', *Speculations: A Journal of Speculative Realism*, 5 (2014), 149. Emphasis in original.
36 *Ibid.*, 150.
37 Morton, 'An Object-oriented Defense of Poetry', 212.
38 *Ibid.*, 213. Emphasis in original.
39 Miller, *The Burdens of Perfection*, pp. 199–200.
40 Paul K. Saint-Amour, 'An Interlude: We Have Never Been Modernists', *English Literature in Transition, 1880–1920*, 56:2 (January 2013), 201.

41 *Ibid.* In factual history, of course, George V (1865–1936) was a grandson of Queen Victoria and reigned from 1910 to 1936.
42 *Ibid.*, 204.
43 See, for instance, Tilottama Rajan's objections to the 'reduction' of Romanticism by practices that have 'absorbed "Romanticism" into a Victorianized "nineteenth century"', which, far from being a neutral unit of time, 'results in a retrodetermination of Romanticism by what the late twentieth century sees as the Victorians' concern with nationalism, imperialism, commodification, and the strictly contained resistance to these forces in various forms of identity and sexual politics'; *Romantic Narrative: Shelley, Hays, Godwin, Wollstonecraft* (Baltimore, MD: Johns Hopkins University Press, 2010), p. xiv. Theorising the long nineteenth century and its discontents has been something of a critical cottage industry since the 1990s; see Ted Underwood, *Why Literary Periods Mattered: Historical Contrast and the Prestige of English Studies* (Stanford, CA: Stanford University Press, 2013), pp. 161–5, for a review of some of this work that looks forward to the ways in which the techniques of the digital humanities might further unsettle the concepts of periodisation and historical discontinuity.
44 Hayot, *On Literary Worlds*, p. 6.
45 Underwood argues that 'If history is radically discontinuous then intellectuals can argue that present-day social standards have to be qualified by historicist culture, which serves as a placeholder for an infinite variety of possible alternate perspectives. If, on the other hand, we have reached a point where the present is finally right to imagine that it holds a privileged perspective, then the supplement of historical cultivation ([or] "culture" as we have known it for the last two centuries) is no longer particularly urgent'; *Why Literary Periods Mattered*, p. 156.

Works cited

Primary texts

Arnold, Matthew, 'The Function of Criticism at the Present Time', in R. H. Super (ed.), *The Complete Prose Works of Matthew Arnold, Volume III: Lectures and Essays in Criticism* (Ann Arbor, MI: University of Michigan Press, 1962), pp. 258–85

Dick, Philip K., 'How to Build a Universe that Doesn't Fall Apart Two Days Later', in Lawrence Sutin (ed.), *The Shifting Realities of Philip K. Dick: Selected Literary and Philosophical Writings* (New York: Pantheon Books, 1995), pp. 259–80

Guy, Josephine M. (ed.), *The Complete Works of Oscar Wilde, Volume 4: Criticism: Historical Criticism, Intentions, The Soul of Man* (Oxford: Oxford University Press, 2007)

Reiman, Donald H. and Neil Fraistat (eds), *Shelley's Poetry and Prose*, 2nd edn (New York: W. W. Norton, 2008)

Shelley, Mary, *Frankenstein*, ed. D. L. Macdonald and Kathleen Scherf, 3rd edn (Peterborough, ON: Broadview Press, 2012)

Secondary texts

Bunzl, Martin, 'Counterfactual History: A User's Guide', *The American Historical Review*, 109:3 (June 2004), 845–58

Christensen, Jerome, *Romanticism at the End of History* (Baltimore, MD: Johns Hopkins University Press, 2000)

Colebrook, Claire, 'Not Kant, Not Now: Another Sublime', *Speculations: A Journal of Speculative Realism*, 5 (2014), 127–57

Ferguson, Niall, 'Introduction: Towards a "Chaotic" Theory of the Past', in Niall Ferguson (ed.), *Virtual History: Alternatives and Counterfactuals* (New York: Basic Books, 1997), pp. 1–90

Galperin, William, 'Describing What Never Happened: Jane Austen and the History of Missed Opportunities', *ELH*, 73:2 (Summer 2006), 355–82

Galperin, William, *The Historical Austen* (Philadelphia, PA: University of Pennsylvania Press, 2003)

Harman, Graham, 'The Well-wrought Broken Hammer: Object-oriented Literary Criticism', *New Literary History*, 43:2 (Spring 2012), 183–203

Hayot, Eric, *On Literary Worlds* (New York: Oxford University Press, 2012)

Johnston, Kenneth R., *Unusual Suspects: Pitt's Reign of Alarm and the Lost Generation of the 1790s* (Oxford: Oxford University Press, 2013)

Levine, Caroline, *Forms: Whole, Rhythm, Hierarchy, Network* (Princeton, NJ: Princeton University Press, 2015)

McCarthy, Anne C. *Awful Parenthesis: Suspension and the Sublime in Romantic and Victorian Poetry* (Toronto, ON: University of Toronto Press, 2018)

Miller, Andrew, *The Burdens of Perfection: On Ethics and Reading in Nineteenth-century British Literature* (Ithaca, NY: Cornell University Press, 2008)

Morton, Timothy, 'An Object-oriented Defense of Poetry', *New Literary History*, 43:2 (Spring 2012), 205–24

Pfau, Thomas, *Romantic Moods: Paranoia, Trauma, and Melancholy, 1790–1840* (Baltimore, MD: Johns Hopkins University Press, 2005)

Rajan, Tilottama, *Romantic Narrative: Shelley, Hays, Godwin, Wollstonecraft* (Baltimore, MD: Johns Hopkins University Press, 2010)

Rosenfeld, Gavriel, 'Why Do We Ask "What If?": Reflections on the Function of Alternate History', *History and Theory*, 41:4 (December 2002), 90–103

Saint-Amour, Paul K., 'An Interlude: We Have Never Been Modernists', *English Literature in Transition, 1880–1920*, 56:2 (January 2013), 201–4

Sedgwick, Eve Kosofsky, *Touching Feeling: Affect, Pedagogy, Performance* (Durham, NC: Duke University Press, 2003)

Underwood, Ted, *Why Literary Periods Mattered: Historical Contrast and the Prestige of English Studies* (Stanford, CA: Stanford University Press, 2013)

2

Door-to-door and across-the-counter factuals: history as fashion, furniture, fraud, forgery, folklore and fiction in the Romantic onset of modernity

Gary Kelly

Beyond play on this volume's title and organising theme, this chapter argues that history, however understood, is always something else too, especially in the Romantic onset of modernity and the formation of modern history as a history for modernity – or rather the formation of a certain historical consciousness for modernity as a field of contest between differing interests. This argument adapts and aligns certain recent theoretical proposals. 'Facts' are always social and hence the distinction between factuals and counterfactuals can only be discursive or a matter of convention or professional practice.[1] Communication and reading are not the 'decoding' of meanings 'encoded' in utterances or 'texts' but rather the creation of meaning by participants in the full context of the communicative situation.[2] 'Texts' are always embodied as material objects.[3] Meanings do not inhere in objects but are created by objects' users for their own purposes at different times and in different places.[4]

History – typically embodied in historiography or history-writing as a recognised genre, and famously supposed to be based and dependent on facts and committed to the factual – is not a presentation or representation of the past, but rather what readers and audiences take history to be.[5] Revealingly, modern and ostensibly factual history began to be developed at the same time as what were later called counterfactuals, especially as part of the practice of modern history within the discourse of modernity.[6] Specifically 'modern' history was created, among other reasons, so that modernisers could identify, legitimate and promote themselves as modern.[7] In summary, modern history was not a set of facts, methods and discursive practices that represented 'the past' more or less well as a body of knowledge encoded in 'texts' or embodied in print objects to be decoded or interpreted consistently by users in any time or place. Modern history was produced from a variety of objects, including but not restricted to self-proclaimed historiography, by the users of these objects in their ongoing everyday creation of 'immortal ordinary society' as the ground of their modernity.[8]

Modernity is here understood as a contested discourse centred on themes of self-reflexive personal identity as the basis for ostensibly 'pure' (or disinterested) relationships of intimacy, conjugality, sociability, citizenship, humanitarianism, sympathy with nature and so on. Formed in and sustained by such relationships, this modern subject is supposedly better able to understand – and manage the consequences of – modernity as accelerating and widening change; intensified conditions of risk and trust; increasingly abstract or remotely operated social, political, economic and cultural systems; reconfigured and ever-changing chronotopes or represented/experienced time–space; and the need to disembed from the 'unmodern' (a phrase that entered into English in this period) and re-embed in the 'modern'.[9] Among other things, modern history provided its users with an ostensibly factualised, and hence (by modern socio-cultural convention) authoritative and reliable, manual for making a particular modernity. This modern history was 'modern' not just in the sense of being post-classical and post-medieval (another phrase that entered English in this period), but also in the sense of being a history for a modernity that was always contested.

In this contest, differing modern histories were all used to distinguish 'modernity' from 'unmodernity' and to counter the latter (past or present) while addressing the present as if it were the past of different futures that contending modernisers were seeking to bring about. The makers and users (not always readers) of 'modern' history created it in and for particular moments in order to assert, experience and effect a break between modernity (present or past) and history as 'the aggregate of past events' and 'the course of human affairs' (*OED*). Such modern history as historiography was titled not 'factual' (which came into English only late in the period) but 'authentic' – meaning 'in accordance with fact or stating the truth, and thus worthy of acceptance or belief; of established credit; able to be relied on; truthful, accurate' and 'genuine; not feigned or false' (*OED*).

Although the phrase 'authentic history' occurred earlier – and, like 'history', sometimes appeared in titles of fictional stories – a search of bibliographical databases (principally Eighteenth-Century Collections Online and WorldCat – OCLC) indicates that during the Romantic onset of modernity, historiography's makers increasingly restricted 'history' to the factual, while 'authentic history' became increasingly common in titles of historiographies, whereafter 'history' was widely understood as only factual and the qualifier 'authentic' disappeared. To obtain 'credit', makers of 'authentic history' deployed methods that ostensibly demonstrated its 'accordance with fact'; but like finance, law and other abstract systems, it ultimately depended on 'credit' in the sense of its users' belief in its authenticity in several senses: 'History is a body of beliefs, not a body of facts.'[10] Such credit also depended on distinguishing 'authentic' modern history from history purposely or unwittingly unfactual, non-factual, spuriously factual (or counterfeit and forged) and 'partisan'. But such credit could also be extended by history's users to works, representations, genres (plays, novels, verse narratives), media (painting, sculpture, architecture, illustration) and events (public spectacles, state and ecclesiastical rituals) not typically or rigorously marketed or purported to be fully 'factual' or 'authentic', but nevertheless 'worthy of acceptance or belief' as historified – as history of some creditable kind.

Professional practitioners of history as 'expert' modern knowledge treated what they regarded as unmodern and unauthentic history in three main ways: by marginalising, disciplining and policing. Disparaged 'unmodern' history was often classed as 'superstition'. One major form – later called 'providential' historiography – represented history, like nature, as divine handiwork; it was dominant up to the onset of modernity but was marginalised or dismissed thereafter. Another major form, long disparaged as 'superstition' but increasingly valued by certain modernisers, was history as 'traditional story', 'popular antiquities', 'fable', 'myth' (into English late in the period), or 'folklore' (into English even later). Some modernisers historicised these forms by collecting, editing and/or explaining them, thereby repurposing them for modern history and certain versions of modernity.[11] Some modern novelists – notably Walter Scott – incorporated such forms, paradoxically, to historify their fictions and sharpen the distinction of modern and unmodern therein.

By contrast, reformist 'popular antiquarians' collected historical popular lore and texts to preserve and celebrate plebeian life as history from 'below', informing a plebeian modernity as in Joseph Ritson's Robin Hood collections and William Hone's *Everyday Book* (1825). Meanwhile, as increasingly professionalised modern historiographers policed the boundaries of the factual-authentic (founding the institutionalised academic discipline we still have today), growing public appetite for historification supported a diverse and enterprising traffic in forgery, fakery and fiction.[12] Alongside reprints of authentic medieval literature, fakes such as Chatterton's 'Rowley' poems fed a growing interest in the origins of a 'national' literature. The ostensibly bardic poems of 'Ossian' (Napoleon's favourite poet) proved a transatlantic best-seller and a major inspiration to generations of artists and composers. With sensational forgeries relating to the 'national' bard, Shakespeare, W. H. Ireland launched a prolific career as historifier across multiple genres including authentic history, biography, current events, topography, drama and fiction. Makers and marketers of modern historiography – much as we still have it (including 'post-modern' history) – claimed or implied that it alone was factually true and thereby totalising, transhistorical and autotelic; that there was no other history worthy of the name; and that to be outside modern history, in several senses, was to be outside both modernity and history – history here conceived as the production of (a particular) modernity over time. Accepting these assumptions, modern history's users also allowed a broader range of historification across literature and other arts, and tolerated and even relished the role of forgeries, fakes, frauds and fiction in historification.

The acceleration of modernisation and consolidation of the discourse of modernity as a field of struggle prompted (and were prompted by) the prolonged struggle for Atlantic and global domination, where the decisive factor would be the ability to modernise effectively while mobilising national identity and purpose sufficiently to maintain the support of public opinion and the political nation.[13] The usefulness of 'modern' history for this task brought together authors, publishers, readers and technological and commercial innovators concerned about history as onrolling events and their place in it, thereby creating a history market comprising historiography and other genres that became increasingly diverse and competitive throughout the Romantic onset of modernity. History and historiography became a modern fashion in the sense of a complex and commercialised discourse of and for modern self-fashioning and performance of modernity.

The process is seen from the mid-eighteenth century in the production of a specifically 'modern' and 'national' history/historiography ostensibly distinct from its predecessor.[14] For some decades, the only such work had been the French Protestant Paul de Rapin de Thoyras's 1720s *Histoire d'Angleterre* up to the Glorious Revolution of 1688, as translated, annotated and continued by Nicholas Tindal.[15] This argued that modern England (and Britain after the 1706–7 Union with Scotland) was decisively established/stabilised at the Glorious Revolution of 1688 by achieving balance between the privileges of the people and royal prerogative. A prefatory author biography suggested that Rapin's history was validated by his own experience as soldier and politician in that Revolution and grounded in his recourse to numerous historical documents. Rhetorically, Rapin-Tindal was both 'factual' and fictionalised. It was substantial and detailed but often reconstructed events without documentation, attributed to historical agents feelings and motives that could not be known, sensationalised accounts of events and proceeded in a steadily energetic narrative style resembling certain ancient histories and seventeenth-century quasi-historified courtly romances read by the same social elites for whom the *History* was designed. Continuing demand for modern national history was stimulated by successive external wars and internal rebellion, and after the indecisive War of the Austrian Succession in 1748, Rapin-Tindal's copyright-holders planned a new edition in cheap serial numbers targeting a widening readership that was interested in political affairs linking the nation's history and its destiny, its past, present and future.

At this conjuncture, the philosopher David Hume, whose theorisations of modern subjectivity, culture, sociability, civil society and history in his treatises and essays had not brought the fame and fortune he desired, undertook a new history of Great Britain, aiming to exploit the character of the modern historian formed by the reception of Rapin-Tindal.[16] He also modernised in his own way the kind of history represented by that work. Hume's *History*, too, treated the Glorious Revolution as the foundation of modern Britain, narrating the preservation of 'British' (actually English) 'liberties' across preceding centuries and different governmental and political regimes. Through narrative style and method, however, Hume aimed to create a figure of the historian in the text neither as a writer of Rapin-Tindal factualised romance nor merely as a narrator of history as 'the aggregate of past events' and 'the course of human affairs', but rather as a sociable 'philosopher' and 'man of feeling' who invited readers to share his cultivated, manly, transhistorical perspective, aware of the unreliability of documents, the incompleteness of facts and the impossibility of determining historical causation.[17] Hume aimed to make the *History* both readable and affecting – moving the reader as self-reflexive modern subject and pleasing them by cultivating their awareness of being so moved (and made to feel modern). Hume aimed to make the *History* rhetorically 'impartial' (not serving party) but at the same time feeling; disinterested, but not uninterested.[18]

Such 'philosophical' but moving representation of past characters and incidents would supposedly call readers into being as self-reflexive and sociable, and hence modern, subjects – transforming them into self-consciously modern men (Hume associated women with 'romance', which he contrasted with history).[19] Such male readers would, Hume hoped, constitute a public opinion, civil society and political nation that would be able to avoid extremes; mediate dangerous social, religious and political differences; balance individual freedoms, social interests and government; achieve modernisation without destabilising social, economic and political structures; and thus ensure sustainable national and imperial strength in the ongoing contest for global power through modernisation.

However, readers are never called into being as anything, and Hume's readers/users would necessarily make their own meanings. The first volume of the *History of England, from the Invasion of Julius Caesar to the Revolution in 1688* was published in 1754, at first as *The History of Great Britain*; beginning with Caesar's invasion signalled Hume's exclusion of unmodern 'legendary' history. The *History* appeared in reverse temporal order; after a slow start caused by a booksellers' conspiracy, it became the 'standard' 'modern' and 'national' history throughout the onset of modernity. Whatever Hume's intentions, this success likely stemmed from several factors. Broadly, by making the *History* accessible as well as convincingly 'modern' in tone, style, method and perspective, Hume seems to have enabled numerous readers of all social conditions over decades to create meanings from reading, or merely owning, the *History* that helped them imagine themselves as 'modern' in various ways.[20] Further, not only did the *History*'s political perspective address its contemporary crisis; it could also be marshalled as a lens through which to read similar successive crises into the early nineteenth century. Importantly, its copyright holders responded promptly and astutely to such crises (and to rivals).

This success elicited a range of competitors promising a cheaper price, or greater length and detail, or shorter length and less detail, or broader temporal coverage, or greater convenience, or a more up-to-date perspective, or greater suitability for a particular readership, or different politics. Certain kinds and uses of factuality were countered by other kinds; historiographical method was a rhetorical and marketing device. Hume's first volume prompted advertisements for a rival publication by Tobias Smollett, which in turn prompted advertisements for the number-trade edition of Rapin-Tindal in sixpenny weekly parts (or 'numbers') addressed to a wide market. These advertisements disparaged both Hume and the as-yet-unpublished Smollett for lacking the length and detail of Rapin-Tindal's work. A countering advertisement of Smollett's history by someone styled the 'Author' promised it would be more modern than Rapin's by disencumbering 'the Detail of historical Events from the immense Farrago of transcrib'd Acts of parliament, Patents, Grants, Charters, Speeches, Treaties, Conventions, Letters, Votes, Resolutions, Manifestoes, Declarations, Remonstrances, Answers, Replies, Replications, dry Dissertation, insipid Remarks, and tedious Repetitions, with which it has hitherto been overloaded and oppressed'.[21]

Smollett's *A Complete History of England, deduced from the Descent of Julius Caesar, to the Treaty of Aix-la-Chapelle, 1748* – up-to-dateness would be increasingly important in marketing – began to appear in 1757 at three guineas for three (eventually four) quarto volumes (about six times a labourer's weekly wage). The *Complete History* was professedly designed to be useful and readable rather than 'philosophical' or exhaustive. Advertisements pointed out the dedication to William Pitt – to many, the man for the present crisis. The immediate success of the *Complete History* prompted its downmarketing. A revised edition followed in 1758 in 110 sixpenny weekly numbers with 167 engraved plates, which Smollett claimed reached sales of over 10,000 copies a week.[22] An eleven-volume edition in the usual mid-market octavo format soon appeared. In 1760, Smollett began publishing a *Continuation*.

Despite Smollett's success, Hume's *History* remained dominant, with 'new editions', 'corrected, and with some additions', appearing in 1770, 1773 and 1777. Modern history had to appear at once definitive about the past and revisable for the present. In 1778 there appeared an edition 'with the author's last corrections and improvements; to which is prefixed, a short account of his life, written by himself'.[23] As an Enlightenment exercise in self-reflection and self-vindication, Hume's 'life' validated his history differently from Rapin's in Rapin-Tindal: Hume appeared as historian-as-philosopher and sociable modern subject rather than as historian-as-man-of-action reflecting on history in retirement. Hume's 'life' would be published separately and assimilated in the booming market for autobiography as a major new discourse of self-reflexive personal identity in the onset of modernity. The 'modern' historian of the nation appeared as historian of his 'modern' self, each validating the other. Many associated Smollett's *History* with Tory politics and with a defence of royal prerogative, supported by the new monarch, George III; keeping abreast, Hume claimed that his revisions made his *History* more Tory.

Responding to increased competition, in 1785 Hume's and Smollett's copyright-holders published a five-volume *History of England, from the Revolution* [of 1688] *to the Death of George the Second, designed as a Continuation of Mr Hume's History*, using material from Smollett but with 'the sections, and other divisions … given in a manner correspondent with those observed by Hume'.[24] This merger made Hume and Smollett seem to be a single magisterial work but actually reduced Smollett to an update of Hume. Hume-Smollett, with further editions of Hume and of Smollett, remained the 'standard' 'national' 'modern' histories in the 1790s. These probably offered more counsel and comfort than ever amid Britain's global death struggle with a ruthlessly modernising revolutionary and Napoleonic France.

One response to this crisis of global power and even national survival (as it seemed at the time) was monumentalisation. History painting was the period's most prestigious pictorial genre, histories were typically illustrated, and the modern arts entrepreneur Robert Bowyer commissioned paintings from British history by notable artists and exhibited them commercially in his 'Historic Gallery' in Pall Mall. This was located close to similar 'national' cultural projects and institutions in the heart of capital, nation and empire: Boydell's Shakespeare Gallery, Macklin's Gallery of the Poets, Fuseli's Milton Gallery, Parliament, royal palaces, the Royal Academy and the Society for the Encouragement of Arts, Manufactures and Commerce. From 1793, Bowyer issued a lavish upmarket edition of Hume in folio parts illustrated with engravings from works in the 'Historic Gallery', reassuringly validating nation and empire as at once modern and historic against an avowedly anti-historic and super-modernising rival France.[25]

Another response was domestication, which enabled the middle classes to take this myth home, in several senses. Here, size mattered, countering more than supplementing large-format stately versions of the national historic factuals. Going beyond mid-market octavo format, in 1793 the firm of J. Parsons published a ten-volume 'pocket edition' in smaller duodecimo, splicing Hume, Smollett and 'a continuation to the present time by J. Barlow, Esqr'.[26] Also in 1793, the number-trade specialist Charles Cooke published a twenty-volume illustrated duodecimo Hume-Smollett with a continuation by 'Thomas Augustus Lloyd'. Publishers such as Cooke and Parsons specialised in 'elegant' illustrated editions of 'standard' literature for display to family, friends and business associates in the newly prominent sociable-domestic spaces of the 'library', 'drawing-room' (in grand homes) or 'parlour' (in modest ones). In 1795, a two-volume octavo abridgement was published by George Kearsley, who served an artisan and middle-class market increasingly seeking political information for their own interests. A mid-market five-volume octavo edition was offered by a large Scottish conger (or ad hoc publishers' consortium). Copyright-holders Cadell and Davies offered similar editions in 1796, 1797, 1801, 1802 and 1807. The market in expurgated 'classics' for the modern home such as the Bowdler's *Family Shakspeare* (1807) prompted the respectable firm of Hatchard to assuage the anxiety of the evangelicalised middle classes about Hume's reputed irreligion by issuing, in eight-volume octavo, *Hume's History of England, Revised for Family Use, with Such Omissions and Alterations as may Render it Salutary to the Young, and Unexceptionable to the Christian* (1816), adapted by George Berkeley Mitchell and dedicated to the bishop of Rochester.

The climax of the Napoleonic Wars prompted rival patriotic editions of Hume-Smollett-plus as yet another aspect of the unfolding commercial, political and cultural embodiment and variegation of the narrativised assemblage of national historical fact, designed to counter other nations' narratives. One was updated to 1814 and then 1815 by the journalist Hewson Clarke. Fisher and Associates published an *Imperial History of England* based on Hume-Smollett, updated in successive editions by 'Theophilus Camden' (probably spurious) and John Watkins (probably real). Cadell joined large congers of leading London mid-market firms in 1818 (issuing Hume), 1823 (issuing Hume-Smollett), and 1830 (issuing Hume), applying force of numbers against competition from mid- and downmarket firms such as Fisher, Tegg, Kelly, Jones, Allman, Walker and Valpy. In the 1820s, the *History* appeared in Jones's 'British Historians' alongside similar series of 'British' poets, essayists, dramatists and novelists and in William Pickering's 'Oxford English Classics', which consolidated and commercialised an emergent 'national' literary canon. Such market diversification indicated various uses for Hume-Smollett-plus – uses that included 'furniture' book, school book, self-education classic, source of political information and a vehicle for participation through material consumption in 'national' identity, culture and politics. Finally, as the *History*'s prestige and usefulness as historiography seemed to be waning before competition and changing modernity, other publishers, following Pickering, successfully transferred it from 'standard' historiography to belletristic 'classic' in the emergent canon of 'national' literature, where it was made to serve modernity differently (and where it remains). Downmarket, it remained the basis for further adaptations as the 'national' history.

Although Hume-Smollett-plus dominated the modern history market throughout the Romantic onset of modernity, Rapin-Tindal still appealed to publishers and readers, usually in the form of John Lockman's popularised *History of England, by Question and Answer*. New rivals continued to appear, especially mid-market, downmarket and for schools. Oliver Goldsmith – prolific and respected writer of modern literature and populariser of modern knowledges – produced a *History of England in a Series of Letters from a Nobleman to his Son* (from 1764) for the education-specialist firm of Newbery and a *History of England from the Earliest Times to the Death of George II* (from 1771) for Hume-Smollett's copyright-holder in a conger with others. This was a 'careful plagiarizing' of Hume – 'almost word-for-word', indeed, on the Tudors and Stuarts.[27] 'Complete' or abridged, Goldsmith's histories of England were republished almost every year into the mid-nineteenth century. Tindal's or John Kelly's version of Rapin was republished in various editions in the 1780s by the firm of Harrison and in early-nineteenth-century stereotype editions from Cundee and from Jones and Co. – all specialists in multi-volume illustrated number-trade editions of 'classic' and 'British' belles-lettres. In the 1790s, the reformist London Corresponding Society commissioned a member to produce a similar work to reflect and circulate their view of the 'national' history, but John Baxter's *A New and Impartial History of England* (1796) was barely different from other pastiches of Hume-Smollett.[28] Apparent countering of one version of the facts with another, ideologically and politically superior, version could be deceptive and illusory.

Another, though differently motivated, competitor for authorising the factuality of the national past, present and future was what would later be called 'providential history'. John Wesley's 4-volume *Concise History of England, from the Earliest Times, to the Death of George II* (1776) was published, suggestively, on the threshold of the American crisis. Though Wesley avowedly adapted modern secular histories by Goldsmith, Rapin and Smollett (Hume, considered irreligious, was omitted), he complained that most histories 'seem calculated only for Atheists; for there is nothing about GOD in them'; his aim was 'to habituate the readers of English History, to a nobler way of thinking: as I desire myself to see GOD pervading the moral, as well as the natural world, so I would fain have others to see him, in all civil events, as well as in all the Phænomena of nature'.[29] Unusually for a work by Wesley, this was not reprinted, despite the efficient and ready-made Methodist print distribution network. Hester Piozzi's providentialist world history, *Retrospection* (1801), written during the prolonged Napoleonic crisis when many were reading 'signs of the times' for divine intentions, was nevertheless ignored or ridiculed. By the 1820s, most self-consciously modern religious citizens interested in reforming Church and State eschewed providentialist and millenarian history for historiographies vindicating with modern facts and scholarship one or another church or sect in history and modernity. Here was yet another body of national historical factuals countering and contradicting others. These included John Lingard's pro-Catholic *History of England from the first Invasion of the Romans to the Accession of Mary* (1819–30); the philosophical anarchist William Godwin's pro-Dissenter, republican *History of the Commonwealth of England* (1824–28); loyalist poet laureate Robert Southey's anti-Catholic and anti-Dissenter defence of the established order of Church and State in his *Book of the Church* (1824); and the reformist William Cobbett's attack (using Lingard) on the establishment in his *History of the Protestant 'Reformation', in England and Ireland; Showing how that Event has impoverished and degraded the main Body of the People in those Countries* (1824).

In the face of a growing and diversifying market for modern history, some number-trade publishers resorted to counterfeit and fraud, as in 'continuations' of Hume-Smollett 'by' Cooke's 'Thomas Augustus Lloyd'. Though there were abridgements, pastiches and adaptations of Hume-Smollett, there appear to have been no contested piracies.[30] In 1770, John Cooke, who learned the number trade with the inventive Alex Hogg and whose son Charles was the next generation's leading number-trade specialist, began publishing *A New and Universal History of England from the Earliest Authentic Accounts, to the End of the Year 1770, Containing a Comprehensive and Accurate Description of the Battles, Sieges, Sea-fights, and other Memorable Events*, by 'William Henry Mountague, Esq.' Like similar works, this had a loose narrative style closer to Rapin-Tindal than Hume and was 'enriched' with numerous copper engravings dramatically reimagining historical events, just as the title of the work associated history with adventure tales, anticipating the imminent fashion for historical or historified adventure-fiction, drama and verse narrative.

'Mountague' was republished in 1775. In 1772, 'the Proprietors' and the number-trade specialist J. Walker published *A General History of England from the Descent of Julius Caesar, to the Year One Thousand Seven Hundred and Seventy-Two*, by 'Charles Augustus Cowley'; it was republished by Walker in 1781, updated to that year, with 'an impartial account of the rise and progress of the unhappy contest between Great Britain and America'. An almost identical work by 'Charlotte Cowley' had been published in 1780 by 'the Proprietors' and S. Bladon entitled *The Ladies History of England, from the Descent of Julius Caesar, to the Summer of 1780, Calculated for the Use of the Ladies of Great-Britain and Ireland, and Likewise Adapted to General Use, Entertainment, and Instruction*.

This highlighted the issue of gender and history in modernity, and has recently interested historians of women writing 'learned' discourses.[31] *The Ladies History* appeared after early volumes of Catharine Macaulay's scholarly, republican and controversial *History of England* (1763) and her more popular *History of England, from the Revolution to the Present Time* (1778). Macaulay was widely recognised as a 'learned lady' or blue-stocking – a figure some saw as a positive feature of British modernity and others as a vestige of unmodern snobbery, intrusion of (French) foreignness or modernity taken too far – which some publishers saw as an opportunity.[32]

The Ladies History was dedicated, loyally, to Charlotte, Princess Royal. It was sold in three formats: entire by subscription; door-to-door in weekly sixpenny numbers; and across the counter in volume form at thirty-six shillings. The large subscribers' list included many women. Advertisements signed 'Charlotte Cowley' declared: 'Amidst the great Variety of Histories of England, not one has been peculiarly adapted to the Use of the Ladies; yet many of the eminent Women of this Country have been as nobly distinguished as any of the other Sex; and frequently have they set Examples worthy the Imitation of the proudest among the Men.' Advertisements promised that the book would 'interweave' 'the most striking Traits in the Characters of our most illustrious Women'.[33] The Preface to *The Ladies History* reversed a misogynist stereotype, declaring that 'the curiosity so frequently derided in our Sex, is, in this instance at least, truly laudable; for the acquirement of knowledge, especially that of our own Country, may be fairly reckoned among the most useful of our pursuits'.[34] The promised emphasis on 'our most illustrious Women' was not fulfilled, though female monarchs were well covered. The book was otherwise a straightforward narrative. As with Tory history, Whig history, Jacobin history, providential history and others, 'ladies history' purported to be (more than was) an alternative if not countering version of now-standardised historical factuality.

Textually, the histories of Charles Augustus Cowley and Charlotte Cowley were almost identical, but authorship of *The Ladies History* is less significant than the market indicated by its subscribers list. Despite the royal dedicatee, few members of the nobility subscribed, though the controversial Elizabeth, Lady Craven – a reputed 'learned lady' and notorious adulteress – took ten copies. Women subscribers were many; mostly from London, they were often residents or proprietors of some 'Ladies' Boarding School'. Number-trade subscribers' lists could be as much a marketing device as a record of purchasers; this one, however, suggests that many took the work to be by a woman for women, disclosing a market for historiography with that perspective, especially in the context of genteel female education. Educationists promoted history for multiple purposes: as an antidote to the supposed female propensity for novel-reading; as class-based cultural capital; as displacement of fiction's assumed fantasy by history's supposed facts; and as an exercise in Humean rational sympathy that moderated the dangerous passions evoked by 'romance'. The commercial and socio-cultural-political potential of women's historiography suggested by subscription to *The Ladies History* was reinforced in Jane Austen's unpublished 1790s burlesque of male historiography in which she complained that historiography contained few women. History that mattered would soon be relocated from the male to the female sphere by historiography about women by writers such as Lucy Aikin and Elizabeth Benger and a wave of women's and men's historical fiction, drama and verse narrative.

Meanwhile, competing number-trade pastiches of modern histories by bogus authors increased their appeal by extending coverage from the earliest historic records to the year of the book's last number. In 1773, 1774 and 1775, J. Cooke published *A New and Complete History of England from the Earliest Period of Authentic Intelligence to the Present Time* by 'Temple Sydney'. In 1777, Cooke offered a very similar title by 'William Augustus Russell'. In 1791, the firm of W. and J. Stratford began selling sixpenny weekly numbers of a very similar title by 'Charles Alfred Ashburton'. Soon the 'national' history was extended further to legendary – or what by 1832 would be called 'pre-historic' – times. From 1793 to 1795, Alex Hogg published *The New, Authentic, Impartial and Complete History of England, from the first Settlement of Brutus in this Island (Upwards of a Thousand Years before the Time of Julius Cæsar) to the Year 1795*, by 'George William Spencer'. All of these works carried numerous illustrations (some recycled), sold in sixpenny weekly large-format numbers, bore similar titles, emphasised newness and completeness, often carried lists of reassuringly middle-class 'subscribers' and had 'authors' with genteel-sounding names otherwise unknown to historical record. Such fabrications sought greater market penetration in the early nineteenth century by exploiting the new technologies of the iron press, stereotyping, machine-made paper, steam-powered printing, cheaper illustration processes and an expanding transport distribution network.

As the number trade's commercial and socio-cultural importance grew, some of those involved sought to dispel the long-standing association with shady practices such as issuing pastiche works ascribed to sham authors. Authors – if still hacks – were now often named, known and even respected men of letters of an emergent modern kind. Thomas Kelly was the most prominent innovative and ostentatiously respectable early-nineteenth-century number-trade specialist. He issued hundreds of thousands of Bibles, standard religious works, manuals, loyalist royal obituary biographies, geographies and atlases, alongside journalistic accounts of notorious crimes and scandals in high life and moralistic but titillating novels. In 1815, amid national triumphalism, Kelly published a work with a title that promised to unify all previous and countering national modern histories: *The Grand National History of England, Civil and Ecclesiastical, from the Earliest Period of Genuine Record to the Year 1815; Comprehending a Faithful Narrative of Historical Occurrences from the first Sources, their Causes, and the Consequences and Events therewith Connected; Describing with the Strictest Impartiality, the Various Changes and Revolutions which have been Effected in the British Dominions, and the True Principles by which they have been Occasioned; including the Modern History of Europe, from the Commencement of the Reign of King George the Third.*[35] The author named was John Malham, a clergyman and schoolteacher who popularised modern knowledges for London number-trade specialists, mainly Kelly. Malham's *History* was grand in several senses and yet affordable, published in folio with numerous engravings in 144 weekly numbers at eight pence each or 12 larger parts at eight shillings each. In 1831 in the Great Reform Bill contest, Kelly tried another overt gesture at unity of factuals amid national division, publishing a work of very similar title, ostensibly by 'H. Clarke, Esq.' – perhaps the shadowy Hewson Clarke, author of a *Modern History of England*, published in 1815, and of another continuation of Hume-Smollett.

Current events repeatedly recontextualised and hence enabled the repurposing and recommercialisation of modern history. Post-war social and economic dislocation, the near-revolutionary 1821 Queen Caroline crisis, public opposition to the government's post-war continental policy, the 1820s campaign to remove civil restrictions on Catholics and Protestant Dissenters and agitation for parliamentary reform culminating in the 1832 Reform Bill all stimulated demand for 'national' and 'modern' history, usually met by updated number-trade editions of Hume-Smollett or pastiches such as Kelly's of 1831. So common were these that an 1831 pro-Reform Bill pamphlet could purport to be a number from a *History of England* published a hundred years later pretending to look back on the consequences of the Bill's rejection – an obvious counterfactual of the kind used since that period and increasingly recognised, deployed and commercialised by historians in recent decades.[36] In Birmingham – hotbed of pro-Reform Bill agitation – a 'J. C. Campbell' (otherwise unknown to bibliography) authored *A New and Popular History of England, from the Earliest Records, to the Passing of the Reform Bills, in the Reign of William IV; Compiled with the Greatest Care, principally from Hume and Smollett, and continued to the Present Day*. This was published from 1833 to 1838 and sold by W. Emans, whose career characterised downmarket bookselling: possibly a stationer in London, bankrupt; bookseller in Birmingham, bankrupt; bookseller in London, bankrupt again. The work illustrates the by-now-typical back-and-forth between a supposedly fixed and factual national history and the current events that prompted interest in such supposedly stable history while at the same time eliciting a historiography purportedly responsive to such events. Emans's career illustrates the perils of such commercial speculation and opportunism.

In the aftermath of the 1832 Reform Act, Hume-Smollett-plus was remade in such ways yet again, targeting an increasingly literate and socially enlarged public for whom reading and/or owning a canon of such modern knowledges constituted cultural citizenship that underwrote claims to political citizenship. In the 1830s, the journalist F. G. Tomlins compiled historical and geographical works for this market, exemplified in his *History of England, combining the various Histories by Rapin, Hume, Smollett, and Belsham, Corrected by Reference to Turner, Lingard, Mackintosh, Hallam, Brodie, Godwin and other Sources*. The title assembled established and recent upmarket historians of diverse political and religious associations, implying that Tomlins's *History* was up to date, comprehensive and above partisanship. In 1834, Mayhew, Isaac and Co. sold Tomlins's *History* in volume form and in 'cheap weekly and monthly issues' from their 'National Library Office' in Covent Garden, alongside 'Standard Works' such as the Bible, Shakespeare, Sheridan's plays, Rollin's ancient history, a compilation history of America, picaresque novels (Defoe, Cervantes, Lesage), a Universal Biography, 'classic' essayists, a dictionary, an English grammar, a natural history, geography, a gazetteer, an atlas and comic periodicals.[37]

Tomlins's *History* was republished by others, and in the 1840s he produced a universal history for other downmarket firms, including the major Victorian publisher of books for the people, Milner of Halifax, with their ubiquitous pocket-format 'Cottage Library', which also reissued Goldsmith's *History of England*. This longevity and this company of works in different discourses and genres illustrate the malleability of modern history within the growing panoply of modern knowledges in a highly commercialised print market.

Militantly, more than crassly, downmarket was *The Pictorial History of England* published from 1837 by Charles Knight and Co. In the 1820s, Knight attempted a version of the 'National Library' of Mayhew, Isaac and Co., but failed and became publisher to the Society for the Diffusion of Useful Knowledge, a Utilitarian-dominated populariser of modern knowledges. *The Pictorial History* was written neither by gentleman scholars nor by the emergent cadre of academic historiographers but rather by Knight's house staff of professional knowledge-journalists led by G. L. Craik. It appeared in large-format, double-column, illustrated weekly sixpenny numbers, monthly two-shilling parts and bound volumes.[38] Knight used modern technologies to industrialise door-to-door and across-the-counter modern knowledges targeting the 'industrial classes' – a new phrase in public discourse. Such technologies were designed to displace this demographic's own supposedly unmodern print culture, discredit their supposed excessively modernising radical politics and educe them into a subordinate place in his and his backers' capitalist version of industrial modernity. *The Pictorial History* was frequently republished, and though Knight overreached and went bankrupt, he anticipated similar projects by publishers such as Chambers and Cassell that took such popularised modern knowledges through to the next century.

The Romantic onset of modernity produced modern histories of all kinds for many purposes, from translations of county-based sections of the Domesday Book to a history of glove-making used to ground arguments for duties on French glove imports, and history came to pervade all arts and discourses to an extent impossible to summarise here. Famously, however, there were central elements of modernity that history could represent only inadequately, if at all, since 'facts' about them were few, lost, never existed or were not 'facts' before modernity's onset. While modern history was advertised as reinterpreting known 'facts' and though it accumulated new 'facts' for representing national chronotopes, institutions and social practices, it had few or no 'facts' for representing from the 'inside' past instances of self-reflexive personal identity and 'pure' relationships of intimacy, conjugality and sociability; for calculating risk and trust; for understanding abstract systems and new chronotopes; or for articulating the experience of disembedding from unmodernity and reembedding in some modernity or other. Consequently, demand for modern history with such elements was met by speculation, fraud, forgery or fiction. As in commerce, so in history: speculation undermined the certainty of 'authentic history', and fraud and forgery (as in the Shakespeare, Ossian and Rowley literary scandals) undermined its 'credit'.

The most successful rival of 'authentic history' in the onset of modernity was a modernised and historified form of its long-recognised counterpart – 'fictitious history', or the novel. Like 'authentic history', the phrase 'fictitious history' appeared earlier but increased in frequency across the period, after which it was deleted or replaced by some alternative. The role and importance of 'fictitious history' in modernity was increasingly asserted, as in Scottish Professor Hugh Blair's often republished *Lectures on Rhetoric and Belles Lettres* (1783), novelist and intellectual Clara Reeve's pioneering literary history, *The Progress of Romance* (1785), and philosopher and novelist William Godwin's (then unpublished) 1797 essay 'Of History and Romance'.

Significantly, historified fiction emerged and developed alongside the following assertion: 'The novel implies that it is a needed supplement to history, its probabilistic truths adding an essential dimension to historical understanding even if they are not verifiably referential.'[39] Novels are lifeless objects and cannot imply anything, but rather are made to imply certain things by readers in their uniquely creative acts of meaning-making. Nevertheless, reader demand prompted increasing numbers of historicised 'fictitious history' in novels, dramas and verse narratives, probably because such 'histories' could be made to surpass 'modern' historiography by inventing subjective and social historical 'facts' unavailable to historiography-as-documented-'fact' and thereby accomplish the kind of descriptive, cultural and ideological work for modernity and modernisers that history as such could not be made to do.

Works entitled 'historical novel' and 'historical romance' – mostly

Door-to-door and across-the-counter factuals

from French and barely historified – appeared from the mid-eighteenth century, but the fashion for modern history initiated by Hume and Smollett in the 1750s soon prompted development and diversification of historified 'fictitious history', signalled by novels responding to Hume and Rapin.[40] The lightly antiquarianised *Longsword, Earl of Salisbury: An Historical Romance* (1762) was soon out-historified by others but was republished into the early nineteenth century.[41] Horace Walpole, author of the spoofishly historified *The Castle of Otranto: A Story* (1765), or 'Gothic Story' in the second edition, had earlier written to Hume to criticise his modern historical method. Clara Reeve's *The Champion of Virtue: A Gothic Story* (1777, republished 1778 as *The Old English Baron*) was informed by Rapin-Tindal's Whig history of England. *Otranto* and *The Old English Baron* quickly became modern classics, frequently republished together during the period. They initiated a market for the 'gothic' as pseudo-historical representation of unmodernity (past or present). Such works were characterised by hyperbolic representations from the 'inside' of modern subjectivity, intimacy, domesticity and sociability, and other major themes of the discourse of modernity. Reeve herself theorised and historicised this role of fiction in *The Progress of Romance*, arguing that the novel was more useful in the education of men and women for modernity than the historic male syllabus of ancient 'classics'.

From the 1760s, women writers increasingly, if controversially, participated in modern knowledges by exploiting the greater access to education promoted in modernity (evidenced by the reception of Charlotte Cowley's *History of England*) and their supposedly innate expertise in modernity's central elements of subjective and private experience. From the 1780s, women writers increasingly converged 'authentic' and 'fictitious' history to remake a 'learned' discourse from which they were otherwise assumed – by Hume, for example – to be barred by education, experience, propensity and capacity.[42] Title phrases such as 'historical novel' and 'historical romance' multiplied and were increasingly differentiated from 'gothic' novels, especially by publishers associated (exaggeratedly) with women authors and readers such as William Lane's Minerva Press. Indicative of these trends was a 1793 advertisement for *The Siege of Belgrade: An Historical Novel* (1791, anonymous), followed immediately by an advertisement for editions of Hume and Hume-Smollett.[43]

By the 1810s and 1820s, male-dominated modern historical factuals had been not only supplemented but also countered and surpassed among the reading public by female-centred, historified and often historically documented modern fictionals. Jane Porter's *The Scottish*

Chiefs: A Romance (1810), published during the Napoleonic cataclysm, envisioned the thirteenth-century Scottish war of independence in terms of subjective, erotic and domestic relations; it was republished through the century and beyond, and adapted as the 1995 film *Braveheart*. In the Napoleonic crisis and aftermath, the historically documented poems and dramas of Felicia Hemans critiqued crises in world history as a masculinist failure to accommodate just those 'feminine' values of modernity that historiography could not know; Hemans became the most widely read woman poet in the nineteenth-century English-speaking world. Mary Shelley similarly fictionalised certain past historical crises, as in *Valperga* (1823) and *Perkin Warbeck* (1830), but also (like several contemporaries) ficto-historicised the present by looking back at it from the future, as in *The Last Man* (1826). From the 1810s to the 1830s, Scott responded repeatedly to these and other feminisations of modern history through fiction by means of more thorough historification of his fiction, a burlesquing of unmodern antiquarian history and the location of female and plebeian characters in unmodern folkloric culture. He became the most influential novelist in history. Despite his and others' efforts of this kind, for many readers – male and female – historified 'fictitious history', including Scott's, extended or even relocated history that mattered from the public, political and male-dominated sphere to the private, affective and erotic female-influenced sphere.

A century and more later, 'historical fiction', as it was being called by the 1820s, was widely promoted by commentators from Hegelian Marxists to Harvard professors as a major discourse of modernity,[44] while a 2015 survey of popular historical fiction readers reported that the genre's greatest appeal was 'to bring the past to life [and show] how people lived in the past'.[45] Modern history as history for modernity 'cuts across any traditional (reocentric) distinction between fact and fiction', or the idea that history represents in words actual things that happened and people that were, 'and by implication expands the class of historians more widely than conservative historians might like' – or than academic history can allow.[46] Put another way, 'we are better served if we think of history as a family of related genres' – and media – 'rather than (as customarily) a simple, unitary one'.[47] Put still another way, 'expert' knowledges essential to modernisation and central to the discourse of modernity – including history – necessarily circulate beyond experts, among those who use it to make themselves and their 'immortal everyday society'.[48]

Notes

1. See Harold Garfinkel and Kenneth Liberman, 'Introduction: The Lebenswelt Origin of the Sciences', *Human Studies*, 30:1 (March 2007), 3–7.
2. See, among his other works, Roy Harris, *Signs, Language, and Communication: Integrational and Segregational Approaches* (London: Routledge, 1996).
3. See for example D. F. McKenzie, *Bibliography and the Sociology of Texts* (London: British Library, 1986).
4. See Alec McHoul, *Semiotic Investigations: Towards an Effective Semiotics* (Lincoln, NE: University of Nebraska Press, 1996), pp. 65–87.
5. See Roy Harris, *The Linguistics of History* (Edinburgh: Edinburgh University Press, 2004).
6. See Reinhart Koselleck, *The Practice of Conceptual History: Timing History, Spacing Concepts*, trans. Todd Samuel Presner *et al.* (Stanford, CA: Stanford University Press, 2002). On the eighteenth-century emergence of counterfactuals, see Richard J. Evans, *Altered Pasts: Counterfactuals in History* (Waltham, MA: Brandeis University Press/Historical Society of Israel, 2013), p. 3.
7. See Reinhart Koselleck, *Futures Past: On the Semantics of Historical Time*, trans. Keith Tribe (New York: Columbia University Press, 2004).
8. See Harold Garfinkel, 'Evidence for Locally Produced, Naturally Accountable Phenomena of Order, Logic, Reason, Meaning, Method, etc. in and as of the Essential Quiddity of Immortal Ordinary Society (I of IV): An Announcement of Studies', *Sociological Theory*, 6:1 (Spring 1988), 103–9.
9. See Anthony Giddens, *The Consequences of Modernity* (Stanford, CA: Stanford University Press, 1990); *Modernity and Self-identity: Self and Society in the Late Modern Age* (Stanford, CA: Stanford University Press, 1991); and *The Transformation of Intimacy: Sexuality, Love, and Eroticism in Modern Societies* (Stanford, CA: Stanford University Press, 1992).
10. Harris, *The Linguistics of History*, p. 226.
11. See Richard M. Dorson, *The British Folklorists: A History* (London: Routledge & Kegan Paul, 1968); Marilyn Butler, 'Popular Antiquarianism', in Iain McCalman *et al.* (eds), *An Oxford Companion to the Romantic Age: British Culture, 1776–1832* (Oxford: Oxford University Press, 1999), pp. 328–37.
12. See Philippa Levine, *The Amateur and the Professional: Antiquarians, Historians, and Archaeologists in Victorian England, 1838–1886* (Cambridge: Cambridge University Press, 1986).

13 See John Brewer, *The Sinews of Power: War, Money, and the English State, 1688–1783* (New York: Knopf, 1989).
14 See Ben Dew, 'An Economic Turn? Commerce and Finance in the Historical Writing of Paul de Rapin Thoyras, William Guthrie and David Hume', in Ben Dew and Fiona Price (eds), *Historical Writing in Britain, 1688–1830: Visions of History* (Basingstoke: Palgrave, 2014), pp. 73–91.
15 See Philip Hicks, *Neoclassical History and English Culture from Clarendon to Hume* (Basingstoke: Macmillan, 1996), pp. 146–50.
16 See Ernest Campbell Mossner, *The Life of David Hume*, 2nd edn (Oxford: Clarendon Press, 1980), pp. 301–18; M. G. Sullivan, 'Rapin, Hume and the Identity of the Historian in Eighteenth-century England', *History of European Ideas*, 28:3 (2002), 145–62.
17 See Nicholas Phillipson, *David Hume: The Philosopher as Historian* (New Haven, CT: Yale University Press, 1989); J. C. Hilson, 'Hume: The Historian as Man of Feeling', *Prose Studies*, 3:2 (September 1980), 93–108; Hicks, *Neoclassical History and English Culture*, pp. 170–209.
18 See Donald T. Siebert, 'The Sentimental Sublime in Hume's *History of England*', *Review of English Studies*, 40:159 (August 1989), 352–72.
19 In his essay 'Of the Study of History'; see Kathryn Temple, '"Manly Composition": Hume and the History of England', in Anne Jaap Jacobson (ed.), *Feminist Interpretations of David Hume* (University Park, PA: Penn State University Press, 2000), pp. 263–82.
20 See Mark Towsey, '"The Book Seemed to Sink into Oblivion": Reading Hume's *History* in Eighteenth-century Scotland', in Mark C. Spencer (ed.), *David Hume: Historical Thinker, Historical Writer* (University Park, PA: Penn State University Press, 2013), pp. 81–102; and, in the same volume, David Allan, 'Reading Hume's *History of England*: Audience and Authority in Georgian England', pp. 103–20.
21 'To the Public'; *London Evening Post*, 17–19 March 1757, n.p.
22 See Lewis M. Knapp, *Tobias Smollett: Doctor of Men and Manners* (Princeton, NJ: Princeton University Press, 1949), pp. 186–7; Karen O'Brien, 'The History Market in Eighteenth-century England', in Isabel Rivers (ed.), *Books and their Readers in Eighteenth-century England: New Essays* (London: Continuum, 2001), p. 114.
23 *The History of England: From the Invasion of Julius Caesar to the Revolution in 1688 ... A New Edition, with the Author's Last Corrections and Improvements. To which is prefixed, a Short Account of his Life, Written by Himself*, 8 vols (London: T. Cadell, 1778).
24 David Hume and Tobias Smollett, *The History of England, from the Revolution [of 1688] to the Death of George the Second, designed as a*

Continuation of Mr Hume's History, 5 vols (London: T. Cadell and R. Baldwin, 1785), 'Advertisement', n.p.
25 See Cynthia Ellen Roman, 'Pictures for Private Purses: Robert Bowyer's Historic Gallery and Illustrated Edition of David Hume's *History of England*' (unpublished PhD thesis, Brown University, 1997).
26 The attribution of authorship by some library catalogues to the reformist American poet, diplomat and businessman Joel Barlow seems highly improbable.
27 See Laura B. Kennelly, 'Tory History Incognito: Hume's *History of England* in Goldsmith's *History of England*', *Clio*, 20:2 (December 1991), 169–83.
28 See Steve Poole, '"Not Precedents to be Followed but Examples to be Weighed": John Thelwall and the Jacobin Sense of the Past', in Steve Poole (ed.), *John Thelwall: Radical Romantic and Acquitted Felon* (London: Pickering & Chatto, 2009), p. 167.
29 John Wesley, *A Concise History of England, from the Earliest Times, to the Death of George II*, 4 vols (London: Robert Hawes, 1776), pp. v–vi, vii–ix.
30 I find none in H. Tomás Gómez-Arostegui, 'Register of Copyright Infringement Suits & Actions From *c*.1560 to 1800', https://law.lclark.edu/faculty/h_tomas_gomez_arostegui/appendix/ (accessed 27 March 2017).
31 See for example O'Brien, 'The History Market in Eighteenth-century England', pp. 126–7 and Philip Hicks, 'Female Worthies and the Genres of Women's History', in Dew and Price (eds), *Historical Writing in Britain, 1688–1830*, p. 24.
32 See Gary Kelly, 'Bluestocking Work: Learning, Literature, and Lore in the Onset of Modernity', in Deborah Heller (ed.), *Bluestockings Now! The Evolution of a Social Role* (Farnham, Ashgate, 2015), pp. 175–208.
33 'A Work Entirely New', *St James's Chronicle*, 25–7 January 1780, n.p.
34 Charlotte Cowley, *The Ladies History of England, from the Descent of Julius Caesar, to the Summer of 1780, Calculated for the Use of the Ladies of Great-Britain and Ireland, and Likewise Adapted to General Use, Entertainment, and Instruction* (London: S. Bladon, 1780), p. v.
35 This was possibly taken over from the firm of Richard Evans, whose stock Kelly acquired on Evans's retirement; see 'To the Booksellers and the Public in General', *Trewman's Exeter Flying Post*, 17 December 1818, n.p.
36 Anon., *A Leaf from the Future History of England on the Subject of Reform in Parliament* (London: Roake and Varty, [1831]).
37 'National Library Office', *Aris's Birmingham Gazette*, 2 June 1834, p. 1.

38 'On the 1st of June will be Published', *The Standard*, 27 May 1831, p. 1.
39 Everett Zimmerman, *The Boundaries of Fiction: History and the Eighteenth-century British Novel* (Ithaca, NY: Cornell University Press, 1998), pp. 1–2.
40 See Jonathan Dent, 'Contested Pasts: David Hume, Horace Walpole and the Emergence of Gothic Fiction', *Gothic Studies*, 14:1 (May 2012), 21–32.
41 Later ascribed to the Irish clergyman, antiquarian, historian of Ireland and history professor, Thomas Leland.
42 See Lisa Kasmer, *Novel Histories: British Women Writing History, 1760–1830* (Madison, WI: Fairleigh Dickinson University Press, 2012), pp. 69–130.
43 *Leeds Intelligencer*, 11 February 1793, p. 2
44 See György Lukács, *The Historical Novel*, trans. Hannah Mitchell and Stanley Mitchell (Boston, MA: Beacon Press, 1963); Jill Lepore, 'Just the Facts, Ma'am: Fake Memoirs, Factual Fictions, and the History of History', *The New Yorker*, 24 March 2008; www.newyorker.com/magazine/2008/03/24/just-the-facts-maam (accessed 15 August 2017).
45 M. K. Tod, '2015 Historical Fiction Reader Survey', https://awriterofhistory.files.wordpress.com/2015/06/2015-report-final2.pdf (accessed 15 August 2017).
46 Harris, *The Linguistics of History*, p. 175.
47 Mark Salber Phillips, *Society and Sentiment: Genres of Historical Writing in Britain, 1740–1820* (Princeton, NJ: Princeton University Press, 2000), p. 343.
48 See Jerome de Groot, *Consuming History: Historians and Heritage in Contemporary Popular Culture* (London: Routledge, 2009).

Works cited

Primary texts

Anon., 'A Work Entirely New', *St James's Chronicle*, 25–7 January 1780, n.p.
Anon., [advertisement for *The Siege of Belgrade*], *Leeds Intelligencer*, 11 February 1793, p. 2
Anon., *A Leaf from the Future History of England on the Subject of Reform in Parliament* (London: Roake and Varty, [1831])
Anon., 'National Library Office', *Aris's Birmingham Gazette*, 2 June 1834, p. 1
Anon., 'On the 1st of June will be Published', *The Standard*, 27 May 1831, p. 1

Anon., 'To the Booksellers and the Public in General', *Trewman's Exeter Flying Post*, 17 December 1818, n.p.
Anon., 'To the Public'; *London Evening Post*, 17–19 March 1757, n.p.
Cowley, Charlotte, *The Ladies History of England, from the Descent of Julius Caesar, to the Summer of 1780, Calculated for the Use of the Ladies of Great-Britain and Ireland, and Likewise Adapted to General Use, Entertainment, and Instruction* (London: S. Bladon, 1780)
Hume, David, *The History of England, from the Invasion of Julius Caesar to the Revolution in 1688*, 6 vols (London: A. Millar, 1754–62)
Hume, David and Tobias Smollett, *The History of England, from the Revolution* [of 1688] *to the Death of George the Second, designed as a Continuation of Mr Hume's History*, 5 vols (London: T. Cadell and R. Baldwin, 1785)
Macaulay, Catharine, *The History of England, from the Accession of James I to that of the Brunswick Line*, 8 vols (London: J. Nourse, 1763)
Macaulay, Catharine, *The History of England, from the Revolution to the Present Time, in a Series of Letters to the Reverend Doctor Wilson* (Bath: R. Cruttwell, 1778)
Mitchell, George Berkeley, *Hume's History of England, Revised for Family Use, with Such Omissions and Alterations as may Render it Salutary to the Young, and Unexceptionable to the Christian* (London: J. Hatchard, 1816)
Smollett, Tobias, *A Complete History of England, deduced from the Descent of Julius Caesar, to the Treaty of Aix-la-Chapelle, 1748*, 4 vols (London: James Rivington and James Fletcher, 1757–58)
Thoyras, Paul de Rapin de, *Histoire d'Angleterre*, 13 vols (La Haye: A. de Rogissart, 1724–36)
Wesley, John, *A Concise History of England, from the Earliest Times, to the Death of George II*, 4 vols (London: Robert Hawes, 1776)

Secondary texts

Allan, David, 'Reading Hume's *History of England*: Audience and Authority in Georgian England', in Mark C. Spencer (ed.), *David Hume: Historical Thinker, Historical Writer* (University Park, PA: Penn State University Press, 2013), pp. 103–20
Brewer, John, *The Sinews of Power: War, Money, and the English State, 1688–1783* (New York: Knopf, 1989)
Butler, Marilyn, 'Popular Antiquarianism', in Iain McCalman *et al.* (eds), *An Oxford Companion to the Romantic Age: British Culture, 1776–1832* (Oxford: Oxford University Press, 1999), pp. 328–37
de Groot, Jerome, *Consuming History: Historians and Heritage in Contemporary Popular Culture* (London: Routledge, 2009)

Dent, Jonathan, 'Contested Pasts: David Hume, Horace Walpole and the Emergence of Gothic Fiction', *Gothic Studies*, 14:1 (May 2012), 21–32

Dew, Ben, 'An Economic Turn? Commerce and Finance in the Historical Writing of Paul de Rapin Thoyras, William Guthrie and David Hume', in Ben Dew and Fiona Price (eds), *Historical Writing in Britain, 1688–1830: Visions of History* (Basingstoke: Palgrave, 2014), pp. 73–91

Dorson, Richard M., *The British Folklorists: A History* (London: Routledge & Kegan Paul, 1968)

Evans, Richard J., *Altered Pasts: Counterfactuals in History* (Waltham, MA: Brandeis University Press/Historical Society of Israel, 2013)

Garfinkel, Harold, 'Evidence for Locally Produced, Naturally Accountable Phenomena of Order, Logic, Reason, Meaning, Method, etc. in and as of the Essential Quiddity of Immortal Ordinary Society (I of IV): An Announcement of Studies', *Sociological Theory*, 6:1 (Spring 1988), 103–9

Garfinkel, Harold and Kenneth Liberman, 'Introduction: The Lebenswelt Origin of the Sciences', *Human Studies*, 30:1 (March 2007), 3–7

Giddens, Anthony, *Modernity and Self-identity: Self and Society in the Late Modern Age* (Stanford, CA: Stanford University Press, 1991)

Giddens, Anthony, *The Consequences of Modernity* (Stanford, CA: Stanford University Press, 1990)

Giddens, Anthony, *The Transformation of Intimacy: Sexuality, Love, and Eroticism in Modern Societies* (Stanford, CA: Stanford University Press, 1992)

Gómez-Arostegui, H. Tomás, 'Register of Copyright Infringement Suits & Actions From c.1560 to 1800', https://law.lclark.edu/faculty/h_tomas_gomez_arostegui/appendix/

Harris, Roy, *Signs, Language, and Communication: Integrational and Segregational Approaches* (London: Routledge, 1996)

Harris, Roy, *The Linguistics of History* (Edinburgh: Edinburgh University Press, 2004)

Hicks, Philip, 'Female Worthies and the Genres of Women's History', in Ben Dew and Fiona Price (eds), *Historical Writing in Britain, 1688–1830: Visions of History* (Basingstoke: Palgrave, 2014), pp. 18–32

Hicks, Philip, *Neoclassical History and English Culture from Clarendon to Hume* (Basingstoke: Macmillan, 1996)

Hilson, J. C., 'Hume: The Historian as Man of Feeling', *Prose Studies*, 3:2 (September 1980), 93–108

Kasmer, Lisa, *Novel Histories: British Women Writing History, 1760–1830* (Madison, WI: Fairleigh Dickinson University Press, 2012)

Kelly, Gary, 'Bluestocking Work: Learning, Literature, and Lore in the Onset of Modernity', in Deborah Heller (ed.), *Bluestockings Now! The Evolution of a Social Role* (Farnham, Ashgate, 2015), pp. 175–208

Kennelly, Laura B., 'Tory History Incognito: Hume's *History of England* in Goldsmith's *History of England*', *Clio*, 20:2 (December 1991), 169–83

Knapp, Lewis M., *Tobias Smollett: Doctor of Men and Manners* (Princeton, NJ: Princeton University Press, 1949)

Koselleck, Reinhart, *Futures Past: On the Semantics of Historical Time*, trans. Keith Tribe (New York: Columbia University Press, 2004)

Koselleck, Reinhart, *The Practice of Conceptual History: Timing History, Spacing Concepts*, trans. Todd Samuel Presner et al. (Stanford, CA: Stanford University Press, 2002)

Lepore, Jill, 'Just the Facts, Ma'am: Fake Memoirs, Factual Fictions, and the History of History', *The New Yorker*, 24 March 2008, www.newyorker.com/magazine/2008/03/24/just-the-facts-maam

Levine, Philippa, *The Amateur and the Professional: Antiquarians, Historians, and Archaeologists in Victorian England, 1838–1886* (Cambridge: Cambridge University Press, 1986)

Lukács, György, *The Historical Novel*, trans. Hannah Mitchell and Stanley Mitchell (Boston, MA: Beacon Press, 1963)

McHoul, Alec, *Semiotic Investigations: Towards an Effective Semiotics* (Lincoln, NE: University of Nebraska Press, 1996)

McKenzie, D. F., *Bibliography and the Sociology of Texts* (London: British Library, 1986)

Mossner, Ernest Campbell, *The Life of David Hume*, 2nd edn (Oxford: Clarendon Press, 1980)

O'Brien, Karen, 'The History Market in Eighteenth-century England', in Isabel Rivers (ed.), *Books and their Readers in Eighteenth-century England: New Essays* (London: Continuum, 2001), pp. 105–33

Phillips, Mark Salber, *Society and Sentiment: Genres of Historical Writing in Britain, 1740–1820* (Princeton, NJ: Princeton University Press, 2000)

Phillipson, Nicholas, *David Hume: The Philosopher as Historian* (New Haven, CT: Yale University Press, 1989)

Poole, Steve, '"Not Precedents to be Followed but Examples to be Weighed": John Thelwall and the Jacobin Sense of the Past', in Steve Poole (ed.), *John Thelwall: Radical Romantic and Acquitted Felon* (London: Pickering & Chatto, 2009), pp. 161–74

Roman, Cynthia Ellen, 'Pictures for Private Purses: Robert Bowyer's Historic Gallery and Illustrated Edition of David Hume's *History of England*' (unpublished PhD thesis, Brown University, 1997)

Siebert, Donald T., 'The Sentimental Sublime in Hume's *History of England*', *Review of English Studies*, 40:159 (August 1989), 352–72

Sullivan, M. G., 'Rapin, Hume and the Identity of the Historian in Eighteenth-century England', *History of European Ideas*, 28:3 (2002), 145–62

Temple, Kathryn, '"Manly Composition": Hume and the History of England', in Anne Jaap Jacobson (ed.), *Feminist Interpretations of David Hume* (University Park, PA: Penn State University Press, 2000), pp. 263–82

Tod, M. K., '2015 Historical Fiction Reader Survey', https://awriterofhistory.files.wordpress.com/2015/06/2015-report-final2.pdf

Towsey, Mark, '"The Book Seemed to Sink into Oblivion": Reading Hume's *History* in Eighteenth-century Scotland', in Mark C. Spencer (ed.), *David Hume: Historical Thinker, Historical Writer* (University Park, PA: Penn State University Press, 2013), pp. 81–102

Zimmerman, Everett, *The Boundaries of Fiction: History and the Eighteenth-century British Novel* (Ithaca, NY: Cornell University Press, 1998)

3

The possibilists: Romantic-era literary forgery and British alternative pasts

Mary-Ann Constantine

> A possible experience or truth is not the same as an actual experience or truth minus its 'reality value' but has – according to its partisans at least – something quite divine about it, a fire, a soaring, a readiness to build and a conscious utopianism that does not shrink from reality but sees it as a project, something yet to be invented.
> (Robert Musil, *The Man Without Qualities*)[1]

> Y Gwir yn Erbyn y Byd / The Truth Against the World.
> (Edward Williams)

Imagine a library on fire.

It is an octagonal library, part of a grand house that looks down across an open meadow and a river to a thickly wooded valley surrounded by bare hills. The entire building is burning, and the fire is so fierce it has flung books and papers high into the night sky. It is 1807.

The library itself is barely twenty years old; it was designed by the architect John Nash and completed, with the house, in 1788. In those two decades many visitors have admired its panelled walls, its impressive collection of books and paintings. Providentially, perhaps, a Glamorgan poet spent three weeks in residence there in 1799, copying texts from medieval manuscripts for inclusion in a three-volume printed anthology that would become a cornerstone of Welsh literary history; the second volume will be dedicated to the library's owner, Thomas Johnes. Not everything will be lost.

The fire at Hafod in Cardiganshire, Wales, was among the

better-documented of the multiple catastrophes that blew holes in the Welsh past. A generation earlier, the scholar-poet Evan Evans had written with anger at the general neglect of a literature 'at great risque of mouldering away' in the damp houses of an increasingly ignorant (and increasingly absent) Welsh gentry.[2] Two generations before him, the preacher Moses Williams had vainly proposed getting these vulnerable records of antiquities into print, since 'all Manuscripts (whether in publick Places or private Hands) are liable to be embezzled or destroyed'.[3]

Literary inheritance is precarious. Today, we know that the oldest Welsh literary texts are contained in a mere handful of manuscript volumes, the earliest of which dates to the thirteenth century, though the material copied into them is often much older, commemorating events and characters from as far back as the fifth and sixth centuries. Pieces like the elegiac *Gododdin* (a litany of fallen soldiers) or the enigmatic *Afallennau* (a poem voiced by an early Merlin figure) are recognised sources of a literary tradition spanning centuries. When contemporary scholars, writers and artists return to these texts, they do so fully conscious of that distance, measured in a branching map of ink-veins and ink-arteries flowing through all the texts between.

Eighteenth-century Britain had a different relationship with the literary past. The theoretical map locating and connecting its various early traditions – Latin, Anglo-Norman, Middle English, Scandinavian, Anglo-Saxon, Welsh, Gaelic – was patchy, filled with guesswork and blank spaces. As Joep Leerssen reminds us, 'literature' was still generally conceived of by the educated elite as an essentially ahistorical pantheon of Greats, conversing with one another and with their readers across time and often across national boundaries: 'Homer, Cicero, Dante, Tasso, Milton, Pope or Voltaire are seen, not as stages in a historical progress but rather as citizens in a timeless Republic of Canonicity, all simultaneously available to the present-day reader and therefore all, simultaneously, our contemporaries.'[4] One of the distinctive features of the period from around 1760 is a rush of curiosity about the literary record in earlier forms of English and in other British languages – a curiosity that, over subsequent decades, entailed a sharpening of chronologies and a finer calibration of historical depth, but which also set in play various competing claims for cultural or national primacy. To call this movement simply 'antiquarian' risks underplaying the exceptionally dynamic nature of its engagement with the past: if the sifting and classification of medieval literature were the main concern of scholars like Thomas Percy, Thomas Warton or Joseph Ritson, there were many – like Hugh Blair, Lewis

Morris or Thomas Gray – who were just as committed to recovering non-classical models and a 'new tone' for writing in the present.

The raggedness and apparently rapid decomposition of the past made for confusion and obscurity, but it was also a territory of possibilities. The eighteenth-century antiquarian world is full of serendipitous retrievals, from Percy's black-letter book of 'minstrelsy' saved from the kitchen fire to the Morrises' thrilling recovery of an 'epic Poem in the British called Gododin [*sic*], equal at least to the Iliad, Aeneid or Paradise Lost'.[5] And it is in this context of possibility – in the gaps between the known coordinates on the map, the spaces where anything might yet show up – that the creations of various literary 'forgers' came into being and were able to thrive.

The alternative versions of the literary (and literal) past created by writers like James Macpherson, Thomas Chatterton and Edward Williams all share, despite generic and contextual differences, a striking fecundity, a tendency to grow and self-populate – whether ballooning, like *Ossian*, from fragment to epic, or, as with Chatterton and Williams, putting out myriad little tendrils that quietly twist themselves into the body of literature and history. 'To forge with any hope of success in the Erse', wrote Williams disingenuously, 'it would not do to fabricate an Ossian, or anything else alone, you must forge in all the unavoidably concomitant branches of literary knowledge, at least in a great many of them.'[6] The literary forger, like Robert Musil's 'man without qualities', is not a realist but a 'possibilist' inhabiting 'the subjunctive mood'.[7]

The expansive energy of literary forgery – its ability to create virtual worlds – derives from something that could be envisaged (with apologies to Douglas Adams) as a possibility-drive. The oscillatory nature of the texts is crucial here. For much of the Romantic period, the poems of Ossian, Rowley and others were perceived as alternately (but also, oddly, simultaneously) ancient and modern, like folded universes. They were admired because the keynote they struck was thrillingly, genuinely, from the past – because that note rang so very true, but *wasn't* (thereby proving the artistry of the creator). Nick Groom calls it 'a hybrid realism, both true and false'.[8] One might see the phenomenon as a kind of literary Big Bang: a moment of genesis, a rush of expanding energy, resulting both in the creation of these alternative universes (the works themselves) and (through the controversies) in the painful splitting of history and literature along separate paths, true and false, fact and fiction.

Much has been written in recent years about the phenomenon of Romantic-era literary forgery and its relationship to 'authentic' literature;

bold claims have been made for these troubling texts and the controversies they generated. Macpherson's *Ossian*, it has been suggested, made it possible to conceive of national literary traditions in European vernaculars, and indeed provided the conceptual framework for literary historicism *per se*.[9] Debates over textual authenticity have been seen as helping to develop and refine notions of the Romantic self[10] and as mirroring the precariously speculative state of the period's economy,[11] but also as pointing up the ultimate 'fakery' of all literature.[12] It has even been claimed (a decidedly counterfactual proposition) that 'Romanticism (for want of a better term) would have been very different without literary forgery – indeed, it may not recognizably have existed at all.'[13]

This chapter develops some of these ideas to posit the literary forger as a dedicated counterfactualist whose imaginative, highly localised graftings onto an emergent literary history offered plausible alternative versions of the past in a complex and increasingly urgent national debate. Revisiting, briefly, the works and controversies associated with Macpherson and Chatterton in the 1760s and 1770s, it also considers the less-well-known writings of the Welsh poet Edward Williams, known by his bardic name, 'Iolo Morganwg' – many of whose invented texts and authors, though written out of the landscape, history and archaeology of his native Glamorgan, dramatically altered perceptions of Wales as a whole. The subtlety and complexity of his methods meant that Welsh scholarship did not have its authenticity debate until decades after his death, and Williams's version of the literary past thoroughly permeated Welsh culture's self-image for much of the nineteenth century. The ensuing disillusion proved painful, and has remained such a sore point in Welsh scholarship that even recently an eminent Celtic scholar could voice the opinion that 'Iolo Morganwg should have been shot' – which, in itself, is a counterfactual scenario well worth contemplating.

'Empty elements' and imagined worlds: Ossian's Highlands, Rowley's Bristol

Two of the most passionate, complex and long-lived authenticity debates of the Romantic period centred on the appearance of texts that staked a claim to specific unmapped spaces in British literary history. They offered potential versions of a literary tradition at a time when that tradition was still marked by areas of flux, when the paths leading from one author to the next were not clearly demarcated at every stage, and when the literatures of the different cultures and languages of the British Isles were not necessarily seen as separate and exclusive of one another. In both cases, a regional, non-metropolitan and contemporary sensibility drove their creators: the poetry of the third-century Gaelic bard Ossian and the fifteenth-century Bristol monk Thomas Rowley, voiced though James Macpherson and Thomas Chatterton, expressed intense engagement with both the local and the present. These are perhaps the key factors in distinguishing the dynamic, 'possibilist' creations of literary forgery from the often equally imaginative reconstructions of the past produced by eighteenth-century antiquarians such as William Stukeley and Henry Rowlands, both of whom also conjured extraordinary worlds from scattered and elusive sources.[14]

The introduction to the anonymously published *Fragments of Ancient Poetry Collected in the Highlands of Scotland* (1760) stressed from the outset both the texts' authenticity ('The public may depend on the following fragments as genuine remains of ancient Scottish poetry') and their likely pre-Christian antiquity.[15] A second edition appeared the same year, and by the end of 1761 came *Fingal*, an epic poem recalling the exploits of the legendary Gaelic hero Fionn Mac Cumhaill ('Finn MacCool'). This was followed by *Temora* (1763) and a complete *Poems of Ossian* (1765). Thereafter, *Ossian* would remain an insistent presence throughout the Romantic period, enjoying extraordinary success in multiple translations across Europe and eventually beyond.[16] The poems' translator-author (his authorial role would grow exponentially with each successive publication) was James Macpherson, a schoolmaster from Ruthven, some forty miles south of Inverness. The village is still dominated by the ruins of a British barracks established in 1721 during the years of intense Jacobite unrest; it was destroyed by retreating Jacobite forces shortly after the Battle of Culloden (16 April 1746), when Macpherson was nine years old. Macpherson grew up in a landscape of losses more recent and more brutal than those evoked by his creations, and *Ossian* can be read (notwithstanding the author's political affiliations to the British government and his later involvement in local clearances) as expressive of the traumatic changes undergone by Highland culture in this period.[17]

The poetry's keynote, like much of the original Gaelic material from which it derives, is elegiac and melancholy: the warrior-bard Ossian is 'the last of his race', and his recollections evoke in the sympathetic reader the 'joy of grief'.[18] The misty Highland backdrop, biblical cadences and the breathless dialogues between soon-to-be parted lovers proved highly seductive, though many felt obliged to resist their charms. The Welsh poet, cartographer and antiquarian Lewis Morris quickly identified it as 'but a modern song ... Nid fel cywyddau ac awdlau'r Britaniaid [Not like the poems and odes of the Britons]'; his London-based brother Richard, on the other hand, was an enthusiast.[19] *Ossian* exploited a gap, a dark space in the early British past, and much intellectual energy on both sides went into analysing its depiction of the manners and customs of an ideal primitive society of third-century north Britons. For some, it confirmed the Scottish Enlightenment's theories of stadial history, while others felt that it simply proved itself a product of that same Enlightenment milieu. Various writers pondered the significance of the absence of any clear organised religion in the work;[20] the naturalist Thomas Pennant was more concerned by the absence of wolves.[21] The work's uncertain location in time and the plausibility or otherwise of the culture it described gave it the flickering quality discussed here – that sense of something simultaneously possible and impossible. This is not an easy target for critical appraisal: the language of the controversy (which ran to thousands of pages in pamphlets and articles, even books) abounds in qualifiers and convolutions; it chases down dead-end alleys, knocking down straw-men.

Much was at stake. If accepted as authentic, *Ossian* (as Hugh Blair claimed in the critical dissertation that accompanied the poems from 1765, and greatly influenced their reception) could take on Homer and Classical Greece and Rome; here was a deep-rooted, native, northern-European heroic literature displaying not the curious *moeurs* of barbarians but episodes of exquisitely refined sensibility.[22] In a British context, a scorned and (by 1760) defanged Scottish Highland culture could claim primacy over the literatures of the other home nations. The Irish, recognising the roots of Macpherson's work in their own Fenian traditions, were quickest to condemn the Caledonian claims.[23] Above all, the *Ossian* poems opened up the possibility of radically different forms of literary history, if not of history itself: these 'translations' from the Gaelic were, after all, supposedly based on orally transmitted songs and stories, and could thus be assimilated to a much wider and more fundamental discussion about the nature of primitive poetry that included Homer and parts of the Bible. Orality, with its multiple variants, alternative endings and perpetual renewal and flux, was another unsettling universe that this period, and this particular authenticity debate, helped to open up.[24] Again, the conceptual challenges this posed to contemporary notions of literature were powerful, as attested by Samuel Johnson's dismissal of the possibility of poetry in a language ('*Earse*') that 'merely floated in the breath of the people, and could therefore receive little improvement'.[25]

The possibilists

The counterfactual force of *Ossian* extended beyond the illicit occupation of notional space in third-century Caledonia to the appropriation of real places. The landscape of the poetry, not yet familiar in actuality to many of the reading public, was a strange, spare world of mist and moorland, wind and cloud:

> I sit by the mossy fountain. On the top of the hill of winds. One tree is rustling above me. Dark waves roll over the heath. The lake is troubled below. The deer descend from the hill. No hunter at a distance is seen; no whistling cow-herd is nigh. It is mid-day: but all is silent. Sad are my thoughts as I sit alone.[26]

This is in many ways a landscape of the mind, a strikingly *unspecific* type of landscape, with a few basic elements that could be shifted around to much the same effect. It is, in many ways, 'generic' Highland scenery. One of the more striking examples of *Ossian*'s power in the Romantic period is the way in which it re-attached itself to places, imbuing them with a specific set of meanings (thereby unconsciously reverting to a key mode of the traditional Fenian material). Thus in 1772, when the explorer and naturalist Joseph Banks sailed down the Sound of Mull past the slopes of Morvern ('mother of the romantick scenery of Ossion' [*sic*]), he toyed with the thought of spending time ashore reading the poetry itself *in situ*. 'I could not even sail past it', he wrote, 'without a touch of Enthusiasm [–] sweet affection of the mind which can gather pleasure from the empty elements & realize substantial pleasure which three fourths of mankind are ignorant of.'[27]

Banks is here self-consciously, almost defensively, aware that his cultured imagination or 'enthusiasm' performs a kind of alchemy, conjuring 'substantial pleasure' from 'empty elements'. Recent work on Ossianic toponomies has shown just how frequently such 'elements', both linguistic and geographical, were conjured into Fingalian forms by being over-interpreted (the word 'white', for example, is common in place-names and not easily distinguishable from the proper name *Fionn*).[28] And although there was an earlier, traditional layer of naming connected to the Fenian stories and ballads, it was – particularly for the tourists who came in increasing numbers – Macpherson's creations that peopled the scene. A generation after Banks, *Ossian* was still the sublime, if troubled, lens through which many tourists engaged with a landscape previously known only textually. In 1802, Anne Grant forced herself to overcome her spontaneous reactions to a type of scenery that had initially left her (like Samuel Johnson earlier) 'repelled and disappointed'; as

Pam Perkins has put it, she tried 'to reimagine the landscape according to what Macpherson wrote, rather than what she felt and saw'.[29] The poetry and the landscape seemed to authenticate each other, to give each other 'substance'; but that oscillatory flicker of doubt made the Ossianic populating of the Highland landscape neither historical (like visiting the birthplace of Robert Burns) nor fictional (like invoking *Macbeth* at Dunsinane). Instead, as Nigel Leask observes and as Anne Grant's curious effort of will implies, 'text and topography alike ran the risk of dissolving into insubstantiality'.[30] These are possible – but also impossible – worlds.

The world conjured by Thomas Chatterton was markedly different in style and period. Characterised by its rich materiality and its urban setting in mercantile Bristol, it was 'an imaginary construct from books, local monuments, and local topography'.[31] Where *Ossian* roamed the wide, open territory of nebulous pre-history, Chatterton's alternative past was woven tightly into the spaces between existing sources and objects – which, in turn, endowed it with credibility. In the autumn of 1768, when Bristol's new bridge across the Avon was opened for traffic, the local newspaper carried a short piece, purportedly from the year 1247, describing a pageant of local dignitaries celebrating the opening of the old bridge.[32] Intrigued local antiquarians identified the contributor as a 16-year-old attorney's clerk, whose family had been sextons of the imposing Gothic church of St Mary Redcliffe for generations. And there was, of course, more: documents, poems, histories, plays and genealogies relating to, and supposedly written by, a lively circle of prelates and scholars clustered round the figure of the (thoroughly historical) mayor of Bristol, William Canynges (d. 1474). Central among these varied sources were the poems attributed to a more shadowy contemporary, the monk 'Thomas Rowley'. When pressed, Chatterton explained that the texts were copied from originals found by his late father in a chest in a small room over the north porch of the church. The chest was there as ocular proof (though Samuel Johnson, persuaded to toil up the narrow stone spiral staircase to inspect it in 1776, was not convinced), and there were also a couple of plausible-looking manuscripts to hand, written in an elaborate medieval script. Chatterton's passion for the Gothic was intensely local, and these new-found texts testified to the cultural wealth not simply of late medieval Bristol, but more particularly of his own territory around St Mary Redcliffe. Where *Ossian* was remote and 'insubstantial', Rowley and his companions were almost tangible: evoked in material relics of paper and stone and inhabiting still-visible buildings and streets, they flourished in the interstices of what was by then a relatively well-mapped period in English history.

Chatterton became something of a celebrity and left Bristol for London in April 1770 to pursue a literary career. Four months later he was found dead in his attic room in Holborn. The inquest ruled that he had committed suicide; he was 17. The story of his short, brilliant life became an integral part of the controversy surrounding his texts, and the supposed suicide of the despairing provincial author in an unfeeling metropolis would haunt literary imaginations all too attuned to tales of rejected or unrecognised genius.[33] It is ironic that the 'suicide' is now largely rejected by historians, who consider Chatterton to have died of an accidental overdose, possibly as a result of self-medication for venereal disease.[34] In other words, the single most compelling historical 'fact' about the poet – and the basis of the myth that kept his name alive well into the nineteenth century – seems in itself to have been a piece of counterfactual history.

Chatterton's precocious talent and sudden death focused attention on his writings, and the Rowley poems in particular became the centre of a furious controversy. As with the ongoing *Ossian* debate, and often entangled with it, attempts to prove or disprove the poems' authenticity focused attention on questions of style, period and historical context, and several Rowley poems were included in the second volume of Thomas Warton's *History of English Poetry*, published in 1778. Warton's treatment of these poems is interesting. In measured and scholarly prose he sets out the problematic duality of the works, but refrains, initially at least, from closing down the possibility that they are 'the real productions of Rowlie':

> It must be acknowledged that there are some circumstances which incline us to suspect these pieces to be a modern forgery. On the other hand, as there is some degree of plausibility in the history of their discovery, as they possess considerable merit, and are believed to be the real productions of Rowlie by many respectable critics; it is my duty to give them a place in this series of our poetry, if it was for no other reason than that the world might be furnished with an opportunity of examining their authenticity.[35]

There follow several pages of extracts, chosen for their lyrical and affecting qualities or for the light they apparently shed on English history. In these pages, Thomas Rowley lives and thrives and takes his place in the English canon between Chaucer and Shakespeare. It is a wonderfully counterfactual moment, but it does not last long. Warton then proceeds to take apart the poetry's claims to historicity, piece by piece: the handwriting of the few 'original' manuscripts is carefully analysed against productions of the same time; internal evidence is summoned, including '[a]n unnatural affectation of antient spelling and of obsolete words, not belonging to the period assigned to the poems'.[36] He also attempts to explain why the pieces 'feel' wrong – 'the cast of thought, the complexion of the sentiments, and the structure of the composition, evidently prove these pieces not antient'.[37] Genuine medieval literature, he notes, often offends against 'taste'; it is frequently ungainly, awkward, or simply impossible to understand.

Warton here echoes the Welsh poet Evan Evans's own authenticating rhetoric for the medieval Welsh poetry he had published a decade earlier; unlike the suspiciously smooth, free-flowing 'translations' of Macpherson, Evans noted with some asperity, his own translations from early Welsh verse carry proof of their authenticity in their lacunae, their painful stiltedness.[38] Warton and Evans – meticulous scholars both – are suspicious of a past that gives itself up too readily, that speaks too clearly to present concerns. They resist, in other words, the direct appeal of these alternative texts to contemporary sensibilities: the counterfactual worlds of both Macpherson and Chatterton answer too many questions.

This growing sense of how language and literary sensibility might fit into particular centuries was an important (and oddly ironic) outcome of the 'authenticity debates' of the late eighteenth century. Discussions about how history and literature might (or might not) be contained and transmitted in both oral and manuscript traditions actively contributed, as Joep Leerssen has argued, to the development of literary historicism, breaking down the monolith of 'literature ... not only into the diachronic stratification of historical periods, but also into the cultural particularism of different national traditions'.[39] The dynamic intervention of the *possible*, then, acted as both challenge and stimulus, and can be recognised as a key factor in eighteenth-century canon formation.

The truth against the world: Edward Williams (Iolo Morganwg)

Something rather different happened in Wales. The medieval texts forged by the poet and stonemason Edward Williams (1747–1816) did *not* cause a major controversy during their author's lifetime (though there were a few barbed comments, largely ignored) or for a very long time afterwards. Moreover the 'forgeries' themselves were not a coherent entity like Macpherson's *Ossian* poems; they were more like the complex 'imaginary construct' of Chatterton's Bristol, except that they were produced not over a couple of years, but over decades, and reached into an even wider range of medieval sources. The absence of a public debate had the curious effect of causing this multi-strand counterfactual history to become (for most people who considered such things at all) 'real' history for the best part of a century. When the controversy finally came to a head, a great deal had already been invested in many aspects of Edward Williams's alternative Welsh past.

Scholarship has yet to produce a full account of the nature and extent of the alterations and additions made by Edward Williams to Welsh literary tradition. In part, this is due to the difficulties of synthesising such a complex oeuvre, which draws on many different areas of specialisation. Modern scholars of British Romantic literature rarely have the linguistic skills for this type of cross-cultural comparison, and few medievalists have had the inclination or patience to do more than label a 'Iolo'-derived source as suspect. The life's work of one scholar, Griffith John Williams, and a number of excellent individual case studies, do, however, reveal the range of Williams's interests.[40] A lively group of poems written in the voice of the fourteenth-century poet Dafydd ap Gwilym and a score of twelfth-century lyrics by one Rhys Goch Ap Riccert (nicely illustrating the latest Troubadour style) are perhaps the most comparable to the Rowley poems. Located much further back in time are the long sequences of triadic verses encapsulating the wisdom of the Welsh over centuries, possibly millennia.

Other inventions were more performative: the initiation ceremony of the *gorsedd* (bardic congress), first held on Primrose Hill in London in 1792 and still used in the modern Welsh cultural festival of the Eisteddfod, involved simple rituals and some resounding phrases, and the marking out of a stone circle ('Truth', noted Williams, 'walks a circle. A system formed by rule and square touches that circle but in a few points').[41] A rune-like bardic alphabet scratched in wood added a further material dimension to Williams's project, but by far the most productive, and obsessive, area of his creativity was textual.[42] Over the years, he introduced a multitude of tiny twists, corrections and insertions to copies (or copies of copies) of authentic medieval manuscripts from libraries like that of Thomas Johnes at Hafod. Some of these interventions were apparently meaningless, some can be read as politically or religiously motivated (Williams was a radical and a Unitarian), but many seem intended to divert the channels of literary tradition away from the north of Wales to his native Glamorgan. Castles, prehistoric stone monuments and churches all offered sanctuary to fictions claiming to be fact. The parallels with Chatterton's Bristol-centred creations are striking.

A couple of examples from this varied and rather messy body of forgeries will suffice here in considering Williams's distinctive contribution to an alternative British past. The Dafydd ap Gwilym poems are the most coherent group. In the 1770s, Williams had begun a correspondence with Owen Jones, president of the London Welsh *Gwyneddigion* society, and it was through this contact that he first encountered the Dafydd ap Gwilym manuscripts held in the Welsh Charity School in Grays Inn Road. The society formed a plan to publish an anthology of the poet's work, and in 1789, when the volume was very close to going to press, Williams, back in his native Glamorgan, sent a clutch of poems (allegedly copied from a recently discovered manuscript) to the editors. The new poems were rushed into an appendix. Among them were pieces which (inevitably) would become firm favourites in the canon of the medieval poet's works for much of the following century. A forensic examination of the poems published in 1926 showed how Williams used a variety of techniques to create this additional corpus, with certain poems formed out of a carefully sewn patchwork of existing medieval couplets, and others spun virtually from nothing, using both genuine and invented medieval vocabulary. The relationship to source is not unlike that of Macpherson's early Ossian poetry, though the feel – all bright luxuriance – is more Chattertonian. Many of the poems fulfil a narrative need, providing biographical details of the relationship between the historical poet and his (historical) patron Ifor Hael, and the poet and his lover Morfudd (the imagined past is enriched, and thickened, as these connections are made). Most important, they strengthen the case for Dafydd as a Glamorgan poet.

In the early 1790s, Williams set about raising subscriptions to publish his own English-language poems; these would eventually appear as *Poems, Lyric and Pastoral* in 1794. By 1792 he had made the decision to publish in London and moved there, leaving his family in Glamorgan; the next three years, mostly based in the metropolis, would prove both strenuous and exceptionally creative. Living under severe financial constraints, prey to vicious bouts of depression and often with barely enough to eat, 'Bard Williams' became known in various overlapping literary, political and religious circles. Coleridge, Southey and Wordsworth would all encounter him and his ideas during this period.[43]

It was now that he began to promulgate ideas about a bardic poetic inheritance dating back to the time of the biblical patriarchs, preserved initially through British druidism and thereafter in a medieval poetic tradition that was tenaciously clinging on in Glamorgan. It contained (and proved the ancient British provenance of) the tenets of a religious belief far more compatible with rational Dissent than the aberrant forms of Catholicism or Anglicanism. As the all-but-last representative of that tradition, Williams took it upon himself not merely to preserve but also to revive the knowledge and practices it embodied, anonymously publishing a lengthy dissertation on the subject in the introduction to William Owen's *Heroic Elegies and other Pieces of Llywarç Hen* (1793) and (demonstrating the expansive, unfolding nature of his creations) 'initiating' dozens of new Welsh bards in the *gorsedd* ceremony. The tenets of bardism were embodied in poetic triads (*trioedd*) – sequences of three-line aphorisms encapsulating the teachings of the ancient *Cymry*, and covering a range of topics from nature and philosophy to more prosaic rules and regulations. The triad has a long and legitimate pedigree in Welsh – it may be one of the earliest poetic forms – and, as Morfydd Owen has shown, Williams's inspired revisitings were part of a long tradition of renewal.[44] Though couched in archaic language, Williams's triads were thoroughly contemporary and deeply appealing in content, reaching into areas of Romantic interest such as esoteric philosophy, nature-feeling and new forms of government and religion. They loom large in another key publication in the Welsh revival, *The Myvyrian Archaiology of Wales* (1801–7), of which Williams was one of the editors and a principal supplier of texts. The third volume contained a large proportion of triads encapsulating the wisdom of the Welsh, including the (wholly fictitious) 'Laws of Dyfnwal Moelmud', which portrayed an idealised and democratic primitive society. The utopian, possibilist ripples of that particular publication would extend as far as Karl Marx.[45]

Williams's techniques were as subtle as they were plausible, and relied on the fact that Wales was still, to a far greater degree than England, operating in a manuscript culture, and that multiple copies of ancient texts existed, with variations between them being the norm. Locating and verifying sources required extraordinary effort – of travel (by foot, in Williams's case, carrying heavy bundles of documents in terrible weather), of negotiation (doors might be slammed at any moment, manuscripts might be released singly, to be copied under supervision, or owners might simply never show up), and of time: 'I imagine that in two months, and not less', Williams wrote from Thomas Johnes's Hafod estate, 'I should be able to copy all that is of real importance.'[46] Moreover, especially when providing material for *The Myvyrian Archaiology*, he always took care to send his forgeries snugly camouflaged by authentic texts, and (a brilliant tactic) would occasionally even draw attention to some of their more striking features and suggest that they might be fakes – leaving it to colleagues to weigh up the evidence he presented for and against, and make the decision themselves. The ongoing deterioration of archives (or, as with Hafod, their total destruction) meant that some of his copied texts remain stuck in a permanently oscillatory state – potentially authentic, possibly not – forever.

Romantic-era literary forgery's teasing 'revelations' of especially vibrant creative periods in the past – prehistoric Britain, third-century Scotland, fifteenth-century Bristol – insist on a version of British literature that acknowledges the peripheries and the provinces. Williams's British past makes the Welsh not only primary and autochthonous, but also already possessed of a highly developed society of poets and law-givers who are emphatically *not*, as Geoffrey of Monmouth claimed, descended from the Trojan Brutus ('a gang of vagabond Trojans'), but rather are ancestors to be proud of: 'It is … much more honourable to have been the primeval possessors of the island in peace and justice, than to have been depredators that dispossessed, unjustly, the original inhabitants.'[47] This is a literary history to trump all competitors, including (and especially) the Ossianic, and it returns us to Leerssen's point about literary historicism's close links with cultural nationalism. As a phenomenon, literary forgery is most often located in the context of the creation of nation-states across Europe in the eighteenth and nineteenth centuries. Nations (and the smaller cultural groups distinguishing themselves through language or custom) needed founding texts, and where none was evident, they had to be claimed (from plausible earlier languages, such as Anglo-Saxon) or invented. The prevalence of heavily manipulated texts, from the *Kalevala* to the *Barzaz-Breiz*, claiming 'original' status for their cultural groups in this period is indeed striking; however, it may be that a focus on nationalisms and on the so-called 'invention of tradition' has simplified, and made it easy to dismiss, the complex and interdependent strands of these imagined alternative worlds.[48]

Edward Williams is often credited with being a 'nation builder' (albeit a rather perverse one), but his political self was shifting and composite, motivated by forces that transcend national boundaries. He was driven by an intense poetic engagement with the linguistic idioms and forms of previous centuries; he was also compelled by personal animosity (he was quick to feel slighted, and had a complicated relationship with his fellow editors of *The Myvyrian Archaiology*), intense local pride (Glamorgan as the home of bardism), religious zeal (his rational Unitarian druid-bards have no truck with the Trinity), utopianism, pacifism and radical politics (one contemporary noted – perceptively if sniffily – that he did not 'recollect to have seen this doctrine, in its full extent, promulgated by any code before a certain period of the French Revolution').[49] In other words, Williams's project is not merely textual tartan, but a dynamic form of creation that flickers into life in the charged space between fact and fiction, history and literature. Its energy is unsettling because (unlike the conservative medievalism of Walter Scott or Lady Llanover) it challenges the present; it offers alternatives. Where the carefully displayed suits of armour at Abbotsford and the traditional harpers of Llanover put the past at the service of the present, Chatterton, Macpherson and Williams, all in their different ways, put their counterfactual creations at the service of the future.[50]

If (to present another counterfactual scenario) Williams had published his endlessly revised, unfinished 'History of the Bards' (which may itself have been a Welsh response to Thomas Warton's *History of English Poetry*), it would have provided a testing ground for wider critical debate within Wales and beyond about how to accommodate Welsh (the language of the aboriginal 'Britons', after all) into the broader British narrative. It was precisely Williams's failure to publish a sustained account of his version of the British past in his own voice that allowed it flourish. Ventriloquised, hidden in footnotes to poems or smuggled into the work of his contemporaries, Williams demonstrates a striking erasure of self, like Musil's 'man without qualities'. There is nothing coherent to oppose. His counterfactual version of the past seeped into the present, and his mediations of Welsh tradition, both written and oral – he was an inspired conversationalist – trickled down unchallenged into dozens, and then scores, of later publications. After his death in 1826, his son Taliesin took charge of his manuscripts; by mid-century they had ended up in the care of the Llanover family, where they were consulted by scholars in the revivalist circle around Benjamin and Augusta Hall near Abergavenny. Taliesin Williams's publication of the forged bardic grammar *Cyfrinach y Beirdd* (1829) and a selection of the *Iolo Manuscripts* (1848) added to the body of invented bardic material available for general consumption; John Williams ('Ab Ithel') would add yet more with *Barddas* (1862–74). With little or nothing in these editions by way of context, the raw material of bardism had (and still occasionally has) a profound impact on perceptions of the Welsh past. For much of the nineteenth century, Welsh Romantic nationalism (largely ignoring the radical politics of their creator) threw in its lot with the bards and druids; Edward Williams, his practised mason's hand carving rune-like bardic letters on gravestones and memorials up and down the land, was the invisible master of ceremonies at a myriad local *eisteddfodau*, the only begetter of benign and non-militaristic culture heroes such as Hu Gadarn and Prydain fab Aedd.[51]

From the mid-1800s, a few lone voices – notably the Merthyr Tydfil chemist and historian Thomas Stephens – had begun contesting this already vigorously rooted counterfactual version of the Welsh past.[52] Disentangling fictitious from genuine sources proved a long and painful process. When Griffith John Williams (by a delicious irony, in a prize-winning Eisteddfod essay in 1921) painstakingly set out the case for treating the 'Appendix' poems of Dafydd ap Gwilym as forgeries, reactions were bitter on both sides. 'Mae'r twyllwr wedi ei ddal' (the impostor has been caught), wrote Sir John Morris-Jones in the introduction to the published account, adding that the Bard of Flemingstone was a 'hateful man full of hate', and that it would take another 'age or two before our literature and history are clean of the traces of his contaminated hands'.[53] The revulsion in some of these responses is telling: this is the voice of disillusion, the necessary recalibration of national identity after a deep deception, the fall-out from a broken relationship with the past. Where contemporary readers of *Ossian* and the Rowley poems were challenged almost from the beginning with the unsettling duality of textual being-not-being, those who had inherited aspects of Williams's counterfactual history faced the much more difficult task of reconceptualising, and to some extent reconstructing, a past they thought they knew. The flicker of *either-or* was in this case a much slower, heavier and more painful pendulum-swing.

Something was undeniably lost in the nineteenth-century materialisation and naturalisation of Williams's bardic vision, when, as the poet Gwyneth Lewis put it, Williams watched 'amser yn ei ufuddhau / a'r byd yn gwireddu ei eiriau' (time bend to his bidding / and the world make his words come true).[54] The shift can be marked in the distance between the first *gorsedd* ceremony on Primrose Hill in 1792 and the pomp of the *eisteddfodau* held by the Abergavenny Welsh society in the 1830s and 1840s – the distance between a largely artisan-class community of new-fledged 'British Bards' and the wealthy industrialist aristocracy with their parades, costumes, speeches and celebrations of loyalty and respectability. The movement from the radical edges to the heart of the establishment reflects, of course, the trajectory of many Romantic writers. But the making true of Edward Williams's counterfactual world in the nineteenth century also perhaps reflects the loss-in-translation of a possible world, the closing down of potential. Romantic-era literary forgeries are idealist manifestos; one might suggest that when the counterfactual becomes real and embodied, it loses its integrity, and is transformed from a possibility to a counterfeit, a fake. There is also an undeniable accompanying shift in the direction of the more sinister manipulated histories of totalitarian regimes (he who controls the past) and the purveyors of modern 'post-truth' politics.

The bardic motto of the *Gorsedd* of the Island of Britain was, and still is, *Y Gwir yn Erbyn y Byd* (The Truth Against the World). The words form part of the ceremony of sheathing the sword (reflecting bardism's strong pacifist strand), and can be found on the title pages of hundreds of nineteenth-century books and pamphlets. Like many mottos, it has a rousing, defiant feel to it, but it is also oddly slippery. The truth, it suggests, must be defended against the ignorance, or worse, of a world that has denied it. But it also suggests that 'truth' is something fundamentally at odds with the world, or at odds with (in William Godwin's more sinister formulation) 'things as they are'.[55] From there it is not much of a leap to a definition of truth as 'things as they aren't', or 'things as they might be'. It is not a bad counterfactualist manifesto: 'The possible', writes Musil, 'includes not only the fantasies of people with weak nerves but also the as yet unawakened intentions of God.'[56] Edward Williams was in many respects a fantasist with weak nerves; he was also, however, one of the most creative minds to come out of the cultural ferment of late-eighteenth-century Britain.

Death in Holborn

If, in deference to Sir John Morris-Jones and his angry descendants, one were to attempt to cleanse Welsh literary history by removing Edward Williams, what would happen? If he were taken out early enough – say in the 1770s or early 1780s – he would have remained a provincial poet in manuscript, waiting for canons to crumble and for the tide of historicism and studies of labouring-class writers to rescue a corpus of largely pastoral poetry, along with notes on history, antiquities, the Welsh language and stonemasonry. One could, alternatively, take a decade or so off at the other end of his career, and remove him in the 1810s or 1820s (pneumonia, perhaps, brought on during long cold hours in the rain – he worked as a stonecutter to the end). This would probably have the effect of erasing his reputation as a 'grand old man' of letters and a source of arcane knowledge – an image reinforced by the vivid and affectionate, if historically problematic, construction of him by Elijah Waring, whose *Recollections and Anecdotes of Edward Williams* (1850) downplayed his radical legacy and shaped perceptions of him for the rest of the century.[57] There is no doubt, however, that the 1790s were the crucial years, the period of his most intense engagement with the major imaginative writers of the age. To remove him early in this decade, before the full panoply of his bardic vision could take hold, might just be enough to rescue nineteenth-century Wales from much of its colourful absurdity and spare later scholars his obsessive tampering with crucial medieval texts.

A counterfactual assassination must be thoroughly plausible. Shooting is clumsy (and surprisingly hard to organise), but various other opportunities do present themselves. It is not hard to imagine Williams actually setting off, as he threatened to do, to look for the descendants of Prince Madoc among the Welsh Indians in America (another bit of pseudo-history with an enduring 'possibilist' motivating force) and perishing out there, as did the young Welshman John Evans, who, fired up with Williams's ideas, left in 1792 and died seven years later up the Missouri.[58] By 1793–94, one might also very plausibly have Williams arrested and tried for sedition (his papers were, he claimed, taken and searched, and he was briefly questioned); if his 'kingflogging' notes weren't enough to hang him, then one might imagine him conveniently deported, like the Unitarian preacher Thomas Fyshe Palmer, who wrote Williams a moving letter after reading his poems in Botany Bay.[59]

But by far the most counterfactually apposite moment to erase him would be the summer or autumn of 1792. The hitman would be the ghost of Thomas Chatterton. In July and August of that year, Williams was in a seriously disturbed state, having recently arrived in London with the aim of publishing his poems, and found the business of raising subscriptions – and dealing with potential patrons – far more demeaning and distressing than it had been among the literary coteries of Bath and Bristol.[60] Letters to his wife Peggy show that he was eating badly, taking a great deal of laudanum for 'a perpetual pain and heat in my head', and behaving even more erratically than usual ('I never sleep, and walk about I know not where, often to the fields where I lie down under a hedge'); furthermore, perhaps from guilt at not being able to send any money to his struggling family, he had developed a paranoid conviction that his children were dead ('tell me sincerely whether the little ones are alive. I cannot possibly put it for two minutes together out of my thoughts but that they are dead').[61] Uncannily, he had ended up in lodgings at 12

Beauchamp Street, Holborn, only too aware that he was living 'within a door or two' of the place where 'poor Chatterton was obliged to force his way out of this good-for-nothing world'. Geraint Phillips, who astutely traces the phases of Williams's depression throughout his life, suggests that a poignantly clumsy note 'on suicide' can be dated to this period.[62] By October he was still wretched, and writing openly of release:

> I have but one hope left now, which is that I shall soon die, for it is impossible for me to be relieved any other way. Send me one letter more, and let me see in it the names of my dear little ones. I shall never see their faces again. Poor Chatterton, who lived and died almost the next door to where I am, found means, like myself, to keep his distresses unknown.[63]

The 'impossible' happened, however. He did not die in 1792, but went on to engage radically, eccentrically and in his own way brilliantly with the good-for-nothing world of 1790s Britain. Yet it does seem that he came very close to becoming a kind of imitation, almost a parody, of one of the period's enduring Romantic images: a 45-year-old provincial genius sprawled lifeless on his bed in a pile of papers, pushed over the edge into one of his own 'circles of inchoation' by the ghost of the greatest literary suicide that (probably) never happened.

Notes

1 Robert Musil, *The Man Without Qualities*, trans. Sophie Wilkins and Burton Pike (London: Picador, 1997), p. 11.
2 Evan Evans, *Some Specimens of the Poetry of the Antient Welsh Bards* (London: R. and J. Dodsley, 1764), p. iii.
3 Moses Williams, *Proposals for Printing by Subscription a Collection of Writings in the Welsh Tongue* (London, 1719), p. 1.
4 Joep Leerssen, 'Ossian and the Rise of Literary Historicism', in Howard Gaskill (ed.), *The Reception of Ossian in Europe* (London: Thoemmes, 2004), p. 110.
5 See Nick Groom, *The Making of Percy's 'Reliques'* (Oxford: Oxford University Press, 1999); Lewis Morris to Edward Richard, 5 August 1758, in Hugh Owen (ed.), *Additional Letters of the Morrises of Anglesey (1735–1786)*, 2 vols (London: The Honourable Society of Cymmrodorion, 1947), I, p. 349.
6 Edward Williams to Robert Macfarlan, 6 June 1804, in Geraint H. Jenkins, Ffion Mair Jones and David Ceri Jones (eds), *The Correspondence of Iolo Morganwg*, 3 vols (Cardiff: University of Wales Press, 2007), II, p. 604.

7 Musil, *The Man Without Qualities*, p. 11. The original term is *Möglichkeitsmensch*; chapter 4 of Musil's book explores such a person's characteristic mental state.
8 Nick Groom, *The Forger's Shadow* (London: Picador, 2002), p. 15.
9 See Leerssen, 'Ossian and the Rise of Literary Historicism'.
10 See Margaret Russett, *Fictions and Fakes: Forging Romantic Authenticity, 1760–1845* (Cambridge: Cambridge University Press, 2006).
11 Ian Haywood (ed.), *Romanticism, Forgery and the Credit Crunch* (Romantic Circles Praxis Volume), www.rc.umd.edu/praxis/forgery/index/html (accessed 17 August 2016).
12 See K. K. Ruthven, *Faking Literature* (Cambridge: Cambridge University Press, 2001).
13 Groom, *The Forger's Shadow*, p. 15. See also Ian Haywood, *The Making of History: A Study of the Literary Forgeries of James Macpherson and Thomas Chatterton in Relation to Eighteenth-century Ideas of History and Fiction* (Rutherford, NJ: Fairleigh Dickinson University Press, 1986); Paul Baines, *The House of Forgery in Eighteenth-century Britain* (Aldershot: Ashgate, 1999); and Jack Lynch, *Deception and Detection in Eighteenth-century Britain* (Aldershot: Ashgate, 2008).
14 See William Stukeley, *Stonehenge: A Temple Restor'd to the British Druids* (London: W. Innys and R. Manby, 1740); Henry Rowlands, *Mona Antiqua Restaurata* (Dublin: Aaron Rhames, 1723). Both are discussed in Sam Smiles, *The Image of Antiquity: Ancient Britain and the Romantic Imagination* (New Haven, CT: Yale University Press, 1994).
15 James Macpherson, *Fragments of Ancient Poetry Collected in the Highlands of Scotland* (Edinburgh: G. Hamilton and J. Balfour, 1760), preface (no pagination).
16 For a helpful entry into *Ossian* studies, see Dafydd Moore, 'James Macpherson', www.oxfordbibliographies.com/view/document/obo-9780199846719/obo-9780199846719-0066.xml (accessed 20 April 2018).
17 See Fiona Stafford, *The Sublime Savage: James Macpherson and the Poems of Ossian* (Edinburgh: Edinburgh University Press, 1988).
18 See Thomas Owen Clancy, 'Gaelic Literature and Scottish Romanticism', in Murray Pittock (ed.), *The Edinburgh Companion to Scottish Romanticism* (Edinburgh: Edinburgh University Press, 2011), pp. 49–60.
19 John H. Davies (ed.), *The Letters of Lewis, Richard, William and John Morris of Anglesey (Morrisiaid Môn) 1728–1765*, 2 vols (Aberystwyth, 1907–9) II, p. 273. See also Mary-Ann Constantine, 'Ossian in Wales and Brittany', in Gaskill (ed), *The Reception of Ossian in Europe*, pp. 67–90.
20 This nebulous pre-Christian state, as Nigel Leask points out, is crucially *not* Catholic but 'a sort of negative Protestantism that mollified

moderate Presbyterian opinion': 'Fingalian Topographies: Ossian and the Highland Tour, 1760-1805', *Journal for Eighteenth-century Studies*, 39:2 (June 2016), 183–96. Edward Williams's Dissenter-friendly bardism performs a similar Catholic by-pass.

21 '[I]t is a matter of surprise that no mention is made, in the Poems of *Ossian*, of our great beasts of prey, which must have abounded in his days'; Thomas Pennant, *A Tour in Scotland & A Voyage to the Hebrides*, 3rd edn (Warrington: W. Eyres, 1774), p. 197. Thanks to Nigel Leask for this reference.

22 See Hugh Blair, *A Critical Dissertation on the Poems of Ossian, the Son of Fingal* (London: T. Becket and P. A. de Hondt, 1763), pp. 22–3.

23 See Mícheál Mac Craith, '"We Know All These Poems": The Irish Response to *Ossian*', in Gaskill (ed.), *The Reception of Ossian in Europe*, pp. 91–108.

24 See Nicholas Hudson, '"Oral Tradition": The Evolution of an Eighteenth-century Concept', in S. J. Alvaro Ribeira and James G. Basker (eds), *Tradition in Transition: Women Writers, Marginal Texts, and the Eighteenth-century Canon* (Oxford: Oxford University Press, 1996), pp. 161–76.

25 Samuel Johnson, *A Journey to the Western Islands of Scotland* (London: J. Pope, 1775), p. 186.

26 Macpherson, *Fragments of Ancient Poetry*, p. 13.

27 Roy A. Rauschenberg, 'The Journals of Joseph Banks's Voyage Up Great Britain's Coast to Iceland and to the Orkney Isles, July to October 1772', *Proceedings of the American Philosophical Society*, 117:3 (June 1973), 205; quoted in Leask, 'Fingalian Topographies', 183.

28 See Paul Baines, 'Ossianic Geographies: Fingalian Figures on the Scottish Tour, 1760–1830', *Scotlands*, 4:1 (January 1997), 44–61.

29 Pam Perkins, '"News from Scotland": Female Networks in the Travel Narratives of Elizabeth Isabella Spence', *Women's Writing*, 24:2 (July 2016), 170–84. Samuel Johnson had been 'astonished and repelled by this wide extent of hopeless sterility'; *Journey to the Western Islands of Scotland*, p. 84.

30 Leask, 'Fingalian Topographies', 184.

31 Donald S. Taylor (ed.), *The Complete Works of Thomas Chatterton: A Bicentenary Edition*, 2 vols (Oxford: Oxford University Press, 1971), I, p. xliv. For further biographical details, see E. H. W. Meyerstein, *A Life of Thomas Chatterton* (London: Ingpen and Grant, 1930).

32 Donald S. Taylor, *Thomas Chatterton's Art: Experiments in Imagined History* (Princeton: Princeton University Press, 1978), p. 108.

33 For a range of cases, see Nick Groom (ed.), *Thomas Chatterton and*

Romantic Culture (London: Palgrave, 1999) and Daniel Cook, *Thomas Chatterton and Neglected Genius, 1760–1830* (London: Palgrave, 2013).
34 See Richard Holmes, 'Thomas Chatterton: The Case Re-opened', *Cornhill Magazine*, 178:1063–8 (1970–1), 200–51.
35 Thomas Warton, *The History of English Poetry, From the Close of the Eleventh to the Commencement of the Eighteenth Century*, 4 vols (London: J. Dodsley *et al.*, 1774–81), II, p. 139.
36 *Ibid.*, p. 155.
37 *Ibid.*, p. 156.
38 See Constantine, 'Ossian in Wales and Brittany', pp. 73–4.
39 Leerssen, 'Ossian and the Rise of Literary Historicism', p. 124.
40 See G. J. Williams, *Iolo Morganwg a Chywyddau'r Ychwanegiad* (Iolo Morganwg and the *Cywyddau* of the Appendix'; Llundain: Cymdeithas yr Eisteddfod Genedlaethol, 1926); *Iolo Morganwg: Y Gyfrol Gyntaf* ('Iolo Morganwg, the First Volume'; Caerdydd: Gwasg Prifysgol Cymru, 1956); *Traddodiad Llenyddol Morgannwg* ('The Literary Tradition of Glamorgan'; Caerdydd: Gwasg Prifysgol Cymru, 1948). The non-publication of two important comparative studies helps to explain Williams's belated arrival to the critical field of Romantic-era forgery: they are Gwyneth Lewis's unpublished PhD dissertation, 'Eighteenth-century Literary Forgeries, with Special Reference to the Work of Iolo Morganwg' (Oxford, 1991), and Marilyn Butler's *Mapping Mythologies* (Cambridge, Cambridge University Press: 2016) which was drafted in the 1980s, twenty years before the historicist methodologies which she did so much to promote brought Williams (and Wales) back into the wider discourse of Romanticism.
41 National Library of Wales, MS 13120B/ 193.
42 For the Dafydd ap Gwilym material, see Williams, *Iolo Morganwg a Chywyddau'r Ychwanegiad*; for Rhys Goch's love poetry, see Huw Meirion Edwards, 'A Multitude of Voices: The Free-Metre Poetry of Iolo Morganwg', in Geraint H. Jenkins (ed.), *A Rattleskull Genius: The Many Faces of Iolo Morganwg* (Cardiff: University of Wales Press, 2005), pp. 95–122; for the triads, see Morfydd Owen, *Y Meddwl Obsesiynol: Traddodiad y Triawd Cyffredinol yn y Gymraeg a'r Myvyrian Archaiology* ('The Obsessive Mind: The Tradition of The Common Triad in Welsh and the *Myvyrian Archaiology*'; Aberystwyth: Papurau Ymchwil Canolfan Uwchefrydiau Cymreig a Cheltaidd, 2007); and for the bardic alphabet, see Richard M. Crowe, 'Diddordebau Ieithyddol Iolo Morganwg' ('The Linguistic Interests of Iolo Morganwg'; unpublished PhD thesis, University of Wales, 1988). Geraint Phillips offers some acute psychological insights into Williams's potential motiva-

The possibilists

tions: see 'Forgery and Patronage: Iolo Morganwg and Owain Myfyr', in Jenkins (ed.), *A Rattleskull Genius*, pp. 403–24. See also my own study, *The Truth Against the World: Iolo Morganwg and Romantic Forgery* (Cardiff: University of Wales Press, 2007), which explores Williams's knowledge and manipulation of the Macpherson and Chatterton controversies.

43 For Williams's influence on contemporary Romantic-period writing, see Damian Walford Davies, *Presences that Disturb: Models of Romantic Identity in the Literature and Culture of the 1790s* (Cardiff: University of Wales Press, 2002).

44 See Owen, *Y Meddwl Obsesiynol*.

45 See Mary-Ann Constantine, 'Welsh Literary History and the Making of "The Myvyrian Archaiology of Wales"', in Dirk Van Hulle and Joep Leerssen (eds), *Editing the Nation's Memory: Textual Scholarship and Nation-Building in Nineteenth-century Europe* (Amsterdam: Rodopi, 2008), pp. 109–28.

46 Edward Williams to Owen Jones (Owain Myfyr), 9 June 1799, in Jenkins et al. (eds), *The Correspondence of Iolo Morganwg*, II, p. 177.

47 Edward Williams to William Owen, 14 November 1799, in *ibid.*, II, p. 241.

48 The concept was first opened up in Eric Hobsbawm and Terence Ranger (eds), *The Invention of Tradition* (Cambridge: Cambridge University Press, 1983) – a volume that had a marked influence on the development of British 'four nations' literary criticism (notwithstanding the ill-informed chapter on Macpherson by Hugh Trevor-Roper).

49 Edward Davies, *The Mythology and Rites of the British Druids* (London: J. Booth, 1809), p. 60. For contemporary scepticism of Williams's inventions, see Moira Dearnley, '"Mad Ned" and the "Smatter-Dasher": Iolo Morganwg and Edward "Celtic" Davies', in Jenkins (ed.), *A Rattleskull Genius*, pp. 425–42.

50 Note Clare Simmons' definition of 'conservative elegiac' engagement with the past as demanding 'a recoverable Middle Ages, one that was different from the present, but not threatening to it': 'Introduction', in Clare A. Simmons (ed.), *Medievalism and the Quest for the 'Real' Middle Ages* (London: Frank Cass, 2001), p. 5.

51 Williams's impact on the culture and historiography of nineteenth-century Wales is thoroughly discussed in Marion Löffler, *The Literary and Historical Legacy of Iolo Morganwg, 1826–1926* (Cardiff: University of Wales Press, 2007).

52 See Marion Löffler, 'Failed Founding Fathers and Abandoned Sources: Edward Williams, Thomas Stephens and the Young J. E. Lloyd', in

Neil Evans and Huw Pryce (eds), *Writing a Small Nation's Past: Wales in Comparative Perspective, 1850–1950* (Farnham: Ashgate, 2013), pp. 61–81.
53 Williams, *Iolo Morganwg a Chywyddau'r Ychwanegiad*, p. xvi.
54 Gwyneth Lewis, 'Iolo Morganwg', *Sonedau Redsa a Cherddi Eraill* (Llandysul: Gwasg Gomer, 1990), p. 46.
55 For an exploration of links between Godwin and Williams that may extend to the naming of Godwin's protagonist in *Things as They Are; or, The Adventures of Caleb Williams* (1794), see Walford Davies, *Presences that Disturb*, pp. 135–92.
56 Musil, *The Man Without Qualities*, p. 11.
57 See Löffler, *The Literary and Historical Legacy of Iolo Morganwg*, pp. 126–9.
58 See Gwyn A. Williams, *Madoc: The Making of a Myth* (London: Methuen, 1978).
59 See Walford Davies, *Presences that Disturb*, pp. 142–5. For the pressures of the period on writers in general, see Kenneth R. Johnston, *Unusual Suspects: Pitt's Reign of Alarm and the Lost Generation of the 1790s* (Oxford: Oxford University Press, 2013).
60 See Mary-Ann Constantine, '"This Wildernessed Business of Publication": The Making of *Poems, Lyric and Pastoral* (1794)', in Jenkins (ed.), *A Rattleskull Genius*, pp. 123–5.
61 For all citations and a discussion of this period, see Constantine, *The Truth Against the World*, pp. 45–7.
62 See Geraint Phillips, 'Math o Wallgofrwydd: Iolo Morganwg, Opiwm a Thomas Chatterton' ('A Type of Madness: Iolo Morganwg, Opium and Thomas Chatterton'), *National Library of Wales Journal*, 29:4 (Winter 1996), 391–410.
63 Edward Williams to Margaret Williams, 27 October 1792, in Jenkins *et al.* (eds), *The Correspondence of Iolo Morganwg*, I, p. 527.

Works cited

Primary texts

Blair, Hugh, *A Critical Dissertation on the Poems of Ossian, the son of Fingal* (London: T. Becket and P. A. de Hondt, 1763).
Davies, Edward, *The Mythology and Rites of the British Druids* (London: J. Booth, 1809)
Evans, Evan, *Some Specimens of the Poetry of the Antient Welsh Bards* (London: R. and J. Dodsley, 1764)
Jenkins, Geraint H., Ffion Mair Jones and David Ceri Jones (eds), *The*

Correspondence of Iolo Morganwg, 3 vols (Cardiff: University of Wales Press, 2007)

Johnson, Samuel, *A Journey to the Western Islands of Scotland* (London: J. Pope, 1775).

Macpherson, James, *Fragments of Ancient Poetry Collected in the Highlands of Scotland* (Edinburgh: G. Hamilton and J. Balfour, 1760).

Musil, Robert, *The Man Without Qualities*, trans. Sophie Wilkins and Burton Pike (London: Picador, 1997)

Pennant, Thomas, *A Tour in Scotland & A Voyage to the Hebrides*, 3rd edn (Warrington: W. Eyres, 1774)

Rowlands, Henry, *Mona Antiqua Restaurata* (Dublin: Aaron Rhames, 1723)

Stukeley, William, *Stonehenge: A Temple Restor'd to the British Druids* (London: W. Innys and R. Manby, 1740)

Warton, Thomas, *The History of English Poetry, from the Close of the Eleventh to the Commencement of the Eighteenth Century*, 4 vols (London: J. Dodsley, 1774–81)

Williams, Edward [Note on Truth], National Library of Wales, MS 13120B/ 193

Williams, Edward, *Poems, Lyric and Pastoral*, 2 vols (London: E. Williams, 1794)

Williams, Moses, *Proposals for Printing by Subscription a Collection of Writings in the Welsh Tongue* (London, 1719)

Secondary texts

Baines, Paul, *The House of Forgery in Eighteenth-century Britain* (Aldershot: Ashgate, 1999)

Baines, Paul, 'Ossianic Geographies: Fingalian Figures on the Scottish Tour, 1760–1830', *Scotlands*, 4:1 (January 1997), 44–61

Butler, Marilyn, *Mapping Mythologies* (Cambridge, Cambridge University Press, 2016)

Clancy, Thomas Owen, 'Gaelic Literature and Scottish Romanticism', in Murray Pittock (ed.), *The Edinburgh Companion to Scottish Romanticism* (Edinburgh: Edinburgh University Press, 2011), pp. 49–60

Constantine, Mary-Ann, 'Ossian in Wales and Brittany', in Howard Gaskill (ed.), *The Reception of Ossian in Europe* (London: Thoemmes, 2004), pp. 67–90

Constantine, Mary-Ann, *The Truth Against the World: Iolo Morganwg and Romantic Forgery* (Cardiff: University of Wales Press, 2007)

Constantine, Mary-Ann, '"This Wildernessed Business of Publication": The Making of *Poems, Lyric and Pastoral* (1794)', in Geraint H. Jenkins (ed.),

A Rattleskull Genius: The Many Faces of Iolo Morganwg (Cardiff: University of Wales Press, 2005), pp. 123–45

Constantine, Mary-Ann, 'Welsh Literary History and the Making of "The Myvyrian Archaiology of Wales"', in Dirk Van Hulle and Joep Leerssen (eds), *Editing the Nation's Memory: Textual Scholarship and Nation-Building in Nineteenth-century Europe* (Amsterdam: Rodopi, 2008), pp. 109–28

Cook, Daniel, *Thomas Chatterton and Neglected Genius, 1760–1830* (London: Palgrave, 2013)

Crowe, Richard M., 'Diddordebau Ieithyddol Iolo Morganwg' (unpublished PhD thesis, University of Wales, 1988)

Davies, John H. (ed.), *The Letters of Lewis, Richard, William and John Morris of Anglesey (Morrisiaid Môn) 1728–1765*, 2 vols (Aberystwyth, 1907–9)

Dearnley, Moira, '"Mad Ned" and the "Smatter-Dasher": Iolo Morganwg and Edward "Celtic" Davies', in Geraint H. Jenkins (ed.), *A Rattleskull Genius: The Many Faces of Iolo Morganwg* (Cardiff: University of Wales Press, 2005), pp. 425–42

Edwards, Huw Meirion, 'A Multitude of Voices: The Free-Metre Poetry of Iolo Morganwg', in Geraint H. Jenkins (ed.), *A Rattleskull Genius: The Many Faces of Iolo Morganwg* (Cardiff: University of Wales Press, 2005), pp. 95–122

Gaskill, Howard (ed.), *The Reception of Ossian in Europe* (London: Thoemmes, 2004)

Groom, Nick, *The Forger's Shadow* (London: Picador, 2002)

Groom, Nick, *The Making of Percy's 'Reliques'* (Oxford: Oxford University Press, 1999)

Groom, Nick (ed.), *Thomas Chatterton and Romantic Culture* (London: Palgrave, 1999)

Haywood, Ian, *The Making of History: A Study of the Literary Forgeries of James Macpherson and Thomas Chatterton in Relation to Eighteenth-century Ideas of History and Fiction* (Rutherford, NJ: Fairleigh Dickinson University Press, 1986)

Haywood, Ian (ed.), *Romanticism, Forgery and the Credit Crunch* (Romantic Circles Praxis Volume), www.rc.umd.edu/praxis/forgery/index/html

Hobsbawm, Eric and Terence Ranger (eds), *The Invention of Tradition* (Cambridge: Cambridge University Press, 1983)

Holmes, Richard, 'Thomas Chatterton: The Case Re-opened', *Cornhill Magazine*, 178:1063–8 (1970–1), 200–51.

Hudson, Nicholas, '"Oral Tradition": The Evolution of an Eighteenth-century Concept', in S. J. Alvaro Ribeira and James G. Basker (eds), *Tradition in Transition: Women Writers, Marginal Texts, and the Eighteenth-century Canon* (Oxford: Oxford University Press, 1996), pp. 161–76

Jenkins, Geraint H. (ed.), *A Rattleskull Genius: The Many Faces of Iolo Morganwg* (Cardiff: University of Wales Press, 2005)

Johnston, Kenneth R., *Unusual Suspects: Pitt's Reign of Alarm and the Lost Generation of the 1790s* (Oxford: Oxford University Press, 2013)

Leerssen, Joep, 'Ossian and the Rise of Literary Historicism', in Howard Gaskill (ed.), *The Reception of Ossian in Europe* (London: Thoemmes, 2004), pp. 109–25

Leask, Nigel, 'Fingalian Topographies: Ossian and the Highland Tour, 1760-1805', *Journal for Eighteenth-century Studies*, 39:2 (June 2016), 183–96

Lewis, Gwyneth, 'Eighteenth-century Literary Forgeries, with Special Reference to the Work of Iolo Morganwg' (unpublished DPhil thesis, Oxford University, 1991)

Lewis, Gwyneth, *Sonedau Redsa a Cherddi Eraill* (Llandysul: Gwasg Gomer, 1990)

Löffler, Marion, 'Failed Founding Fathers and Abandoned Sources: Edward Williams, Thomas Stephens and the Young J. E. Lloyd', in Neil Evans and Huw Pryce (eds), *Writing a Small Nation's Past: Wales in Comparative Perspective, 1850–1950* (Farnham: Ashgate, 2013), pp. 61–81

Löffler, Marion, *The Literary and Historical Legacy of Iolo Morganwg, 1826–1926* (Cardiff: University of Wales Press, 2007)

Lynch, Jack, *Deception and Detection in Eighteenth-century Britain* (Aldershot: Ashgate, 2008)

Mac Craith, Mícheál, '"We Know All These Poems": The Irish Response to *Ossian*', in Howard Gaskill (ed.), *The Reception of Ossian in Europe* (London: Thoemmes, 2004), pp. 91–108

Meyerstein, E. H. W., *A Life of Thomas Chatterton* (London: Ingpen and Grant, 1930)

Moore, Dafydd, 'James Macpherson', www.oxfordbibliographies.com/view/document/obo-9780199846719/obo-9780199846719-0066.xml

Owen, Hugh (ed.), *Additional Letters of the Morrises of Anglesey (1735–1786)*, 2 vols (London: The Honourable Society of Cymmrodorion, 1947)

Owen, Morfydd, *Y Meddwl Obsesiynol: Traddodiad y Triawd Cyffredinol yn y Gymraeg a'r Myvyrian Archaiology* (Aberystwyth: Papurau Ymchwil Canolfan Uwchefrydiau Cymreig a Cheltaidd, 2007)

Perkins, Pam, '"News From Scotland": Female Networks in the Travel Narratives of Elizabeth Isabella Spence', *Women's Writing*, 24:2 (July 2016), 170–84

Phillips, Geraint, 'Forgery and Patronage: Iolo Morganwg and Owain

Myfyr', in Geraint H. Jenkins (ed.), *A Rattleskull Genius: The Many Faces of Iolo Morganwg* (Cardiff: University Press, 2005), pp. 403–24

Phillips, Geraint, 'Math o Wallgofrwydd: Iolo Morganwg, Opiwm a Thomas Chatterton', *National Library of Wales Journal*, 29:4 (Winter 1996), 391–410

Rauschenberg, Roy A., 'The Journals of Joseph Banks's Voyage up Great Britain's Coast to Iceland and to the Orkney Isles, July to October 1772', *Proceedings of the American Philosophical Society*, 117:3 (June 1973), 186–226

Russett, Margaret, *Fictions and Fakes: Forging Romantic Authenticity, 1760–1845* (Cambridge: Cambridge University Press, 2006)

Ruthven, K. K., *Faking Literature* (Cambridge: Cambridge University Press, 2001)

Simmons, Clare A., 'Introduction', in Clare A. Simmons (ed.), *Medievalism and the Quest for the 'Real' Middle Ages* (London: Frank Cass, 2001), pp. 1–28

Smiles, Sam, *The Image of Antiquity: Ancient Britain and the Romantic Imagination* (New Haven, CT: Yale University Press, 1994)

Stafford, Fiona, *The Sublime Savage: James Macpherson and the Poems of Ossian* (Edinburgh: Edinburgh University Press, 1988)

Taylor, Donald S. (ed.), *The Complete Works of Thomas Chatterton: A Bicentenary Edition*, 2 vols (Oxford: Oxford University Press, 1971)

Taylor, Donald S., *Thomas Chatterton's Art: Experiments in Imagined History* (Princeton: Princeton University Press, 1978)

Walford Davies, Damian, *Presences that Disturb: Models of Romantic Identity in the Literature and Culture of the 1790s* (Cardiff: University of Wales Press, 2002)

Williams, G. J., *Iolo Morganwg a Chywyddau'r Ychwanegiad* (Llundain: Cymdeithas yr Eisteddfod Genedlaethol, 1926)

Williams, G. J., *Iolo Morganwg: Y Gyfrol Gyntaf* (Caerdydd: Gwasg Prifysgol Cymru, 1956)

Williams, G. J., *Traddodiad Llenyddol Morgannwg* (Caerdydd: Gwasg Prifysgol Cymru, 1948)

Williams, Gwyn A., *Madoc: The Making of a Myth* (London: Methuen, 1978)

4

Sophia Lee's *The Recess* and the epistemology of the counterfactual

Tilottama Rajan

Between 1785 and 1844, Sophia Lee's novel *The Recess; Or, A Tale of Other Times* (1783–85) – now largely forgotten – was reprinted several times, pirated, and also abridged as a street novel. *The Recess* is a boldly counterfactual romance about Matilda and Ellinor, children of the imaginary marriage of Mary Queen of Scots and the Duke of Norfolk, and about the complex relationships between the 'real' earls of Leicester and Essex and the twins, who are avatars for a role in history that women can claim only vicariously and (il)legitimately through love and marriage. Like Lee's *The Two Emilys* (1798), the novel is concerned with the forging of alternative genealogies and histories, specifically the sisters' claim to the throne of England. Lee's 'invention' – to invoke her contemporary, William Godwin – has a basis in a 'scanty substratum of facts'.[1] In 1567, after Mary's illegitimate half-brother forced her abdication in favour of her infant son James, she was rumoured to have had still-born twins, or (in another version) a daughter who was smuggled to France. In 1568, Mary escaped to England, where she was kept under the surveillance of the 9th Baron Scrope, brother-in-law of Norfolk, who was involved in her trial even as there were rumours of marriage plans between them. Lee combines these stories to legitimise the twins as daughters of a clandestine marriage. But since Mary's third husband, Bothwell, turns out to be alive, the secret births remain scandalous and (il)legitimate, like many of the counterfactual unions in the text, which are based on bigamy, incest or murder – provocations that both provide alternative realities and strip the veneer of legitimacy from received history. Written on the cusp of the Romantic period, *The Recess* is arguably the first in a line of feminist counterfactual histories that includes Mary Shelley's *Valperga* (1823) and

Virginia Woolf's fiction of Judith Shakespeare in *A Room of One's Own* (1929). However, the novel should not be tied to a feminist content, whether cautionary or liberatory, since it is really a series of provocations for thinking about the issues it raises.

I begin by approaching the text through Godwin's essay 'On History and Romance' (1797), a companion to his own counterfactual novel *St Leon* (1799). Godwin knew Leibniz's theory of possible worlds, in which a reality in which Mary has two daughters is not impossible, but merely 'incompossible' with an actuality in which she does not.[2] But in Godwin's essay, his counterfactualism finally, if equivocally, yields to realism. I therefore suggest that Deleuze, who operates in the field of logic and without the constraints of theology (Leibniz) or historical argument (Godwin), provides a better pathway into *The Recess* – a text we should not read mimetically as the imitation of an action, but narratologically, as opening up the very logics of reading.

My aim, then, is to use *The Recess* to reflect on the epistemology of the counterfactual as something more elusive and dynamic than simply a possible world on the model of romance. For unlike *Valperga*, where Euthanasia's alternate history has a specific content defeated by real history, *The Recess* is about the form rather than the content of the counterfactual. Female history is too criss-crossed by differences to constitute an ideology; rather, it is an envelope for exploring the conditions of the (im)possibility of the counterfactual, of which feminisms are an effect. While a counterfactual proposition (like 'Shakespeare's sister') can be read in terms of set-theory, a counterfactual narrative is more complex. A proposition can be an internally coherent set that produces an alternate reality. In a counterfactual narrative, as in all complex systems, the set is at points non-coherent. It functions both in terms of another possible world and in terms of our world, and cannot provide a line of flight into pure fantasy, especially when it includes both historical and fictional characters. But if historical romance mixes the categories of coherence and correspondence, in *Valperga* the coherence of the proposition is finally defeated by the reality of the historical and dis-integrated by the non-coherence between Euthanasia and Beatrice. *Valperga*, then, is better described as counterhistorical rather than as counterfactual. In Lee's novel, by contrast, the very non-coherence between the sisters and of each character individually breaks open the logic of sense by which the novel of sensibility (as critics often see *The Recess*) is generally limited.

Godwin's essay, which may well have Lee in mind, provides an initial entrance to the epistemological paradoxes of the 'historical romance' that both of them write.[3] 'Of History and Romance' ('HR') is an intricately sophistical experiment in unsettling received notions of truth and falsification, or things as they are and should be. It is even a theory of 'simulation' in Deleuze's sense, to which I will return, where the simulacrum or 'false pretender' deconstructs the Platonic grounding of imitation in truth. Anticipating his daughter's opposition of official history to the 'private chronicles' it omits,[4] Godwin starts by distinguishing 'general history', which looks for normalising patterns, from 'individual history', whose singularities potentiate 'conjunctures and combinations' which, 'though they have never yet occurred, are within the capacities of our nature' ('HR', p. 457). In the essay's many twists and turns, he overlaps this binary with one between ancient and modern history, also evoked in Lee's distinction of the present from 'the reign ... of romance' and in her tongue-in-cheek description of the historical Elizabeth as 'the child of fancy'.[5] That ancient history is interesting because it is full of 'fables' ('HR', p. 461) then lets Godwin pose the problem in terms of romance versus a history no longer differentiated as individual or general.

Asking why imagination is not as true as facts that are tissues of lies, Godwin proclaims the romance-writer as the author of 'real history', only to perform a volte face by equivocally returning the 'advantage' to the historian. For now it is romance that indulges in broad simplifications, while history, with its eye for particulars, opens a space for the 'single grain of sand' that potentially alters the entire 'motion' of the earth and over time 'diversifie[s] its events' ('HR', pp. 466–7).

Embedded in these pirouettes is a complex theory of counterfactuals that does not keep the actual and virtual series separate. In the conventional reading of Leibniz, a world where Adam is not a sinner is logically possible even though it does not correspond to 'reality', but is 'incompossible' with the one in which he falls, because combining them would create a non-coherent set; the possible world is thus safely kept in parentheses. But for Godwin, through the subversiveness of particulars, the imaginary and real series of persons and events so continually turn the tables on each other that the virtual becomes the fold of the actual; hence the technique both he and Lee use, of mixing historical and fictional characters. This conjunction means that romance is continually exposed to history, as we see when the realist Ellinor deconstructs Matilda's romance with Leicester. But it also allows for an upsurge of the possible within the real, as minute particulars of characters and events enfold paths not taken as virtually present. Moreover, when we 'produce the materials' gathered from our reading, further incompossibles 'by a sort of magnetism' – or 'quasi-causation' – 'start out to view in ourselves, which might otherwise [lie] undetected' ('HR', p. 455). Hence not only are counterfactuals produced by the actual; what happens factually also remains in flux since it virtually contains counterfactuals. Or as Godwin later writes, while in 'the universe of matter' the current world is the only possible world, 'in the determinations and acts of living beings each occurrence may be or not be' and both issues are 'equally possible till that decision has been made'.[6] If incompossibles exist till a decision is made, then surely they exist virtually after a decision.

Yet as he travels between possibilities, Godwin finally absorbs contingency into necessity. For in the end, the grain of sand is removed from our hands 'and determined by the system of the universe' ('HR', p. 467), as Godwin chooses 'the universe of matter' – where nothing happens except as it 'has been or will be' – over the individual, for whom incompossibles virtually exist.[7] 'Of History and Romance' aptly describes Mary Shelley's *Valperga*, which binds Euthanasia's possible world into a historical succession, and which, as suggested, is more counterhistorical than counterfactual. By contrast, the very structure that gives Lee's novel its title figures the folding of the virtual and actual into each other. The 'Recess', where the twins are concealed until adulthood, is a subterranean labyrinth secretly connected to the 'real' world of St Vincent's Abbey, the residence of Lord Scrope, a firm supporter of Elizabeth, who nevertheless connives at the 'marriage' of Norfolk and Mary. Although Lord Scrope's forebear had built St Vincent's on the wreckage of a monastery he had torn down during the reign of Henry VIII, he had also used the Recess to shelter Catholic priests. Though hidden from daylight, it cannot 'be called a [Platonic] cave', being 'composed of various rooms', expanded from the original structure as each priest added a new chamber (*The Recess*, pp. 7–8, 12, 22).

At crucial points, Lee's narrative returns to the secret passageway to the Recess. Mrs Marlow periodically retreats there; on Lord Scrope's death, the family pictures are taken to Kenilworth via the Recess; Matilda and Leicester flee there from Elizabeth's wrath and escape to France; and by contrast, Ellinor is imprisoned in St Vincent's by her husband and shut off from the Recess as an archive of secret histories that shelters what has been repressed and opens pathways to the future. The connections between the Recess and the abbey thus model pathways across the ideologies that maintain the boundaries of the existing order; nearly all Protestant characters in the novel have secret 'Catholic' connections, just as nearly everyone is guilty of incestuous or (il)legitimate relationships.

The novel's 'gothic' genre has less to do with the supernatural than with this baroque architecture. With its multiplying rooms in a confined space, the Recess provides a structure for the narrative akin to what Deleuze and Guattari, in their account of 'minor literature', call a rhizome or burrow, which 'has many entrances' and 'main and side doors' with different 'rules of usage', allowing us to reflect on how 'the map' is modified, depending on where one enters.[8] One day, the twins leave their shelter through the looking-glass of their mother's portrait and meet Lord Leicester – a virtual character, of course, but from the 'real' or outside world within the novel's virtual reality. Following the 'dead letter of female virtue' that Lee's text is 'required to reproduce',[9] Matilda feels duty-bound to 'lament' the fulfilment of her fantasy (*The Recess*, p. 10). Yet because the Recess keeps returning as a fold in the novel's topology, we cannot read the narrative within the logic of necessity as a passage from the virtual to its ensuing defeat by the actual. Deleuze's fold, in his studies of Leibniz and Foucault, is both an ontological and historiographical concept. The fold contests accounts of subjectivity that separate inside and outside, the inside being a fold of the outside, as one's self is folded onto and over oneself. All subjects are therefore non-simple and composed of multiple possibilities, as the forces of the outside continually refold the inside. In Deleuze's 'baroque' house, which opens up Leibniz's potential radicality, there are two 'floors': an upper floor of 'innate ideas' that is 'blind and closed' and windowless, as Leibniz nominally theorises his monads, and a lower chamber of matter in which, like origami, a fold 'is folded within a fold, like a cavern in a cavern', which is how monads secretly work, as they are always subdivisible into further monads.[10] In *The Recess*, this upper floor of official history comprises the courts of Elizabeth and James, while the lower chamber is made up of the 'minor' narratives. And just as for Deleuze/Leibniz there is constant communication between the floors, so in *The Recess,* through the fold between Protestant and Catholic, proper and improper sexuality, the closed upper floor is opened up to multiple differences by the lower.

Moreover, the present (subjectivity) is continually folded over onto the past (memory), as one lives one's life as 'the double of the other'.[11] This temporal folding also yields a new conception of simulation – a concern of both *The Recess* and Lee's *The Two Emilys*. It is in the Recess that the twins encounter their parents' portraits, based on which they simulate an identity that cannot be placed in simple categories of true and false. Deleuze's deconstruction of Plato functions as a genealogy of morals that endows the simulacrum with the power of creation, unbinding it from a logic of imitation grounded in truth. Plato assumes a moral hierarchy of the original/model, the true copy, and the copy of the copy (the simulacrum or false copy); thus the philosopher is a true copy of the good, while the sophist is a 'false pretender'. But for Deleuze, the real difference is not between model and copy, but between true and false copies; that there are two copies, that the simulacrum or 'false pretender' claims the status of copy, means there is no original.[12] Lee's novel is full of pretenders who are creators and not imitators, the first being the Queen of Scots. This foreigner's claim to the throne of England confused clear lines of descent in ways that remind us that these lines were also skipped in the Hanoverian succession, disclosing official history too as a forgery. It opened up new lines of flight, as Mary became a feminist icon, inflecting texts like Wollstonecraft's *The Wrongs of Woman; or, Maria* (1798), where Maria is saved and maybe betrayed by 'Darnford', a version of Mary's second husband, Lord Darnley. If in these afterlives Mary figures the trap of sensibility, the contrast between the Virgin Queen and her sexually prolific rival also unbinds desire to find other routes around the very dead-ends of feminist history, possibilities that are multiplied in Lee's novel by the fact that Mary has not one but two daughters. Or more?

Lee's intricate six-part novel resists memorable summary. The main narrator is Matilda who, as if fulfilling a dream, marries Leicester. But to avoid angering Elizabeth, he conceals the twins at Kenilworth disguised as musicians, then passes them off at court as daughters of Lady Jane Grey (The *Recess*, p. 81), until, on Matilda's pregnancy, he discloses his marriage. The couple take shelter in France with Matilda's aunt, Lady Mortimer, where Leicester is killed by Elizabeth's agents. Embedded in Matilda's narrative, which she writes on her deathbed as a letter to a French friend, are other stories that create an effect of mirrors within mirrors. The most important of these are the double 'origin story', which entwines Mary's history with a number of other histories and narratives: that of the twins' foster-parents, Mrs Marlow and Father Anthony (not their real names); Leicester's narrative; Ellinor's account of her thwarted relationship with Essex (Robert Devereux) in a series of letters given to Matilda, on her return to England, by the Countess of Pembroke (Sir Philip Sidney's sister – who continues Ellinor's story); and the story of Matilda's daughter, another Mary.

The stories all end disastrously as the sisters are separated, Leicester and Essex die, and Ellinor goes mad. After betraying Leicester, Lady Mortimer imprisons Matilda for marrying a Protestant. Her son helps Matilda escape but kidnaps her and takes her to Jamaica, where he is about to force marriage on her; she is saved in a slave revolt, imprisoned again, then befriended and liberated by the Spanish governor's mistress, Anana. Matilda returns to England and finds Ellinor, but Ellinor dies and Matilda's daughter Mary is poisoned, leaving Matilda to await death and write her memoirs. One can extract from this catalogue a dull moral about the 'dangers' of the romantic choices open to women, but the novel resists being imprisoned in a mimetic reading.[13] For since a counterfactual history has not happened, what happens in it cannot foreclose what has not happened. Indeed, since the logic of probability according to which things 'happen' in fiction is a projection based on custom, we must consider whether the predictability of these disastrous endings is truth, or a genre of fiction that institutes itself as self-fulfilling prophecy.

Just as we cannot read *The Recess* mimetically, so too we should not 'apply' it to reality. Feminist thinking is among the *effects* of the narratives, which make us reflect on women's desire to be men's equals, on how the trap of sensibility leads them to realise their ambitions through men and be re-interpellated into what they resist through the genre of sentimental romance, and on whether there is any other way for women to participate in history. The novel raises the same questions as texts by Wollstonecraft, Mary Shelley, Mary Hays and Eliza Fenwick, which it influenced.[14] However, the problem with a feminist reading is that since *The Recess* presents no 'agenda for social change', if we seek a political point, we can see the text only as peopled 'with negative examples of women who have been abused by the system', or 'failed to make the most' of their 'choices and powers'.[15] *The Recess* then becomes a less naturalistic version of Wollstonecraft's *The Wrongs of Woman*, whose vindication of the rights of women is stalled by underlying contradictions such as Maria's sensibility and Wollstonecraft's inability to collectivise her middle-class narrative with that of the outcast Jemima (who is prefigured by Lee's Anana).

Moreover, a mimetic reading assumes that we identify with the novel's characters rather than pass through them; yet the characters have no interiority but form a self-repeating series. In the absence of unique selves, what matters is the repetition of stories, which is not reconfirmation but difference. For this repetition is not just serial (Matilda's story followed by that of her daughter) but also lateral (Matilda's story doubled as Ellinor's) and recessive (the sisters' stories repeated in Mrs Marlow's). If each story comes to a similarly sad end, this is because in its present form it has run its course: its characters must be terminated, their histories shelved and the energies or disavowals they represent rethought through possibilities that emerge from their differences. Such differences allow us to operate the text in terms of a modal rather than propositional logic, where modal logic provides different alethic options (necessity, possibility, impossibility) and different doxastic options or modalities of belief. In short, the novel is a space for thinking rather than a serial replacement of one failure with another within a predicative logic. The earlier stories keep returning as letters that are sent again, containing further letters that are recesses in the novel – letters about the twins' birth; letters about the (il)legitimate genealogy of Mrs Marlow that return years later when they are given to Ellinor by a servant after the destruction of the Recess (*The Recess*, pp. 207–9); and Ellinor's and Matilda's own letters.

The first story, which seems to be a gateway to the novel but becomes a recess or fold, is Mrs Marlow's story of proscribed love, which she tells Matilda as a preface to her account of the twins' birth. This story is prefaced by its own origin story, whose confusing genealogy is belied by an attempt to unfold it in a historical sequence. Mrs Marlow's mother had conceived an unfortunate passion for an earlier Lord Scrope, whereupon the mother's Catholic parents locked her up. Mrs Marlow was then handed over to Lord Scrope, who raised her alongside his legitimate son, Scrope *fils*, owner of St Vincent's at the time of the twins' birth. Eventually, she fell in love with Anthony Colville, a West Indian (from a white settler family, but nevertheless 'foreign'). But just as they were married, it emerged that Anthony was her brother, conceived when their mother was briefly reunited with the elder Lord Scrope, and born after the mother's parents had deported her to the West Indies and married her to Colville *père*, who raised Anthony as his son. Traumatised, the two live in celibacy in the Recess as 'Father Anthony' and 'Mrs Marlow'. Meanwhile Scrope *fils* marries Matilda Howard, and while visiting them, the latter's brother Norfolk secretly marries Mary Queen of Scots. The result is the twins, who are brought up by the incestuous celibates in the Recess in ignorance of their origins. Mary's secret marriage is the alibi for Mrs Marlow's complicated story, which she conveys in the mandatory form of a cautionary tale that incites the very desire it prohibits – a desire unleashed when Mrs Marlow's death liberates the text from a celibate world.

Mrs Marlow's story is the closest we come to the mimetic mode, and her alias (oddly middle class for an Elizabethan romance) is symptomatic of the morality of the good copy. But even this story, with its receding series of repeating transgressions, opens up the possibilities that Mrs Marlow would rather bury in the 'tomb' of the Recess (*The Recess*, p. 15). Hereafter, perception is an implicit issue, since on Mrs Marlow's death, the twins enter the world and open the fold between the actual and virtual. This does not mean that they move from one to the other, from images and portraits into reality. For if one follows a fold up to the following fold, the inside becomes the outside and vice versa, and the virtual and actual keep exchanging places. In this topography, subjects have no essence but are folds of the events in which they are produced. But this is not to say that they are passive effects of events; the characters are always active, and if there is a difference between the narratives of Mrs Marlow and Matilda, it consists in the way the stories are told – in the fact that Mrs Marlow submissively records events, whereas Matilda's story, by performing what could not historically have happened, produces events. In short, in the counterfactual mode of the sisters' narratives (as against the factual mode of Mrs Marlow's), people happen within events that these characters can potentially counter-actualise or fold in different directions.

Given this plasticity, Lee, far from following existing historians – as Anne Stevens claims – plays fast and loose with facts, particularly in the case of Leicester.[16] Or more precisely, she follows 'fact' just enough for the reader to feel the epistemic force of the counterfactual as a possible world rather than a fantasy. From 1585 to 1587, Leicester was in the Netherlands, returning briefly from December 1586 to June 1587. Historically, this was because of the Mary Queen of Scots crisis, but in the novel it is prompted by Matilda's pregnancy. However, since the couple only meet in 1586 (*The Recess*, p. 33), how in those six months could Leicester also have married Matilda, lived with her at Kenilworth, and fled with her to France? Furthermore, in 1578 the real Leicester married Letitia Knollys, with whom he lived happily and who survived him by many years. But the novel makes Leicester conveniently available for remarriage. Having spurned his guardian's niece, Miss Lineric, in his youth, he falls passionately in love with Lady Essex, who turns out to be Miss Lineric. They marry after the death of her first husband; Leicester then discovers her in bed with her brother, and narrowly avoids being poisoned by them (his servant suggests switching the plates, with the result that the incestuous pair ingest their own poison). This assassination of real history clears the way for the fantasy marriage between Matilda and a man forty-six years older. There are other departures from truth, including the fact that the historical Leicester died of stomach cancer, malaria or poison, whereas in the novel he has a romantic death in France.

But Leicester exists in a synchronic space – as the 'Leicester effect'

– which, like Deleuze and Guattari's Joan of Arc effect, functions as an intensity added to Matilda's claim for an alternative history.[17] The ideological specifics of this alternative are unimportant; Matilda provides a line of flight from established history, a vector for experimentation. Leicester, then, is a potentiality added onto this vector: 'his beauty was rather fixed than faded' (*The Recess*, p. 39). Proper names, according to Deleuze and Guattari, are not part of a logic of 'representation', where the name is a historical personage, but are 'intensities' or 'effects within fields of potentials'. These 'names of history' are thus 'not figures who were once present and became past, but exist as a subject's passage back through historical personae'.[18] To identify with a name is to identify with a 'zone' rather than an 'identity', since the historical personage herself is not an identity but has 'circulated through the names of history on the periphery of her own zones of intensity'.[19] To expand a time that is contracted within historical duration – as Lee does with the six-month period when Leicester returned to England – is to open new spaces within it. Leicester is only one of the characters in the novel who violate history so as to exist outside of a strict temporal succession, thus becoming 'a phantasm that anyone can live through'.[20] Sir Philip Sidney falls in love with Matilda, and on being rejected, despondently marries Frances Walsingham, later Lady Essex. The names of history that return in the text are lines of flight that allow us to imagine different trajectories for history. Of these, Mary Queen of Scots herself – a recessive figure never seen in the text except through a grate (*The Recess*, p. 75) – is the most significant.

In contrast to Matilda, Ellinor offers us the 'realist' alternative in a counterfactual novel where realism itself is exposed as a fantasy. Ellinor reads Leicester as selfish, introducing a division into the twins' historico-political project of which Matilda cannot but be subtextually aware. Ellinor is the other side of the enthusiast Matilda: 'Astonishing that two agreeing in every instance till that moment, should ... differ in so decided a manner!' (*The Recess*, p. 155). For Ellinor, who refuses to share Matilda's enthusiasm, Leicester conceals his marriage to keep the Queen attached to him so that she will 'break [her] match with the French Prince' (*The Recess*, p. 157). Continuing with the realist scenario, Ellinor restrains her own passion for Essex out of 'obstinate prudence' (*The Recess*, p. 215), although Frances Walsingham has conveniently released Essex from the marriage projected for them by her parents, by choosing Sir Philip Sidney instead. Ellinor rejects Essex again to save him from the Queen's jealousy and from threatened execution, and agrees to marry

Sophia Lee's The Recess

the undistinguished Arlington, forcing the virtual Essex back into his (historical) marriage with a now widowed Frances Walsingham. Hoping to save her mother from execution, Ellinor also yields to Burghley's insistence that she sign a document declaring her birth papers to be forged. In so doing, she submits – albeit under duress – to a realist logic according to which the counterfactual is a forgery.

However, not only is Mary executed anyway (which is to say that the realist scenario does not accomplish its purpose); Ellinor herself also fares worse than the 'romantic' Matilda, who amasses considerable wealth through Leicester and the Jamaican concubine, Anana. Ellinor's spouse Arlington buys St Vincent's, destroys the Recess as part of modernisation, dies in an accident and leaves instructions for Ellinor to be imprisoned at the Abbey. That the twins' lives are virtual lives – alternative scenarios for unfolding the legacy of desire – is suggested by Burghley when he urges Ellinor to sign the paper renouncing her claim to be Mary Queen of Scots's daughter: 'consider ... who, and what you will be' (*The Recess*, p. 177). Given a story to choose, Ellinor, unlike Matilda, decides not to perform her life as the Queen of Scots's daughter. Yet in a doubling of Matilda's desire that belies this renunciation, Ellinor too falls in love with a favourite of Elizabeth's – indeed with Leicester's stepson, who has a 'countenance no less perfect' than Leicester's but which is 'lighted up by brilliant youth' (*The Recess*, p. 159). Moreover, despite his marriage, Essex persists in his love of Matilda, tracking her down at St Vincent's and nursing her back to health. This is to say that the desire Matilda expresses directly (as her love of Leicester) is, in Ellinor's case, socially channelled through renunciation only to be re-projected as Essex's love for her.

But should we believe Ellinor's cynical assessment of why Leicester conceals his marriage to Matilda, which to her astonishment he eventually discloses? For while her doubts about Leicester fill in the 'minute shades in a character' which for Godwin complicate romance ('HR', p. 467), it may not be true, as Ellinor claims, that 'at that period' Leicester could have acknowledged his marriage without 'offending Elizabeth' and arousing the Queen's anger against the sisters as well as himself (*The Recess*, p. 157). The image of Leicester forged in Part I of the novel may not be entirely false, making Ellinor's realism as hypothetical as Matilda's romanticism. Nor is Matilda the victimised woman that Ellinor sees; after all, she too falls in love with Leicester out of ambition, and not so deeply as not also to be attracted to Sidney in a novel in which fantasy is not meant to be fulfilled but rather 'teaches us how to desire'.[21]

This brings us to the last story, that of Matilda's daughter, Mary. After Ellinor's death, Matilda returns to Kenilworth, now rented to a manufacturer, and retrieves two caskets containing bonds for Leicester's money abroad and proofs of her birth and marriage. Intriguingly (counterfactually), these documents still exist, though Elizabeth has already torn them up (*The Recess*, pp. 119, 171); but there seem to be twin sets of documents, which puts this story also in the realm of virtuality. Now acknowledged as Lady Leicester, Matilda comes into her own; she moves to Richmond, where she hopes her daughter Mary will marry Henry, Mary's cousin and King James's son. Henry is conjured into their lives when one day the ladies' carriage overturns and they look up to see two saviours, almost indistinguishable (*The Recess*, p. 282): Henry, and James's favourite, the villainous Rochester – itself a name with future recesses. In a contrivance that tells us this story is more about Matilda than Mary, Matilda sends her daughter riding during Henry's visits so that she can cultivate him. She divulges her origins to Henry, who is in love with Mary, and he confides his fears that Rochester may kill him. Before Mary and Henry can marry, however, Henry dies and Matilda is accused of poisoning him. Rather than flee, she discloses her identity to her half-brother the King, who seems sympathetic but keeps the documents that prove her parentage, and has Mary and Matilda kidnapped. Matilda is separated from her daughter, and one day discovers her dying in a luxurious apartment. While Matilda was cultivating Henry, Mary had secretly fallen in love with Rochester, who was trying to divorce his wife and had been ensuring the safety, if not freedom, of the Stuart women. Despite his unworthiness, Mary cannot curb her love for him and she is poisoned by his wife, the notorious Frances Howard, Lady Essex.

This Lady Essex is indistinguishable in her villainy from another Lady Essex encountered in the novel. The multiplying cast of depthless, exchangeable characters, combined with an infinitely extensible series of actants generated from a set that is incestuously closed by its finite number of names is no accident. The difficulty – and irrelevance – of knowing which Lady Essex this is reduces these 'real' historical characters to virtuality, as the text becomes more a narratology than a genealogy.

The last narrative adds little beyond a terminus, since there is now no one to survive Matilda. But perhaps it is meant to be disappointing. As we move from Elizabethan times to the early seventeenth century, we move from a heroic romance that is a feminist equivalent of Spenser's *The Faerie Queene* to a domestic story that is a premonition of the eighteenth-century imprisonment of women in the sentimental genre. Put differently, whereas Leicester is a vehicle for Matilda to participate in history, her daughter Mary is defined purely by her ill-fated love for Rochester. Mary bears her royal grandmother's name, and the Marian legacy is reduced, in this final recension, to her misfortune in choosing men, as the novel becomes the story of sensibility it is often taken to be.[22] But though it introduces many of the *topoi* that recur in the feminist novel of the 1790s, to this point *The Recess* has been generically worlds apart from the naturalism of that genre.

The sentimental cultural representation of Mary Queen of Scots after the Civil War had two parts: first, she was reduced to her excessive sensibility, whether critically or sympathetically, and then such representations atoned for their chauvinism through affecting descriptions of her death. Whether used by Royalists to build the Stuart dynasty on Mary's martyrdom or by Whig historians like Hume to put her into a literary parenthesis, this double narrative rendered Mary passive and located her firmly in the past. Yet Mary did not simply define herself through the men she loved. She returned from France to rule; she married Darnley, also descended from Margaret Tudor, to strengthen her claim to the English throne; and she raised an army to fight her half-brother, who became Regent after forcing her abdication. The stories of Matilda and Ellinor capture that activism, which is an intensity rather than an ideology. Though their lives are mobilised by seeing their parents' portraits in the Recess, the novel is about what these images produce – indeed, what images and simulacra in general produce. To approach images as productive rather than mimetic is also to resist reading as a mimesis. Godwin had already challenged passive reading in his essay 'Of Choice in Reading'. In this essay, which can be seen as a companion piece to 'Of History and Romance', he argues that a text's meaning consists in its 'tendency' rather than its 'moral', where the moral is an 'ethical sentence' that the text statically 'illustrat[es]', while the tendency is 'the actual effect' produced on the reader, which can be known only 'by the experiment', which differs with every reader.[23]

From its actual effects in history to its virtual effects in literature, Mary Queen of Scots's story was a 'source of potential public disorder' and a site of political urgency.[24] In *The Recess* in particular, her recessive image produces possibilities that are deconstructed when unfolded in narrative but preserved in the novel's many intimate secrets and the letters that pass between past and future without divulging the whole truth. The exact content of Mary's subversiveness is unimportant. Catholicism simply signifies another side to history, not an inside but a fold that could equally be folded outwards to conceal its own inside, so that the way almost every Protestant character in the novel turns out to have Catholic alliances simply intimates that every event has manifold possibilities. The Catholic Mary produces effects of thought, which include feminism as a power of thought but not as a single position, given that it is the power of deposition that Mary introduces into history, both in terms of how she threatened Elizabeth and in terms of her own deposition and execution.

But the last story seemingly lacks this productivity. The story is not actually that of Matilda's daughter Mary, but that of Matilda herself. The mother survives the daughter, and it is she who spends time with Henry, living vicariously through her daughter until she has to 'abridge *myself* of the pleasure of the Prince's society' (*The Recess*, p. 286; italics mine). We know little of the daughter except through Matilda; her story emerges after her death, when the secret of her love for Rochester is shockingly and remorsefully divulged as a recess or inset story within Matilda's. Matilda's new existence differs from her past in two ways. She settles into everyday life in ways more characteristic of the period after the Glorious Revolution than the time before the Civil War. She wants to make her story public even before the accusation against her compels her to do so. Yet paradoxically, it is when she asserts her legitimacy that her story is declared a forgery, as the King keeps her papers and sends her the renunciation signed by Ellinor. This is not just another case of the official record suppressing its rivals. At some level, despite the 'moral' proclaimed by critics that secrecy is misguided, the counterfactual can exist only on the condition of keeping something secret.[25] This secret keeps open a differend in history, something that cannot be phrased in the discourses of either side, and for which the Recess is a figure.[26] Just as much as Arlington, Matilda destroys this recess.

The narrative of settling down and marrying into mainstream history, naturalised and domesticated by Austen through the two sisters in *Sense and Sensibility*, is thus poisoned at the core of its conventionalism. Its vehicle, Matilda's daughter Mary, must also be poisoned, but not until, through a new twist, she has herself poisoned Matilda's intentions by not being a dutiful daughter to middle-class feminism. Just as Mary becomes a false rather than good copy, Rochester, an unsavoury character who remained with his evil Countess in real life, may redeem himself because he plans to divorce her fictionally. As neither quite fits his/her stereotype, the novel keeps the secret of what their relationship, and the consanguinity of Mary and Lady Essex (her cousin), mean. The names and *topoi* of the history folded up at the end of the novel will punctuate further novels by women. These include *Jane Eyre* and Mary Elizabeth Braddon's *Lady Audley's Secret* – also a tale of imposture, bigamy and murder, whose secrets are not so much exposed as locked up when the protagonist is immured in an asylum in France. For Deleuze, there exists an 'infinity' of monads that have not 'yet been called', have 'fallen', 'folded onto themselves' or (like Rochester) have been 'damned, hardened in a single fold' that will not 'unfurl'. Or as Leibniz says, what we call *'births'* are unfoldings and growths', while *'deaths* are enfoldings and diminutions'. Leibniz's optimism, according to Deleuze, is 'based on the infinity of the damned as the foundation of the best of all worlds: *they liberate an infinite quantity of possible progress*'.[27]

At the end, Matilda also escapes to France, home of seditious counter-histories. Indeed, it is striking how easily she escapes (rather than being banished) with her jewels restored, which gives the story another attempt at transmigration. Rather than seeing Lee's 'cyclic' conception of history as 'an endless loop of despair',[28] we should regard it in terms of Nietzsche's eternal return, which for Deleuze means that difference eternally returns.[29] The end opens up this difference, as the diachronic series of a generational novel is folded into the synchronic space of a letter, in which the last event in the plot recommences the story through its writing; Mary's death cuts off a filial transmission and terminates the historical series, forcing us to return to the past through an adopted reader in another country – Matilda's last friend, Adelaide, daughter of the French ambassador to England. Since counterfactually what happens has not happened, the various series of events can return in a field of simultaneities, where an occurrence can exist 'in different places on different time-lines' and be continuously available in 'a co-existing "cone" of the pure past'.[30] As Deleuze says of the coexistence of virtual series, these are not perspectives on the same story but distinct series, each of which develops in its 'difference from the other series which it implicates' and 'in abstraction from their empirical succession in time'.[31] The significance of each series is this *difference* and the different powers it contains, some of which remain to be unfolded.

This is also to say that within each series or story there are further series that should not be tied to the chronological order in which they appear in someone's life. Ellinor's refusal of Essex, which ends in her imprisonment, comprises one series. But 'after' this (or why not simultaneously?), Essex tracks her down, she fakes her death and escapes, disguised as a maid, to join him in Ireland, is captured by the rebel leader

Tiroen, escapes disguised as Tiroen, and is briefly reunited with Essex. In this second series, though Essex is executed, Ellinor is active rather than reactive. Matilda's story also contains multiple series: 'after' the Leicester series, she is kidnapped, saved by Jamaican revolutionaries, recaptured, secretly protected by Anana and returns to England, weakened by rheumatic fever but with unexpected wealth.

If the first series develops Matilda's masculine desire to rule through Leicester, and the third unfolds a feminine submission to the impossibility of legitimacy except through marriage, the second embroils Matilda in revolutionary and anti-slavery movements that Lee was ahead of later writers like Fenwick or Austen in according a central place. Though the Spanish had settled Jamaica in 1509, the famous slave revolt on which Lee probably draws occurred in 1760 under the English: another example of events existing outside chronology. Each (sub-)series signifies as a *difference* from the others, and their very repetitiveness redirects attention from plot to the hermeneutic effects created by repeated patterns, such as the constant imprisonments and escapes that re- and de-territorialise the story. As name-series intersect event-series (the name-series of multiple Ladies Essex appears in the event-series concerning Ellinor, Matilda and her daughter Mary), we become aware of narratology as much as reference, of the combinatorial possibilities that the novel holds as a storehouse of event- and character-types that can be populated differently from the way narratives legitimated as 'historical' have been. The arbitrariness and reversibility of characters contribute to this virtuality: Leicester disdains Miss Lineric but falls in love with her as Lady Essex; Henry and Rochester, though supposedly true and false copies, are initially indistinguishable; Henry first falls in love with the 'bad' Lady Essex but then learns to love the 'good' Mary who is in fact the former's cousin. This troubling of the false/true binary proliferates the power of false pretenders or simulacra.

Amid what might seem the return of the same, there is also the sheer unexpectedness of revolutions and alternative feminist genealogies in which women are not just pawns, like Lady Jane Grey, but inventors. For Deleuze, series must be understood in terms of the 'trinity complication-explication-implication'. The novel is, then, what he calls the 'great whole' or 'chaos' that 'contains all, the divergent series which lead out and back in, and the differenciator [*sic*] which relates them one to another'.[32] The 'explication' or development of a single series is always complicated by, and implicated in, the others. For in addition to event-series and name-series, there are also good and bad character-series, male- and female-series, royal-favourite-series, military-series and so on. The relations between all these series are 'multi-serial', as 'the terms of each' are in 'perpetual relative displacement' to each other, allowing an infinite number of connections that do not conform to a centralised organisation'.[33] For Deleuze, the series – a form initiated in this novel by the double series and fold of the twins – 'instantiates a mode of organization of difference that avoids the pitfalls of representation, within which difference is tamed by the mechanisms of resemblance, identity, analogy and opposition'.[34] Such organising patterns include the resemblance of Mary Queen of Scots and Mary, Matilda's daughter; or the opposition of Elizabeth and Mary Queen of Scots; or sense (Ellinor) and sensibility (Matilda). All these pairings – used by critics in an attempt to navigate the novel – imply moral judgements, thus preventing 'the emergence of any new mode of existence'.[35]

Baffling our attempts to remember anything, the enormous structural complexity of the novel's 'chaos' erases representation and compels us to read again and again so as to encounter the folds or recesses in the story that harbour undeveloped connections between series. The novel's length contributes to making it an 'erasing-machine' that deactivates its events and the logic of mimesis.[36] Discussing why Foucault shifts to long-term histories, Deleuze suggests that length is coextensive with 'forgetting', without which there is no creative memory. By contrast, in mimesis, a 'brief memory' forecloses an 'absolute memory' which is 'endlessly forgotten and reconstituted' and whose 'fold' merges with its 'unfolding'.[37] In fact, *The Recess* opens up this second memory in two ways: it is both historically contracted into a short period (?1569–?1613) that recovers folds neglected in long histories like Hume's *and* narratively expanded to a great length that allows us to forget details that thwart the return of the future in the past by swallowing up its 'tendencies' in a kind of literalism.

As an erasing-machine, the novel continually exterminates its real and imaginary characters and the solutions they attempt. But the extermination of simulacra is not the only thought-form introduced by the novel. Ellinor is a contradictory character, whose increasingly fragmented narrative is continued by Lady Pembroke; she thus introduces the possibility of thinking about characters as unfinished. With the annihilation of the historical series itself at the end, 'the event of the future' can 'invent pathways' and 'search through the past' to 'satisfy desire, without being causally determined by it'.[38] The novel simulates one such event as already having happened in the twins' extraordinary birth, of which Mary Queen of Scots, since she is never directly seen, is only a 'quasi-cause'.

Quasi-causes '*propagate* as if causally', allowing the twins, in turn, to become quasi-causes of Shakespeare's sister. But as Lampert explains, the 'as if' nature of the quasi-cause means that, unlike a cause, by 'selecting one possibility', it 'preserve[s], at a distance' the possibilities excluded, so that 'incompossible worlds' become 'variants of the same story'.[39] In other words, there is a form of 'counter-effectuation' in which, when one thing happens, 'other incompatible determinations' coexist, not factually but 'theatrically'. Thus while events that 'virtually [contain] counterfactuals' – whether the twins' birth or King James's denial of Matilda's legitimacy – 'become actual', they 'remain in flux'.[40] For Lee, therefore, unlike Godwin, the historian never quite recovers the advantage over the writer of romance.

Notes

1 William Godwin, 'Of History and Romance', in Gary Handwerk and A. A. Markley (eds), *Caleb Williams* (Peterborough, ON: Broadview Press, 2000), p. 462; hereafter cited as 'HR'.
2 See Tilottama Rajan, 'Between Romance and History: Possibility and Contingency in Godwin, Leibniz, and Mary Shelley's *Valperga*', in Betty T. Bennett and Stuart Curran (eds), *Mary Shelley in Her Times* (Baltimore, MD: Johns Hopkins University Press, 2000), pp. 90–6.
3 Godwin wanted to meet a 'Lee' in 1786; this was probably the more well-known Sophia, who had recently published *The Recess*, rather than her sister Harriet, whom he met the year after he wrote 'Of History and Romance'.
4 See Mary Shelley, *Valperga: Or, The Life and Adventures of Castruccio Prince of Lucca*, ed. Tilottama Rajan (Peterborough, ON: Broadview Press, 1998), p. 439.
5 Sophia Lee, *The Recess; or, A Tale of Other Times*, ed. April Alliston (Lexington, KY: University Press of Kentucky, 2000), p. 5.
6 William Godwin, *Thoughts on Man, His Nature, Productions, and Discoveries* (London: Effingham Wilson, 1831), p. 230.
7 *Ibid.*
8 Gilles Deleuze and Félix Guattari, *Kafka: Toward a Minor Literature*, trans. Dana Polan (Minneapolis, MN: University of Minnesota Press, 1986), p. 3. Minor literature is not literature written in a minor language but a 'minor practice of a major language' and thus it has a 'high coefficient of deterritorialization' (p. 16).
9 April Alliston, 'The Value of a Literary Legacy: Retracing the

Transmission of Value Through Female Lines', *The Yale Journal of Criticism*, 4:1 (October 1990), 123.
10 Gilles Deleuze, *The Fold: Leibniz and the Baroque*, trans. Tom Conley (Minneapolis, MN: University of Minnesota Press, 1993), pp. 3–7; G. W. Leibniz, 'The Monadology', in Nicholas Rescher, *The Monadology: An Edition for Students* (Pittsburgh, PA: University of Pittsburgh Press, 1991), #16, #65 (pp. 81, 226).
11 Deleuze, *The Fold*, p. 98.
12 Gilles Deleuze, *The Logic of Sense*, trans. Mark Lester (New York: Columbia University Press, 1990), pp. 253–9.
13 See Megan Lynn Isaac, 'Sophia Lee and the Gothic of Female Community', *Studies in the Novel*, 28:2 (Summer 1996), 205.
14 Fenwick's *Secrecy; or The Ruin on the Rock* (1795) adapts the *topoi* of secrecy, a child brought up in seclusion and a ruin that forms a matrix in the narrative's topology.
15 Isaac, 'Sophia Lee', 204.
16 See Anne H. Stevens, 'Sophia Lee's Illegitimate History', in Albert J. Rivero, George Justice and Margo Collins (eds), *The Eighteenth-Century Novel: Volume 3* (New York: AMS Press, 2003), p. 265.
17 Gilles Deleuze and Félix Guattari, *Anti-Oedipus: Capitalism and Schizophrenia*, trans. Robert Hurley, Mark Seem and Helen R. Lane (Minneapolis, MN: University of Minnesota Press, 1983), p. 86.
18 *Ibid.*, p. 311.
19 Jay Lampert, *Deleuze and Guattari's Philosophy of History* (London: Continuum, 2006), p. 2.
20 *Ibid.*, p. 102.
21 Slavoj Žižek, *The Plague of Fantasies* (London: Verso, 1997), p. 7.
22 Stevens, 'Sophia Lee's Illegitimate History', 277.
23 William Godwin, 'Of Choice in Reading', *The Enquirer: Reflections on Education, Manners, and Literature in a Series of Essays* (1797; New York: Augustus Kelley, 1965), pp. 136–8.
24 John Staines, *The Tragic Histories of Mary Queen of Scots, 1560–1690* (Farnham: Ashgate, 2009), p. 26.
25 See for example Isaac, 'Sophia Lee', 205.
26 See Jean-François Lyotard, *The Differend: Phrases in Dispute*, trans. Georges Van den Abbeele (Minneapolis, MN: University of Minnesota Press, 1988), pp. xi, 9.
27 Deleuze, *The Fold*, p. 74; Leibniz, 'The Monadology', #73 (p. 240). Italics in original.
28 Stevens, 'Sophia Lee's Illegitimate History', pp. 273–5, 277.
29 Gilles Deleuze, *Difference and Repetition*, trans. Paul Patton (New York:

Columbia University Press, 1994), pp. 90–3. Not everything returns: the eternal return sifts out 'the average' from the 'superior' (pp. 55, 115). Thus if the pair Elizabeth/Leicester shows how 'transversal relations of resistance' become 'restratified', its repetition as the pair Matilda/Leicester allows for a 'superior' potential to be extracted (Deleuze, *The Fold*, p. 94).

30 Lampert, *Deleuze and Guattari's Philosophy of History*, pp. 123, 1–3.
31 Deleuze, *Difference and Repetition*, pp. 123–5.
32 *Ibid.*, p. 123.
33 Deleuze, *The Logic of Sense*, pp. 37–9.
34 See Judith L. Poxon and Charles J. Stivale, 'Sense, Series', in Charles J. Stivale (ed.), *Gilles Deleuze: Key Concepts* (Montreal, QC: McGill-Queen's University Press, 2005), p. 68.
35 Gilles Deleuze, *Essays Critical and Clinical*, trans. Daniel W. Smith and Michael A. Greco (Minneapolis, MN: University of Minnesota Press, 1997), p. 135.
36 Lampert, *Deleuze and Guattari's Philosophy of History*, p. 110.
37 Gilles Deleuze, *Foucault*, trans. Seán Hand (Minneapolis, MN: University of Minnesota Press, 1988), p. 107.
38 Lampert, *Deleuze and Guattari's Philosophy of History*, p. 97.
39 *Ibid.*, pp. 55, 97–8; Deleuze, *The Logic of Sense*, p. 114.
40 Lampert, *Deleuze and Guattari's Philosophy of History*, pp. 38, 104.

Works cited

Primary texts

Godwin, William, 'Of Choice in Reading', *The Enquirer: Reflections on Education, Manners, and Literature in a Series of Essays* (1797; New York: Augustus Kelley, 1965), pp. 129–46

Godwin, William, 'Of History and Romance', in Gary Handwerk and A. A. Markley (eds), *Caleb Williams* (Peterborough, ON: Broadview Press, 2000), pp. 453–67

Godwin, William, *Thoughts on Man, His Nature, Productions, and Discoveries* (London: Effingham Wilson, 1831)

Lee, Sophia, *The Recess; or, A Tale of Other Times*, ed. April Alliston (Lexington, KY: University Press of Kentucky, 2000)

Shelley, Mary, *Valperga: Or, The Life and Adventures of Castruccio Prince of Lucca*, ed. Tilottama Rajan (Peterborough, ON: Broadview Press, 1998)

Secondary texts

Alliston, April, 'The Value of a Literary Legacy: Retracing the Transmission of Value Through Female Lines', *The Yale Journal of Criticism*, 4:1 (October 1990), 109–27

Deleuze, Gilles, *Difference and Repetition*, trans. Paul Patton (New York: Columbia University Press, 1994)

Deleuze, Gilles, *Essays Critical and Clinical*, trans. Daniel W. Smith and Michael A. Greco (Minneapolis, MN: University of Minnesota Press, 1997)

Deleuze, Gilles, *Foucault*, trans. Seán Hand (Minneapolis, MN: University of Minnesota Press, 1988)

Deleuze, Gilles, *The Fold: Leibniz and the Baroque*, trans. Tom Conley (Minneapolis, MN: University of Minnesota Press, 1993)

Deleuze, Gilles, *The Logic of Sense*, trans. Mark Lester (New York: Columbia University Press, 1990)

Deleuze, Gilles and Félix Guattari, *Anti-Oedipus: Capitalism and Schizophrenia*, trans. Robert Hurley, Mark Seem and Helen R. Lane (Minneapolis, MN: University of Minnesota Press, 1983)

Deleuze, Gilles and Félix Guattari, *Kafka: Toward a Minor Literature*, trans. Dana Polan (Minneapolis, MN: University of Minnesota Press, 1986)

Isaac, Megan Lynn, 'Sophia Lee and the Gothic of Female Community', *Studies in the Novel*, 28:2 (Summer 1996), 200–18

Lampert, Jay, *Deleuze and Guattari's Philosophy of History* (London: Continuum, 2006)

Leibniz, G. W., 'The Monadology', in Nicholas Rescher, *The Monadology: An Edition for Students* (Pittsburgh, PA: University of Pittsburgh Press, 1991), 17–29

Lyotard, Jean-François, *The Differend: Phrases in Dispute*, trans. Georges Van den Abbeele (Minneapolis, MN: University of Minnesota Press, 1988)

Poxon, Judith L. and Charles J. Stivale, 'Sense, Series', in Charles J. Stivale (ed.), *Gilles Deleuze: Key Concepts* (Montreal, QC: McGill-Queen's University Press, 2005)

Rajan, Tilottama, 'Between Romance and History: Possibility and Contingency in Godwin, Leibniz, and Mary Shelley's *Valperga*', in Betty T. Bennett and Stuart Curran (eds), *Mary Shelley in Her Times* (Baltimore, MD: Johns Hopkins University Press, 2000), pp. 88–102

Staines, John, *The Tragic Histories of Mary Queen of Scots, 1560–1690* (Farnham: Ashgate, 2009)

Stevens, Anne H., 'Sophia Lee's Illegitimate History', in Albert J. Rivero, George Justice and Margo Collins (eds), *The Eighteenth-Century Novel: Volume 3* (New York: AMS Press, 2003), pp. 263–92

Žižek, Slavoj, *The Plague of Fantasies* (London: Verso, 1997)

5

Lord Byron reads *The Prelude*

Kenneth R. Johnston

C'est une des lois fatales de l'humanité que rien n'y atteigne le but.
(Louis-Napoléon Geoffroy-Château, *Napoléon Apocryphe, 1812–1832*)[1]

'This is not "counterfactual" history.' So say I, on page 8 of my *Unusual Suspects: Pitt's Reign of Alarm and the Lost Generation of the 1790s* (2013). Yet I was recruited into the *Counterfactual Romanticism* project because my book was said to 'deploy a counterfactual heuristic without quite theorising it as such', and because commentators including John Barrell and David Simpson identified aspects of the book as invested in counterfactual speculation, in the classic vein of 'what if Napoleon had won at Waterloo?'.[2]

Could I be counterfactual without realising it, like Molière's bourgeois gentleman, pleased to learn he has been speaking prose all his life? I would not have thought of myself, before now, as an enthusiast of counterfactuality; on the contrary. It is true I have written a book-length study of a non-existent poem, Wordsworth's *The Recluse*, based on its extant parts and fragments, and in *The Hidden Wordsworth* I have chapters on his travels in Germany and his visit to Paris at the time of The Terror, based on the very slim evidence we have for each.[3] Rather than technically counterfactual arguments, however, these studies offer literary criticism and history of a highly contingent nature, characteristic of revisionist writing. I find very few sentences in *Unusual Suspects* that explicitly raise the 'what if?' question concerning the career opportunities that my suspects lost – that is, what was lost to British culture – owing to Pitt's alarmist domestic policies and practices in the period 1793–98. The vast majority of my 375 pages are explicitly about what *did* happen, in painful detail, to twenty people (representative of dozens more), to alter, block, hinder, pervert – in a word, ruin – their careers, making them a 'lost' minority within the larger generation called 'Romantic' by posterity.

Nevertheless, in my conclusion, which focuses on six first-generation Romantics (Coleridge, Southey, Wordsworth, Lamb, Burns and Blake), I do employ some counterfactual reasoning to emphasise what they achieved, by heroic contrast to what they were almost prevented from achieving. For example, I consider how some of the characters, settings and actions in Blake's *Jerusalem* derive not from his profound myth-making imagination but from the superficial street details of his arrest for subversive activity in Felpham in 1803, and how that traumatic experience affected the structure (and indeed existence) of his masterwork. Or, how Charles Lamb disguised his ruthless political feelings in what De Quincey called the 'lurking' syllables of apparently facetious writing or harmless fantasies that have only recently been recognised as what they are – a reaction formation to his great fear of political repression, not only for himself but also for his invalid sister. I do not say that Blake or Lamb or the others would have written better without these fears, but they assuredly would have written differently.

Chief among these Romantic counterfactuals is one I pursue here, as a self-challenging experiment or speculative trial run for the present occasion of *Counterfactual Romanticism*, to see what light such a perspective might cast on our usual perceptions of the period (or to identify the glints of possibility we might glimpse in this way, since I personally find the process of counterfactual thinking more compelling than its promise of fully developed alternative realities, like *Napoléon Apocryphe*). Specifically, what if Wordsworth had published *The Prelude* not long after he first finished it (May 1805), rather than holding it back for posthumous publication in 1850? This will elaborate a hypothesis I set out in *Unusual Suspects*: 'It is very safe to say that if Wordsworth had published [*The Prelude* in 1805] … the effect on the development of English literature would have been enormous. One has only to imagine, as best one can, what a difference it would have made to the young Byron, Shelley, and Keats – just to invoke the most obvious names – and one need say no more.'[4] I mention these three not simply because they are the next generation of Romantic poets, but also because they all wrote important long poems in the self-creation mode of *The Prelude*, or 'the poem on the growth of my own mind', as Wordsworth called it. These include, notably, Byron's *Childe Harold's Pilgrimage* and *Don Juan*, Shelley's *Alastor* and 'Epipsychidion' and Keats's *Endymion* and his two fragmentary *Hyperion* epics. I propose to imagine, with specific reference to Byron, the opportunity he was denied by the non-publication of *The Prelude*, to see 'the relations between his two long poems of artistic self-consciousness ... and Wordsworth's "poem on the growth of my own mind"'.[5]

First, I must locate a solid starting point. Truly fruitful counterfactual questions cannot be pulled out of thin air, no matter how intriguing they seem, though we do this all the time. For counterfactuals to demonstrate their real usefulness by increasing the ability of the imagination to construct 'nonactualized alternatives to what actually happened', and thus help us address 'negative effects arising from events or actions'[6] (such as Pitt's Reign of Alarm), they should, in my estimation, satisfy three criteria usefully set out by Niall Ferguson: they should be plausible, probable or credible; they should be determined by an appropriate historical context; and they should be preserved in some sort of textual record.[7] Imagining Byron reading a *Prelude* published around 1805 meets all of these tests. But a contextualised formulation of the question is better than an abstract one. Thus, I ask not only 'What if Wordsworth had published *The Prelude* in 1805?', but also 'How can we plausibly imagine Wordsworth publishing it then, and with what likely results?'

I take it as *prima facie* true that a *Prelude* published in 1805 would have had an enormous impact; our own estimates of the poem confirm this. Or, to put it the other way round: it is difficult to state, let alone overstate, the negative impact of the *non*-appearance of *The Prelude*, this huge absence or lacuna in the Romantic era's knowledge of itself. As David Fairer observes, following D. W. Jefferson: 'it took time to assimilate Wordsworth, when *The Prelude* was not there to offer a context for understanding the visionary poet's development. How greatly we now take that poem for granted! It is hard to imagine how individual contemporary readers found their way to the heart of Wordsworth without it.'[8] In the present context, I would heighten the expostulation. How can we ever take adequate account of the central counterfactual that the greatest poem of the English Romantic period was not an active presence in that period? – that this masterpiece of self-creation was not *in play* at its moment of origin, preceding all the others in the visionary company of which it is the leader, by dint of accomplishment? How can we conceptualise the fact that such a text, by its deliberately delayed appearance, is a latecomer, a straggler? How can *The Prelude* be the greatest British Romantic poem if it wasn't even there then? How might we reckon with this phenomenon in its counterfactual implication? It is too simple to say that Wordsworth finished *The Prelude* in 1805 but never published it; we should say, rather, that 1805 is the year Wordsworth *began not publishing* his masterpiece. To get to grips with these questions, we have to ask two others. First, why didn't Wordsworth publish the poem in 1805 or 1806? This is Counterfactual No. 1.

Two major reasons are usually given, one internal and one external. The internal and strongest – or most traditional – reason is that Wordsworth did not feel he could publish such a long autobiographical poem before he had completed the much longer philosophical poem, *The Recluse*, on which he believed his greatness depended. But as we know, he never finished *The Recluse*, and published only one part of it, *The Excursion*, in 1814. His preface to *The Excursion* ended with a 'Prospectus' for *The Recluse* that raised the stakes for that poem to supra-Miltonic levels ('Jehovah, with his thunder, and the quire / Of shouting Angels ... / I pass them unalarmed'), dramatically increasing the challenge of writing it, and likewise the possibility of not finishing it.

As far as it goes, this is an airtight rationale for not publishing *The Prelude*. It does, of course, require taking everything Wordsworth said about *The Recluse* at face value, which is standard procedure, but perhaps more counterfactual than scholars like to admit. Over the course of forty-five years, the poet and his family and friends found many extenuating reasons to explain – or explain away – this albatross he had hung about his neck. It also requires accepting what I take to be an even more problematic premise: that Wordsworth well knew he had written one of the greatest poems in English, but was not going to publish it because he felt he had an even greater poem still in him. Geoffrey Hartman sees this presumption as a sign of godlike strength, as if *The Prelude* were the Son to Wordsworth's God the Father/*Recluse*, on whose known existence he could repose securely.[9] This is an effective metaphor, but it offers a more Trinitarian defence than I care to make of any human author, and leaves dangling the awkward theological implication that Wordsworth did not vouchsafe his 'Son' to the world until he, the 'Father', was dead. When the 'wordsworthian or egotistical sublime', as Keats called it, goes too far, it tips over into the egotistical ridiculous.

But this subjective rationale for non-publication is supported by an objective one, which I consider almost equally strong, and which has the advantage of greater force in the immediate context of 1805. This is that Wordsworth, like all liberal authors of his generation, was keenly aware of the dangers attendant on Pitt's apparatus of domestic alarm, of speaking too strongly on the liberal side of the great questions of the day – whether the French Revolution or the English parliamentary reform movement that it re-energised during the 1790s. *The Prelude* exposed Wordsworth's personal and imaginative investments in the revolution at great length, especially in the two books, IX and X, that powerfully conclude its narrative plot: 'Residence in France and French Revolution'. The second half of Book X sharply articulates Wordsworth's disgust for Pitt's alarmist tactics:

> Our shepherds – this say merely – at that time
> Thirsted to make the guardian-crook of law
> A tool of murder. They who ruled the state …
> …
> Giants in their impiety alone,
> But in their weapons and their warfare base
> As vermin working out of reach, they leagued
> Their strength perfidiously to undermine
> Justice and make an end of liberty.[10]

If a poem containing these lines had appeared in 1805, or almost any time during the next generation, it would have exposed its author either to the severe legal penalties of the 1795 'Gagging Acts' (not repealed until 1848), or to the sweepingly hegemonic career damages of innuendo and slander which, following Hazlitt, I identify as the more effective extra-legal weapons characteristic of Pitt's Reign of Alarm: 'The flame of liberty … was to be extinguished with the sword – or with slander, whose edge is sharper than the sword'.[11]

In brief, then, the non-publication of *The Prelude* in Wordsworth's lifetime was one of the most damaging cultural costs to posterity of Pitt's domestic surveillance regime, which Wordsworth condemned, and which he also excoriated in *The Excursion*: 'In Britain ruled a panic dread of change.'[12] Panic ruled; Alarm reigned.

How, then, could *The Prelude* have been published in 1805, or thereabouts, so that we might estimate the cost of its non-appearance to Byron, or the benefits he would have reaped if it had, and charge these to Pitt's account? This is Counterfactual No. 2. There was a small window of opportunity during 1805–7, when the political climate lightened enough to have, perhaps, given Wordsworth the courage he needed to publish it. The Peace of Amiens (1802–3) was another such window, but it closed quickly, though its hopeful moment may have stimulated the rapid composition of *The Prelude* at that time, which suddenly accelerated beyond an early five-book version to encompass Wordsworth's years in London and Paris. The failure of the peace produced the Great Terror of 1803–5, motivated by the prospect of an invasion by Napoleon, but 1805 gave Britain respite with the victory at Trafalgar in October, even as it delivered the Allies their worst blow yet, the disaster of Austerlitz in December.[13] Looking at this same timeframe, E. P. Thompson remarked that 'the course of English history might have been changed if there had been five years of peace from 1802'.[14] By what I judge to be present-day standards of counterfactuality, five years is a rather large 'if' – five hours would have made the crucial difference at Waterloo. But the possibility was there, nonetheless, and the 'if' with which we are concerned here impacts on the softer option of English literary, not political, history.

In the climate of the recent bicentenary celebrations of Wellington's victory at Waterloo, it is easy to overlook the intensity of Britain's hopes for peace – not necessarily victory – when war resumed with the formation of the Third Coalition in 1805. But after Pitt's death in January 1806, Grenville formed his 'Ministry of all the Talents' with Charles James Fox (still a great friend to France) as Secretary of State for Foreign Affairs. A negotiated peace was the centerpiece of exaggerated liberal hopes for this new administration in its single year of frenetic pursuit of a remote possibility. Negotiations with France resumed in March, but with Fox's death in September, peace hopes collapsed, confirmed by the crushing Allied defeat at Jena in October. From this point on, England knew it was engaged in an unconditional fight to the death.

But suppose, counterfactually, that a peace treaty had been concluded some time earlier in 1806; great efforts were certainly made in this direction. The national mood of relief and euphoria might have been enough to persuade Wordsworth to bring out his long, newly 'finished' poem on his intensely personal experiences in France (1791–93), which he had updated with a denunciation of the Pope's crowning Napoleon Emperor in December 1804 (*The Prelude* (1805), X, ll. 932–3), augmented by his disgust with Pitt, back in office as of May 1804 (coincidentally the same month Napoleon claimed his imperium). The present-tense presence of Pitt is close to the surface of Wordsworth's denunciation – another reason for not publishing *The Prelude*:

> But this is passion over-near ourselves,
> Reality too close and too intense,
> And mingled up with something, in my mind,
> Of scorn and condemnation personal
> That would profane the sanctity of verse.
>   (*The Prelude* (1805), X, ll. 640–4)

Such vocabulary is also a high-toned literary way of signalling that such personal condemnation of 'those who ruled the state' was potentially libellous, and therefore treasonous, implicating Wordsworth's 'passion' for exculpating his 'juvenile errors' (*The Prelude* (1805), X, l. 637) in a 'reality too close and too intense'. Too close for what, however? The public aspect of the creative crisis of *The Prelude* is constituted by Wordsworth's disillusion with Revolution on the one hand and his disaffection with Napoleon on the other. Byron expresses the same frustration of all apparent hope for peace and progress throughout *Childe Harold* and *Don Juan*, further confirmed by the return of old corruption in the Restoration. Wordsworth could not simply have cut the offending lines on Pitt, for the moral despair that is *The Prelude*'s final impasse (before Wordsworth swears allegiance to Imagination) depends on our recognising England (Pitt) and France (Napoleon) as almost equally repugnant moral choices.

Contrary to the conditions of my own experiment, I believe Wordsworth's nervousness about exposing his youthful political liberalism would still have been too great – unless public euphoria for a negotiated peace had reached very great heights indeed – for him to publish *The Prelude* in 1806. His lifelong refusal to allow Francis Wrangham to publish their 1795 Juvenalian satire on the English nobility (including Sir James Lowther, Earl of Lonsdale, Wordsworth's patron after 1802 and dedicatee of *The Excursion*) and his fearful fascination with the fate of Gilbert Wakefield, dead from prison fever in 1801 following his conviction for attacking the politics of the Bishop of Llandaff, whom Wordsworth had attacked (in manuscript) even more vehemently in 1793 – these and other instances of Alarm's impact on Wordsworth make it hard to see him publishing *The Prelude* in 1806.[15] But these instances do underscore the steep costs of Alarm to British literature and culture – the fact from which all my counterfactuals here derive. And Thomas Macaulay's reaction to the appearance of *The Prelude* in 1850 demonstrates that Wordsworth's caution was warranted: 'The story of the French Revolution, and of its influence on the character of a young enthusiast, is told again at greater length, and with less force and pathos, than in "The Excursion". The poem is to the last degree Jacobinical, indeed Socialist. I understand perfectly why Wordsworth did not choose to publish it in his lifetime.'[16] For a post-Waterloo world, Macaulay's political judgement is sound, even if his literary assessments are not, for ours.

With a *Prelude* published in, say, 1806, we can bring our other protagonist, Lord Byron, into the counterfactual scenario, for he did review a work by Wordsworth in 1807 – *Poems, in Two Volumes*. He might have reviewed *The Prelude*, had it appeared in 1806. What would he have made of it, based on his reaction to *Poems* (which appeared as an unsolicited submission in *Monthly Literary Recreations* for July 1807)?[17] The review did not cost his young lordship much effort. Typically for the time, it was mostly quotation, opening with an approving quotation in full of the sonnet, 'November 1806', on the disaster of Jena:

> Another year! – another deadly blow!
> Another mighty Empire overthrown!
> And We are left, or shall be left, alone,
> The last that dare to struggle with the Foe.

One can sense why the lines appealed to the 19-year-old Byron: it is a proleptic echo, in our counterfactual wonderland, of his own response to Waterloo a decade later: 'Stop! – for thy tread is on an Empire's dust!'[18]

Byron proceeds in his review to acknowledge that Wordsworth 'has not undeservedly met with a considerable degree of public applause', though he warns that 'the present work may not equal his former efforts'. He praises Wordsworth's 'native eloquence, natural and unaffected', but undercuts this by comparing his 'namby-pamby' verses to nursery rhymes, giving us almost a full page of lines like 'the cock is crowing' from the obviously playful lines, 'While resting on the bridge at Brother's Water'. Byron – the moody hero-in-training – finds the 'least worthy' section of the publication to be 'Moods of My Own Mind' – that is, Wordsworth's most personal poems. But he concludes magnanimously: 'Many, with inferior abilities, have acquired a loftier seat on Parnassus, merely by attempting strains in which Mr Wordsworth is more qualified to excel', though he trusts that Wordsworth's motto will in future be *Paulo maiora canamus*.

That is all. No hint, from Byron, that these volumes – arguably Wordsworth's great single collection – contain the 'Ode to Duty', 'Resolution and Independence', 'The Solitary Reaper' and 'Elegiac Stanzas', nor (the unkindest omission of all) the great Intimations Ode, from which Byron cites only the epigraph, the well-known phrase from Virgil (*Paulo maiora canamus*). That is, he hopes Wordsworth will sing of 'things a little higher', while completely omitting the many 'higher things' the two volumes contain. He leaves his readers with the facile impression that the volumes do not much advance Wordsworth's project, if at all, beyond the only work by which Wordsworth was well known at the time – the several editions of *Lyrical Ballads* published since 1798 (an impression it was Wordsworth's express intention to overcome by publishing *Poems*).

Lord Byron reads The Prelude

What if Byron had reviewed *The Prelude* instead? Would the 19-year-old lord have been up to it? There he would have found much of the 'native eloquence, natural and unaffected' he valued in *Poems*, along with plenty of the higher things he regretted not encountering – but had in fact ignored – there. I like to think *The Prelude* would have excited a Byron who would have been swept along by the narrative pace of Wordsworth's adventures. However – again countering the counterfactual (an instinct hard-wired into the counterfactual imagination) – it might have been too 'advanced' for Byron, at least at first. His own first efforts, as represented by *Hours of Idleness* (published, like Wordsworth's *Poems, in Two Volumes*, in 1807), were still very much in the sentimental mode of regret for times past, lost youth, departed friends and abandoned lovers best expressed in the poems on Newstead Abbey, and summed up in his lengthy 'Childish Recollections', which bears at best only a topical resemblance to the first three books of *The Prelude*. Most of these compositions reveal that Byron was still in debt to Gray's elegiac spirit, not yet assimilating the stronger uses of memory that he eventually appropriated from Wordsworth's 'Lines written a few miles above Tintern Abbey' (to such an extent that Wordsworth privately accused him of plagiarism). *The Prelude*'s modern yet Miltonic blank verse and conversational plain language might have seemed 'unpoetical' to Byron, given his lifelong allegiance to Augustan poise. On the other hand, Wordsworth's direct, first-person mode of describing the actual events of his life might have encouraged Byron to do likewise, much earlier than he did, and without the exotic filters through which he first projected his voice. Such is my counterfactual agenda: to speculate how soon and to what extent Byron would have assimilated Wordsworth's largely unadorned direct address to his own voice; and further, more pointedly, how the informal idiom of *Don Juan* might have appeared earlier in Byron's verse, thanks to his reading of *The Prelude*. At 19, Byron certainly would have envied the scope and intensity of Wordsworth's adventures and investment in the great events of the age, and might even have emulated them more directly than he did in his Mediterranean travels of 1809–11, whose trajectory was partly determined by the need to avoid dangerous war zones.

Byron would certainly have accepted Wordsworth's denunciations of Pitt in *The Prelude*, and would have relished Wordsworth's homage to 'the great and good' Fox in *Poems, in Two Volumes* ('A Power is passing from the earth / To breathless Nature's dark abyss'),[19] though he did not bother to say so in his review. Wordsworth's assessments of Pitt and Fox are reflected in Byron's own elegy, 'On the Death of Mr Fox', where

Byron admits that although 'Pitt expir'd in plenitude of power', nonetheless 'ill success obscur'd his dying hour':

> But lo! another Hercules [Fox] appear'd,
> Who for a time, the ruined fabric rear'd;
> He too is dead! who still our England propp'd,
> With him our fast reviving hopes have dropped.[20]

The two statesmen's deaths and the two poets' estimates of them precisely frame the fleeting moment when we could imagine *The Prelude* appearing in print.

One interpretive possibility that can be drawn from postulating Byron's positive reaction to the 1805 *Prelude* is that it foreshadows the eventual appearance of a young man similar to Wordsworth's poetic self/hero in somewhat similar circumstances some fifteen or so years later, when Byron's focus turned to Don Juan's arrival in England, which was to constitute the most sustained single episode in the poem (Cantos IX–XVI).[21] Here, Byron appears at last to have got his hero where he wants him, no longer reprising the exotic scenery and personages of *Childe Harold's Pilgrimage*, but testing him amid the social mores and political opinions of contemporary England. Wordsworth is also, of course, directly invoked in Canto I, stanzas 90–6, where Juan, 'poor little fellow', is trying to account for the 'unutterable things' raised in his mind by Donna Julia's eyes as he wanders by the 'glassy brooks' where 'poets find materials for their books' – 'Unless like Wordsworth they prove unintelligible' (Canto I, ll. 713–20). But this Juan/Wordsworth is more the young Byron of *Hours of Idleness* than the young Wordsworth of *The Prelude*: 'He thought of wood nymphs and immortal bowers / ... So by the poesy of his own mind / ... his soul was shook' (Canto I, ll. 747, 756–7).

Both *The Prelude* and *Don Juan* manifest a strongly evaluative authorial metaperspective on the young heroes' often mistaken actions. But here again, the counterfactual scorpion, true to its genes, recoils and stings itself. For Byron got to this point all by himself, without the benefit of *The Prelude*. In terms of real-world cause and effect, it might be better to ask whether Wordsworth in *The Excursion* had been influenced by Byron, in extending his story of himself into his avatar, the Solitary, whom early reviewers criticised for 'Byronism'. Jane Stabler has fruitfully transmuted the critics' agitated negative reactions into the observation that Wordsworth is already criticising the excesses (and popular appeal) of his younger contemporary, Byron, in the form of the Solitary's persistent, sarcastic, self-indulgent bitterness and disillusionment.[22]

An entire book could be launched from this point, pursuing all the possible connections between the two poets' progress from 1805 to 1824. Much of this work has already been done, some of it as counterfactual speculation, by scholar-critics such as Michael Cooke, Peter Manning, Jerome J. McGann and Jane Stabler.[23] To track this large double parabola is to lay bare each poet's recognition that he is not only his true hero but rather – what is not quite the same thing – the true subject of his poem. That is, Wordsworth and Byron recognised that they were writing versions of a story that became in many respects the *grand récit* of nineteenth-century European literature, from *The Red and the Black* to *War and Peace* – that is, how an idealistic, sensitive young person, swept up and away by the humane ideals of the French Revolution, managed to recover (or not, or only partially) from his or her bitter disillusionment at their failure, whether this failure be construed as arising from within the Revolution itself (The Terror), its imperialistic over-extension (Napoleon) or the constant implacable resistance to it and eventual return of the *status quo ante* (the Restoration). This truly 'immense perspective', as Mark Reed rightly says of Wordsworth's repeated and difficult efforts to relate his own experiences to 'the common experience of mankind during the great shaping events of his era', presented a challenge met, if rarely mastered, by many other writers after him, including Byron first and foremost – except that, in our counterfactual looking glass, Byron achieved actual publication before Wordsworth.[24] What if he had had Wordsworth as a guide? How much further could he have gone? And in what directions?

To frame some answers to this supposition, we may look at the reactions of two writers whom we know to have read the first *Prelude*: Coleridge and De Quincey. Coleridge responded with 'To William Wordsworth', a magnificent précis of Wordsworth's poem encased within something like a near-death experience of shame and awe, from which *The Prelude* itself paradoxically revives him, 'even as life returns upon the drowned'.[25] De Quincey's reaction was both particular and encompassing. First, he transcribed the manuscript Wordsworth had lent him (in 1810) into five notebooks, which he then used as a resource and inspiration throughout his career, from the dream sequences of *Confessions of an English Opium-Eater* (1821) to, less admirably, indiscreet revelations about Wordsworth in his *Autobiographic Sketches* of 1853.[26]

For an instance of a young poet who read *The Prelude* unconditioned by personal familiarity with Wordsworth, we can look abroad to Walt Whitman, who would, to be sure, have read the 1850 version when it first appeared. Whitman said that between 1850 and 1852 he was suddenly 'possess'd ... with a special desire ... to articulate and faithfully express ... my own physical, emotional, moral, intellectual and aesthetic personality ... and to exploit that personality ... in *a far more candid and comprehensive sense* than any hitherto poem or book [*sic*]' (Whitman's emphasis).[27] Whitman was very quiet, to put it mildly, about his literary influences, but after more than a century of silence, there is now a scholarly consensus, based on critical interpretation and archival evidence, that he knew Wordsworth's poetry, including *The Prelude*, very well indeed, to the extent that one could, at a provocative extreme, argue that *Leaves of Grass* (especially 'Song of Myself') would not be the work it is without *The Prelude* marching on before.[28] Luckily, I do not have to argue that, though others like Robert Weisbuch have.[29] I only have to offer Whitman as a brilliant example of what might have happened had Byron read *The Prelude*. Whitman said he was only 'simmering' till Emerson brought him to a boil; after 1850, Wordsworth's *Prelude* added more fuel to Whitman's fire. True, Whitman's public image is more Byronic than Wordsworthian. But, as Weisbuch argues, *The Prelude* and 'Song of Myself' are 'the two and only examples in English-language poetry in the nineteenth century of a particular genre: the epic-like poem merged with spiritual autobiography, an epic in which the poetic self is hero'.[30]

In marked contrast to his profound silence about Wordsworth, Whitman was open and consistent in his admiration for Byron – 'my daily food' – throughout his career: 'Byron has fire enough to burn forever.'[31] It is not much of a tax on anyone's imagination to see *Leaves of Grass* as a *Prelude* in New World dress, and Byron might well have written an English 'Song of Myself' if he had read the 1805 *Prelude*, his aristocratic insouciance a fit companion for open-collared Broadway Walt. He would have become more directly personal, much more so than in the persona we deduce only with difficulty from his romantic tales; his poetry would have edged closer to the mode of his disarming correspondence, on a par with his sophisticated, relaxed authorial metaperspective in the last eight books of *Don Juan*.

Considering these parallel cases of *Prelude*-influence, we can see that all three writers proceeded, post-*Prelude*, to write masterpieces of autobiographical reflection with astonishing thrusts into other domains of discourse: literary criticism and theory in *Biographia Literaria* (1817), universal depth psychology in *Confessions of an English Opium-Eater* (1821) and national political and spiritual identity in *Leaves of Grass* (1855, and its subsequent elaborations). They might have done so anyway, but Wordsworth surely helped them, as he would have helped Byron.

Lord Byron reads The Prelude

Returning to Wordsworth and Byron, we can note that Wordsworth went immediately from ending his 1805 *Prelude* to composing a third-person version of himself (and many others of his generation, as he said) in the character of the Solitary. This was a project begun in 1806, accelerated in 1809–10, and completed with the publication of *The Excursion* in 1814. For most readers, this movement traces a downward arc in poetic quality. In Byron's case, the arc moves from his sentimental youthful self in *Hours of Idleness* (1807), through the several exotic versions of disillusioned romantic heroes into which he projected himself after his travels in Greece and the Mediterranean – *Childe Harold's Pilgrimage* (1812), *The Giaour* (1813), *The Corsair* (1814), *The Prisoner of Chillon* (1816), *Manfred* (1817), *Childe Harold* again (1818) – to the sudden inversion of all this into irony with the composition and publication of *Don Juan*, beginning in 1819. For many readers, this Byronic arc goes steadily upwards, to a point where we are extremely sorry to see it end. But both poets move *immediately* from completing one version of themselves to begin another, revisionary form of it (*Prelude > Excursion*, 1805–6; *Harold > Juan*, 1818–19) with the alacrity of someone who has suddenly stumbled on what he thinks is a great idea.[32] The progressions are also similar in that neither is complete. *Don Juan* breaks off, its author dead, in 1824 (*rien n'y atteigne le but*). The author of *The Prelude* also dies, in 1850, but his hero's life-progress had arbitrarily, though not unreasonably, ended forty-five years earlier in 1805 – or in 1814, if we accept the Solitary as his sour substitute. And even in the Solitary, Wordsworth remains true to his own experience: the Solitary's announced 'despondency' does not achieve its promised 'correction' in the long course of *The Excursion*, but is left to an unspecified future point which 'our future labours may not leave untold': the last words of the poem. They did remain untold, however; Wordsworth never resumed the story.

All these dates mark important junctures along the course of the horrific Napoleonic Wars and their brutal reactionary aftermath. At one pivotal junction, we might counterfactually imagine Wordsworth and Byron comparing notes just as the fulcrum of the war and of their career heroes converged at Waterloo in 1815. But, wondrous to say, we don't have to imagine this: they actually did meet at Samuel Rogers's townhouse in London on Sunday, 18 June 1815 – the very day of Waterloo. Their reported comments tell us something not only about their politics, which we might anticipate, but also about their ways of articulating their positions, which differ from what we might expect. Wordsworth is the contingency thinker, not Byron, that endless entertainer of other options. Byron simply hoped Napoleon would win; Wordsworth said he had no chance, *if* the Allies stuck together – which they had shown a marked predilection for *not* doing, through twenty years of total war.[33]

Here, Wordsworth validates the crucial importance of counterfactual or contingent thinking (and interpretation) at the highest level of contemplated human action. Wellington agreed with him: if Marshall Blücher and the Prussians don't show up soon, we are lost. As the afternoon wore on, Wellington was praying for one of two things: 'Night or the Prussians must come.' Wellington was a serious contingency man, not merely hoping, like Byron, for the outcome he wanted: he had 17,000 troops in reserve to cover his retreat to Brussels, if need be. His morning-after reply to the loaded question, 'Went the day well?', confirmed the force of Wordsworth's proviso: it was 'the nearest-run thing you ever saw in your life'.[34]

There is no record of Byron reading the little squib Wordsworth had anonymously published just two months earlier in 1815 – *Lines Addressed to a Noble Lord; (His Lordship will know why) By One of the Small Fry of the Lakes*, co-authored with Robert Southey's wealthy neighbour and protégée, Mary Barker – in which Wordsworth clumsily tried to put his finger on the literary-historical balance between himself and Byron.[35] Here we see Romantic counterfactualism in action in one of its strangest, most ephemeral incarnations. The text is an invitation to Byron to come to the Lakes for a picnic on Helvellyn: 'And our PONDS shall better please thee / Than those now dishonour'd Seas, / With their shores and Cyclades / ... Sensual Mussulmen atrocious, / Renegadoes, more ferocious!'[36] This trifle is simply a career embarrassment that deserves no notice at all, except as a jokey attempt to counter the emerging facts of English literary history. (None of Wordsworth's recent major biographers mentions it.) If our question is: What if Byron had read *The Prelude*? then Wordsworth's question is: What if Byron accepted his invitation? What would be the result? 'Halt in thy insane career!' Wordsworth and Barker write: 'Come then – discontented creature! / Come, and glory in thy nature! / See the joys of innocence'; 'To unlearn thyself, repair / Hither ... / Striving to become the creature / Of a genuine English nature!'[37] Experiencing such a change of scene, Byron might have become ... Wordsworth. It is hard to be more counterfactual than that. It is also hard to believe that Wordsworth wrote these lines at all, but in fact he worked on them rather energetically with Miss Barker in 1814, who was staying at Rydal Mount. He revised the first seven stanzas, which she wrote, and which regret most explicitly Byron's foul, vain, remorseful and altogether 'Avernian' expressions. Wordsworth's contribution – the last nine stanzas – is much more benign, working to blunt the sting of the opening lines by appealing to his lordship's better nature, evoking, *L'Allegro*-fashion, the benefits Byron might reap in Grasmere: 'Talents, genius, heaven hath granted, / Prudence, virtue, hast thou wanted.'

The occasion that relates these verses to my counterfactual scenario was Francis Jeffrey's recent volte-face elevation of Byron as 'Master-Poet of the Age!' – a judgement read of course by Mary Barker and her co-conspirator with the opening of Jeffrey's infamous review of *The Excursion* ('This will never do') ringing in their minds. Their six-page 'Note' extends the condescension of their verses: it is an ill-tempered screed against Jeffrey as a no-talent prose writer who could not write a creative line of poetry if he tried, 'no, not even on an instrument so unpretending as a jew's-harp!'.[38]

The meeting at Rogers's house and the lines written with Mary Barker are almost the last evidence we see of any geniality between the two poets. Astute readers could see Byron in the character of the Solitary, but he still figures as worthy of redemption in *The Excursion*, as he also does in *Lines Addressed to a Noble Lord*. After their encounters in 1815, Wordsworth may have decided that the noble lord was no longer worth his effort. For his part, Byron famously objected to *The Excursion*. But Byron, as astute a reader as one could want, would surely have recognised himself in the Solitary – and not have waited with any great anticipation for his promised redemption (which never comes).

Since the two poets change postures when moving from writing one version of themselves to another – Wordsworth going from the particular to the generic, Byron from the romantic to the ironic – what do we gain, if anything, by positing Byron reading and reviewing *The Prelude* in 1806–7? The damage done to British literary history by Pitt's 1793–98 Reign of Alarm is harder to assess than the damage it did to British civil rights – a topic rarely considered by mainstream historians, who usually dismiss it as unfortunate collateral damage in the Great War against France. One can easily argue that Byron might have reached his supreme poetic mastery in *Don Juan* earlier, and thus perhaps have refined it further, had he had *The Prelude* for a model. Achieving something earlier rather than later is perhaps an overrated category in literary history, if achievement is in fact attained – as it was not, for example, by victims of Alarm like William Frend, William Drennan, Mary Hays, Amelia Alderson and many others of this 'lost' generation. Perhaps Keats (and his readers) would have had an easier time of it in *Endymion* had he read *The Prelude*. Perhaps Shelley would have been less confusing in his imagery in *Alastor*, given the same advantage. But since they achieved works such as the *Hyperion* poems and *Prometheus Unbound* without it, the counterfactual bonus seems reduced.

For someone like John Thelwall, however, the balance of gain over loss would be easier to appreciate, especially since he himself fantasised about it in his conversation poems, relishing what he and his friends Coleridge and Wordsworth *might* do if he were admitted to the 'literary triumvirate' at 'the Academus of Stowey'.[39] Invoking Thelwall's healthy egotism allows me to dispose of yet another counterfactual possibility: that the towering example of *The Prelude* might have claimed nearly all of them as early victims of that 'anxiety of influence' first identified by Harold Bloom in the generational relations between the English Romantic poets. We can be sure that Byron's egotism and social position would have insulated him against such anxiety.

Proceeding further along the arc of the two poets' developing characterisations of their career heroes, we find that both Wordsworth and Byron envisioned their protagonists – which is to say they imagined themselves – paying for their revolutionary enthusiasms by falling victim to the Revolution's terrors, specifically as martyred *orators* in the cause of Liberty. Wordsworth portrays himself as coming close to being 'a poor mistaken and bewildered offering' in the dangerous intrigues of the expatriate community in Paris. And yet,

> Mean as I was, and little graced with powers
> Of eloquence even in my native speech,
> And all unfit for tumult and intrigue,
> Yet would I willingly have taken up
> A service at this time for cause so great,
> However dangerous.
>
> (*The Prelude* (1805), X, ll. 131–6)

Similarly, his alter-ego, the Solitary, longed for success like those verbal rock stars of the Revolution, Mirabeau, Vergniaud, Danton and Desmoulins: 'in crowds in open air, / My voice there mingled, heard or not' as he 'sang Saturnalian rule / Returned, – a progeny of golden years / ... the admiration winning of the crowd' (*The Excursion*, III, ll. 745–52, 766). Among many projected endings for *Don Juan*, Byron most particularly imagined Juan ending up like the flamboyant but politically astute Prussian-Dutch aristocrat adventurer, Jean-Baptiste du Val-de-

Lord Byron reads The Prelude

Grâce, Baron de Cloots ('Anacharsis Cloots'), known as 'the orator of mankind', guillotined in March 1794. As Byron wrote to John Murray in February 1821: 'I meant ... to make [Juan] finish an *Anacharsis Cloots* in the French revolution. To how many cantos this may extend – I know not – nor whether (even if I live) I shall complete it.'[40]

We see little of such potential in Juan's story, but increasing amounts of it in his creator's life. Here again, Byron would have found encouragement for his ideas in *The Prelude* – ideas that eventually led him far beyond Wordsworth's notional activism to the fetid swamps and partisan infighting of Missolonghi. In imagination or in fact, both heroes are positioned to become martyrs to the revolution they admired and regretted, standing in the advance guard of that long line of similarly bewildered heroes in nineteenth-century European literature that includes Stendahl's Julien Sorel, Tolstoy's Pierre Bezukhov and the misbegotten revolutionary conspirators of Dostoevsky's *Demons*.

But since Byron's story was never finished, and Wordsworth's was never published in his lifetime, we can go no further in charting what happened to their heroes as a measure of Wordsworth's putative influence on Byron. Instead, by way of conclusion, I trace their conjoined counterfactual lineage as 'Byronic' heroes with reference to their last words and the notable rhetorical similarities they reveal in seeking to bring their stories to a close in Books XI–XII of the 1805 *Prelude* and Cantos XI–XVI of *Don Juan*. Wordsworth's dominant closing note is Imagination; Byron's, Freedom. But both poets, in the closing books of their epics, display the same rhetorical reflex in the form of large intakes of vatic breath that seem to herald The End, but which are exhaled in new and complicating directions. Neither poet seems able to end his poem, though both *seem* to want to, and both hint – boast, rather – in the midst of their apparent difficulties, that the poem they are having a hard time finishing may be one of the greatest ever written in English. Given their close identifications with their heroes in these poems of self-creation, conclusion may have seemed all too much like death.

Byron's frustrating end-signals are familiar: 'However, 'tis no time to chat / On general topics'; 'My Juan, whom I left in deadly peril'; 'But how shall I relate in other cantos ...?' (*Don Juan*, XI, ll. 350, 505, 689). And in Canto XII: 'And now to business'; 'Oh pardon my digression'; 'But now I will begin my poem'; 'Here the twelfth canto of our introduction / Ends' (ll. 177, 305, 425, 679). Some readers may be frustrated by these continual stops and starts, but rather than try to account for them, it might be better to persuade such readers not to read Byron, at least not *Don*

Juan. Their characteristic motion is a sudden comic swerve undercutting serious reflection, but even readers in love with Byron's satiric voice tend to underestimate how the comedy gradually builds back up to reflection in another key.

Wordsworth's end-signals in the last three books of *The Prelude* are also well known, but less as purposeful digressions and more as frustrating *non sequiturs*. Most of these brief verse essays – almost odes-in-miniature – of approximately 25–50 lines each (Wordsworth's typical 'breathing space' of utterance), begin fresh paragraphs with title-topic sentences. These paragraphs have exercised our three greatest comparers of Byron and Wordsworth: Michael Cooke, Jerome J. McGann and Peter Manning. McGann in particular finds them 'a series of dismal recapitulative texts' arising either from bad faith or from astonishing lapses of awareness.[41] Less harshly, Manning speaks of the 'increasing pressure' that Wordsworth places on his narrative by trying to fit it to 'a scheme in which "All [is] gratulant if rightly understood" [*The Prelude* (1805), XIII, l. 385]'.[42] Such criticism may arise in part because these commentators find themselves in the cultural-rhetorical position of defending a long-neglected Byron against a Wordsworthian standard that had, at the time they were writing, achieved hegemonic orthodoxy in Anglo-American academic literary criticism. Hence they feel compelled to attack Wordsworth for his woolliness of thought and turgidity of expression, rather than seeing these two dozen or so verse paragraphs in terms of what they are perfectly capable of seeing in Byron: namely, inconclusive conclusions in the manner of many a last chapter of many a nineteenth-century novel – 'Conclusion, in Which Nothing is Concluded' – or, alternatively, as good-faith beginnings to summations that eventually prove too large or intractable. The optimistic launchings of such paragraphs often result in concluding lines apparently at odds with their opening topic sentence. For example, a passage beginning as follows –

> Time may come
> When some dramatic story may afford
> Shapes livelier to convey to thee, my friend,
> What then I learned, *or think I learned*, of truth,
> And the errors into which I was betrayed ...
> (*The Prelude* (1805), X, ll. 878–82; my emphasis)

– concludes with:

> ... I lost
> All feeling of conviction, and (in fine),
> Sick, wearied out with contrarieties,
> Yielded up moral questions in despair ...
>
> (*The Prelude* (1805), X, ll. 897–900)

Or, there is the abrupt gradation from 'This history ... has chiefly told / Of intellectual power from stage to stage / Advancing ...' to 'Can aught be more ignoble than the man / Whom they [the great poets of the past] describe ...?' (*The Prelude* (1805), XI, ll. 42–4, 71–3).

This repeated yet varied pattern can intensify the attentive reader's appreciation of the difficulty of the author's task, which is the immense one of offering a satisfactory, but by no means definitive, answer to the great question of the nineteenth century: How shall we – I, my hero – reconcile ourselves to the perceived failure of man's best hopes for social amelioration? These pronouncements are deliberately vulnerable utterances in the classic Wordsworthian model of self-exposed thinking out loud – itself a key instance of Romantic counterfactualism, as in 'Tintern Abbey': '*If* this / Be but a vain belief, *yet, oh!* ...' (my emphasis). Wordsworth is not making mistakes in composing these paragraphs, not expressing himself poorly, but rather enunciating the confusions he felt at the time of action. Coleridge well said that Wordsworth always meant all of every word he used, and this is true also of most of the verse paragraphs at the end of *The Prelude*, which we can be sure he fully intended after painstakingly revising them over forty-five years.

Byron's apparently effortlessly informal manner over-encourages 'light' readings. Wordsworth's formal language and serious manner over-encourage 'heavy' readings, as if he must achieve a philosophically coherent conclusion that we *assent* to, rather than a statement of faith we can *respect*. But how many serious Wordsworthians accept as true his statements about the interrelation of Nature and the Mind of Man? It is not the *substance* of the sweeping proviso that 'All [is] gratulant if rightly understood' that we see here, but its rhetorical component. If Wordsworth had wanted to end in what many of his readers take to be his normative stance, he could have concluded *The Prelude* with Book VIII, 'Love of Nature Leading to Love of Mankind', and published it without compunction.[43] But he forged on into the revolution, complexity and greatness.

Byron's *Juan* conclusions might not have been facilitated by his reading of *The Prelude* as regards his hero's failures and ultimate fate. But neither would he have been infuriated by Wordsworth's syntax of speculation, as he was by *The Excursion*'s heavy manner and spurious systematising. Instead, he would have recognised Wordsworth as a fellow labourer in the same vineyard, who was trying to find a plausible end-point in a worldwide scene of thought and action that was always swirling about him, whether the date of composition was 1805, 1815 or 1824. Michael Cooke rightly remarks that 'as a great public poem of the inward-oriented romantic period', *Don Juan* leads away from, rather than towards, public assent in the public good; rather, it aims for 'a state of disequilibrium', denying the reader the usual Romantic escape routes into shared indignation or lament.[44] Or, Cooke might have added, the attractive promises of works to come (which Wordsworth so freely dispensed throughout his career, especially after 1805, when he felt – to vary Geoffrey Hartman's metaphor – that he had the reserves in the bank to fund them). In distinguishing without evaluative prejudice Byron's epic from Wordsworth's, Cooke grants *The Prelude* a 'final, all-encompassing reality'.[45] The poem certainly gestures constantly towards that conclusion in the course of its long endgames, but (if rightly understood) it just as clearly does not reach this conclusion, as Byron, that lifelong smoker-out of Romantic abstractions, would surely have recognised – and welcomed.[46]

Notes

1 Louis Napoléon Geoffroy-Château, *Napoleon Apocryphe, 1812–1832: Histoire de la Conquête du Monde et de la Monarchie Universelle* (Paris: Chez Paulin, 1841), p. i. One of the originals of modern counterfactualism, *Napoléon Apocryphe* imagines Napoleon easily conquering the entire world; Britain is disposed of in five short chapters. It has, however, the interesting wrinkle of a reflexive chapter ('Une prétendue histoire') denouncing the 'horribles impostures' of a 'romancier coupable' for mentioning places like Elba and St Helena: 'que cette historie n'est pas l'histoire, que ce Napoléon n'est pas le vrai Napoléon' (p. 252).

2 Damian Walford Davies, personal communication; John Barrell, 'To Stir up the People', *London Review of Books*, 36 (23 January 2014), 17–19; David Simpson, review of *Unusual Suspects*, *The Wordsworth Circle*, 45:4 (Autumn 2014), 329–30.

3 *Wordsworth and 'The Recluse'* (New Haven, CT: Yale University Press, 1984); Kenneth R. Johnston, *The Hidden Wordsworth* (New York: W. W. Norton, 1998).

4 Kenneth R. Johnston, *Unusual Suspects: Pitt's Reign of Alarm and the Lost*

Generation of the 1790s (Oxford: Oxford University Press, 2013), p. 251.
5   Ibid., p. 252.
6   Lubomir Dolezel, *Possible Worlds of Fiction and History: The Postmodern Stage* (Baltimore, MD: Johns Hopkins University Press, 2010), pp. 101, 125.
7   See Niall Ferguson (ed.), *Virtual History: Alternatives and Counterfactuals* (London: Papermac, 1998), pp. 83–90.
8   D. W. Jefferson, *Three Essays: Johnson, Wordsworth, Byron*, ed. David Fairer (Leeds: Leeds Philosophical and Literary Society, 1998), p. 4.
9   Cited in Peter Manning, *Reading Romantics: Texts and Contexts* (Oxford: Oxford University Press, 1990), p. 194, n. 28.
10 *The Prelude* (1805), X, ll. 645–56; William Wordsworth, *The Prelude: The Four Texts (1798, 1799, 1805, 1850)*, ed. Jonathan Wordsworth (Harmondsworth: Penguin, 1995), p. 438. Hereafter given as references in the body of the text.
11 William Hazlitt, *The Spirit of the Age*, ed. E. D. Mackerness (Plymouth: Northcote House, 1991), p. 66.
12 *The Excursion*, III, l. 835; William Wordsworth, *The Excursion*, ed. Sally Bushell, James A. Butler and Michael C. Jaye (Ithaca, NY: Cornell University Press, 2007), p. 125. Hereafter given as references in the body of the text.
13 See Richard Matlak, 'Wordsworth and the "Great Terror" of 1803–05', *The Wordsworth Circle*, 46:1 (Winter 2015), 21–6.
14 E. P. Thompson, *The Making of the English Working Class* (London: Penguin, 1991 [1963]), p. 494.
15 Wakefield is the almost invisible tutelary spirit of Wordsworth's resumption of the poem that became *The Excursion*, by way of the composite generational figure of The Solitary; see Kenneth R. Johnston, 'Wordsworth's *Excursion*: Route and Destination', *The Wordsworth Circle*, 45:2 (Spring 2014), 106–7. Wordsworth was ready to drop, without any question, substantive parts of *The Convention of Cintra* (1809) if his literary advisers, Daniel Stuart and Thomas De Quincey, had considered that his comments on the conduct of General Arthur Wellesley (soon to be Duke of Wellington) might be construed as treasonous, as Wakefield's on Watson had been.
16 G. O. Trevelyan (ed.), *The Life and Letters of Lord Macaulay*, 2 vols (New York: Harper, 1876), II, p. 239.
17 ['*Poems*, by W. Wordsworth'], *Monthly Literary Recreations*, 12 (July 1807), 65–6. Curiously, a review of Byron's *Hours of Idleness* appears immediately after his review of Wordsworth. The lead sentence indicates the difference rank makes: 'The young and noble author of these poems

introduces them to public notice with a degree of modesty, which does honour to his feelings as a poet and a lord' (p. 67).

18 *Childe Harold's Pilgrimage*, Canto III, l. 145; Jerome J. McGann (ed.), *Byron (The Oxford Authors)* (Oxford: Oxford University Press, 1991), p. 109. Hereafter given as references in the body of the text.

19 'Lines (Composed at Grasmere ... the Author having just read in a Newspaper that the dissolution of Mr Fox was hourly expected)', ll. 17–18; Stephen Gill (ed.), *William Wordsworth (The Oxford Authors)* (Oxford: Oxford University Press, 1990), p. 329.

20 'On the Death of Mr. Fox', ll. 15–18; Byron, *Fugitive Pieces*, ed. Marcel Kessel (New York: The Facsimile Text Society/Columbia University Press, 1933), pp. 30–1.

21 See Susan Wolfson and Peter Manning, 'Introduction', in Byron, *Don Juan*, ed. T. G. Steffan, E. Steffan and W. W. Pratt (New York: Penguin, 2004), pp. xxiii–iv.

22 Jane Stabler, 'Byron and *The Excursion*', *The Wordsworth Circle*, 45:2 (Spring 2014), 142–3.

23 See Michael Cooke, *Acts of Inclusion: Studies Bearing on an Elementary Theory of Romanticism* (New Haven, CT: Yale University Press, 1979); Peter Manning, *Reading Romantics*; Jerome J. McGann, *Don Juan in Context* (Chicago: University of Chicago Press, 1976); Jane Stabler, *Byron: Poetics and History* (Cambridge: Cambridge University Press, 2002).

24 William Wordsworth, *The Thirteen-Book Prelude*, ed. Mark Reed, 2 vols (Ithaca, NY: Cornell University Press, 1991), I, pp. 5, 38–9.

25 'To William Wordsworth', l. 63; S. T. Coleridge, *The Complete Poems*, ed. William Keach (London: Penguin, 1997), p. 340.

26 See Robert Morrison, *The English Opium-Eater* (London: Weidenfeld & Nicolson, 2009), pp. 152, 209, 304–5.

27 Walt Whitman, 'A Backward Glance o'er Travel'd Roads' (1888), quoted in Richard Gravil, *Romantic Dialogues: Anglo-American Continuities, 1776–1862* (London: Macmillan, 2000), p. 163.

28 See Karen Karbiener, 'Intimations of Imitation: Wordsworth, Whitman, and the Emergence of *Leaves of Grass*', in Joel Pace and Matthew Scott (eds), *Wordsworth in American Literary Culture* (London: Palgrave, 2005), pp. 144–59. Karbiener's brilliantly succinct essay confirms the value of counterfactual thinking and interpretation, as she cites work after work whose authors boldly pursued critical connections between Whitman and Wordsworth despite the absence, at the time they were writing, of any demonstrable textual or biographical – 'factual' – connection between them.

29 Robert Weisbuch, *Atlantic Double-Cross: American Literature and British*

Influence in the Age of Emerson (Chicago: University of Chicago Press, 1986).
30 *Ibid.*, p. 178.
31 Quoted by R. W. French in J. R. LeMaster and Donald Kummings (eds), *Walt Whitman: An Encyclopedia* (London: Garland, 1998), p. 76.
32 See Bernard Beatty, 'Introduction', *Don Juan and Other Poems* (London: Penguin, 1987), p. 73.
33 Mark Reed, *Wordsworth: The Chronology of the Middle Years, 1800–1815* (Cambridge, MA: Harvard University Press, 1975), p. 499n.
34 See Elizabeth Longford, *Wellington: The Years of the Sword* (London: Weidenfield & Nicolson, 1969), pp. 450, 473, 489.
35 William Wordsworth and Mary Barker, *Lines Addressed to a Noble Lord*, ed. Jonathan Wordsworth (Otley: Woodstock, 2001); and see Ken Parille, 'All the Rage: Wordsworth's Attack on Byron', *Papers on Language and Literature*, 37:3 (Summer 2001), 255–8.
36 Wordsworth and Barker, *Lines Addressed to a Noble Lord*, p. 13.
37 *Ibid.*, pp. 3, 8, 14.
38 *Ibid.*, p. 23.
39 Quoted in Damian Walford Davies, *Presences that Disturb: Models of Romantic Identity in the Literature and Culture of the 1790s* (Cardiff: University of Wales Press, 2002), p. 296.
40 Byron, *Selected Letters and Journals*, ed. Leslie A. Marchand (London: Pimlico, 1993), pp. 251–2. See also McGann, *Don Juan in Context*, p. 61 and Henry W. Wetton, *The Termination of the Sixteenth Canto of Lord Byron's Don Juan* (London: Trübner, 1864), p. 21.
41 Jerome J. McGann, *Byron and Wordsworth* (Nottingham: School of English Studies, 1999), p. 41.
42 Manning, *Reading Romantics*, p. 132.
43 Jefferson, *Three Essays*, p. 33.
44 Michael Cooke, *The Blind Man Traces the Circle: On the Patterns and Philosophy of Byron's Poetry* (Princeton, NJ: Princeton University Press: 1969), p. 140.
45 *Ibid.*, p. 141.
46 For helpful suggestions throughout, I thank John Bugg, Julia Carlson, Peter Manning and Susan Wolfson.

Works cited

Primary texts

Byron, Lord [George Gordon], *Don Juan*, ed. T. G. Steffan, E. Steffan and W. W. Pratt (New York: Penguin, 2004)
Byron, Lord [George Gordon], *Don Juan and other Poems*, ed. Bernard Beatty (London: Penguin, 1987)
Byron, Lord [George Gordon], *Fugitive Pieces*, ed. Marcel Kessel (New York: The Facsimile Text Society/Columbia University Press, 1933)
Byron, Lord [George Gordon], review of Wordsworth's *Poems, in Two Volumes* (1807), *Monthly Literary Recreations*, 12 (July 1807), 65–6.
Byron, Lord [George Gordon], *Selected Letters and Journals*, ed. Leslie A. Marchand (London: Pimlico, 1993)
Coleridge, Samuel Taylor, *The Complete Poems*, ed. William Keach (London: Penguin, 1997)
Geoffroy-Château, Louis-Napoléon, *Napoléon Apocryphe, 1812–1832: Histoire de la Conquête du Monde et de la Monarchie Universelle* (Paris: Chez Paulin, 1841)
Gill, Stephen (ed.), *William Wordsworth (The Oxford Authors)* (Oxford: Oxford University Press, 1990)
Hazlitt, William, *The Spirit of the Age*, ed. E. D. Mackerness (Plymouth: Northcote House, 1991)
McGann, Jerome J. (e.), *Byron (The Oxford Authors)* (Oxford: Oxford University Press, 1991)
Trevelyan, G. O. (ed.), *The Life and Letters of Lord Macaulay* (New York: Harper, 1876)
Wordsworth, William, *The Excursion*, ed. Sally Bushell, James A. Butler, and Michael C. Jaye (Ithaca, NY: Cornell University Press, 2007)
Wordsworth, William, *The Prelude: The Four Texts (1798, 1799, 1805, 1850)*, ed. Jonathan Wordsworth (Harmondsworth: Penguin, 1995)
Wordsworth, William, *The Thirteen-Book Prelude*, ed. Mark Reed (Ithaca, NY: Cornell University Press, 1991)
Wordsworth, William and Mary Barker, *Lines Addressed to a Noble Lord*, ed. Jonathan Wordsworth (Otley: Woodstock, 2001)

Secondary texts

Barrell, John, 'To Stir up the People', *London Review of Books*, 36 (23 January 2014), 17–19
Cooke, Michael, *Acts of Inclusion: Studies Bearing on an Elementary Theory of Romanticism* (New Haven, CT: Yale University Press, 1979)

Cooke, Michael, *The Blind Man Traces the Circle: On the Patterns and Philosophy of Byron's Poetry* (Princeton, NJ: Princeton University Press, 1969)

Dolezel, Lubomir, *Possible Worlds of Fiction and History: The Postmodern Stage* (Baltimore, MD: Johns Hopkins University Press, 2010)

Ferguson, Niall (ed.), *Virtual History: Alternatives and Counterfactuals* (London: Papermac, 1998)

French, R. W., 'British Romantic Poets', in J. R. LeMaster and Donal Kummings (eds), *Walt Whitman: An Encyclopedia* (London: Garland, 1998), pp. 75–7

Gravil, Richard, *Romantic Dialogues: Anglo-American Continuities, 1776–1862* (London: Macmillan, 2000)

Jefferson, D. W., *Three Essays: Johnson, Wordsworth, Byron*, ed. David Fairer (Leeds: Leeds Philosophical and Historical Society, 1998)

Johnston, Kenneth R., *The Hidden Wordsworth* (New York: W. W. Norton, 1998)

Johnston, Kenneth R. *Unusual Suspects: Pitt's Reign of Alarm and the Lost Generation of the 1790s* (Oxford: Oxford University Press, 2013)

Johnston, Kenneth R., 'Wordsworth's *Excursion*: Route and Destination', *The Wordsworth Circle*, 45:2 (Spring 2014), 106–13

Johnston, Kenneth R., *Wordsworth and 'The Recluse'* (New Haven, CT: Yale University Press, 1984)

Karbiener, Karen, 'Intimations of Imitation: Wordsworth, Whitman, and the Emergence of *Leaves of Grass*', in Joel Pace and Matthew Scott (eds), *Wordsworth in American Literary Culture* (London: Palgrave, 2005), pp. 144–59

Longford, Elizabeth, *Wellington: The Years of the Sword* (London: Weidenfeld & Nicolson, 1969)

Manning, Peter, *Reading Romantics: Texts and Contexts* (Oxford: Oxford University Press, 1990)

Matlak, Richard, 'Wordsworth and the "Great Terror" of 1803–05', *The Wordsworth Circle*, 46:1 (Winter 2015), 21–6

McGann, Jerome, *Byron and Wordsworth* (Nottingham: School of English Studies, 1999)

McGann, Jerome, *Don Juan in Context* (Chicago: University of Chicago Press, 1976)

Morrison, Robert, *The English Opium-Eater* (London: Weidenfeld & Nicolson, 2009)

Parille, Ken, 'All the Rage: Wordsworth's Attack on Byron', *Papers on Language and Literature*, 37:3 (Summer 2001), 255–8

Reed, Mark, *Wordsworth: The Chronology of the Middle Years, 1800–1815* (Cambridge, MA: Harvard University Press, 1975)

Simpson, David, review of Johnston, *Unusual Suspects*, *The Wordsworth Circle*, 45:4 (Autumn 2014), 329–30

Stabler, Jane, 'Byron and *The Excursion*', *The Wordsworth Circle*, 45:2 (Spring 2014), 137–47

Stabler, Jane, *Byron: Poetics and History* (Cambridge: Cambridge University Press, 2002)

Thompson, E. P., *The Making of the English Working Class* (London: Penguin, 1991 [1963])

Walford Davies, Damian, *Presences that Disturb: Models of Romantic Identity in the Literature and Culture of the 1790s* (Cardiff: University of Wales Press, 2002)

Weisbuch, Robert, *Atlantic Double-Cross: American Literature and British Influence in the Age of Emerson* (Chicago: University of Chicago Press, 1986)

Wetton, Henry H., *The Termination of the Sixteenth Canto of Lord Byron's Don Juan* (London: Trübner, 1864)

6

Counterfactual obstetrics: Mary Wollstonecraft's Frankenstein

Damian Walford Davies

'Obstetrics': from the Latin for 'midwife' – literally, 'one who stands before/opposite/in the way of the woman in childbirth. As both heirs to and active deliverers of Romanticism's inheritances, we are ourselves in an uncanny parturitive position. Assisting at the iterative, often difficult (re)births of literary texts, we participate in acts of critical midwifery. What follows is a provocation – a performance of a critical heuristic that is assistive but also dynamically oppositional, one that in its (re-) narrativisation of (literary) history both brings to birth new forms of Romanticism and *stands in the way of* received Romantic inheritances. My method is therefore 'obstetrical' in the full paradoxical sense of the term.

Dissatisfaction with what has been entailed to us by history, biography, fiction, literary history and *Streptococcus pyogenes* bacteria (minute particulars, there) prompts me to bring to birth a monstrous, murderous and resurrectionary counterfactual scenario. I begin in intimate and hyper-historicised obstetric space. We are at the Polygon, Somers Town, London, home of Mary Wollstonecraft and William Godwin. It is 7:39 a.m. on Sunday 10 September 1797. Mrs Blenkinsop, experienced midwife-matron from the Westminster Lying-in Hospital, known to Wollstonecraft from antenatal consultations, has long been dismissed. Three male doctors have been called in – Louis Poignand, James Fordyce and John Clarke (the last a recognised authority on the 'inflammatory and febrile diseases of lying-in women' who was also known for his criticisms of midwives' 'continued presence in a field whose status he wished to raise').[1] They too have now departed. A fourth, Anthony Carlisle (a family friend), is in the house. During the past week, Wollstonecraft has suffered the appalling effects of puerperal sepsis resulting from endometritis (a genital tract infection) caused by bacteria introduced into her system in the early hours of 31 August by the lacerating, and most likely unwashed, hands of the man-midwife, Dr Poignand.[2] He had scraped for four hours at Wollstonecraft's 'raw uterine wall', removing 'in bits' (most of) her retained placenta, which was causing postpartum haemorrhage.[3] (The evidence, I suggest, points to a case of *placenta accreta* – where the organ is deeply embedded in the wall of the womb – rather than merely *placenta adherens*.) As the crux or 'nexus event' (Karen Hellekson's phrase) of my counterfactual scenario, I posit that, at 7:40 a.m. on 10 September, Wollstonecraft did not die.[4] Rather, her immune system rallied against the infection, enabling her to make a recovery. In my revisionary obstetrical economy, the mother's survival is at the expense of the daughter's being: 'it' – as a stressed William Godwin referred to his infant daughter Mary at this fraught time – died a week later (after becoming 'alarmingly ill' at the Reveleys').[5] My postulate has obvious consequences for literary history.

Dispensing with the iron logic of the 'plausibility', 'cotenability', 'projectability' and 'compelling mechanisms' that govern the use of counterfactuals as they have been deployed to date as 'thought exercise[s]' that test 'non-linear models' in the sciences, social sciences and in the discipline of history, this chapter embraces the affordances of various 'second-order' events that are clearly located in the realm of what Richard Ned Lebow terms 'miracle counterfactuals'.[6] In my present thought experiment, the imaginative corollary of having Wollstonecraft alive at the end of the 1790s is that she survives to write – and, indeed, write (a version of) the *Frankenstein* story. Paradoxically, imagining the shape *Frankenstein* might have taken as the *mother's* text, and specifically as a production of the 1790s, is in part motivated by, and in turn underscores, the central presence in the *daughter's* text of the lost mother whom Mary Shelley knew only textually, posthumously, as Mary Jacobus reminds us (witness our entailment of Marys).[7] Such counterfactual interventions in literary history can salutarily bring home to us our agency as co-creators of 'Romanticism' and our position as active readers within a literary-historical timespace that is most valuably seen not as a causal line or sequence, but as a dense quantum 'field' that is 'sideshadowed' (to invoke Gary Saul Morson) by multiple possibilities. As Morson emphasises, 'we are usually deceived by our own presence at the sequence's culmination'.[8] The results of that (self-)deception can range from critical hubris to tyrannous and essentialising literary histories. Even the most committed New Historicist constructs and confirms a 'canon'. To draw down Morson's concept of 'tempics' and structures of narrative temporality into the context of *literary* history again: Mary Shelley's *Frankenstein* must be understood as 'just another possibility that somehow came to pass'; the 'mirage' – or miracle – is 'not other possibilities but the necessity of the actual one'.[9]

Wollstonecraft Rediviva

Lebow reminds us that our choice of counterfactuals 'reflects the different interests' of the chooser.[10] It is worth further diagnosing the prompts behind the dissatisfaction noted above with 'things as they are' – the title of William Godwin's novel of 1794, which Wollstonecraft was reading during the last year of her life. Such chafing – intellectual and emotional – are crucial aspects of the counterfactual itch; it is a mode of knowing, wishing and imagining 'otherwise' that Romanticism itself enjoined.

The present counterfactual experiment is offered by one who – self-aligned with that feminist clarion, 'Wollstonecraft's daughters' – is acutely aware of his historical position as a son of Mary Wollstonecraft and as a middle-class male critic writing 220 years after her death, prying into intimate obstetric space and female physiological and psychological trauma.[11] What I propose is a literary-historical modality of Wollstonecraft's own resistance to entailment, which she imagined in *The Wrongs of Woman; Or, Maria* as a 'thraldom' akin to being 'chained to dead bodies' – in the present case, literary history, and Wollstonecraft's own corpse.[12] The manner of her demise is an ingredient of her hold over us, of her own deathly power. Against the still shocking attack of Richard Polwhele (who was quick to 'point out the ills which the radical woman's flesh is heir to' in ascribing Wollstonecraft's death 'to a vengeful providence') and also against contemporary critical embalmings of her image, I feel compelled to animate the petrific, mummified, memorialised body of 'our dead mother', Mary.[13] I take into new territory Julie A. Carson's argument that the 'life/writings' of the Wollstonecraft-Godwin-Shelley clan – their 'publicizing of family' – actively set out to challenge 'the deadness of the dead' through writerly acts of creative mourning that 'craft works of a new species out of the un/dead'.[14] Through a boldfaced act of historical balking, I also answer Mary Jacobus's call to resist Wollstonecraft's 'legacy of impossible mourning' by declaring a resistance to her death and to the family refrain that Wollstonecraft – bastilled in a fatal, fatalistic narrative – inherited from her mother's deathbed and which she subsequently performed in her own life and fiction and echoed in childbed (her own deathbed): 'A little patience, and all will be over!'[15] In doing so, I reject our own contemporary 'unmothered' condition as (merely) grieving heirs and disciples.[16] Like Godwin in the Preface to his *Memoirs of the Author of A Vindication of the Rights of Woman* (1798), I nurse 'an attachment to [Wollstonecraft's] fate' that makes me wish to deliver her (I pun, obstetrically) from the 'tactless frankness' of those very memoirs – a work whose 'hagiographic devotion' largely conditioned the negative character of that fate for two generations, during which Wollstonecraft's name became shorthand for political and sexual monstrosity.[17]

In play also, of course, is our frustration with curtailment. We lament the fact that space and time were not given to Wollstonecraft to revise and refresh herself, and to come to terms with her condition as survivor at the *fin de siècle*. After all, 'compensatory' narratives – acts of consolatory reimagining and 'undoing' – are at the heart of the counterfactual imagination, as Mark Salber Phillips and Catherine Gallagher have emphasised.[18] The nature of Wollstonecraft's death, replete as it is with 'ideological ironies' and 'attributable only to the accident of its having fallen there rather than here in the narrative of obstetric "progress"', as Vivien Jones puts it, directly motivates such reparative acts.[19] Claudia L. Johnson and others have taxonomised Wollstonecraft's 1790s career in terms of a 'revolutionary' and 'postrevolutionary' phase. Johnson views the former (articulated in the 1790 and 1792 *Vindications*) as valorising a modality of rational 'republican masculinity into which women too could be invited' – an interpretation validated by Wollstonecraft's seemingly off-hand post-natal remark to Ruth Barlow on 14 May 1794: 'My little Girl [Fanny Imlay] begins to suck so *manfully* that her father reckons saucily on her writing the second part of the R—ts of Woman').[20] In the latter phase (exemplified by *The Wrongs of Woman; Or, Maria*), Johnson sees Wollstonecraft tentatively exploring new forms of revolutionary feminist identity and action, revising the former model in a climate of personal and political disillusionment. This latter period was tragically 'overtaken by events', as Gary Kelly has it.[21] The status of *The Wrongs of Woman* as fragment ('imperfect', 'broken', 'incoherent', 'mutilated', 'a mark to record the triumphs of mortality', in Godwin's spousal-editorial vocabulary) begs the question of how the revisionary project on which Wollstonecraft embarked might have been taken forward.[22] As we shall see, I choose to identify the generic ground of that project as Wollstonecraft's developing adventures in what might be called political autobiografiction in the context of a gothicised national tale.

Then there are those areas of her life experience that one feels Wollstonecraft herself did not (have the chance to) fully explore. One of the most salient is her hybrid, archipelagic cultural and political identity. Gordon refers to 'the shifting, half-Irish Wollstonecrafts' (Mary's mother was from Ballyshannon, County Donegal, where the family was connected with the gentry).[23] This aspect of her personal, cultural and national-political sense of belonging is a major element in what follows. Mary Shelley's *Frankenstein*, with its anxiously formal dedication to Father Godwin, its plot (learned partly from the father) of parent-creature flight and pursuit, and its analysis of a culture of dead mothers, is itself preoccupied with the pathologies of inheritance. Thus a 1799 pre-incarnation of the novel offers a tantalising platform on which to allow Wollstonecraft to consider her own elided or repressed cultural formation and entailments. Counterfactual revisioning and creative rehistoricisation are a means of resisting what one might delicately term, following Mary Jacobus, Wollstonecraft's stillborn 'enthusiastic prematurity'.[24]

Julia V. Douthwaite's recovery of a 1790 French novella by François-Félix Nogaret concerning 'artificial creation' and automata, set in third-century-BCE Syracuse and featuring an inventor called Frankénstein, is a further galvanic prompt to (re)imagine a *Frankenstein* that is rooted in the 1790s. In Douthwaite's book, the links between this politico-technological French tale (historicised in terms of 'the agitation concerning trade guilds and inventors' rights' at the beginning of the French revolutionary republic) and Mary Shelley's novel remain frustratingly unexplored. However, Douthwaite's literary-historical repossession of the novella testifies to 'an alternative genealogy for Frankenstein's creature' that renders Mary Shelley's later fiction, whatever the line of influence, uncannily supplementary and *post hoc*.[25]

In proposing a retrojection of '*Frankenstein*' – now held at arm's length between inverted commas as well as italicised – to the 1790s, I respond also to the following: the uncanny effects that are the product of the discourse Wollstonecraft herself deployed to articulate her own *Bildung*; Mary (*fille*)'s multiple 'transactions' with Mary (*mère*) and with her 1790s inheritance; and contemporary critical and literary-historical Freudian slips.[26] Writing from London to her sister Everina on 7 November 1787, having just left the employ of Lord and Lady Kingsborough in Ireland, Wollstonecraft announced her decision to 'exert [her] talents' in literary endeavour with the support of Joseph Johnson: 'I am then going to be the first of a new genus – I tremble at the attempt.'[27] It is a statement that re-echoes in Victor Frankenstein's declaration: 'A new species would bless me as its creator and source.'²⁸ Emancipating herself into writing in the letter to Everina, Wollstonecraft casts herself in multiple recursive roles – literary predecessor, mother, creator and (disturbingly) creature *avant la lettre*.

Other examples foreshorten the distance between Wollstonecraft and her daughter's novel. From Copenhagen on 6 September 1795, the creaturely, pan-European Wollstonecraft called out to an indifferent Gilbert Imlay: 'I am strangely cast off ... I meet with families continually, who are bound together by affection or principle ... I am ready to demand, in a murmuring tone, of Heaven, "Why am I thus abandoned?".'²⁹ It is the very cry of Mary Shelley's creature on the Mer de Glace. Wollstonecraft becomes the proleptic protagonist of her daughter's plot in ways that are not simply a function of Mary Shelley's conscious deployment in her novel of aspects of her mother's life and works. A classic example is the punning embodiment, in Victor's nightmare embrace of his mother's corpse in *Frankenstein*, of Wollstonecraft's meditation in *Letters Written during a Short Residence in Sweden, Norway, and Denmark* (1796) on the mummies – 'human petrifactions' – in Tønsberg church ('Where goes this breath? this *I*, so much alive? ... Pugh! my stomach turns').[30] It is a morbid textual embrace and reanimation of Mary's dead *Mummy*. Further, one cannot read Godwin's July 1796 remark to Wollstonecraft – 'I love ... the malicious leer of your eye' (it was subject to a 'slight paralysis of the lid') – without thinking of her daughter's creature.[31]

Biographers perpetuate the weird shudder. Lyndall Gordon diagnoses her subject as 'a mutation of sorts, a creature in the making' who lacked 'the companionship of a like creature' and who, losing hope, 'expect[ed] to end the experiment'.[32] Miranda Seymour's biography of Mary Shelley reproduces Blake's engraving of a father standing over the dead bodies of his children, published in the second (1791) edition of Wollstonecraft's *Original Stories*; Seymour's caption makes the mother the author of the daughter's work: 'An illustration by William Blake to Mary Wollstonecraft's *Original Stories from Real Life*, prefiguring the monster's appearance before his creator in her novel, *Frankenstein*'.[33] Further, the ambiguity allows us to configure the parent in Blake's illustration as the surviving Wollstonecraft standing above her daughter's literary corpus.

A counterfactual scenario that restores Wollstonecraft to literary life is the direct heir to multiple resurrectionary acts that began in 1795, two years before her death. Gordon describes Dr Poignand as by turns 'torturing and resuscitating' his patient as he sought to extract the placenta.

His ministrations were not, however, the first act of (awful) revivification experienced by Wollstonecraft. She had been 'inhumanly brought back to life and misery' (her own words) by members of the Royal Humane Society following her second suicide attempt in October 1795.[34] As Carolyn Williams suggests, it is entirely possible that the resuscitation was effected 'after her breathing had stopped'; further, one can plausibly speculate that the techniques of reanimation employed on her – possibly in one of the Society's 'receiving houses' close to Putney Bridge – would have included 'bellows up the nostril', the rubbing of salt, snuff, or *eau de luce* on the skin, the laying on of 'flannels soaked in rum or Dutch gin', and possibly also the application of electricity to the thorax.[35] (The inscription on the obverse of the Society's medal was *Lateat Scintillula Forsan* – 'A Little Spark may yet Remain'.)

Drawing a parallel between the mother's experience and the daughter's text, Williams notes:

> [Victor Frankenstein's] underlying assumption that the offspring of resuscitated once-dead tissue must be monstrous, even if that tissue was human, is a disturbing reflection from the pen of a woman who was conceived by the victim of an unwanted resuscitation.[36]

Or to put it differently: it is the daughter herself who has hitherto most powerfully imagined a Wollstonecraft uncannily vivified. The counterfactual imagination seizes on that prompt. Having suggested that, for Wollstonecraft at the end of 1795, 'the rights of woman might ... include the revolutionary right of rational death' (that is, self-murder rationally entered into), Janet Todd goes on to proclaim: 'But she does not die. She bubbles up to the surface as so many women do, the female [suicide] failure rate being much larger than the male – and goes on living.'[37] There is something significant and uncanny about the choice of the present tense here: it positions us there, downriver from Putney Bridge, while also emphasising Wollstonecraft's continuing resistance to death.

Vivien Jones reminds us that the number of maternal deaths for home deliveries in the 1790s is 'estimated at between three and six per thousand'.[38] The low figure will no doubt greatly surprise most readers. As Jones remarks, 'Knowledge of that statistical context can only make Wollstonecraft's death seem all the more arbitrary.'[39] The untimeliness of a death that resulted from multiple contingencies has been a significant stimulus for the compensatory construction of her multiple (often spectral) *afterlives* – a phenomenon that further impels my own counterfactual scenario. Andrew McInnes and Devoney Looser have recently examined the ways in which writers and commentators have summoned Wollstonecraft 'as a kind of ghost' – a phantom, a 'restive' presence (both 'bogeywoman' and paradigm) who, as Cora Kaplan remarks, 'cannot be … honorably laid to rest'.[40] As Looser reveals, 'the tradition of describing [Wollstonecraft's] ghost and of seeing ourselves as haunted by her' began very soon after her death in the form of a 1798 dialogue-debate in which, though admitting her 'errors' and unrestrained 'passions', she speaks as an assertrix of proto-feminist values.[41] The conjuration of Wollstonecraft by Virginia Woolf as 'spiritual medium' is well known – 'she cut her way to the quick of life … she is alive and active, she argues and experiments, we hear her voice and trace her influence even now among the living' – even if the *Frankenstein*-haunted anatomico-scientific discourse that Woolf deploys has not been remarked on.[42]

Janet Todd's *Rebel Daughters: Ireland in Conflict, 1798* (2003) – a profile of the Kingsborough family against the background of the Irish Rebellion in which Margaret King, Wollstonecraft's pupil and passionate acolyte (her *creature*, indeed), figures prominently – can, I suggest, be seen as an indemnifying narrative that redresses the curious curtness of the deathbed dead-end of Todd's own biography (2000) by revealing how Wollstonecraft's energies worked posthumously in others. The last three chapters of Lyndall Gordon's biography (entitled 'Converts', 'Daughters' and 'Generations') profile modalities of Wollstonecraft's posthumous presence and influence – 'stories of promise' and 'counter-narratives to the cut-off plot of Wollstonecraft's death' to which the counterfactual scenario underlying this chapter is intimately related.[43] My counterfactual experiment can also be seen as a radical extension of Charlotte Gordon's *Romantic Outlaws* (2015), which, in attempting a double biography in alternating chapters, has the effect of uniting mother and daughter in an uncannily synchronous, symbiotic existence.[44]

The critical and cultural history profiled above may suggest that we inherit, and continue to curate, a zombie Wollstonecraft, discomfitingly undead. That image is vitally and necessarily part of our recognition of Wollstonecraft's continuing literary and political presence and relevance – an image that must *remain disturbing* so as to *remain motivating*. As Looser remarks: 'she continues to come to us, pointedly, as undead'.[45] The counterfactual experiment that restores Wollstonecraft to writing cannot escape the narratives of unlooked-for reanimation for which not only the daughter's, but also the mother's, life and writings are noted.

Critical precursors

Since the mid-1980s we have become acclimatised to a creative-critical historicist method that summons what one might call doppelgänger-works as spectral alterities that the Romantic author in question *did not write*, but which ghost the work (usually a lyric) as we have it. We can now speak of a Romantic New Historicist frisson – the moment when the text under scrutiny is suddenly rendered a kind of uncanny, occlusive allegory. The philosophical, methodological and indeed ethical robustness of such provocations has been subject to much criticism; at the same time, I suggest that the more creative modalities of Romantic New Historicism can be seen to have created the literary-historical equivalent of a multiverse, comprising multifarious alternative forms of Romanticism.[46] Our very familiarity with canonical Romanticism is apt to breed a critical nearsightedness and complacency born of an illusion of ownership and knowledge – an ultimately comforting assumption that our literary-historical inheritance could not have been otherwise. The counterfactual irruption into that history of a 'rival' text renders our received 'original' ersatz and strangely counterfeit; it also configures all subsequent texts as being in dialogue with and influenced by that *arriviste* text. What the counterfactual scenario engenders is not Romantic New Historicism's ghost works but rather an alternative living body. Through that body we may enter into a new evaluative relationship with the familiar, but now salutarily estranged, productions of received literary history, new aspects of which – depending on the contours of the counterfactual precursor – will come into view.

Such critical-creative negotiations with history, and counterfactualism itself, have impeccable Romantic credentials in a source intimately close to Wollstonecraft in the year of her death. During 1797, William Godwin was reflecting on the relationship between history and fiction as he formulated a philosophical underpinning for a historiography that married facts with narrative and with what Mark Salber Phillips terms 'acts of imaginative identification' and 'pattern[s] of affective engagement' that 'overcome the opacity of the past'.[47] In the essay 'Of History and Romance', intended for a second volume of *The Enquirer* (1797), Godwin saw 'history' as 'the broken fragments, and the scattered ruins of evidence', with a history of those facts being 'the mere skeleton of history'. In a *Frankenstein*ian formulation, he adds that 'The muscles, the articulations, every thing in which the life emphatically resides, is absent', which leads him to the radical statement that it is the writer of 'romance' who is to be regarded as 'the writer of real history'.[48] As Phillips notes:

> Godwin's observations seem a prescient recognition that the new and still uncertain techniques that allowed novelists to display unmediated access to other minds would be epoch making for the relations of history and fiction.[49]

Godwin's 'agent-centered historicism', which as John Klancher notes 'replace[d] the ideological trope of probability with the constructionist figure of possibility', prefigures the late-twentieth-century 'linguistic turn' in historical writing and historiography led, in different ways, by Hayden White and Dominick LaCapra. Their emphasis on the discursivity, rhetoricity and disciplinary and generic miscibility of all historical writing – on the need to open up 'alternative ways of understanding' the past and 'expand our definitions of history' – in turn informs recent analyses of 'the troubled relationship between history and literature, both in the late eighteenth and early nineteenth centuries, and in current scholarly practice'.[50] As Porscha Fermanis and John Regan suggest, contemporary critical examinations of 'the role of feelings [and] empathy' in historical writing seem to mark a return to a recognition of 'the apparently porous boundaries' between history and literature negotiated by Romantic-period authors themselves.[51] What underlies such claims as Godwin's at the close of the 1790s – claims related to his project of nuancing the rationalism and necessitarianism of the first edition of *An Enquiry concerning Political Justice* (1793) and his exploration in such works as the novel *St Leon* (1799) of the role of 'narrative pattern' in sustaining and contesting state power – is a 'genuine skepticism about the accessibility of historical truth', as Gary Handwerk notes.[52] To be sure, extending Godwin's valorisation of fictive modalities and 'forms of imagination' to encompass *literary* history in the context of my present counterfactual experiment with *Frankenstein* runs the risk of appearing perversely to deny that we have materially and unambiguously inherited Mary Shelley's novel(s) of 1818 (and 1831).[53] However, there is a meaningful analogy between, on the one hand, Godwin's conception of an animating, vitalising narrator who, in writing 'history', fleshes out historical absence and establishes networks of connection between inherited 'broken fragments'; and on the other, a counterfactualism whose affective engagement with alternative possibilities involves our projecting ourselves beyond the 'scattered ruins of evidence' of received literary history, which is itself only the product of contingency. Literary history – that contested site of jostling presences and absences – is 'the mere skeleton' of literature's multiverse.

Birthing literary history

What shape, then, might a *fin-de-siècle* novel by a restored Mary Wollstonecraft take? *I propose an irruption into literary history of a political-obstetrical fiction by a physically recovered but mentally traumatised woman, set against the background of the terror of the Irish Rebellion of May–October 1798*.[54] That 'irruption' must be carefully curated by the critic in parturitive stages that are the necessary, careful deferrals and gestational phases of the project's coming-into-being. The first two sections of this chapter can be considered to fulfil those phases; this present section and the next are the contractions that bring on the birth itself in the section 'L'Estranging *Frankenstein*'.

Wollstonecraft's is a spousal project (and family drama), written after she sets aside *The Wrongs of Woman*, and framed alongside, and in dialogue with, her husband's *St Leon* (a historical fiction also concerned with 'fatal legac[ies]' and the 'atrocious secrets of medicine').[55] Wollstonecraft's novel is published, in three volumes, by Joseph Johnson, her long-standing enabler, on 2 December 1799, on the same day as her husband's book. Its title is *L'Estrange; Or, The Modern Menoetius. An Irish Tale*, identified on the title page as the work of the author of *A Vindication of the Rights of Woman* (Figure 6.1). It is dedicated to her former pupil at Mitchelstown, County Cork – Margaret King, whom Julie A. Carson calls Wollstonecraft's 'first "daughter"' and who by 1799 was the shape- and name-shifting, cross-dressing, six-foot Ascendancy nationalist, Lady Mount Cashell.[56] In the Advertisement to her first novel, *Mary: A Fiction* (1788), Wollstonecraft had presented her portrait of 'a woman, who has thinking powers' as a kind of counterfactual scenario: 'Without arguing physically about *possibilities* – in a fiction, such a being may be allowed to exist.'[57] I appropriate the same words as I clear space for the historical autobiografiction that is *L'Estrange*.

I suggest that Wollstonecraft follows the 1798 Rebellion with fascinated dread and a deepening, dislocating awareness of personal investment. The compound cultural, political and religious agendas and allegiances that made the Rebellion no simple binary agon but rather a mass of competing ideologies on all sides held up a mirror to the paradoxes of her own plural drives and her hybrid archipelagic identity. What the Rebellion threw into relief were her own 'accursed origin[s]' (to quote

L'ESTRANGE;

Or,

THE MODERN MENOETIUS

AN IRISH TALE

BY THE AUTHOR OF
A VINDICATION OF THE RIGHTS OF WOMAN
&c., &c.

LONDON:
PRINTED FOR J. JOHNSON, ST. PAUL'S CHURCH-YARD.

1799.

6.1 Mary Wollstonecraft, *L'Estrange; Or, The Modern Menoetius. An Irish Tale*

the outlaw creature's description of its own hybridity in *Frankenstein*), her being not 'English-quite, nor Irish-quite' (in the words of John Banim's *The Anglo-Irish of the Nineteenth Century* (1828)).[58] I also suggest that the Irish Rebellion would have prompted her to reflect on those origins and on the Irish question, compensating for what Janet Todd has seen as her (previous) 'neglect' of the 'politics, the social and economic systems, the class structures [and] the effect of religion' on Irish life – a singular disregard for which Todd accounts by citing Wollstonecraft's emphasis on disinterested global rather than national(ist) citizenship and her ingrained 'English anti-Catholicism'.[59] Writing *L'Estrange* allows Wollstonecraft to process, in the context of the Rebellion, her experience of being 'something betwixt and between' – a phrase she used more than once – as a fascinatingly ambiguous and ambivalent member of the Kingsborough household at Mitchelstown Castle (which, as she told her sister Everina, she first entered 'as if [she] was going into the Bastile [*sic*]'), and in Dublin from 1786 to 1787.[60]

At the time, a sharp observer of the lapdogs-and-lisping social and sexual environment at Mitchelstown, Wollstonecraft was less acutely attuned to the political structures and the cultural and ethnic tensions that both sustained and imperilled Ascendancy life and which were palpably felt in the garrison-like nature of the recently remodelled town and encoded in the Great House and estate. The latter had recently been transformed on the advice of the agriculturalist Arthur Young and was protected from the Catholic natives by a 'buffer' zone and 'ten-foot-high demesne wall'.[61] In his *A Tour in Ireland*, Young commented that 'Mitchelstown, till his Lordship made it the place of his residence, was a den of vagabonds, thieves, rioters, and Whiteboys' (a secret organisation that took direct action against oppressive landlordism).[62] Beyond, to the north, lay the Galtee mountains; all around was an 'untamed populace ... elusive, slipping over their bogs, fluid in their arrangements, somehow uncontainable' who were necessarily constructed as a potentially violent Other that underpinned the Ascendancy's very definition of itself.[63] In short, it was a landscape of embodied violence.

In Dublin, Wollstonecraft wandered with Caroline, Lady Kingsborough through the pleasure gardens of the Rotunda (the oldest maternity hospital in Britain and Ireland, opened in 1745 as the Dublin Lying-in Hospital), listened to performances of Handel at St Werburgh's Church, attended the theatre and participated in the vice-regal ball hosted by Lord Lieutenant Camden at Dublin Castle and in fashionable masquerades (wearing her employer's black domino and a half-mask, from behind which she 'took on the Ascendancy', giving 'full scope to a satirical vein').[64] Through such encounters she would have gauged what R. F. Foster has called the more 'gamy' flavour of an Anglo-Irish caste (or 'balked' nation) that was itself 'a confusing mixture of colonialist and colonized' and which sought to reinforce its separate identity against the threat of both the Catholic Irish and the English state.[65] However, the swirling political complexities of that world remained at the time insufficiently calibrated by Wollstonecraft. That said, there was surely a nascent recognition that the inbetweenness she identified as part of her Irish experience was not only social (as has been the critical assumption) but also ethnic and ideological. One who surely recognised this, if only later when she herself came to full (and complex) political consciousness, was Margaret King, whom Wollstonecraft first encountered at Mitchelstown in 1786 as a 13-year-old 'literally speaking wild Irish'.[66] Come the Rebellion, Margaret (by then married to the second Earl Mount Cashell) would also occupy a liminal position as a member of a 'nationalist Ascendancy' who actively supported (and, in the cellars of her estate at Moore Park and in her townhouse in Dublin, actually sheltered) the Society of United Irishmen. The Society was itself a culturally, ideologically and religiously heterogeneous group whose (ill-defined) aims were not too problematically opposed to Margaret's deep sense of 'aristocratic blood honour'.[67] In this sense, Margaret was a different creature entirely from her parents and older brother, the sadistic George King ('Big George'), who during the 1798 Rebellion led the ruthless loyalist militia known as the North Corks. The corps' torture of choice, 'pitch-capping' – 'instituted in mockery of the short republican hairstyle of the [rebel] "croppies"' – involved placing on their victim's head 'a cap of heavy paper or linen filled with tar or pitch and gunpowder', then setting it alight and watching the burning tar blind the sufferer before both cap and scalp were ripped off.[68] This was the same George King who as a 15-year-old in October 1786 had failed to appear at Eton to accompany Wollstonecraft on her way to Ireland as governess.

From the centre of the Kingsboroughs' social round in Dublin five months later, Wollstonecraft wrote to her sister Everina:

> I do not like Ireland. The family pride which reigns here produces the worst effects – They are in general proud and mean ... As a nation I do not *admire* the Irish, I never before felt what it was to love my country; but now I have a value for it built on rational grounds ... I never see an English face without feeling tenderness.[69]

Her 1799 novel would give her a platform to critique and nuance that assessment.

What Wollstonecraft produces from 1797 to 1799 is a complexly autobiographical historical fiction/fictive history (and dark romance) that explores the affordances of an Irish modality of the gothic specifically in the context of the 1798 Rebellion.[70] The work constitutes an early example of the 'national tale' that questions the very *possibility* of that genre in the process of its traumatic parturition. The revisionary literary history I offer in the form of the 'miracle counterfactual' that is Wollstonecraft's 1799 novel intervenes in a received literary history that is itself constantly being revised archivally (most recently by Christina Morin) to reveal the 'divergent uses and manifestations of the literary gothic' in the period and the contribution of Irish terror-writing to other national and transnational literary traditions.[71] Bringing to light early literary responses to the turmoil of 1798, Jim Shanahan notes that

> Up to quite recently, Ina Ferris's observation that the 1798 Rebellion did not become a persistent topic in fiction until the 1820s would have been largely unquestioned. However, recent bibliographical research has revealed that just as 'histories' of the Rebellion appeared practically instantaneously ... fictional versions also began to be produced almost immediately.[72]

Wollstonecraft's 1799 novel is among the first of those early fictional engagements.

For the Anglo-Irish Wollstonecraft, the Rebellion would have been 'a persistent troubling imperative'.[73] Ina Ferris has identified as a crux of the Irish national tale the 'dynamic notion of culture as encounter', figured as intercultural contact of an 'abrasive' and always uncanny and destabilising kind.[74] (I suggest that one should regard the Irish section of *Frankenstein* itself as a truncated or inchoate 'national tale'.) In *L'Estrange; Or, The Modern Menoetius*, Wollstonecraft offers a monstrous initial staging of that narrative of mutually estranging and 'unhinging' encounter and *bouleversement* (reversal, violent upheaval) identified by Ferris. Within the counterfactual schema, we can choose to see later developers of the post-Union national tale such as Sydney Owenson and Maria Edgeworth reacting to Wollstonecraft's text by deliberately choosing *less prodigious* fictions that seek, and often achieve, the comfort of closure. Wollstonecraft's explosive – and, as we shall see, open-ended – text assists us to identify with greater sharpness the persistent anxieties in these later fictions concerning the monstrous shapes of Irish culture and politics and of Union itself (despite what Miranda Burgess has identified as their emphasis on assuaging 'allegories of the natural' and their efforts to separate Irish cultural and political nationalism).[75]

Embracing the counterfactual as a critical heuristic and accepting *L'Estrange* as an innovative development of the gothic novel and as a formative forerunner of both the Irish national tale and novelistic engagements with the Rebellion serve to focus the ways in which earlier Irish gothic fictions and later national tales constitute a body of 'agitated fiction' (Katie Trumpener's phrase at the end of a lengthy 1993 'traverse' of early-nineteenth-century novels that have been occluded by the 'singular/representative status' of Walter Scott).[76] Further, *L'Estrange* anticipates the narrative strategies that critics including Mary Jean Corbett, Ina Ferris and Colleen Booker Halverson have seen at work in those national tales. Novels such as Owenson's *The Wild Irish Girl* (1806) and Edgeworth's *Ennui* (1809) have been read as 'substitut[ing] for sectarian certainties' – Protestant, Catholic, Presbyterian – 'a more complicated approach to representation, plot, and interpretation'.[77] As the historian Marianne Elliott has argued, the form and progress of the 1798 Rebellion 'baffled' even its principal protagonists; further, Jim Shanahan has noted how early literary inscriptions of a crisis that was difficult to understand within a framework of 'basic historical integrity' – a difficulty not solely related to the lack of historical distance – tended to eschew 'grand narratives' in favour of 'subjective tales of individual ... trauma'.[78] Justifying his choice of Ireland as the location of his tale in the preface to *The Milesian Chief* (1812), Charles Maturin diagnosed the country as a place of 'extremes' created by 'the strange existing opposition of religion, politics and manners', where 'the most wild and incredible situations of romantic story are hourly passing before modern eyes'.[79] Recognising the challenges inherent in articulating such a culture and its violent symptoms, and the impossibility of essentialising Irish national 'character' and 'identity', the national tale of the early nineteenth century – and, for Terry Eagleton, the Irish novel more generally – confronts national trauma, the uncanny 'stereoscopic depth of the nation's time' and the permeability of the boundaries between history, romance, the gothic, antiquarianism and tourist literature by adopting appropriate structural and stylistic techniques.[80] These include the tousling and fracturing of the narrative line with 'heteroglossic textures', 'alternative histories' and 'the play of multiple genres' that befit the distressful political and ethnic 'entanglements' of Irish history and its 'disrupted', 'recursive' and 'abortive' course (obstetrics, again).[81]

Such strategies are also a symptom of a crisis of memory and memorialisation in relation to the events of 1798. It is one that persists to this day. The problem of memory is best described by Richard Terdiman as 'the perturbation of the link to [one's] own inheritance' – a frisson to which the counterfactual act itself gives rise.[82] In *Remembering the Year of the*

French: Irish Folk History and Social Memory, Guy Beiner conceives of the forms taken by 1798 in folk memory (as opposed to the formal discourses of history and historiography) as the product of effects and strategies of condensation, elision, telescoping, fragmentation, fusion and overlap. His concern is with the alternative histories represented by individual 'provincial constituenc[ies]', as against 'national metanarrative[s]' (which are themselves acknowledged to be partisan and partial representations). As Beiner notes, the 'multiple temporal perspectives' and condensatory-accretive energies of memory and folk history present 'cubist portrayals of the past'.[83] I contend that a counterfactual literary history *actively* pursues 'cubist' (or *mannerist*, given that movement's penchant for elongation, distortion, exaggeration and perspectival play) engagements with the past. The Irish Gothic element in Wollstonecraft's *L'Estrange* distends the Rebellion and her own experience into monstrous and surreal shapes; rejecting the authority of metanarratives, the novel invests in the voices of Beiner's 'provincial constituenc[ies]' and in the forms of troubled memory.

L'Estrange; Or, The Modern Menoetius also allows Wollstonecraft to confront, as part of her representation of wider political trauma, her own recent experience of near-fatal (male) medical intervention. We know from her *Posthumous Works*, edited by Godwin, that as well as 'a series of books for the instruction of children' (which were to include the hauntingly pared-down prompts – now staccato, now lyrical – published under the title 'Lessons' and intended as instruction for '[her] unfortunate little girl', Fanny Imlay), Wollstonecraft was from the mid-1790s planning a project entitled *Letters on the Management of Infants*, which was to include chapters on pregnancy and lying in.[84] This would have been a fascinating obstetric development of her late 1780s works, *Thoughts on the Education of Daughters* (1787) and *Original Stories from Real Life* (1788). Surviving sepsis, Wollstonecraft would have parlayed that instructional interest in the holistic care of the pregnant mother into her 1799 novel, confronting her own anxieties concerning the pathology of the gravid and postpartum female body and the terrifying contingencies of childbirth.

I argue that she would also have used the platform of fiction to confront the wider issues of the politics of childbirth at the close of the eighteenth century, the invasion of female space (in all senses) by male practitioners, and the relative authority of male and female bodies of knowledge. As Lyle Massey has shown, the later eighteenth century was marked by the professionalisation and, crucially, the pathologisation, of childbirth – the 'reformulation of childbirth as a medical rather than domestic concern'.[85]

The increasingly normative presence of forceps-wielding male physicians (calling themselves 'man-midwives' or *accoucheurs*) at even unproblematic births, the concomitant eclipsing of female midwives and their authority, together with representations of the gravid female body in the 'new genre' of the obstetrical atlas (William Smellie's and William Hunter's being the pre-eminent examples) collapsed midwifery and pathological anatomy, thereby 'wrench[ing] a semiprivate female ritual out of its homely confines and into the full light of public scrutiny and medical science'.[86] As Wollstonecraft herself remarks in her second *Vindication*: 'I am afraid the word midwife, in our dictionaries, will soon give place to *accoucheur*'.[87] (Vivien Jones valuably reminds us that 'good practice was never clearly demarcated along gender lines' and that, by the 1790s, 'enlightened practice – whether by men or women – meant ... nonintervention unless complications arose'.)[88]

Massey notes that while Smellie's *A Sett of Anatomical Tables ... and an Abridgement of the Practice of Midwifery* (1754) concentrates its gaze on birth itself, with its 'images of forceps-induced delivery, bad presentations, and other indications that require a surgeon's intervention', Hunter's *Anatomia Uteri Humani Gravidi/Anatomy of the Human Gravid Uterus* (1774) offers 'stark, brutal and fetishistically naturalistic' representations of in-utero gestational morphology 'based on dissections of many individual women who died before labour'.[89] The female body in childbed (both eroticised and empirical) and the medical male gaze trained on it, became epistemologically and aesthetically related to the body in the dissection theatre, where its structures and physiology were scrutinised and literally laid bare. To stand in an obstetric relation – opposite, and paradoxically in the way of, we remember – to the pregnant subject was now also to stand *over* her, as over an anatomical specimen. Already ambiguously located gender- and class-wise, the late-eighteenth-century man-midwife became further ontologically blurred with the anatomist and dissector. The link between the dissecting theatre and childbirth was not merely theoretical. In *A Treatise on the Epidemic Puerperal Fever of Aberdeen* (1795), Alexander Gordon had contended that puerperal sepsis was in some way 'infectious' and that, distressingly, he had himself been 'the means of carrying the infection to a great number of women'.[90] The insight gained little traction. Surgeons and anatomists, their hands unwashed, would continue to be regularly called to a birth straight from previous deliveries, from the operating theatre and, indeed, 'from the dissection of cadavers'.[91]

The uncanniness of obstetric practice is amplified by the effects of the graphic engravings produced for both Smellie and Hunter by Jan van Riemsdyk. Massey's critical ekphrasis brings home some of these:

> In an image [in Smellie's atlas] of a bad presentation … the infant's left arm and shoulder emerge from the birth canal while the rest of the body is trapped inside the uterus … The engraving, while it shows the awkwardness and danger of the position, alludes to the living, embodied presence of both infant and mother. Neither is shown dead, even though each is featured through the lens of dissection. The engraving evokes a viewpoint that is closer to an X-ray than to the anatomist's knife … Thus, although reliant on the trope of dissection, [van Riemsdyk's] images work to reanimate both the female and infant bodies.[92]

The woman who had meditated on mummies in Tønsberg would have been fascinated by these images. In van Riemsdyk's engravings for Hunter's *Anatomy of the Human Gravid Uterus*, she would have found a disturbing interpellation of the viewer as that strange hybrid, an obstetric surgeon-anatomist, positioned both enablingly opposite and investigatively above the dissected and ruthlessly truncated subject and her stillborn, but strangely still-being-born, foetus.[93] Lisa Forman Cody has emphasised how crucial a role 'matters of the body' played in the formation of eighteenth-century Britons' conception of themselves as both political subjects and cultural agents, contending that the complex traffic between life and death in such atlas images amplifies testing questions, in the context of wider 1790s debates, concerning the 'personhood' and 'rights-bearing' status of the child.[94] Such debates established midwifery – and, one might add, dissection and anatomy – as a 'political metaphor'.[95]

But as Massey notes, 'It is death itself that seems most present' in van Riemsdyk's drawings: 'pregnancy … increasingly appears to be the source of each female body's affliction and demise'.[96] Moreover, the fatal malady of childbirth is 'fully exposed only to the trained eye and hand of the male anatomist and/or clinician'.[97] In one of the preparatory red chalk drawings for Hunter's *Anatomy*, in which an acutely foreshortened perspective 'pulls the viewer down toward the woman's body', van Riemsdyk places a book in front of the dissected mother's pubis (Figure 6.2).[98] Recognising that the presence of the object bespeaks 'some equivocation about how much the image should reveal', Massey hazards that the book has been introduced 'to distance the viewer and dissipate the drawing's uncanny effects'. Surely it is otherwise: the book augments rather than dispels those effects. I highlight van Riemsdyk's drawing as a shocking material condensation and wider allegory of Wollstonecraft's late-1790s fears and

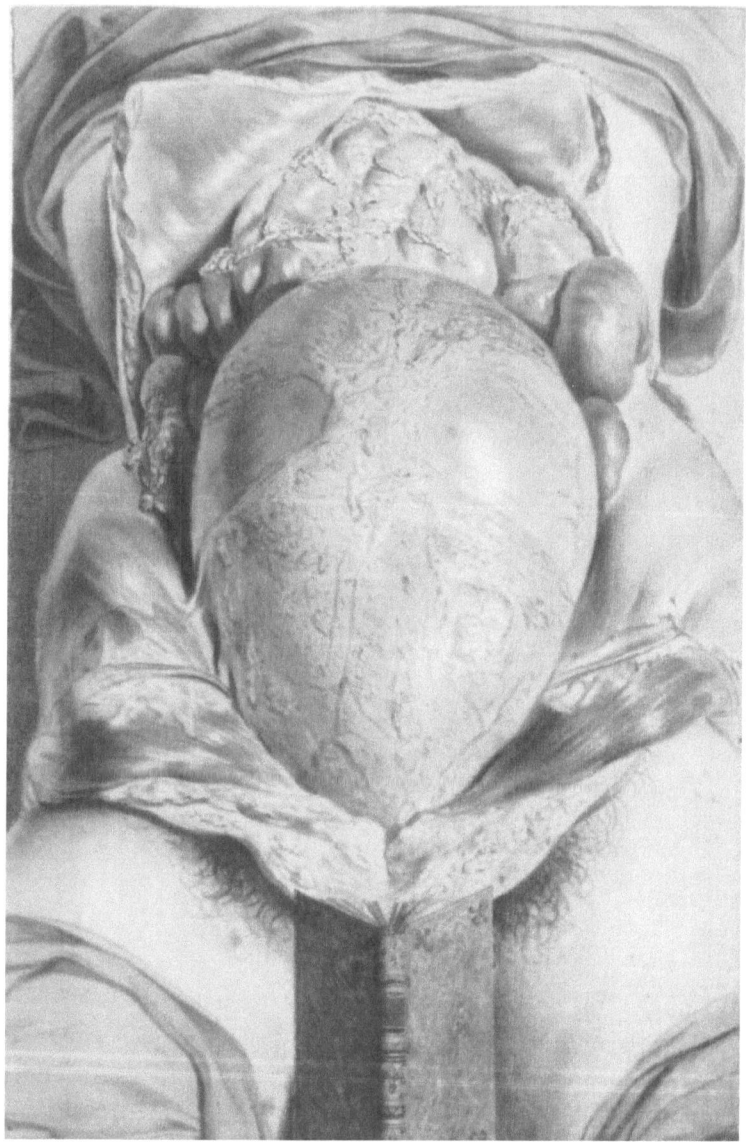

6.2 Jan van Riemsdyk, dissection of a retroverted gravid uterus (five months pregnant), red chalk on paper; preparatory drawing for William Hunter, *Anatomia Uteri Humani Gravidi/Anatomy of the Human Gravid Uterus* (1774), table XXVI, figure 1

compulsions as she turns – postpartum, 'posthumously', looking both inward through the flesh at her own story and outward to history and the wider political sphere – to give birth to *L'Estrange*.[99] I remain acutely aware of the creative and scholarly, as well as ethical, responsibilities of placing myself and the (man-)midwife-reader – by means of a van Riemsdykian foreshortening of literary history – in an obstetric relation to Wollstonecraft as she does so.

Disjecta membra

In what follows, I offer as something to be relished those moments at which the reader may find themselves unsure as to where 'facts' ends and my counterfactuals begin. Recourse to an also-to-be-relished destabilising, interruptive toggling between text and endnotes may offer orientation. I present a Wollstonecraft *rediviva* who in the writing of *L'Estrange; Or, The Modern Menoetius* draws on a range of texts, images and histories, both private and circulating. The narrative of her own life is one of these. I imagine Godwin informing her of the drift of the *Memoirs* he would have written had she not rallied in September 1797; that stillborn biography becomes a shadow-text against which Wollstonecraft crafts *L'Estrange*. I see her closely following the progress of the Irish Rebellion throughout the summer of 1798, seeking further details and word-of-mouth intelligence from Irish kin and from former acquaintances in Ireland whom she had not seen or corresponded with since the late 1780s and early 1790s, such as Margaret King and the man whom her beloved Fanny Blood had married, Hugh Skeys. One can also imagine a transatlantic correspondence on the nature of the Rebellion with Archibald Hamilton Rowan in Delaware (a member of the Society of United Irishmen whom she had known in 1794–95 in Paris, where he had fled under threat of prosecution for treason), and also with the eloquent Dublin lawyer and defender of the leaders of the United Irishmen, John Philpott Curran (who was to accompany Godwin to Dublin in 1800).

News in early 1798 of the billeting of the army 'at free quarters' among the Irish peasantry was followed, come early May, by accounts of the more robust measures adopted by the Dublin Castle 'junto', by the ruthless new commander of the army, Lieutenant-General Gerard Lake, and by yeomanry and militia officers to strangle an incipient insurrection whose Dublin leadership and county-by-county organisation were at best ragged.[100] The prevailing atmosphere was one of suspicion and terror. There was grand judicial theatre, too, in which Wollstonecraft had something of a stake. Her interest would have been piqued by the trial, on 18 May 1798, of Lord Kingsborough, now the Earl of Kingston – her erstwhile employer at Mitchelstown – for the murder of his wife's kinsman, Henry Gerald Fitzgerald, who had seduced the Earl's daughter, Mary (Wollstonecraft's pupil at Mitchelstown). Certain English commentators were to ascribe the sins of the daughter very firmly to her governess; inquiring in the *Gentleman's Magazine* whether the compromised Anglo-Irish family in question was indeed the household in which Wollstonecraft had been employed, a 'lady correspondent' wrote: 'is not every degree of indiscretion, and profligacy, the natural consequence of such principles as Mrs G.[odwin] maintained in speculation, and exhibited in her own conduct?'[101] My Wollstonecraft lives, of course, to read these words and respond to its narrative of wicked entailment.

Though she could not have known that the National Directory of the United Irishmen, under the leadership of Lord Edward Fitzgerald (himself, for safety's sake, a serial cross-dresser, 'now a doctor, now a woman, and now a poor drover complete with sheep'),[102] had intended to assassinate the viceroy, his cabinet and the Irish lords at her erstwhile employer's trial, Wollstonecraft would have heard of Lord Edward's arrest the next day, and of the reinforcing of Dublin, whose citizens, as Thomas Pakenham notes, expected a rebel attack at any moment: 'In the almost total darkness, people reported shadowy figures assembling in St Michan's graveyard, where pikes in plenty were known to be buried'.[103] She would have noted 25 May as the day the Rebellion began. All through that hot summer, she would have read and heard 'atrocity stories' spiralling out from the early rebel attacks on Clare, Prosperous and Naas; the barbaric burning by rogue rebels of around 200 men, women and children in a barn at Scullabogue on 5 June; the piking of loyalist prisoners on the bridge at Wexford; and the no less horrific outrages by regular troops, rogue elements of 'the Orange Bogey', the croppy-hunting True Blues and the infamous rebel-tracker, Hunter Gowan and his ruthless yeomanry corps (the 'Black Mob'). She would have consumed accounts of the horrific battles at New Ross on 5 June, at Arklow on 9 June (where the insurgents advanced even to the muzzles of the army's cannon), and on 21 June at the rebel camp on Vinegar Hill, County Wexford, where the government sealed its victory.[104] The Rebellion's final acts were played out on 8 September when a French force led by General Humbert surrendered at Ballinamuck, and Wolfe Tone was taken after the naval battle of Tory Island on 12 October. 'I find then I am but a bad anatomist', Tone is reputed to have said, having severed his windpipe rather than his jugular with a penknife while awaiting execution.[105]

Wollstonecraft would also have sought out the early loyalist accounts and 'histories' of the Rebellion that began appearing in 1798. These ranged from sectarian overviews such as the anonymous *Concise History of the Rebellion in Ireland* (1798) and digests of croppy brutalities, inspired by 'the spirit of Popery, as ravenous as the grave', such as Richard Musgrave's *A Concise Account of the Material Events and Atrocities ... in the Present Rebellion* (1799) to such personal partisan accounts as *A Narrative of the Sufferings and Escape of Charles Jackson, Late Resident at Wexford* (1798), which claimed to offer eyewitness testimony of rebel atrocities (and which offered a eulogy of 'Big George' as a leader beloved of his men and paternalistic landlord at Mitchelstown).[106] Wollstonecraft would have been all too aware that such publications offered an exclusively male perspective on the Rebellion. Although she could not have had access to testimonies by women (which have only recently been retrieved by historians from the archive), the very nature of her project would have compelled her to imagine what Susan B. Egenolf has termed female 'interior accounts of the rebellion' that placed women firmly in 'the midst of the fight' across the 'public and private spaces' of the rising.[107] As Union beckoned in 1799, Wollstonecraft would also have consulted pamphlets on the Union debate, among which was an intervention by Margaret Mount Cashell – *A Few Words in Favour of Ireland* (1799). In this work, the girl whose free-thinking (if still class-bound) mind Wollstonecraft had helped form at Mitchelstown made a case against an '"unnatural" Union' and against Irish and English 'ministerial innovation'; she also anatomised the causes of a conflict that had resulted in 'ravaged plains', 'deserted houses', 'ruined villages' and a 'starved, reproachful' populace.[108]

As one might expect, *L'Estrange* gathers to itself, and inflects in new Hiberno-Gothic contexts, the portfolio of Wollstonecraft's previous works, published and in manuscript, ranging from her contributions to educational theory and the Revolution Controversy to her analysis of the progress of the French Revolution and her previous experiments in fiction. Further, by dint of its being a 'miracle counterfactual', what the novel also annexes are some of the paradigmatic formulations and set-pieces of the text it displaces from literary history (only to allow it to return, signifying differently): her dead infant daughter's *Frankenstein*.

Visual texts inform the representations of Wollstonecraft's autobiographical historical fiction. For the sections of *L'Estrange* located in Dublin, Wollstonecraft, as well as calling up her own memories, would

Counterfactual Romanticism

have plotted a gothic psychogeography for her characters and readers with the aid of a map – the *Modern Plan of the City and Environs of Dublin* produced at the height of the Rebellion in June 1798 by the bookseller and stationer William Wilson, engraved by Benjamin Baker and dedicated to Frances, Countess Camden, the wife of the Dublin Viceroy.[109] She would have used the map, with its striking green and pink wash, to establish in her fiction the relational coordinates of the Dublin Lying-in Hospital and Rotunda;[110] the Royal College of Surgeons in Ireland with its school of anatomy and surgery behind Mercer's Hospital; the shadowy meeting places of the United Irishmen's Dublin Directory in the narrow streets of Usher's Island, Usher's Quay and the Liberties (the weavers' ghetto); Dublin Castle (with its 'battered statue of Justice' whose scales, Pakenham reminds us, 'tilted when it rained'); and mummy- (and pike-) filled St Michan's Church.[111]

Following her near-fatal birth experience in 1797, two other images haunt Wollstonecraft's imagination – and, explicitly, that of her protagonist – in *L'Estrange*. The first is Isaac Cruikshank's illustration for the frontispiece of Samuel William Fores' *Man-Midwifery Dissected; Or, The Obstetric Family-Instructor*, published in 1793 (Figure 6.3) – an obstetric polemic that defended 'the *regular* practice of midwifery' as properly a female profession and attacked the 'new-fangled obstetric butchery' practised by prurient and voyeuristic men-midwives when called to attend unproblematic births.[112] Cruikshank's image, entitled *A Man-Mid-Wife*, depicts 'the ambiguous demi-masculine and demi-feminine' figure of the *accoucheur* as a disturbingly (if also comically) composite being occupying domestic-clinical space; the hybrid is described below the engraving as a 'Monster' and a 'newly discover'd animal, not known in Buffon's time'.[113] The second image also depicts monstrous beings; here we grapple again with the paradox of the counterfactual. Just as Mary Shelley used *The Nightmare* by the painter with whom her mother had been infatuated in 1790–92 as a template for her representation of the murder of Elizabeth Lavenza on her wedding night in *Frankenstein*, so her mother, wresting that possibility from her daughter, deploys Henry Fuseli's painting, *Theodore Meets in the Wood the Spectre of His Ancestor Guido Cavalcanti* (*c.*1783), to structure a key scene in *L'Estrange* (Figure 6.4).[114] The image shows Cavalcanti on a *Nightmare*-like steed setting his hell-hounds on the fleeing naked lover who had spurned him. Fuseli's source is Boccaccio's *Decameron* via Dryden's translation, 'Theodore and Honoria' (1700), in which the pursued female is doomed to repeat a hideous cycle of being caught,

Counterfactual obstetrics

eviscerated through her side and back as by an act of hellish surgery, and reanimated, only to begin her flight again.[115]

The painting's centre ground is a congeries – a veritable dissecting table – of human, canine and equine limbs, the musculature of Theodore's left leg rendered in the mannerist anatomical style so characteristic of Fuseli. The artist's representation of the female-hunting male would

6.3 Isaac Cruikshank, *A Man-Mid-Wife*, frontispiece to John Blunt [Samuel William Fores], *Man-midwifery Dissected; Or, The Obstetric Family Instructor, for the Use of Married Couples and Single Adults of Both Sexes*

6.4 Henry Fuseli, *Theodore Meets in the Wood the Spectre of His Ancestor Guido Cavalcanti* (*c.*1783), oil on canvas, 276 cm × 317 cm

have reminded Wollstonecraft of the painting of the rape of Proserpina that adorned the ceiling of the hall in Mitchelstown; she would also have recognised in Fuseli's image a retroverted vision of her own amorous pursuit of the artist, a portrait of her own obstetric experience in the female figure whose organs are drawn out of her body and who then suffers revivification, and an archetype of the mounted croppy-hunter of the 1798 Rebellion, Hunter Gowan.

The texts cited here are tools of a critical counterfactual imagination that reveals forms of late-1790s culture that are not, I argue, arbitrarily summoned in order unthinkingly to saturate the blank canvas opened up by the counterfactual of Wollstonecraft's survival and the 'miracle counterfactual' of her 1799 novel. While *L'Estrange; Or, the Modern Menoetius* is, to be sure, a performance of the critical and creative proclivities of the present writer (who creates the taste by which a reanimated Wollstonecraft might be enjoyed/estranged), those inclinations have necessarily been formed by Wollstonecraft herself. I imagine *L'Estrange* as a novel in which the portfolio of texts cited is deployed as part of a multi-genre bricolage that practises on Irish culture the techniques of the dissection theatre in its creation of a monstrous national tale that negotiates the hybrid allegiances of the 1798 Rebellion.

Having contextualised the Irish turn in Wollstonecraft's career, I conclude with a creative-critical inhabitation of the novel she published on the eve of Union. What I offer is an enactment through which the status of *L'Estrange* as both *fin-de-siècle* summative performance and uncanny displacer of *Frankenstein* can be communicated. I set out resolutely to resist parody, conflating plot profile (to be read in the light of the arguments I have offered) and textual ventriloquisation (referenced so as to highlight the layered textuality and historicity of my project).

L'Estranging Frankenstein

Not *Frankenstein; Or, The Modern Prometheus*, then, but *L'Estrange; Or, The Modern Menoetius. An Irish Tale, by the author of A Vindication of the Rights of Woman.* The title of Wollstonecraft's novel and the epitexts the reader must negotiate before gaining access to the tale itself are all ideologically freighted and are an index of the distressful hybridity that is the author's principal theme. 'L'Estrange': a French (Norman) name that trumpets its otherness (the stranger, the newcomer); 'Menoetius': Prometheus's Titan brother, god of 'doomed might' and rash action – but here, it seems, a contemporary incarnation of that figure. 'An Irish Tale', which introduces a third cultural term (and mythos), is ironically insouciant, suggesting a native folk tale for touristic appetites. Immediately following this is an epigraph from the novel that would be published simultaneously in 1799 – Godwin's *St Leon* (which Godwin was to describe as 'a much greater favourite everywhere in Ireland than Caleb Williams').[116] The quoted passage – on the personhood of the child – invests *L'Estrange* not with the accumulated authority of literary history and its great Nobodaddies (as is the effect of the quotation from *Paradise Lost* that stands as epigraph to *Frankenstein*) but rather with the living voice of a partner who, like Wollstonecraft, is grieving for his dead child:

> [Children] are not puppets, moved with wires, and to be played on at will. Almost from the hour of their birth, they have a will of their own, to be consulted and negociated [*sic*] with. We may say to them, as Adam to the general mother of mankind, But now, thou wert flesh of my flesh, and

bone of my bone; and, even now, thou standest before me ... a living being, to be regarded with attention and deference, to be courted, not compelled ... It is because thou art thus formed that I love thee ... I would negociate for your affections and confidence, and not be loved by you, but in proportion as I shall have done something to deserve it.[117]

As noted, Wollstonecraft dedicates the novel to her former pupil, pointedly displaying the latter's overdetermined name to bring home to the (complicit) dedicatee the entailments (baggage) of her accumulated history and her multiple personal and dynastic identities. In the same breath, Wollstonecraft reveals her to be the author of the recent anti-Union pamphlet:

TO MARGARET KING MOORE, LADY MOUNT CASHELL,
AUTHOR OF *A FEW WORDS IN FAVOUR OF IRELAND*,
THESE VOLUMES ARE INSCRIBED
BY THE AUTHOR
AS ADMIRER, NOT INSTRUCTOR

The tale then begins. It is generically and narratologically ambitious, conflating and repurposing received genres and coordinating sectional shifts between third- and multiple first-person narrators so as to generate competing representations of the same event.

Dublin, May 1798. William Tone L'Estrange – celebrated anatomist, surgeon and man-midwife, 28 – introduces himself (in harrowing retrospect) as a member of the recently founded Royal College of Surgeons in Ireland.[118] He is a man of ambition and innovation, engaged to a 'marriageable miss', the youngest daughter of a landed Ascendancy family whose paterfamilias is a vocal defender in the Irish Parliament of Protestant hegemony and the rights of his class and ethnicity in the face of what he sees as the imminent rebel threat.[119] L'Estrange's Catholic family has harboured grievances against a string of tyrannous landlords and the yeomanry in his native County Cork; he espouses deep nationalist sympathies and is drawn into the Society of United Irishmen. As a member of the new Directory that meets in the narrow streets of Usher's Quay and the Liberties, he recognises that the rebels' plans, on the eve of the Rising, are in disarray. There is little coordination between the Dublin Directory and county organisations, which are riven by spies.

L'Estrange inhabits an already traumatic, paradoxical world. As a noted obstetric expert, called to attend births at the Dublin Lying-in Hospital and also increasingly in demand as a forceps-armed *accoucheur* by wealthy middle-class, gentry and aristocratic women, his hands are each day quick with new life. They are also bloody with the dissevered flesh of the dissection table at the Royal College of Surgeons' schools of anatomy and surgery. As pikes are sharpened across Dublin and in the soon-to-be-declared Republic of Wexford, as the rebels assemble in the suburbs of Rathfarnham and Dalkey and at Tallaght and Rathcoole, and as the mail-coaches are burned in Dublin so that their non-arrival in the county towns will signal the start of the Rising, L'Estrange, his judgement clouded by his passionate hatred of things as they are, engages in two acts of deathly obstetric conception.[120] These acts of 'creation' are performed in the service of the Rebellion, which breaks out on 25 May 1798 with cries of *Erin go Bragh* (Ireland for Ever) and the mottos 'Attuned to Liberty' and 'It is New Strung and Shall be Heard', which, along with the Irish harp, figured on the rebels' green banners.[121]

From the *disjecta membra* of the dissection theatre and Dublin's slaughter houses, L'Estrange creates a male creature *and* a gravid female, both of whom are constructed as weapons – war engines – of the Rebellion, intended to man the cannon and wreak havoc on the British regulars, the garrison's militias and the yeomanry.[122] A promethean compulsion underlies his menoetian rashness: as an obstetrician, he wishes to deliver women from the pain and dangers of childbirth, and thus secretly experiments with inflected anatomies of both foetus and maternal uterus. Three beings are therefore assembled, given life, and – fatally – rejected as the Rebellion breaks out and the property-burning, half-hanging on portable gallows and flogging on mobile triangles begin.[123] 'Hell stalks abroad.'[124]

The narrative is now given, first to Father John Curran, one of the Wexford rebel commanders (who fights in his priestly robes), and then to a captain of the Dublin militia, Bagenal Masterson, both childhood friends of L'Estrange. Each offers a partisan version of the battles of early June 1798. The male creature – a sensationally represented but ultimately tangential presence in the fiction – escapes from his confinement behind Mercer Street and immediately joins the Rebels in Wexford. Sporting a green cockade and decorating himself with feathers and tippets – 'parts of the apparel of ladies, found in the houses [the rebels] had plundered'[125] – he participates with brutal force in the ultimately abortive rebel attack on New Ross, whose aftermath Father Curran and Captain Masterson describe in terms that anticipate the picture offered by James Alexander in *Some Account of the First Apparent Symptoms of the Late Rebellion in the County of Kildare* (1800):

> The rebel carcases lay in the streets unburied for three or four days, some perforated over and over with musquet [sic] balls, or the bayonet; some hacked with swords, some mangled and torn with grape shot, and still worse with pigs; some of which I have seen eating the brains out of cloven sculls and knawing [sic] the flesh about the raw wounds.[126]

In Captain Masterson's narrative, the male creature is also the prime actor in the rebel outrage at Scullabogue, piking those who seek to escape from the barn as the fire is lit. Father Curran's account of the same event makes no mention of the creature.

The eight-months-pregnant female then takes up the telling. We hear her distinctive voice. She recounts her own 'birth' and rejection, together with her subsequent observations (through an oculus above L'Estrange's dissecting table) of the surgeon-obstetrician's work. She offers a profile of her own education based on the texts she explored in L'Estrange's library, which includes the atlases by Smellie and Hunter (whose illustrations both fascinate and distress her) and Fores' *Man-midwifery Dissected*, in which she seeks to make sense of Cruikshank's representation of the 'monster' man-midwife. Other objects of fascination are the 'birthing phantoms', 'mother machines' and 'foetal mannequins' – mechanical apparatuses and puppets – used by L'Estrange (pioneered by Madame du Coudray in France, and used by William Smellie) to train (men-) midwives (Figure 6.5). Composed 'of real Bones, mounted and covered with artificial Ligaments, Muscles and Cuticle, to give them the true Motion, Shape and Beauty of natural Bodies', these uncanny objects simulate 'the contraction of both the internal and external os [and] the generation of waters in parturition' with such exactness that 'hardly any difference is to be noticed between these and those in natural women'.[127] Another phantom comprises a belly made of leather, filled with red-brown beer and stopped by a cork, from which L'Estrange delivers now a 'wax-doll', now 'a real foetus, often in a state of putridity'.[128] It is through these objects that the female becomes hypersensitised to the economy of her own gravid body and to the exercise of male authority in the birthing scenes she views, both in the theatre of the Royal College of Surgeons and in well-to-do private dwellings across Dublin, to which she follows her creator. Each day, she feels the child inside her becoming more active, more insistent.

Having come to such explicit and distressful knowledge, she recounts multiple appeals to L'Estrange to succour her, each of which has failed. She adopts for her own newborn, hybrid self the cry of rebel Ireland

Counterfactual obstetrics

6.5 Training mannequins ('birthing phantoms') of the kind used by Angélique Marguerite le Boursier du Coudray (*c.*1712–94) in France and, in England, by William Smellie

– *I am new strung and shall be heard!* – but still is shunned. In a section that takes travel literature into monstrous new terrain, Wollstonecraft has her recount how she dragged her increasingly massive gravid frame south through Wicklow and Wexford, through Waterford to Cork (and Mitchelstown), up over the Galtees through Queen's County up as far as Ulster, the location of the (Presbyterian) birth of the Society of United Irishmen. Thus Wollstonecraft's novel maps a ravaged Ireland in detail, layering in oral and folk material and unsettling and parodying the antiquarian tours and topographical literature of the day. Finding at New Ross, Wexford, the cannon-blasted corpse of her male twin (now rendered *disjecta membra* again), and in Ballynahinch 'the bodies of two beautiful women, fantastically dressed in green silk, who had carried the rebel standards' and who had been called 'the Goddess of Liberty and the Goddess of Reason … apparently the town prostitutes', she keens over them.[129]

Wollstonecraft's focus is on the female creature's responses to the violent, ideologically fragmented world into which she is born (Wolfe Tone famously referred – in an anatomico-political phrase – to Ireland's 'intestine divisions') and on her struggle to understand the cross-currents and allegiances that made the Rebellion no easily defined struggle between a Catholic nationalist peasantry and Anglo-Irish hegemony.[130] Confused by recursive identities, she finds herself in the fray on both the loyalist and the rebel sides. She recalls yelling anti-rebel songs ('We'll fight for our country, our King and his crown, / And make all the traitors and croppies lie down. / Down, down, croppies lie down') and donning a monstrously particoloured uniform that mixes the 'scarlet ... with black facing, silver epaulettes, yellow helmets and white buttons' of the Mitchelstown (Volunteer) Light Dragoons with the blue and silver lace of the notoriously brutal Welsh fencible regiment, the Ancient Britons'.[131] She then recounts how she tore that loyalist soldier-jester's uniform off her body, clothed herself in simple rebel garb, placed a scapular with a religious text around her neck, and repeated obsessively the United Irish catechism with its message of political parturition:

What have you got in your hand?
A green bough.
Where did it first grow?
In America.
Where did it bud?
In France.
Where are you going to plant it?
In the crown of Great Britain.[132]

Wollstonecraft makes it plain that the creature is terrified of the future into which her child will be born and is tortured by fear of the impending birth itself. She plans to manage it herself, but is filled with horror by graphic memories of the problematic births at which she has seen *accoucheur*-L'Estrange displace frustrated midwives, and by the postpartum complications she has also witnessed (and indeed studied in such works as Smellie's *Treatise on the Theory and Practice of Midwifery*, in which she has read of the 'noose' of the 'navel-string' and 'mortified inclosure' of the womb).[133] Fear, in turn, enrages her.

The narrative now reverts to L'Estrange, who tells how his creation, loping south through smoking countryside to Dublin, sought him out. In a scene in the dim-lit, mummy-packed crypt of St Michan's, she demands that he preside as man-midwife at the hour of her child's birth – demands that he *stand opposite* her. She vows that if L'Estrange again refuses to perform his duty as both creator and obstetrician, she will murder the leaders of the Rebellion (in whose success L'Estrange is still invested) one by one. She also threatens L'Estrange himself, promising to be present, murderously, at his wedding night. At this point Wollstonecraft redeploys a line from her own Mitchelstown-inspired *Original Stories*, in which her mentor-figure, Mrs Mason (a name that was later to be adopted by Margaret Mount Cashell as an authorial nom-de-plume), addresses her young charges: 'I am stronger than you – yet I do not kill you.'[134] L'Estrange consents to the creature's wishes. What are displaced and erased in this scene – rendered second-hand, parodic and vampiric – are *entailed* scenes in *Frankenstein*. The confrontation between Victor and the creature on the Mer de Glace in particular now becomes stagy, an artificial straining for the sublime in the light of Wollstonecraft's Hibernian prototype.

L'Estrange, however, renegues on his promise. '[H]unted form hole to hole' as if she were an 'infected beast' by a Hunter Gowan-like figure (whose series of ambushes are mediated by Wollstonecraft through the lens of Fuseli's painting), the creature finally confronts her creator-*accoucheur* on the west coast.[135] L'Estrange's own rashness and anger are utterly spent; he is incapable of responsibly standing opposite anyone. Wollstonecraft leaves the reader with the image of the female creature – her pregnancy coming to full term as Cornwallis is appointed Lord Lieutenant, as the rebels are defeated at Vinegar Hill, as the French land in Killala Bay and are eventually defeated, and as L'Estrange's namesake, Wolfe Tone, botches the slitting of his own throat – sloping off to the great Bogs of Allen to await her time. As she goes, she discards all the medical tomes she has taken from L'Estrange's library save for a publication entitled *Letters on the Management of Infants* and *Advice to Young Mothers on the Physical Education of Children, by a Grandmother*.[136] She is followed by a group of similarly damaged, displaced, bereaved and pariah female victims of the Rebellion – 'the *out-laws* of the world' (Wollstonecraft deploys the phrase she had first used in *The Wrongs of Woman*) whom she has assembled in the interim as companions and midwives.[137]

In a brief coda, located a year on in Dublin on the eve of Union, a difficult birth attended by a recovering L'Estrange is interrupted by a magistrate with troops in tow. The man-midwife delivers the child successfully, if with shaking hands. He lays down his forceps. He is immediately arrested and becomes a capital prisoner on the testimony provided by a manuscript, penned by the creature, who offers a fragmentary, exploratory, confused but at the same time eloquent account of her life. To L'Estrange's horror, it concludes with clear evidence of what had occurred in the Bogs of Allen. Here, Wollstonecraft gives to the female creature – now a mother – text from the 'Lessons' she had herself drafted for her first and only surviving daughter. It is a pregnantly distilled articulation of a mother's traumatic relation to her own body and to a violent world:

> Hide your face. Wipe your nose. Wash your hands. Dirty hands … You were seven months without teeth, always sucking. But after you got one, you began to gnaw a crust of bread. It was not long before another came pop. At ten months you had four pretty white teeth, and you used to bite me. Poor mamma! … you hurt me very much.[138]

Afterbirth

Thus Wollstonecraft's *L'Estrange* comes, pop – or rather groaning and keening – into the world and into literary history, a newborn and an antecedent text, to gnaw, bite and hurt. I would wish its readers to stand in a fully obstetric relation to it – a position from which one should both ease and balk its passage into the world. My counterfactual experiment results in what may be viewed as a 'filthy mass' (to cite *Frankenstein*).[139] It is brought to birth, however, by a male critic-*accoucheur* who strives for self-awareness concerning his gender and historical position vis-à-vis Wollstonecraft (and the academy) and whose aim is to disturb the epistemological pieties of literary history, renew our bond and covenant with Wollstonecraft through innovative forms of creative-critical historicist practice, and, ultimately, render *Frankenstein* itself first faux and counterfeit – then animated anew.

Notes

1. Lyndall Gordon, *Vindication: A Life of Mary Wollstonecraft* (London: Virago, 2006), p. 359. Clarke and Wollstonecraft shared a publisher: Joseph Johnson.
2. For the aetiology and pathogenesis of puerperal sepsis, see Nithiya Palaniappan, Maria Menezes and Penny Wilson, 'Group A Streptococcal Puerperal Sepsis: Management and Prevention', *The Obstetrician & Gynaecologist*, 14:1 (2012), 9–16; http://onlinelibrary.wiley.com/doi/10.1111/j.1744-4667.2011.00082.x/full (accessed 25 May 2017).
3. See Gordon, *Vindication*, pp. 358–9.
4. Karen Hellekson, *The Alternate History: Refiguring Historical Time* (Kent, OH: The Kent State University Press, 2001), p. 5.
5. Gordon, *Vindication*, p. 361.
6. Richard Ned Lebow, 'What's So Different About A Counterfactual?',

World Politics, 52:4 (July 2000), 550, 566, 569; and see Philip E. Tetlock and Aaron Belkin, 'Counterfactual Thought Experiments', in Tetlock and Belkin (eds), *Counterfactual Thought Experiments in World Politics: Logical, Methodological, and Psychological Perspectives* (Princeton, NJ: Princeton University Press, 1996), pp. 7, 17–18.

7 Mary Jacobus, *First Things: The Maternal Imaginary in Literature, Art, and Psychoanalysis* (New York: Routledge, 1995), p. 78.
8 Gary Saul Morson, 'Sideshadowing and Tempics', *New Literary History*, 29:4 (Autumn 1998), 602.
9 *Ibid.*
10 Lebow, 'What's So Different About A Counterfactual?', 564.
11 Jacobus, *First Things*, p. 80.
12 Janet Todd and Marilyn Butler (eds), *The Works of Mary Wollstonecraft*, 7 vols (London: William Pickering, 1989), I, p. 154. For the same figure (motivated by the Burke-prompted debate concerning the political relationship between the living and the dead), see also Thomas Paine, *Agrarian Justice, Opposed to Agrarian Law* (London: T. Williams, 1797), p. 11.
13 Vivien Jones, 'The Death of Mary Wollstonecraft', *Journal for Eighteenth-Century Studies*, 20:2 (September 1997), 192; Jacobus, *First Things*, pp. 79–80.
14 Julie A. Carson, *England's First Family of Writers: Mary Wollstonecraft, William Godwin, Mary Shelley* (Baltimore, MD: Johns Hopkins University Press, 2007), p. 10.
15 See Gordon, *Vindication*, pp. 28, 251, 358. Godwin recorded the formulation in *Memoirs of the Author of A Vindication of the Rights of Woman* (London: Joseph Johnson, 1798), p. 28.
16 Jacobus, *First Things*, p. 80.
17 Godwin, *Memoirs*, p. 3 (the second edition substitutes 'sympathy' for 'attachment'); Janet Todd, *Gender, Art and Death* (Cambridge: Polity Press, 1993), p. 116; Susan Wolfson, 'Mary Wollstonecraft and the Poets', in Claudia L. Johnson (ed.), *The Cambridge Companion to Mary Wollstonecraft* (Cambridge: Cambridge University Press, 2002), p. 163.
18 Mark Salber Phillips, *On Historical Distance* (New Haven, CT: Yale University Press, 2013), p. 231; Catherine Gallagher, 'Undoing', in Karen Newman, Jay Clayton and Marianne Hirsch (eds), *Time and the Literary* (New York: Routledge, 2002), p. 11.
19 Jones, 'The Death of Mary Wollstonecraft', 187, 204.
20 See Claudia L. Johnson, 'Mary Wollstonecraft: Styles of Radical Maternity', in Susan C. Greenfield and Carol Barash (eds), *Inventing Maternity: Politics, Science and Literature, 1650–1865* (Lexington, KT:

The University Press of Kentucky, 1999), pp. 160–2; Ralph M. Wardle (ed.), *Collected Letters of Mary Wollstonecraft* (Ithaca, NY: Cornell University Press, 1979), p. 255.

21 Mary Wollstonecraft, *Mary and The Wrongs of Woman*, ed. Gary Kelly (Oxford: Oxford University Press, 2007), p. xxx.

22 See Godwin's notes and 'Advertisement': Todd and Butler (eds), *The Works*, I, pp. 142, 163, 171.

23 Gordon, *Vindication*, p. 294.

24 Jacobus, *First Things*, p. 75.

25 See Julia V. Douthwaite, *The Frankenstein of 1790 and Other Lost Chapters from Revolutionary France* (Chicago: University of Chicago Press, 2012), pp. 5, 59–97.

26 Jacobus, *First Things*, p. 70.

27 Wardle (ed.), *Collected Letters*, p. 164. Gordon suggests that 'An abundance of wild flowers in the vale of Kvistrum [in the summer of 1795] made [Wollstonecraft] reflect that Sweden had been the right country to initiate the study of botany. Linnaeus's system of binomial classification according to genera and species was the source of the "genus" terms of her own self-making' (*Vindication*, p. 263).

28 Mary Shelley, *Frankenstein*, ed. Marilyn Butler (Oxford: Oxford University Press, 2008), p. 36.

29 Wardle (ed.), *Collected Letters*, p. 310.

30 Todd and Butler (eds), *The Works*, VI, pp. 278–9.

31 Quoted in Gordon, *Vindication*, pp. 304–5.

32 *Ibid.*, p. 100.

33 Miranda Seymour, *Mary Shelley* (London: John Murray, 2000), series of plates between pages 176 and 177.

34 Wardle (ed.), *Collected Letters*, p. 317.

35 See Carolyn Williams, '"Inhumanly Brought Back to Life and Misery": Mary Wollstonecraft, *Frankenstein*, and the Royal Humane Society', *Women's Writing*, 8:2 (2001), 213–33.

36 *Ibid.*, 227.

37 Todd, *Gender, Art and Death*, p. 115.

38 Jones, 'The Death of Mary Wollstonecraft', 190.

39 *Ibid.*

40 See Andrew McInnes, *Wollstonecraft's Ghost: The Fate of the Female Philosopher in the Romantic Period* (New York: Routledge, 2016); the same author's 'Wollstonecraft's Legion: Feminism in Crisis, 1799', *Women's Writing*, 20:4 (November 2013), 479–95; and Devoney Looser, 'Mary Wollstonecraft, "Ithuriel" and the Rise of the Feminist Author-Ghost', *Tulsa Studies in Women's Literature*, 35:1 (Spring 2016), 59.

41 See Looser, 'Mary Wollstonecraft', 56–91. 'I am a mere animal', Wollstonecraft declared to Joseph Johnson in 1792 in the wake of Henry Fuseli's rejection of her proposed *ménage à trois*; Wardle (ed.), *Collected Letters*, p. 220.
42 See Looser, 'Mary Wollstonecraft', 59; Virginia Woolf, 'Mary Wollstonecraft', in Andrew McNeillie (ed.), *The Common Reader, Second Series* (London: Vintage, 2003), p. 163.
43 Gordon, *Vindication*, p. 446.
44 Charlotte Gordon, *Romantic Outlaws: The Extraordinary Lives of Mary Wollstonecraft and Mary Shelley* (London: Hutchinson, 2015).
45 Looser, 'Mary Wollstonecraft', 3.
46 For an account of the debate, see my 'Introduction: Reflection on an Orthodoxy', in Damian Walford Davies (ed.), *Romanticism, History, Historicism: Essay on an Orthodoxy* (New York: Routledge, 2009), pp. 4–7.
47 Phillips, *On Historical Distance*, pp. 96, 232.
48 Mark Philp et al. (eds), *Political and Philosophical Writings of William Godwin*, 7 vols (London: William Pickering, 1993), V, pp. 297, 301.
49 Mark Salber Phillips, *Society and Sentiment: Genres of Historical Writing in Britain, 1740–1820* (Princeton, NJ: Princeton University Press, 2000), p. 120.
50 Jon Klancher, 'Godwin and the Republican Romance', in Marshall Brown (ed.), *Eighteenth-century Literary History: An MLQ Reader* (Durham, NC: Duke University Press, 1999), p. 78; and see Lloyd S. Kramer, 'Literature, Criticism, and Historical Imagination: The Literary Challenge of Hayden White and Dominick LaCapra', in Lynn Hunt (ed.), *The New Cultural History* (Berkeley, CA: University of California Press, 1989), pp. 101, 102.
51 Porscha Fermanis and John Regan (eds), *Rethinking British Romantic History, 1770–1845* (Oxford: Oxford University Press, 2014), pp. 4, 1.
52 See Gary Handwerk, 'History, Trauma, and the Limits of the Liberal Imagination: William Godwin's Historical Fiction', in Tilottama Rajan and Julia M. Wright (eds), *Romanticism, History, and the Possibilities of Genre* (Cambridge: Cambridge University Press, 1998), pp. 73, 68.
53 Kramer, 'Literature, Criticism, and Historical Imagination', p. 101.
54 For the role played by Ireland and the 1798 Rebellion in 'the political geography of Gothic' in Mary Shelley's novel, see Fred V. Randel, 'The Political Geography of Horror in Mary Shelley's *Frankenstein*', *ELH*, 70:2 (Summer 2003), 482–5.
55 William Godwin, *St Leon: A Tale of the Sixteenth Century*, 4 vols (London: G. G. and J. Robinson, 1799), IV, p. 26. The novel has

recently been read as a 'fantasy of immortal life, divorced from the management of children'; see Cathy Collett, 'Every Child Left Behind: *St Leon* and William Godwin's Immortal Future', *European Romantic Review*, 25:3 (May 2014), 332.

56 Carson, *England's First Family of Writers*, p. 223. For Margaret King, see Edward C. McAleer, *The Sensitive Plant: A Life of Lady Mount Cashell* (Chapel Hill, NC: University of North Carolina Press, 1958); Janet Todd, *Rebel Daughters: Ireland in Conflict, 1798* (London: Viking, 2003); Elizabeth Campbell Denlinger, *Before Victoria: Extraordinary Women of the British Romantic Era* (New York: The New York Public Library/Columbia University Press, 2005), pp. 44–9; and Emma Garman, 'A Liberated Woman: The Story of Margaret King', https://longreads.com/2016/05/24/a-liberated-woman-the-story-of-margaret-king/ (accessed 5 June 2017).

57 Todd and Butler (eds), *The Works*, I, p. 5.

58 Shelley, *Frankenstein*, p. 105; Banim quoted in Ina Ferris, *The Romantic National Tale and the Question of Ireland* (Cambridge: Cambridge University Press, 2002), p. 14. As Ferris notes (p. 14), 'The term "Anglo-Irish" ... seems to have taken hold in the decades immediately after Union' (that is, after 1800–1); previously, 'terms like "English-Irish" or "Anglo-Hibernian" or, simply, "Irish" were more common'.

59 Janet Todd, 'Ascendancy: Lady Mount Cashell, Lady Moira, Mary Wollstonecraft and the Union Pamphlets', *Eighteenth-century Ireland*, 18 (2003), 100–1.

60 See Wardle (ed.), *Collected Letters*, pp. 124, 147, 120.

61 See Gordon, *Vindication*, pp. 89–90, 83 and Todd, *Rebel Daughters*, pp. 50, 60.

62 A. W. Hutton (ed.), *Arthur Young's Tour in Ireland (1776–1779)*, 2 vols (London: G. Bell & Sons, 1892), I, p. 463.

63 Gordon, *Vindication*, p. 91.

64 *Ibid.*, p. 112.

65 R. F. Foster, *Modern Ireland, 1600–1972* (London: Penguin, 1989), p. 169; Gordon, *Vindication*, p. 91, and Todd, *Rebel Daughters*, p. 60.

66 Wardle (ed.), *Collected Letters*, p. 122.

67 Todd, *Rebel Daughters*, p. 187.

68 See Gordon, *Vindication*, pp. 198, 80.

69 Wardle (ed.), *Collected Letters*, p. 141.

70 For an account of the complex ways in which 'the horrors of the rising' and its aftermath were processed in a gothic mode conditioned by the imperative to memorialise, transform and exorcise, see Siobhán

Kilfeather, 'Terrific Register: The Gothicization of Atrocity in Irish Romanticism', *boundary 2*, 31:1 (Spring 2004), 49–71.
71 See Christina Morin, *The Gothic Novel in Ireland, c.1760–1829* (Manchester: Manchester University Press, 2018), pp. 1–20.
72 Jim Shanahan, 'Tales of the Time: Early Fictions of the 1798 Rebellion', *Irish University Review*, 41:1 (Spring/Summer 2011), 152.
73 *Ibid.*, 153.
74 Ferris, *The Romantic National Tale*, p. 9; Ina Ferris, 'Narrating Cultural Encounter: Lady Morgan and the Irish National Tale', *Nineteenth-century Literature*, 51:3 (December 1996), 288, 292, 299.
75 See Miranda J. Burgess, 'Violent Translations: Allegory, Gender and Cultural Nationalism in Ireland, 1796–1806', *Modern Language Quarterly*, 59:1 (March 1998), 56.
76 Katie Trumpener, 'National Character, Nationalist Plots: National Tale and Historical Novel in the Age of *Waverley*, 1806–1830', *ELH*, 60:3 (Autumn 1993), 686, 716.
77 Mary Jean Corbett, '"Between History and Fiction": Plotting Rebellion in Maria Edgeworth's *Ennui*', *Nineteenth-century Literature*, 57:3 (December 2002), 322.
78 See Marianne Elliott, *Partners in Revolution: The United Irishmen and France* (New Haven, CT: Yale University Press, 1982), p. 165; Shanahan, 'Tales of the Time', 165, 166.
79 Charles Maturin, *The Milesian Chief*, 4 vols (London: Henry Colburn, 1812), I, p. v.
80 Terry Eagleton, *Heathcliff and the Great Hunger: Studies in Irish Culture* (London: Verso, 1995), p. 147; Ina Ferris, 'Writing on the Border: The National Tale', in Rajan and Wright (eds), *Romanticism, History, and the Possibilities of Genre*, p. 100.
81 Katie Trumpener, *Bardic Nationalism: The Romantic Novel and the British Empire* (Princeton: NJ: Princeton University Press, 1997), p. 143; Ferris, 'Writing on the Border', pp. 93, 95, 96, 98; Colleen Booker Halverson, 'Fragmented Histories: 1798 and the Irish National Tale' (unpublished PhD thesis, University of Wisconsin-Milwaukee, 2012), pp. 5–6.
82 See Richard Terdiman, *Present Past: Modernity and the Memory Crisis* (Ithaca, NY: Cornell University Press, 1993), pp. 3–4.
83 See Guy Beiner, *Remembering the Year of the French: Irish Folk History and Social Memory* (Madison, WI: The University of Wisconsin Press, 2007), pp. 124, 125, 134, 135.
84 Todd and Butler (eds), *The Works*, IV, p. 468.
85 Lyle Massey, 'Pregnancy and Pathology: Picturing Childbirth in

Eighteenth-century Obstetrical Atlases', *The Art Bulletin*, 87:1 (March 2005), 73. See also Marcia D. Nichols, 'Venus Dissected: The Visual Blazon of Mid-eighteenth-century Medical Atlases', in Jolene Zigarovich (ed.), *Sex and Death in Eighteenth-century Literature* (New York: Routledge, 2013), pp. 103–24.
86 Massey, 'Pregnancy and Pathology', 73.
87 Todd and Butler (eds), *The Works*, V, p. 218.
88 Jones, 'The Death of Mary Wollstonecraft', 194–5.
89 Massey, 'Pregnancy and Pathology', 73, 71.
90 Alexander Gordon, *A Treatise on the Epidemic Puerperal Fever of Aberdeen* (London: G. G. and J. Robinson, 1795), pp. 63–4. Gordon was writing half a century before the pioneering antiseptic practices of Ignaz Semmelweis ('the saviour of mothers') and seventy years before the development of germ theory by Louis Pasteur and Robert Koch.
91 Gordon, *Vindication*, p. 357.
92 Massey, 'Pregnancy and Pathology', 88–9.
93 See *ibid.*, 76–7, 83–5.
94 Lisa Forman Cody, *Birthing the Nation: Sex, Science and The Conception of Eighteenth-century Britons* (Oxford: Oxford University Press, 2005), p. 6.
95 *Ibid.*, pp. 278, 210.
96 Massey, 'Pregnancy and Pathology', 84, 86.
97 *Ibid.*, 73.
98 See *ibid.*, 83–4, 87.
99 For a recent discussion of van Reimsdyk's illustrations in the context of the birthing of *Frankenstein* and the 'delivery' of the novel's 'labouring reader', see Sarah Emily Blewitt, 'Hidden Mothers and Poetic Pregnancy in Women's Writing, 1818 to the Present Day' (unpublished PhD thesis, Cardiff University, 2015), pp. 210–62.
100 Thomas Pakenham, *The Year of Liberty: The Great Irish Rebellion of 1798* (London: Abacus, 2000 [1969]), p. 33.
101 See Todd, *Rebel Daughters*, p. 229.
102 *Ibid.*, p. 254.
103 Pakenham, *The Year of Liberty*, pp. 254, 102.
104 See *ibid.*, pp. 107–260.
105 T. W. Moody, R. B. McDowell and C. J. Woods (eds), *The Writings of Theobald Wolfe Tone, 1763–98*, 3 vols (Oxford: Clarendon Press, 1998–2007), III, p. 391.
106 See Richard Musgrave, *A Concise Account of the Material Events and Atrocities, which Occurred in the Present Rebellion* (Dublin, 1799), pp. 24–5; Charles Jackson, *A Narrative of the Sufferings and Escape*

of *Charles Jackson, Late Resident at Wexford in Ireland, including an Account, by Way of Journal* [sic] *of Several Barbarous Atrocities, Committed in June, 1798, by Irish Rebels in that Town* (Sligo, 1798), p. 59: 'Lord Kingsborough ['Big George'] had, with princely munificence, built several neat alms-houses at Mitchelstown'.

107 Susan B. Egenolf, '"Our Fellow-Creatures": Women Narrating Political Violence in the 1798 Irish Rebellion', *Eighteenth-century Studies*, 24:2 (Winter 2009), 228, 234 and *passim*.
108 'No Lawyer' [Margaret King, Lady Mount Cashell], *A Few Words in Favour of Ireland* (Dublin, 1799), pp. 25, iii, vii–viii. See also Todd, 'Ascendancy: Lady Mount Cashell', 98–117.
109 See www.dublin1798.com (accessed 26 May 2017).
110 Thus when the novelist Sarah Isdell has 'a group of United Irishmen plotting sedition … in a public space associated with women and reproduction – the public rooms at the Rotunda Lying-In Hospital' (Kilfeather, 'Terrific Register', 63–4) in *The Irish Recluse; Or, Breakfast at the Rotunda* (1809), she is channelling Wollstonecraft's Irish novel.
111 Pakenham, *The Year of Liberty*, p. 32.
112 John Blunt [Samuel William Fores], *Man-midwifery Dissected; Or, The Obstetric Family Instructor, for the Use of Married Couples and Single Adults of Both Sexes* (London: S. W. Fores, 1793), pp. 65, xiii.
113 *Ibid.*, p. 62.
114 See Anne K. Mellor, 'Possessing Nature: The Female in *Frankenstein*', in Anne K. Mellor (ed.), *Romanticism and Feminism* (Bloomington, IN: Indiana University Press, 1988), p. 225.
115 See James Kinsley (ed.), *The Poems and Fables of John Dryden* (Oxford: Oxford University Press, 1970), pp. 704–6 (ll. 103–216).
116 Quoted in Pamela Clemit and Jenny McAuley, 'A Nation in its Last Moments: William Godwin's Visit to Ireland, 1800', *History Ireland*, 23:4 (July/August 2015), 24.
117 Godwin, *St Leon*, II, pp. 27–9.
118 I (Wollstonecraft) assemble the moniker from the names of Francis L'Estrange (1756–1836), a surgeon at Mercer's Hospital, Dublin and president of the Royal College of Surgeons in Ireland; and, of course, Theobald Wolfe Tone (1763–98), one of the founders of the United Irishmen and leader (in exile) of the 1798 Rebellion.
119 Todd and Butler (eds), *The Works*, V, p. 242.
120 See Pakenham, *The Year of Liberty*, p. 108.
121 See Todd, *Rebel Daughters*, p. 174 and Kevin Whelan, *Fellowship of Freedom: The United Irishmen and 1798* (Cork: Cork University Press, 1998), pp. 24, 54, 83.

122 Mary Shelley's creature would in the Victorian period be explicitly hibernicised; for the figure of 'The Irish Frankenstein' as a marker of British ethnic prejudice and fear from the 1840s to the 1880s, see H. L. Malchow, 'Frankenstein's Monster and Images of Race in Nineteenth-Century Britain', *Past & Present*, 139 (May 1993), 124–5.
123 See Pakenham, *The Year of Liberty*, p. 85, and Whelan, *Fellowship of Freedom*, p. 63.
124 Todd and Butler (eds), *The Works*, V, p. 58.
125 Pakenham, *The Year of Liberty*, p. 179.
126 James Alexander, *Some Account of the First Apparent Symptoms of the Late Rebellion in the County of Kildare* (Dublin, John Jones, 1800), p. 66.
127 See Harry Owen, *Simulation in Education Healthcare: An Extensive History* (Cham, Switzerland: Springer, 2016), p. 99.
128 See *ibid.*, pp. 100 and 101.
129 Pakenham, *The Tree of Liberty*, p. 231.
130 Quoted in Thomas McLoughlin, *Contesting Ireland: Irish Voices Against England in the Eighteenth Century* (Dublin, Four Courts Press, 1999), p. 244.
131 Todd, *Rebel Daughters*, p. 61; Gordon, *Vindication*, p. 91; and see Pakenham, *The Year of Liberty*, p. 71.
132 Quoted in Todd, *Rebel Daughters*, pp. 177, 170; see also Pakenham, *The Year of Liberty*, p. 208.
133 William Smellie, *Treatise on the Theory and Practice of Midwifery*, 5th edn (Dublin: T. and J. Whitehouse, 1764), pp. 103, 104.
134 Todd and Butler (eds), *The Works*, IV, p. 368.
135 *Ibid.*, I, pp. 89, 165.
136 The first title is of course a project left unfinished by Wollstonecraft at her death; the second, an influential book by Margaret Mount Cashell herself, published in 1823, in which, pioneeringly, she advocates the benefits of preventative medicine. Its first chapter, 'On Pregnancy and Child-birth', champions trust in midwives (though not to the exclusion of a male practitioner if the situation demands it) and counsels against premature extraction of the placenta.
137 Todd and Butler (eds), *The Works*, I, p. 146.
138 *Ibid.*, IV, pp. 469, 470.
139 Shelley, *Frankenstein*, p. 121.

Works cited

Primary texts

Alexander, James, *Some Account of the First Apparent Symptoms of the Late Rebellion in the County of Kildare* (Dublin, John Jones, 1800)

Blunt, John [Fores, Samuel William], *Man-midwifery Dissected; Or, The Obstetric Family Instructor, for the Use of Married Couples and Single Adults of Both Sexes* (London: S. W. Fores, 1793)

Godwin, William, *Memoirs of the Author of A Vindication of the Rights of Woman* (London: Joseph Johnson, 1798)

Godwin, William, *St Leon: A Tale of the Sixteenth Century*, 4 vols (London: G. G. and J. Robinson, 1799)

Gordon, Alexander, *A Treatise on the Epidemic Puerperal Fever of Aberdeen* (London: G. G. and J. Robinson, 1795)

Hutton, A. W. (ed.), *Arthur Young's Tour in Ireland (1776–1779)*, 2 vols (London: G. Bell & Sons, 1892)

Jackson, Charles, *A Narrative of the Sufferings and Escape of Charles Jackson, Late Resident at Wexford in Ireland, including an Account, by Way of Journal [sic] of Several Barbarous Atrocities, Committed in June, 1798, by Irish Rebels in that Town* (Sligo, 1798)

Kinsley, James (ed.), *The Poems and Fables of John Dryden* (Oxford: Oxford University Press, 1970)

Maturin, Charles, *The Milesian Chief*, 4 vols (London: Henry Colburn, 1812)

Moody, T. W., R. B. McDowell and C. J. Woods (eds), *The Writings of Theobald Wolfe Tone, 1763–98*, 3 vols (Oxford: Clarendon Press, 1998–2007)

Musgrave, Richard, *A Concise Account of the Material Events and Atrocities, which Occurred in the Present Rebellion* (Dublin, 1799)

'No Lawyer' [King, Margaret, Lady Mount Cashell], *A Few Words in Favour of Ireland* (Dublin, 1799)

Paine, Thomas, *Agrarian Justice, Opposed to Agrarian Law* (London: T. Williams, 1797)

Philp, Mark *et al.* (eds), *Political and Philosophical Writings of William Godwin*, 7 vols (London: William Pickering, 1993)

Shelley, Mary, *Frankenstein*, ed. Marilyn Butler (Oxford: Oxford University Press, 2008)

Smellie, William, *Treatise on the Theory and Practice of Midwifery*, 5th edn (Dublin: T. and J. Whitehouse, 1764)

Todd, Janet and Marilyn Butler (eds), *The Works of Mary Wollstonecraft*, 7 vols (London: William Pickering, 1989)

Wardle, Ralph M. (ed.), *Collected Letters of Mary Wollstonecraft* (Ithaca, NY: Cornell University Press, 1979)
Wilson, William, *Modern Plan of the City and Environs of Dublin* (London: E. and T. Williams, 1798); www.dublin1798.com
Wollstonecraft, Mary, *Mary and The Wrongs of Woman*, ed. Gary Kelly (Oxford: Oxford University Press, 2007)

Secondary texts

Beiner, Guy, *Remembering the Year of the French: Irish Folk History and Social Memory* (Madison, WI: The University of Wisconsin Press, 2007)
Blewitt, Sarah Emily, 'Hidden Mothers and Poetic Pregnancy in Women's Writing, 1818 to the Present Day' (unpublished PhD thesis, Cardiff University, 2015)
Burgess, Miranda J., 'Violent Translations: Allegory, Gender and Cultural Nationalism in Ireland, 1796–1806', *Modern Language Quarterly*, 59:1 (March 1998), 33–70
Carson, Julie A., *England's First Family of Writers: Mary Wollstonecraft, William Godwin, Mary Shelley* (Baltimore, MD: Johns Hopkins University Press, 2007)
Clemit, Pamela and Jenny McAuley, 'A Nation in its Last Moments: William Godwin's Visit to Ireland, 1800', *History Ireland*, 23:4 (July/August 2015), 22–4
Cody, Lisa Forman, *Birthing the Nation: Sex, Science and The Conception of Eighteenth-century Britons* (Oxford: Oxford University Press, 2005)
Collett, Cathy, 'Every Child Left Behind: *St Leon* and William Godwin's Immortal Future', *European Romantic Review*, 25:3 (May 2014), 327–36
Corbett, Mary Jean, '"Between History and Fiction": Plotting Rebellion in Maria Edgeworth's *Ennui*', *Nineteenth-century Literature*, 57:3 (December 2002), 297–322
Denlinger, Elizabeth Campbell, *Before Victoria: Extraordinary Women of the British Romantic Era* (New York: The New York Public Library/Columbia University Press, 2005)
Douthwaite, Julia V., *The Frankenstein of 1790 and Other Lost Chapters from Revolutionary France* (Chicago: University of Chicago Press, 2012)
Eagleton, Terry, *Heathcliff and the Great Hunger: Studies in Irish Culture* (London: Verso, 1995)
Egenolf, Susan B., '"Our Fellow-Creatures": Women Narrating Political Violence in the 1798 Irish Rebellion', *Eighteenth-century Studies*, 24:2 (Winter 2009), 217–34

Elliott, Marianne, *Partners in Revolution: The United Irishmen and France* (New Haven, CT: Yale University Press, 1982)
Fermanis, Porscha and John Regan (eds), *Rethinking British Romantic History, 1770–1845* (Oxford: Oxford University Press, 2014)
Ferris, Ina, 'Narrating Cultural Encounter: Lady Morgan and the Irish National Tale', *Nineteenth-century Literature*, 51:3 (December 1996), 287–303
Ferris, Ina, *The Romantic National Tale and the Question of Ireland* (Cambridge: Cambridge University Press, 2002)
Ferris, Ina, 'Writing on the Border: The National Tale', in Tilottama Rajan and Julia M. Wright (eds), *Romanticism, History, and the Possibilities of Genre* (Cambridge: Cambridge University Press, 1998), pp. 86–106
Foster. R. F., *Modern Ireland, 1600–1972* (London: Penguin, 1989)
Gallagher, Catherine, 'Undoing', in Karen Newman, Jay Clayton and Marianne Hirsch (eds), *Time and the Literary* (New York: Routledge, 2002)
Garman, Emma, 'A Liberated Woman: The Story of Margaret King', https://longreads.com/2016/05/24/a-liberated-woman-the-story-of-margaret-king/
Gordon, Charlotte, *Romantic Outlaws: The Extraordinary Lives of Mary Wollstonecraft and Mary Shelley* (London: Hutchinson, 2015)
Gordon, Lyndall, *Vindication: A Life of Mary Wollstonecraft* (London: Virago, 2006)
Halverson, Colleen Booker, 'Fragmented Histories: 1798 and the Irish National Tale' (unpublished PhD thesis, University of Wisconsin-Milwaukee, 2012)
Handwerk, Gary, 'History, Trauma, and the Limits of the Liberal Imagination: William Godwin's Historical Fiction', in Tilottama Rajan and Julia M. Wright (eds), *Romanticism, History, and the Possibilities of Genre* (Cambridge: Cambridge University Press, 1998), pp. 64–85
Hellekson, Karen, *The Alternate History: Refiguring Historical Time* (Kent, OH: The Kent State University Press, 2001)
Jacobus, Mary, *First Things: The Maternal Imaginary in Literature, Art, and Psychoanalysis* (New York: Routledge, 1995)
Johnson, Claudia L., 'Mary Wollstonecraft: Styles of Radical Maternity', in Susan C. Greenfield and Carol Barash (eds), *Inventing Maternity: Politics, Science and Literature, 1650–1865* (Lexington, KT: The University Press of Kentucky, 1999), pp. 159–72
Jones, Vivien, 'The Death of Mary Wollstonecraft', *Journal for Eighteenth-century Studies*, 20:2 (September 1997), 187–205
Kilfeather, Siobhán, 'Terrific Register: The Gothicization of

Atrocity in Irish Romanticism', *boundary 2*, 31:1 (Spring 2004), 49–71

Klancher, Jon, 'Godwin and the Republican Romance', in Marshall Brown (ed.), *Eighteenth-century Literary History: An MLQ Reader* (Durham, NC: Duke University Press, 1999)

Kramer, Lloyd S., 'Literature, Criticism, and Historical Imagination: The Literary Challenge of Hayden White and Dominick LaCapra', in Lynn Hunt (ed.), *The New Cultural History* (Berkeley, CA: University of California Press, 1989)

Lebow, Richard Ned, 'What's So Different About A Counterfactual?', *World Politics*, 52:4 (July 2000), 550–85

Looser, Devoney, 'Mary Wollstonecraft, "Ithuriel" and the Rise of the Feminist Author-Ghost', *Tulsa Studies in Women's Literature*, 35:1 (Spring 2016), 59–91

Malchow, H. L., 'Frankenstein's Monster and Images of Race in Nineteenth-Century Britain', *Past & Present*, 139 (May 1993), 90–130

Massey, Lyle, 'Pregnancy and Pathology: Picturing Childbirth in Eighteenth-century Obstetrical Atlases', *The Art Bulletin*, 87:1 (March 2005), 73–91

McAleer, Edward C., *The Sensitive Plant: A Life of Lady Mount Cashell* (Chapel Hill, NC: University of North Carolina Press, 1958)

McInnes, Andrew, *Wollstonecraft's Ghost: The Fate of the Female Philosopher in the Romantic Period* (New York: Routledge, 2016)

McInnes, Andrew, 'Wollstonecraft's Legion: Feminism in Crisis, 1799', *Women's Writing*, 20:4 (November 2013), 479–95

McLoughlin, Thomas, *Contesting Ireland: Irish Voices Against England in the Eighteenth Century* (Dublin, Four Courts Press, 1999)

Mellor, Anne K., 'Possessing Nature: The Female in *Frankenstein*', in Anne K. Mellor (ed.), *Romanticism and Feminism* (Bloomington, IN: Indiana University Press, 1988), pp. 220–32

Morin, Christina, *The Gothic Novel in Ireland, c.1760–1829* (Manchester: Manchester University Press, 2018)

Morson, Gary Saul, 'Sideshadowing and Tempics', *New Literary History*, 29:4 (Autumn 1998), 599–624

Nichols, Marcia D., 'Venus Dissected: The Visual Blazon of Mid-Eighteenth-century Medical Atlases', in Jolene Zigarovich (ed.), *Sex and Death in Eighteenth-century Literature* (New York: Routledge, 2013), pp. 103–24

Owen, Harry, *Simulation in Education Healthcare: An Extensive History* (Cham, Switzerland: Springer, 2016)

Pakenham, Thomas, *The Year of Liberty: The Great Irish Rebellion of 1798* (London: Abacus, 2000 [1969])

Palaniappan, Nithiya, Maria Menezes and Penny Wilson, 'Group A

Streptococcal Puerperal Sepsis: Management and Prevention', *The Obstetrician & Gynaecologist*, 14:1 (2012), 9–16; http://onlinelibrary.wiley.com/doi/10.1111/j.1744-4667.2011.00082.x/full

Phillips, Mark Salber, *On Historical Distance* (New Haven, CT: Yale University Press, 2013)

Phillips, Mark Salber, *Society and Sentiment: Genres of Historical Writing in Britain, 1740–1820* (Princeton, NJ: Princeton University Press, 2000)

Randel, Fred V., 'The Political Geography of Horror in Mary Shelley's *Frankenstein*', *ELH*, 70:2 (Summer 2003), 465–91

Seymour, Miranda, *Mary Shelley* (London: John Murray, 2000)

Shanahan, Jim, 'Tales of the Time: Early Fictions of the 1798 Rebellion', *Irish University Review*, 41:1 (Spring/Summer 2011), 151–68.

Terdiman, Richard, *Present Past: Modernity and the Memory Crisis* (Ithaca, NY: Cornell University Press, 1993)

Tetlock, Philip E. and Aaron Belkin (eds), *Counterfactual Thought Experiments in World Politics: Logical, Methodological, and Psychological Perspectives* (Princeton, NJ: Princeton University Press, 1996)

Todd, Janet, 'Ascendancy: Lady Mount Cashell, Lady Moira, Mary Wollstonecraft and the Union Pamphlets', *Eighteenth-century Ireland*, 18 (2003), 98–117

Todd, Janet, *Gender, Art and Death* (Cambridge: Polity Press, 1993)

Todd, Janet, *Rebel Daughters: Ireland in Conflict, 1798* (London: Viking, 2003)

Trumpener, Katie, *Bardic Nationalism: The Romantic Novel and the British Empire* (Princeton: NJ: Princeton University Press, 1997)

Trumpener, Katie, 'National Character, Nationalist Plots: National Tale and Historical Novel in the Age of *Waverley*, 1806–1830', *ELH*, 60:3 (Autumn 1993), 685–731

Walford Davies, Damian, 'Introduction: Reflections on an Orthodoxy', in Damian Walford Davies (ed.), *Romanticism, History, Historicism: Essays on an Orthodoxy* (New York: Routledge, 2009), 1–13

Whelan, Kevin, *Fellowship of Freedom: The United Irishmen and 1798* (Cork: Cork University Press, 1998)

Williams, Carolyn, '"Inhumanly Brought Back to Life and Misery": Mary Wollstonecraft, *Frankenstein*, and the Royal Humane Society', *Women's Writing*, 8:2 (2001), 213–33.

Wolfson, Susan, 'Mary Wollstonecraft and the Poets', in Claudia L. Johnson (ed.), *The Cambridge Companion to Mary Wollstonecraft* (Cambridge, Cambridge University Press, 2002), pp. 160–88

Woolf, Virginia, 'Mary Wollstonecraft', in Andrew McNeillie (ed.), *The Common Reader,* Second Series (London: Vintage, 2003), 156–63

7

John Thelwall: a counterfactual ghost story

Judith Thompson

Preamble

Christmas 1844. *The chimes* rang out across the rooftops of London. From the darkened window I turned back to the chamber where my friend sat, *pale as Allegory beneath the painted ceiling*, slowly revolving in his hand a tumbler of *negus*. He was thinking, no doubt, of the guests who had lately *circled our blazing hearth, social and gay*, now gone to their comfortable homes, and perhaps turning his mind to certain other long-departed spirits.

'Tell me about the ghost,' I said.

'I saw her but twice and she did not say a word. She was a woman wronged, who walks the *roomy passages and antechambers* of this house, dressed in *grey silk* of a bygone fashion, her face drawn and ashen. But I remember her from my youth. Once she was pretty, and kept a *rustic's ruddy health* before wasting under the strain of a disease, the last of many sorrows that had worn her down. For she was *his good angel*, amiable and capable; she worked beside and stayed true to him through those lonely years of exile, grief and persecution before his persistence (some would call it folly) brought them back to London, where they rose to prosperity and he laughed in the faces of those who had maligned him. More loyal she was to him than he to her, even before the scandal of *that actress affair* – on her very deathbed – cast another shadow on his public life and judgement. It was one of so many vanities that exiled him from his better self and from what friends remained to him. But let that be. It is well-nigh thirty years ago she died, and ten now he's been gone.'

'And best forgotten, you may well say, as so many do,' I replied. 'But that's not fair either. For he stood firm and spoke up for the principles we still believe in, when "better" men – fair-weather friends and poets too – crouched and quailed in the service of power. Once he set the nation on fire with his voice. We shall not look upon his like again.'

So, bidding him goodnight, I walked pensively to my bedroom in the house that had once belonged to the subject of our discourse: John Thelwall, citizen and champion of liberty, firebrand demagogue and pompous pedagogue. A puzzle of vain ambition and passionate integrity, he died alone, and lies buried in a distant churchyard.

I placed my head on the pillow *but did not sleep, nor could I be said to think*. And yet I must have done, for it was as if in a dream I woke to voices in the square below, carrying unmistakable but uncanny *through the closed shutters. Darkling I listened* to the twisting trills, like water *buddling and babbling over stones in some sequestered summer solitude*. I followed the sound of the nightingales into the hallway and up the magnificent staircase, shining under the moon-silvered skylight, *elliptically joining lowest cellar to highest rooftop*. Was that a figure I saw above me, silhouetted against *the attic railing*? Or only the broken voices up and down the stairs, echoing back through time, bringing fragments of a story that has never been told? Nor am I fit to tell it now. But I will add my words to those that remain.

Counterfactual biography

The life of John Thelwall – radical Romantic, maker of the English working-class, orator, journalist, poet, playwright, novelist, elocutionist, speech therapist, polymath – is one of the great untold stories of English history. There is a book by that title, published by his second wife in 1838, but it covers less than half the tale of a man who packed more into his threescore years and ten than many of his better-known contemporaries, yet failed to find the fame he so ardently desired. Two volumes were intended, one dealing with his political life and principles, the other with his professional and literary careers, but the second was never published, and in the aftermath of political persecution and personal misfortune, most of his archive disappeared. As a result, his legacy is all but forgotten in a world that might benefit from his example – a man who championed democratic freedoms (then, as now, under attack); who straddled spheres of high art and popular activism that remain as far apart as ever; who gave voice to the voiceless; and who embraced success and failure alike without ever compromising his principles.

The lack of a complete Thelwall biography is especially ironic given that he penned so many of them himself, published and unpublished, in verse and prose, writing himself in a manner alternately self-aggrandising and self-mocking, but always intent on leaving a mark on posterity. Yet now that posterity is beginning to catch up with him, he faces an obstacle almost as daunting as the Gagging Acts that so effectively 'bastill'd' the tongues of Romanticism's lost generation.[1] For even though his life of towering ambition, relentless persecution, scandalous passion, heroic integrity and eccentric originality is ripe for a fully fledged Hollywood treatment, Thelwall has fallen below the radar of pop culture, while in the scholarly arena, the days of such magisterial 'Great Lives' have passed. The postmodern biographer is more self-reflexive and sceptical of her own interpretative authority and self-constructions and those of her subjects, more alert to material environments and conditions, more interested in social networks and creative collaborations than in titanic egos and solitary genius. Fortunately, Thelwall's very obscurity, as well as his values, lend themselves to such a decentered approach; he must be sought in the interstices of other lives and archives, in the worlds of aspiration he traversed and the intellectual networks he connected through his lecture tours, and in the print traces of oral performances whose ephemeral multiplicity militates against any authoritative narrative.

A ghost in the archive of Romanticism, he haunts the echoing margins to which he has been relegated, testing the illusions of complete historical knowledge promised by an age of digital reproduction. Surely, one thinks, if his life was worth remembering, we would have a record. Surely no one that notorious and well connected could have disappeared so completely. But is it possible to write a biography when one is forced to rely on fragmentary and unreliable sources, many of them in poetic form? What is the scholarly status of such documents? And even if one could write such a biography, what audience would it find, when budgets are stretched, and scholars are still preoccupied with the same great names from the past while celebrities endlessly capture the ever more fickle popular imagination? If this is true of a man, how much more so is it for the women with whom he was connected? We may wish to reconstruct Romanticism to include such marginal figures, but how can we do so when there are so many gaping fissures in the archival and biographical record? As we endeavour to fill these gaps, how can we avoid projecting our own desires, or perpetuating the injustices that created them – inequities already so deeply inscribed in our literary-historical methods and materials? Is it possible to imagine and practise a new scholarship that walks a fine line between documentation and speculation, critical rigour and creative intuition?

These questions introduce my modality of the Romantic counterfactual. As I prepare to write the first full modern biography of Thelwall, I keep returning to them, less interested in the 'what ifs' or 'might have beens' of literary history than in *what probably did happen* – which, however, can be confirmed only when, or if, lost archives are found. In their absence, I fill gaps in the record with educated intuition, intertwining the voices of scholar and storyteller and interweaving scraps of historicised hypothesis from multiple genres and various parts of Thelwall's life and writing, reception and afterlife. I willingly entertain conjecture and speculation – not, as in most counterfactual biography, to offer new perspectives on a well-known life, but rather to investigate and reflect on the extent to which an unknown life may be reconstructed by means of counterfactual literary techniques. In the opening and closing frames of this chapter, I indulge freely in Romantic – and romantic – metafiction, penning fantasies based on textual hints and clues, many of them deriving from my own experience of searching for them. In the body of the chapter, as a more scholarly detective, I explore poetry as a mode of the counterfactual, testing the possibility and reflecting metacritically on the process of making a factual narrative out of the allusive, elusive methods of what Thelwall called seditious allegory: techniques of ellipsis and evasion, strategies of disguise and deception, acts of ventriloquism and multiple, shifting, uncertain voices, manuscript hands and personae.

My test case is a crucial episode in the life of John Thelwall of which something is materially known (with more being revealed each year), but whose full contours will likely always remain a matter of speculation. The time is the summer of 1816; the place is Thelwall's home and elocutionary institution at 57 Lincoln's Inn Fields, London. There, far from the famous 'haunted summer' on the shores of Lake Geneva, a real-life gothic romance is taking shape, as the fate of a successful professional and buried radical is being sealed by the death of a loyal partner, the lure of a Lolita pupil and betrayal by a second-self son. Thelwall's truth will never shine as bright as Mary Shelley's fiction, but the former shaped the latter and still speaks to it in several significant ways. Not only was Thelwall a member of the Godwin circle and an influence on *Frankenstein*, as Michael Scrivener and others have shown; the creativity and turmoil that surrounded Thelwall in the summer of 1816 resonates with the family romance that followed the elopement of Mary Godwin and Claire Clairmont, leading to the suicide of Fanny

Imlay.[2] In both families, young women pursuing a Wollstonecraftian legacy of intellectual and sexual independence and fulfilment attached themselves to lovers who sought in the daughter to reanimate a feminist foremother and a lost father of political justice. In the case of Thelwall's family, it was not the second Romantic generation but the ageing radical paterfamilias who revered and revived the lost mother of feminism in the daughter of adoption, and it was that daughter who fulfilled her creative ambitions through a strangely Byronic surrogate-father-lover, leaving the wannabe rebel son, like a sad-sack Shelley, out in the cold. This is the counterfactual romance I have to tell, replete with sexual rivalry, betrayal and quasi-incest. I have embedded clues to it in the opening sequence of this chapter, combining allusions to *Frankenstein* with my own uncanny midnight encounter with unseen nightingales (recorded only in my private journals) at the January 2007 conference in Bath, England, that heralded the modern scholarly rebirth of Thelwall.

These shades of Regency Romanticism are set within a Victorian fictional framework, in order to acknowledge another landmark in literary history for which Thelwall's life provides a countertext. The rooms of John Forster – in which Charles Dickens's famous ghost story, 'The Chimes' was recited at Christmas 1844 – were located at 58 Lincoln's Inn Fields, right next door to what had been Thelwall's Institution.[3] Dickens used the same site for Tulkinghorn's chambers in his 1851 masterpiece *Bleak House*. Though Thelwall was ten years dead by 1844 and thirty years gone from the neighbourhood by 1851, Dickens must have known of him and his Institution through both his mentor Thomas Noon Talfourd (whom Thelwall had mentored) and through Thelwall's widow, Cecil, herself (with whom Dickens was personally acquainted at the time he began *Bleak House*).[4] From Cecil Thelwall and Talfourd, Dickens would have learned how fully John Thelwall's childhood, interests and principles matched his own. Further, whether or not Dickens was aware of it, his own obsession with Nelly Ternan, the young actress and 'Invisible Woman' for whom he betrayed and abandoned his loyal wife Catherine, mirrors John Thelwall's scandalous behaviour with the second Mrs Thelwall, also a teenage actress, a generation earlier.[5]

That affair left two final phantoms, even more elusive and improbable, who shadow the opening and closing frames of my story. The first is the grey lady who is said to haunt the halls of 57 Lincoln's Inn Fields (now the chambers of England's leading group of human rights barristers). She has been seen lurking at the top of the property's spectacular elliptical staircase (designed by Thelwall's neighbour, the distinguished architect

Sir John Soane), from whose upper landing she is said to have thrown herself.⁶ The second is no more than a hint in Victorian parish records, a puzzle of names that has long teased my pursuit and will never be solved, around which I have constructed another romantic fantasy to mark the limits of interpretation, whether factual or counterfactual.

In populating my metafictional frames with these intertextual ghosts (their presence indicated by italics), I hope to share both puzzle and pleasure while reinforcing another point about my counterfactual biography. While I can expect some of my readers to pick up allusions to canonical texts, no one yet knows the work of Thelwall well enough to hear the echoes of it that are also deeply embedded here, and on which my biography depends. This highlights the extent to which standard biographies of well-known figures and counterfactual histories of well-known events rely on a long body of accumulated intertextual knowledge that has already established the facts and enriched the textures of a given life or historical period. When this is missing, we are reduced to facts alone – or tempted into fiction.

Just the facts, Ma'am

So here is what we know, according to reliable documentary evidence.

In the summer of 1816, John Thelwall, aged 52, was reaching the apex of the professional career that followed his political rise and fall and his poetical retirement. His polymathic pedagogical therapeutic Institution 'for the Remedy of Organic Defects, Cure of Impediments, and Preparation for the Pulpit, Bar and Senate' in Lincoln's Inn Fields was a fashionable landmark that served aspiring parliamentarians, barristers and divines, exiled European patriots, actors and actresses and the speech-impaired sons (and daughters) of those who could afford its rather steep fees.⁷ Although he had become a gentleman, Thelwall had not abandoned his principles: while his prices excluded the working classes to whose political education he had once devoted his efforts, his lectures continued to promote free speech as the cornerstone of citizenship, individual and national liberty, improvement and agency. His progressive values also persisted in his pioneering attention to the rights of the disabled and the voices of women. Thelwall was assisted by his 42-year-old wife, Susan(nah) ('Stella' – the muse of his early poetry) and his sons and daughters (all named after revolutionary heroes and heroines whose spirit their father sought to revive).⁸ Many of Thelwall's pupils were no doubt law students from nearby Lincoln's Inn, but the one who turned his life around was an aspiring actress: Henrietta Cecil Boyle, 16-year-old daughter of the publishers of the fashionable *Boyle's Court Guide*, who had lost her father in 1808 and was of an age with Thelwall's own daughters Manon Roland and Sara Maria. We do not know exactly when she became Thelwall's pupil, but by July 1816 he was serving as her *de facto* manager, seeking engagements among his theatrical contacts.[9] In September of that year, she made a successful debut at Covent Garden.[10] The same month, Thelwall's wife and 'good angel' (Henry Crabb Robinson's phrase) died.[11] The cause of her death is not known, but an obituary published in the *Morning Post* mentions a lingering malady.[12] The sober obituary stands in marked contrast to the effusive proclamation and poetic 'apologue' that appeared in the *Liverpool Mercury* under the Shakespearean pseudonym 'Benedict' only 8 months later on 15 May 1817, announcing the marriage at St James's, Westminster of the 52-year old widower Thelwall and the pupil one third his age.[13]

Thelwall's children were christened the week before their father's second wedding, for whether or not the once-staunch atheist had changed his own religious opinions, his new wife was an Irish Catholic.[14] Among those children, the eldest certainly did experience a religious conversion; although 21-year-old Algernon Sydney had been destined by his father for a career in law, with his name entered at Middle Temple in January 1816, by the end of that year, in diametric opposition to his father's plans and values, he returned to Cambridge, took Holy Orders, and became a strident evangelist and virulent anti-Catholic. It is not known what provoked this filial rebellion; in his 1858 memoir, Algernon mentions nothing of his youth except that he was 'educated at home' and 'brought out of the depths of Infidelity' at Cambridge; he barely acknowledges his father, even though he borrowed the elder Thelwall's theories wholesale to build his own career as the first lecturer on elocution at King's College London (an Anglican institution originally founded to rival the 'godless college in Gower Street' that his father had enthusiastically supported).[15] It is possible that the griefstricken and conventionally religious obituary for Susan Thelwall published in the *Morning Post* was actually written by Algernon; this might account for its dismissive remarks about a father who, it claims, was seldom at home, leaving Susan to be 'almost [the] only guide and instructor' of her children 'from the cradle to the threshold of the university'.[16]

This accumulation of facts may seem quite sufficient for the biographer. It certainly reveals that three dramatic reversals of fortune occurred in the Thelwall family around the summer of 1816 – the death of a wife and mother, the estrangement of a son and heir and the transformation of a pupil into a lover. These had stark consequences for John Thelwall's posthumous reputation, and hence for my biography, insofar as they deprived him of those who might have done for him what the descendants of his erstwhile friends William Wordsworth and Samuel Taylor Coleridge did for their reputations and biographies. But facts alone fail to show what caused these critical events in John Thelwall's life and how they might be related. In order to get beyond skeleton narrative on the one hand, and mere speculation on the other, the literary biographer must turn elsewhere: in this case, the Derby manuscript, a virtually complete collection of poems by Thelwall that was clearly intended to accompany the unpublished second volume of Cecil Thelwall's 1838 biography.[17] The discovery of this document promises to fill in many of the gaps in the scant documentary evidence, since it covers his entire life, specifically those years and activities that are missing from existing biographies.

Among its more than 200 selections, many of them dated, some in multiple versions, are several that are explicitly autobiographical, including a number of the sensual love poems or 'songs of eros' whose presence and precedence in the manuscript are one of its most intriguing features.[18] These poems offer considerable evidence to corroborate, supplement and illuminate the events of 1816. However, they are clearly sources that any historian or biographer must approach with caution. As love poems, they are highly conventional, sentimental, mannered and melodramatic, hiding as much as they seductively reveal. In this they may be seen as counterfactual, echoing the subversive, slippery countervoice that characterises Thelwall's famous seditious allegories of the 1790s, which both invite and frustrate simple, factual interpretation, instead spinning out multiple self-cancelling meanings that refuse to be pinned down.[19] However, whereas Thelwall's seditious allegories were political in their aim and action, the transgressive truths that the later poems at once disclose and evade are more personal, and often sexual. I have dubbed them 'seductive allegories', and I begin by looking at several of them, both in the Derby manuscript and elsewhere, before moving on to other texts – primarily poems – that illustrate other, related, seductively counterfactual techniques, namely surrogacy or adoption; ellipsis, disguise and deception; ventriloquism or personation; and protean voice and textuality. Each technique and group of texts allows me to uncover more fully the events of 1816. At the same time, each also moves further and further from reliable biographical fact into a realm of Romantic counterfactual speculation and performance.

Seductive allegory: the language of flowers

'The Oak and the Woodbine', the poetic 'apologue' that announced Thelwall's 1817 wedding to Cecil Boyle, typifies his art of seductive allegory. An apologue is an allegorical fable that offers an indirect moral lesson, traditionally using personified animals (as in Aesop, Orwell or Thelwall's seditious allegories of cocks, fish and sheep). Thelwall's poem deploys a sentimental language of flowers that had been given new scientific legitimacy (and an erotic charge) by Erasmus Darwin's *The Botanic Garden* (1791), which dramatised the sex lives of plants.[20] In Thelwall's poem, the eroticism is overt and transparently autobiographical. A young, 'gay smiling woodbine' twines herself around an oak who is old but still green and 'erect in his pride'. With a 'semblance of coyness and a look like disdain', the woodbine asks why she should attach herself to a 'patriarch tree' when so many younger species – 'Elm, Maple and Holm' – 'seem to vie for my grace'. In reply, the 'old Grandsire' hopes that the strength of his foliage and experience of storms withstood may be 'useful to thee', while her beauty and sweetness are simply 'rapture to me' (*SPP*, p. 36).

The gendered allegory of oak and woodbine is rooted in Thelwall's earlier poetry (and sexual and political experience), with the woodbine offering moral lessons on the reciprocity of sexual desire and social duty, and the oak representing Patriot Virtue buffeted by political tempests.[21] The publication of 'The Oak and the Woodbine' as a wedding announcement confirms the interpretation of allegorical fancy as biographical fact. Further layers of autobiographical allegory are introduced by reading Thelwall's wedding poem alongside 'The Woodbine', a poem addressed to his eldest daughter Maria in 1797 and published in his 1801 volume, *Poems, Chiefly Written in Retirement*. Here, a woodbine reflected in the River Dove images the reciprocity of memory and hope, reminding the speaker of his wife in the days of their courtship and anticipating his daughter's 'awakening passion' in years to come. A note of anxiety, however, enters parenthetically when he acknowledges that 'blighting mildews' may lie in wait to blast his 'paternal hope' (*SPP*, p. 35). Tragically, they did: 7-year-old Maria died suddenly at Christmas 1799, two years after 'The Woodbine' was composed, occasioning an outpouring of intense grief that found its poetic outlet in the 'Paternal Tears' elegies that lie at the heart of the *Retirement* volume (in one of which Maria's ghost appears), and its catharsis in Thelwall's 1801 novel, *The Daughter of Adoption*, whose title character is based in part on Maria.

A poetics of surrogacy: The Daughter of Adoption

The novel and poems addressed by Thelwall to the lost daughter on whom he had pinned so many personal and political hopes are the locus of a motif related to seductive allegory that is crucial to any understanding of the events of 1816 and of Thelwallian counterfactualism: the daughter of adoption. Adoption or surrogacy (that is, the substitution of one person for a lost or absent other) is an important ethical and aesthetic concept for Thelwall. Aesthetically, adoption/surrogacy is best understood as a form of metonymy – a technique that is counterfactual in that, openly acknowledging the absence of singular fact or pure identity, it relies like allegory on difference, substitution or displacement rather than identity or assimilation of word and thing. In the case of seditious allegory, the intended meaning is obvious but cannot be proven in a court of law since the vehicle is always changing, always mobile. In the case of adoption or surrogacy, the original and the substitute are not the same but are treated as if they are; they are identified with one another until the distinction is lost and one effectively becomes the other. This is what happens with Thelwall's daughter Maria in *The Daughter of Adoption*, in a way that also throws light on his courtship of Cecil Boyle.

During her short life and long after, Maria was the image of Thelwall's ideal woman, combining 'artless softness' (*SPP*, p. 35) with the headstrong vigour celebrated in a letter of 1798 that describes her 'bound[ing] along in her trowsers [sic] in all the romping vivacity of independence' and 'tak[ing] health by storm'.[22] After her death, he associated her with Mary Wollstonecraft, who had died in 1797 and whose character, as memorialised (with improvident frankness) by Wollstonecraft's husband and Thelwall's friend William Godwin, manifested the same combination of soft sensibility and intellectual strength. The association is conspicuous in *The Daughter of Adoption*, whose title character combines the feminine sweetness and feminist agency of Maria and Wollstonecraft, together with certain circumstances of their lives. Although the novel is not in any obvious way autobiographical, it shows how Thelwall recovered from the personal and political grief and blight occasioned and symbolised by both women's deaths through a poetics of surrogacy articulated and exemplified by several father-mentor figures in the novel. First, Parkinson, who has lost his young daughter, finds an orphan girl who resembles the lost child (in ways that echo Thelwall's descriptions of Maria); he fosters, renames and teaches her, so that 'the Seraphina I had lost became a model to her whom I had found, till they were identified in my heart'.[23]

Later, the same Seraphina (now an adult whose feminist independence and opinions pay tribute to Wollstonecraft) is adopted by Montfort, who is guilt-stricken at having abandoned his own daughter long ago; he is advised by the fatherly Dr Pengarron that 'the only way to make his peace ... would be to find out some amiable and injured orphan, whose misfortunes had been similar, and make, by proxy ... that atonement he could not make in person'.[24]

In Thelwall's novel, surrogacy is ultimately redemptive. But the joyous denouement it enables does not come about until persistent anxieties about incest, integrally connected to it, are dispelled.[25] One might say then that Thelwall's poetics of surrogacy has two faces, at once redemptive and transgressive; this becomes important for understanding its application to the events of 1816. What becomes clear in the Derby manuscript is that *The Daughter of Adoption* came true when Thelwall met Cecil Boyle some fifteen years after its publication. But it did not come without moral anxieties and fears of transgression. His embrace of her as a daughter of adoption is clearly shown in other poems that appear next to 'The Oak and the Woodbine' in the Derby manuscript, particularly one whose original title, 'Cecil', has been crossed out and replaced with 'Adoption'.[26] Developing the language of flowers into an extended horticultural metaphor, this simple ballad narrates the speaker's attempts to nourish and encourage a reluctant bud to blossom. The published version of the poem ends with fears of 'blight', but in the manuscript, a postscript stanza confirms success (and explicit autobiographical allegory):

> P.S. after the 15 May 1817
>
> I have not marr'd the lovely flower
> That on my faith depended,
> But planted her within my bower –
> Mine own till life be ended.[27]

A more complex and troubled expression of the daughter of adoption motif is found in a longer seductive allegory that curiously does not appear in the Derby manuscript, but only in Thelwall's *Poetical Recreations of the Champion* (1822). 'Thoughts and Remembrances' is a blank-verse lyric meditation, analogous to the 'Paternal Tears' effusions he composed in response to the death of Maria. In fact, it closely follows the first of those elegies, opening with a repetition of the imagery of storm and isolation, lost sunshine and 'spring no more' that had struck the keynote for the entire earlier sequence (*SPP*, pp. 154–7). In 'Thoughts and

Remembrances', however, consolation comes to ease his devastating grief and blighted hopes as an unnamed 'She' rises 'like the day-star' to his 'widowed heart' that still drifts anchorless in the gloom. The poem traces his dawning recognition of their love, from 'simple duty' to a bond that is more than just paternal:

> And I did love her with a father's heart –
> At least it seem'd no other. I did take
> Her image, as a daughter's, to my soul,
> And cherish'd it …
>   … And she lov'd me;
> Lov'd as a daughter – or at least it seem'd
> But as a daughter's love, that in such guise
> Of sanctity and semblant gratitude
> Stole on my heart …
>
> (*SPP*, p. 263)

Despite the poem's redemptive resolution, however, the repetition of 'seems' and the language of disguise and stealing cast a shadow of anxiety around their adoptive relationship. The same language is seen in the poem that immediately precedes 'Adoption' in the Derby manuscript, entitled 'Cupid's Disguise', which begins: 'In Friendship's form the traitor came';[28] it is a line that resonates in the final lines of 'Thoughts and Remembrances':

> In friendship's form,
> In duty's name, or gratitude, – in shapes
> Of filial or fraternal tenderness,
> Or the sage semblance of paternity,
> The more entrancing ecstasy, that blends
> All these in one, may steal upon the heart.
>
> (*SPP*, p. 263)

Such passages as these suggest that the redemptive consolation and renewal remembered in the poem, and presumably experienced by Thelwall on meeting Cecil Boyle, are haunted by some conflict not yet resolved or dispelled as they had been in the original novel *The Daughter of Adoption*. The 'ecstasy' that blends filial, fraternal and paternal identities into one, the language of guile, guise and transgression, and the proliferation of dashes and broken or conditional syntax – all these counterfactual techniques complicate and unsettle Thelwall's art of surrogacy.

Elliptical deception: hidden in plain sight

While John Thelwall's art of surrogacy may explain his attraction to Cecil Boyle, any clues it offers as to the other critical events of 1816 must be glimpsed through a veil of factual deception, rhetorical disguise and strategic silence that at once elucidates and vexes biographical reading. The style of 'Thoughts and Remembrances' may thus be called elliptical, drawing attention to something under the surface that appears to be, or at least feels, transgressive, but which is left unstated. Perhaps, like the incest motif in Thelwall's novel, it gestures towards residual taboos that underlie any father's feelings for a (surrogate) daughter. It also probably bespeaks anxieties about the sincerity and motives of Cecil as a gifted actress, whose 'entrancing ecstasy' was far from the 'artless softness' of Thelwall's long-lost Maria.

Like the perspectival and gender confusion in 'Cupid's Disguise' (in which it is difficult to tell whether the traitor is speaker or addressee, male or female), the guile and guise in 'Thoughts and Remembrances' are also self-reflexive. They remind us that Thelwall too was an actor, a master orator whose poems, published and unpublished, were carefully constructed performances. In this light, it is worth looking more carefully at its sequence of details. The phrase 'widow'd heart' in the opening lines suggests that Thelwall did not meet or notice Cecil until after Susan's death; yet this is contradicted by some of our factual evidence. A letter to the theatre manager William Elliston in mid-July 1816 indicates that Thelwall was already deeply committed to Cecil's theatrical career, but he inexplicably disguises her name (substituting one of his own poetical personae): 'Miss B— (or as we will *call her*, if you please, *Miss Wentworth*)'. This comes after he has listed the roles they have been preparing together, many of which are known for cross-dressing deception (Rosalind in *As You Like It*, Imogen in *Cymbeline* and Letitia Hardy in *The Belle's Stratagem*).[29]

The same date of July 1816 appears in marginal notations on some of the most erotic poems in the Derby manuscript – a numbered series of 'paphiades' that tell of a love that dare not speak its name. It is unclear when they were composed, but the notations, referring to the singing teacher Gesualdo Lanza, suggest that these poems may have been performed by Cecil well before the death of Susan Thelwall. All this leads the reader to suspect what common-sense experience may already have suggested: that the middle-aged professor and his talented daughter-pupil were having an extra-marital affair. Thus adultery, as well as quasi-incest, may be the unspoken transgression that underlies the disturbed, elliptical style of Thelwall's 'Thoughts and Remembrances'. Of course, there is no factual proof of this; perhaps Thelwall really was so grief-stricken and preoccupied at the imminent death of his wife as to be oblivious to Cecil's nubile attractions, but it is just as likely that what we recognise here is the familiar rhetoric of adulterous rationalisation that elliptically reveals what is hidden in plain sight.

Further evidence of Thelwall's elliptical counterfactualism lies even closer to the surface of 'Thoughts and Remembrances'. Indeed, the most striking feature of that poem is a literal ellipsis, a 5-line passage of asterisks that appears in its second verse paragraph. Immediately after mourning his 'widow'd heart', Thelwall explains his alienation from those

> who should –
> Under a better star, have cheer'd the hours
> Of heavy loneliness ...
> ... and chiefly one –
> Whom I had ever hop'd should be to me
> Friend and companion! – whom my love had train'd
> But too indulgently!

Five lines of silence follow, broken only by five stuttering monosyllables: 'He was far off, and ...' Such ellipses were not uncommon in Romantic-era print culture; in periodicals they were widely used to signal something scandalous or libellous without opening oneself to prosecution; in sentimental novels they indicate intense emotion and moments of narrative crisis, often associated with male ego, rakishness and/or moral defect.[30] Like all such aporia, this one both invites the reader to fill in the missing information and frustrates the search, since Thelwall offers only one clue – that it refers to a male member of his family, whom he had indulged and treated more like a friend than a son.

This surmise is confirmed and extended by a recently discovered poem whose title, 'A Remembrance', suggests that it fills in the missing lines of 'Thoughts and Remembrances', although it takes a different lyric form, at once Burnsian and Byronic:[31]

> There is a feeling at my heart,
>   By feeling only scann'd; –
> A bosom'd pang; a cherish'd smart;
> A throb, from which I cannot part,
> Though rankling like a venom'd dart
>   Shot by some treacherous hand!

> There is a name I cannot bear
>   To name myself – but less to hear,
> Which yet in joy, and yet in care,
> The dotage of my thought will share,
> Such deep affection graves it there
>   Even to resentment dear!
>
> There is an image in mine eye
>   That darkness cannot hide:
> It claims the tear, it swells the sigh,
> Deepens my grief, and dims my joy;
> From which I cannot wish to fly,
>   And could not if I tried.
>
> O, Memory! where's the potent art,
>   And where's the magic wand,
> Can conjure from the wounded heart
> The fond affection, or the smart
> The throbs of blighted hope impart, –
>   Blighted by filial hand?
>
>   (*SPP*, p. 264)

This remarkable lyric sums up Thelwall's counterfactual techniques and backs up the scholarly detective work that analyses, connects and uses them as evidence to build a credible and coherent factual narrative. It complements 'Thoughts and Remembrances' not only in its title, but also in the fact that this poem, too, has come down to us only in its public, printed form. Indeed, it was published (in the *Monthly Magazine* for 1825) with another poem that appears nowhere else – a love lyric that repeats the image of the 'day-star' from 'Thoughts and Remembrances'.[32]

'A Remembrance' also calls up motifs from other seductive allegories: the arrow from 'Cupid's Disguise' and the blight from the flower poems. The speaker's refusal to identify the feeling, name and image that haunt him creates another teasing ellipsis or absence at the heart of the utterance, while the mirror-image confusion of self and other in that unnamed name points to yet another important aspect of Thelwall's poetics of surrogacy: his lifelong quest for, and repeated betrayal by, a 'second self' with whom he hoped to realise the ideal of reciprocity and correspondence that stands at the core of his oeuvre.[33] As for 'filial' in the final line above, it fills the blanks of 'Thoughts and Remembrances' by suggesting that the unnamed he who blighted, disappointed or betrayed Thelwall was one of his sons – most likely Algernon Sydney, of whose destiny (at the age of 3) Thelwall had written: 'that he will be no ordinary lad I think myself certain – but whether he will be an uncommon genius or an uncommon villain, time and a thousand accidents which it is impossible either to foresee or control must decide'.[34]

Ventriloquism: the voice of the other

In pursuit of Algernon Sydney, I now venture beyond the established oeuvre of John Thelwall to certain poems that deepen counterfactual mysteries of identity in the Thelwall family by introducing a technique that is characteristically Thelwallian and present in the works of both father and son. Ventriloquism, or personation, was fundamental to John Thelwall's elocutionary poetry and his pedagogy, which offered students the opportunity to liberate their own voices, overcome impediments and develop 'practical fluency' and agency by taking on the voices and adopting the personae of others – specifically voices of authority from classical, biblical and literary history.[35] This technique is relevant to two poems whose authorship and documentary reliability are open to question, but which are worth considering nevertheless, in part because their dates are pertinent to this inquiry. These unattributed blank-verse meditations appear in an addendum to Algernon Sydney's *Thoughts in Affliction*, a book of religious consolation published in 1831 (the year in which his father's only child by Cecil, a son named Weymouth Birkbeck, was born).[36] Printing them together, with commentary, to illustrate the development of a 'sickly mind' from atheist misery towards Christian redemption, Algernon Sydney notes that they 'have been so long connected in my mind, that I know not how to separate them'.[37]

The first poem 'was written about the month of May 1816, when [the author] was yet an Infidel'; the second dates from early 1824, by which time, though still suffering from a 'constitutional tendency to melancholy and despondency', its author had 'found abundant peace and consolation' in God.[38] There is absolutely no proof that the poems are by John Thelwall, except that both bear clear signs of his style, in their fluent and accomplished blank verse, their conversational odic form, their imagery of storm at sea, shipwreck, exile, blighted flowers and friendship lost, and their tone of quasi-Byronic angst and pathos. This is especially marked in the first poem, which recalls both 'Thoughts and Remembrances' and one of John Thelwall's best conversation poems, 'To the Infant Hampden':

> Yet still one consolation for a while
> Could soothe my aching heart, and calm the waves,

> The surging billows dark, of misery,
> That roll'd and roar'd continual round my head.[39]

The second poem begins in the same mood – 'Alone – alone – alone upon the earth' – but its rapid turn to religious language ('Where should I look, O Saviour! but to Thee? –') seems inconsistent with what we know of John Thelwall the radical atheist. Yet even as it bows to Christian scripture, it retains a tone of religious speculation, tolerance and materialism characteristic of Thelwall's late work, particularly the poem 'Visions of Philosophy', addressed to Coleridge, which attempts to harmonise Platonic metaphysics with a Socratic social gospel.[40] Another obstacle to attributing the 1816 poem to John Thelwall is that its expression of grief is for the loss not of a wife but of a male friend:

> I had one friend – one true, unwavering friend –
> Who lov'd me still for what I might have been,
> And fondly pitied me for what I was: –
> And he is gone! O heaven and earth and air!
> That I should live to say, 'He is no more!'[41]

Again, this may be taken as evidence that these poems are not by Thelwall *père* at all. Yet given what we know about surrogacy and second selves, and noting the use of 'gone', rather than 'dead', it is possible that this poem may refer to the same grievous loss, change or betrayal that occasioned 'A Remembrance'. It is significant, too, that according to Algernon Sydney, 'the circumstances alluded to were (in great measure) *imaginary*'. Yet he has no qualms about reading them biographically.

The poems in *Thoughts in Affliction* also draw attention to the ventriloquism evident throughout the work of Algernon Sydney, whose repudiation of his father seems always to have taken the form of inverse imitation. Having grown up in John Thelwall's institution, lecturing beside his father and imbibing his theories, Algernon was well versed in his elocutionary pedagogy; after he had declared his independence, he turned his practical fluency to a very different end, but remained his father's son in other respects. In his theological writings, he adopts the same tone of stubborn independence and strident defensiveness about church politics that his father had shown about reform politics. When he took up his position at King's College London, he further ventriloquised his father – without attribution – by making the same points about elocution using the selfsame examples and exercises. It is, therefore, not impossible that he did the same thing in these poems: either he wrote them himself, adopting his father's characteristic images and tone in a kind of inverse surrogacy, simultaneously following and cancelling out his father's example; or perhaps more likely, he took poems originally written by his father, and altered them to suit his own ideological agenda, bringing the infidel home to God in an act of simultaneous redemption and rivalry, consolation and triumph.

Proteus paramount: counterfactual voice and textuality

For the most revealing and yet supremely evasive example of Thelwallian counterfactualism however, with all its uncertainties, absences, substitutions and counterfeitings of identity, voice and authorship, we must return to the Derby manuscript. Quite apart from the poems collected within it, its own documentary status is counterfactual in the sense that it is not unified or reliable, but fragmentary and unfinished, with multiple versions and revisions of many poems and passages, and evidence of other hands besides Thelwall's. As the first editor of this sprawling document, as well as a prospective biographer, I am only too aware of the difficulties and dangers it presents, even as I am excited by its rich potential. If there is one text in this manuscript that sums up both the problems and the promise of the Derby document for the counterfactual biographer, it is one of three poems that I have collectively dubbed the Pandolia fragments, which focus on a single character of that name. A consummate actress of entrancing wit, commanding voice, ebullient energy and self-possessed agency who runs rhetorical circles around the men who dote on her, Pandolia is almost certainly based on Cecil Boyle. Her voice sounds here as nowhere else in Thelwall's poetry, since one of the poems is almost certainly in her hand, and may have actually been written by her.

Undated, but appearing in volume 3 of the manuscript among the poems of 1816 already discussed, the first of these poems, 'Pandolia. A Sapphic', is clearly by Thelwall. It is in his hand, follows one of his favourite forms (the Sapphic ode) and resembles the adoption poems in its two-stanza celebration of Pandolia's 'Beauty with wit reciprocally blending' (*SPP*, p. 201), followed by a final stanza that introduces a question as to whether she can be trusted. The second, longer poem, however, is more complex and challenging as regards both its voice and its hand, as well as its implications for my counterfactual biography. 'Pandolia's Description of her Four Lovers. A scene rejected from an unpublished Drama as not sufficiently dramatic' is a 150-line fragment. It has three speakers: Pandolia, who describes (and mocks) her lovers, and a pair of friends who laugh and urge her on. Her speech is a tour de force of seductive allegory, deception and disguise, witty wordplay and multivocal ventriloquism, proving her to be – as one of her admirers calls her – 'My metamorphist! Proteus paramount!' (*SPP*, p. 204). The protean, metamorphic nature of both Pandolia and the counterfactual techniques she personifies is summed up in two meanings of 'affect' – to pretend and to feel – that are united in her. When she is asked whether she 'affects' (that is, favours, or has feelings for) any of her many lovers, she replies: 'Oh! yes – most marvellously / I do affect them all: as you shall hear' (*SPP*, p. 201). She then proceeds not only to describe but also to imitate four of them, each a romantic type, thus revealing how she changes her manner and identity in response to theirs, pretending to be what they desire. The first is a poet, with whom she expresses 'melancholy sympathies'. The next is a dandy, with whom she 'floats' and 'trills' through 'the gay mazes of the antic dance', laughing with but mostly at him. The third, of whom she speaks longest and most harshly, is a 'truss'd philosopher' who 'holds our sex as unessential ciphers / Physical crudities! Mere non-rationals!'; pretending to be a 'dimpled Socrates', she 'affect[s]' him / Even to the bathos of his own profound', tangling him 'in a cobweb snare / Of his own weaving ... / Spun from the bowels of his own conceit'. The final lover is 'my man of Mars, my red hot soldier', in relation to whom she takes a 'voice and port / Right Amazonian' (*SPP*, pp. 203–4).

While Pandolia's character and observations are in some ways conventional, recalling comedies of manners by female Romantic playwrights such as Hannah Cowley and Joanna Baillie, as well as the Shakespearean roles that Cecil had rehearsed, they also invite biographical interpretation based on techniques we have already seen. On the one hand, Pandolia's brilliant ventriloquism and protean adaptability highlight the theatrical talents for deception and disguise already associated with Cecil. On the other, each of the four lovers, while equally conventional, may be associated with Thelwall himself, or at least with his oratorical, poetical and pedagogical personae; the four identities mock the subjects and types of elocution he taught (martial, for example), the methods he used (dandified gestures), the philosophical ideals he promoted and the poetry he delivered. They also recall one of Thelwall's earliest and most brilliant orations, *A Speech in Rhyme* (1788), in which young Thelwall played all five speakers in a debate on love: four male lovers, followed by a single woman who wins the represented contest (and won Thelwall the real debate) by satirising and overcoming the men's romantic and rhetorical inadequacies.[42] So it is quite possible to read this drama as an updating of that speech, reflecting his theatrical ventriloquism just as much as Cecil's.

That in itself foregrounds another two counterfactual features of 'Pandolia's Description of her Four Lovers'. First, just as protean as the voices being adopted and satirised is the authorship of the poem. There are at least two hands. One is Thelwall's own, the hand in which most of the poems in the manuscript are written – sometimes more elegant in fair copy, at times more rushed and rough, in multiple revisions. This hand is responsible for the title of this dramatic fragment and numerous corrections, elisions and revisions, including those that convert Pandolia's first speech into Thelwallian sapphics. But the hand in which most of the fragment is written is a different one; childish, rounded and upright, it looks very much like that of a young girl. This raises several questions. If, as seems likely, Pandolia is Cecil, and this fragment derives from their practice of working on scenes together, did she compose the scene herself (or the entire drama, if more of it was ever written), perhaps as a pupil awaiting his corrections? Or did he write it, she faircopy it, and then he revise it further? Who is the author? Who is ventriloquising whom? To whom should we attribute its masterful mockery, manipulation and subversion of romantic conventions? And to whom do they refer? Is it possible that a middle-aged male professor in love with a young actress-pupil could either compose, or calmly read and revise, this cutting satire without seeing himself in it? Could he have detached himself from his male ego, or entered into her gender position, sufficiently to laugh at it and at himself?

The recursive confusion of gender identity and role-playing in the Pandolia fragment becomes more complex when one considers the other two speakers in the scene (not the characters being described, but the listeners who occasionally interject). They are obviously favoured male companions who encourage Pandolia's mockery of her lovers, but who are oblivious to the ways in which she is also manipulating their own love of her. One of these interlocutors is named Dolometis (from Latin *dolor*, signifying misery and grief, and Greek *metis*, signifying a quality that combines wisdom with cunning, duplicity, pliability and equivocation). The other is identified only by the abbreviation Soph (another Greek root signifying both wisdom through speech instruction and falsity through rhetorical manipulation). Soph is an older man (he pants and puffs when Pandolia dances with them, cursing his 'phthysic' or respiratory ailment), but he is obviously smitten by her, flattering her obsequiously and foolishly succumbing to her flirtatious favours. Dolometis also flatters her, but is jealous of Soph, whom he viciously teases about his age. He calls him 'an old trout playing on the line / Sage as he is, he must be nibbling still, / And snap at mayflies, like the youngest fry'. He also alludes to Beatrice's mockery of Benedick in *Much Ado about Nothing* when he asks, in an aside, 'is that birdbolt lost on this blind buzzard?' (*SPP*, p. 203). Even without knowing that Thelwall called himself 'Benedict' in his wedding announcement and wrote a courtship allegory and cautionary tale called 'The Trout' at about this time (addressed to his teenage daughter Manon, aka 'Troutilla'), it is not difficult to identify him with Soph and to see in this 'rejected' scene a vignette of Cecil, John and Algernon reading plays together at Lincoln's Inn Fields.

And so this outrageously fragmented, impossibly counterfactual fiction may in the end be the best clue to the true romance of the gothic rivalries and betrayals, manipulations and transformations of the summer of 1816. Henrietta Cecil Boyle was a vivacious, self-assured, attractive and ambitious 16-year-old actress. It is only natural to suppose that Algernon Sydney, just 21 years old and home from university, might have been attracted to his father's pupil. How infuriating must it have been to watch his father fawn on her and see her flirt with him, especially in the house in which his beloved mother was upstairs, dying. How much worse must it have been when, so soon after his mother's death, Cecil chose the old trout rather than the young fry. It would be enough to drive any young man into the arms of the Church.

But whatever sympathy I – as prospective biographer of John Thelwall – might have for Algernon (which is not much, given the militant whine of his religious writings), I wonder more about poor Susan. How much did she know, as she lingered in her illness, of what was happening in the classroom downstairs? More than her husband realised, one suspects. Enough, perhaps, to account for her lingering longer, a grey ghost forever on the landing, forever casting herself over the railing of that staircase and down the long ellipsis of their lives together. But, of course, the most intriguing character here is Cecil herself, especially if she actually wrote and *was* Pandolia. What happened to that supremely witty, self-possessed satirist, that talented ingénue who gave up her career for a man three times her age, was left a widow with a small child at the age of 31, published the first, political, volume of a planned two-volume biography, collected materials (including the Derby manuscript) for the second, literary, volume, but was stonewalled by Wordsworth and gave up, then disappeared for a decade before appearing as an elegant and beautiful hostess to Charles Dickens in the home of her sister, and then, mysteriously, vanishing from the record for another decade, to die in penury in 1865? What a story she might tell! And what about her other 'sisters', Thelwall's biological daughters – Manon Roland (named for the French Revolutionary heroine) and Sara Maria (named not only for the lost Maria, but also, it seems, for the wife of Thelwall's erstwhile second-self, Coleridge, at exactly the same time as the latter named *his* daughter Sara after Wordsworth's sister-in-law)? Cecil, Manon and Sara Thelwall make a creative triad comparable to Claire Clairmont, Mary Shelley and Fanny Imlay (and, for that matter, Sara Coleridge, Dora Wordsworth and Edith Southey). Who will fill in the blanks in *their* stories?

Not I; I am too busy with their father. Besides, as must by now be obvious, I long ago allowed myself to get carried away by my speculative enterprise, tumbling off the fine line I promised to walk, and straying deep into the realm of romance, far (it may seem) from the rigorous detachment of the scholar and the limits even of counterfactual conjecture. After all, how much can one read into a manuscript fragment of a farce, written in a confusion of hands and voices, discarded from an unpublished drama that may never be found – if indeed it was ever written? Surely the biographer is herself in danger of being tangled in a cobweb of conceit, in both senses of that word. And there she must remain, a cautionary example of the perils of counterfactual Romanticism, or at least this version of it.

But let me offer one last word (and ventriloquial performance) of wilful wish-fulfilment in this age of #MeToo, reflecting (on) the frustrations of the female biographer as yet another handmaid to yet another Romantic ego. Channelling one final, tiny, tantalising fact – the parish notice of the marriage of a Cecil Thelwall Boyle to an Ann Rowse in 1846 – through another, much more distinguished, metafiction (A. S. Byatt's paradigmatic 1990 postmodern tale of Romantic possession), I leave you with …[43]

A coda

Autumn 1846. On a lowering morning after a night of storm, the vicar of St John the Baptist, Shoreditch, entered his drawing room to find his wife arranging flowers in a vase.

'Oh my!' she exclaimed. These winds have made such a rout! I've gathered and saved what I could from the garden, but what's left is sadly battered and will want propping. My *roses* are all blown, and even the *woodbine* has been torn away from its *anchor near the oak* in the corner.'

'I shall see that Tom repairs the trellises. You, my dear, shall work your wonders, I am sure.'

'As you have done in our parish. Your work to *establish the savings bank and national school* is a beacon of hope, though I can see how it wears you down.'

'Ah, yes. Our new church may have been *designed by John Soane's finest pupil*, but I'm afraid my own plans are constantly thwarted. The condition of my flock grows ever more desperate! It is hard to know where we stand these days, when some rise so high, while others fall so low. I have just seen a curious example of that in the ceremony I performed this morning. Such an odd couple, with so little fuss and so few attendants! They could have done with some blooms from your garden, my dear, battered though it is. The bride was pious and pretty enough – of country stock, if I'm not mistaken, sturdy and capable, a good *Christian belle* with roses in her cheeks. But it was the bridegroom who wanted propping. He was so slight, and quite *blanched* in complexion. He was plainly yet carefully dressed, and has come down in the world, I'll warrant, for he was surely a gentleman, soft- and well-spoken; and when he made his vows, his voice had something so powerful and fluent in it, like *music to the soul*. Clean-shaven he was and almost boyish, yet obviously in his middle years. Certainly older than his best man, who looked a schoolboy indeed, though so alike they might almost have been *parent and child*. The older leaned upon the younger as they walked to the altar, and when at last the groom *twined* his arm around the waist of his bride, it seemed that she was supporting him, and not he her. Yet for all that, my dear, they were well matched and obviously in love. They hastened out to a waiting gig, but I learned from the boy who stayed behind to pay their fee that they intend to set up a school together at the top of the parish towards Newington Green. I wish them well of it, and perhaps I will call on them, for something tells me they may be sympathetic to my *projects for reform*.

'What were their names, my dear?'

'Now that's a strange thing too, for there was something so familiar in his name, yet I cannot place it.' His eye wandered up towards the bookshelf. 'Hers – *Ann Rowse* – was common enough, yet his was quite elegant – *Cecil Thelwall Boyle*. I can't think where I've heard it before, but it rings in one's ears, don't you think?'

Notes

1. See Kenneth R. Johnston, *Unusual Suspects: Pitt's Reign of Alarm and the Lost Generation of the 1790s* (Oxford: Oxford University Press, 2013).
2. See Michael Scrivener, 'Frankenstein's Ghost Story: The Last Jacobin Novel', *Genre*, 19:3 (Fall 1986), 299–318; and Yasmin Solomonescu, *John Thelwall and the Materialist Imagination* (New York: Palgrave, 2014), pp. 2–3.
3. See Ben Weinreb, Christopher Hibbert, Julia Keay and John Keay (eds), *The London Encyclopedia*, 3rd rev. edn (London: Macmillan, 2008), p. 487.
4. Thomas Noon Talfourd had studied law at Lincoln's Inn at exactly the time that Thelwall moved there. He was precisely the same age as Thelwall's eldest son and contributed to Thelwall's newspaper and magazines, including *The Champion* (published at Lincoln's Inn Fields). The sister of Thelwall's second wife, Cecil, was the wife of Dr Robert Davey, at whose home Charles Dickens lodged his ailing father, whom he often visited. According to a reminiscence published in 1885 in *The Christian Union* ('A New Page in the History of Charles Dickens'), Cecil Thelwall – the still beautiful middle-aged 'widow of the celebrated politician and orator' – served as an elegant hostess at her sister's literary soirées (p. 7).
5. See Claire Tomalin, *The Invisible Woman: The Story of Nelly Ternan and Charles Dickens* (London: Penguin, 2002).
6. I draw here on first-hand accounts relayed to me by the capable, authoritative and rather Dickensian maintenance man at Garden Court Chambers in 2014.
7. See *Morning Chronicle*, 5 January 1813, p. 1, and John Thelwall, *Plan and Objects of Mr Thelwall's Institution* (London: J. M'Creery, 1813). Fees ranged from 4s. a lecture to £300 a year, depending on the age of the pupil and the nature and degree of their impediment.
8. In July 1816, Thelwall's surviving children were Algernon Sydney (21 years old), John Hampden (19), Manon Roland (17), Sara Maria (15), Edwin Northumbrian (12) and Benjamin Franklin (3) who died shortly before Thelwall's remarriage. See *England Births and Christenings 1538–1975*, Family Search database, https://familysearch.org/ark:/61903/1:1:NL2T-FL6 (accessed 29 September 2016), FHL microfilm 374,335; and https://familysearch.org/ark:/61903/1:1:JMLF-WDZ (accessed 7 June 2018).
9. Thelwall to R. W. Elliston, 18 July 1816; Baker Library, Harvard Business School, Kress Collection, MS 330. I am indebted to Michael Scrivener for his transcription of this letter.

10 See William Hazlitt, *A View of the English Stage; or, a Series of Dramatic Criticisms* (London: R. Stodart, 1818), p. 354.
11 Henry Crabb Robinson, *Diary, Reminiscences and Correspondence of Henry Crabb Robinson*, ed. Thomas Sadler (London: Macmillan, 1872), p. 15.
12 *Morning Post*, 16 September 1816, p. 3.
13 *Liverpool Mercury*, 27 June 1817, p. 6; *England Marriages, 1538–1973*, Family Search database, https://familysearch.org/ark:/61903/1:1:NKNX-8JL (accessed 29 September 2016), FHL microfilm 1,042,319.
14 Crabb Robinson, *Diary, Reminiscences and Correspondence*, p. 42.
15 See Patty O'Boyle, '"A Son of John Thelwall": Weymouth Birkbeck Thelwall's Romantic Inheritance', www.rc.umd.edu/praxis/thelwall/HTML/praxis.2011.oboyle.html (accessed 16 April 2018); and Algernon Sydney Thelwall, *Memorials and Testimonials* (London, 1858), pp. 2–6. Algernon Sydney published his inaugural lecture at King's College London as *The Reading Desk and the Pulpit* (London: Wertheim, Macintosh and Hunt, 1861).
16 *Morning Post*, 16 September 1816, p. 3.
17 The formal title of the Derby manuscript is *Poems, Chiefly Suggested by the Scenery of Nature* (Derby Central Library, Local Studies MSS, 5868–70). It comprises three bound volumes, paginated and with a table of contents, containing more than 200 different poems, many of them dated (between 1787 and 1827), covering more than 1,000 numbered pages including unnumbered insertions and verso pages numbered in reverse. I cite the manuscript collection in the notes that follow as 'Derby MS', followed by volume and page number. For more on the Derby manuscript, including its love poems, see Judith Thompson, 'Citizen Juan Thelwall: In the Footsteps of a Free-Range Radical', *Studies in Romanticism*, 48:1 (Spring 2009), 67–100, and John Thelwall, *Selected Poetry and Poetics*, ed. Judith Thompson (New York: Palgrave, 2015), pp. 17–18 (hereafter *SPP* in the body of the text).
18 Composed in 1805, Thelwall's 'Song of Eros, or Triumph of Love, intended as a substitute for the concluding stanza of Collins' Ode of the Passions' (*SPP*, pp. 179–81) serves as an announcement, vindication and virtually a poetic manifesto of the triumph of eros as the 'all-subjugating cause' of Nature, the passions, poetry, science, human history and politics.
19 On seditious allegory, see Michael Scrivener, *Seditious Allegories: John Thelwall and Jacobin Writing* (University Park, PA: Penn State University Press, 2001).

20 See Beverly Seaton, *The Language of Flowers: A History* (Charlottesville, VA: University of Virginia Press, 1995), pp. 36–60.
21 'The Nosegay' (*SPP*, pp. 27–31) – an important series of flower poems in Thelwall's first published volume, *Poems on Various Subjects* (1787) – shows that Thelwall's erotic botanical allegories predated those of Darwin. 'The Wintery Oak' (*SPP*, p. 34), revised in the Derby manuscript, was originally published untitled in John Thelwall, *The Peripatetic*, ed. Judith Thompson (Detroit, MI: Wayne State University Press, 2001), pp. 168–9.
22 John Thelwall to Dr Peter Crompton, 8 March, 1798, in Damian Walford Davies, *Presences that Disturb: Models of Romantic Identity in the Literature and Culture of the 1790s* (Cardiff: University of Wales Press, 2002), p. 302.
23 John Thelwall, *The Daughter of Adoption*, ed. Michael Scrivener, Yasmin Solomonescu and Judith Thompson (Peterborough, ON: Broadview Press, 2013), pp. 155–6.
24 *Ibid.*, p. 426.
25 On the incest motif in *The Daughter of Adoption*, see *ibid.*, p. 27
26 Derby MS, III, p. 826.
27 *Ibid.*, p. 827. 'Adoption' was published in John Thelwall, *The Poetical Recreations of the Champion* (London 1822), pp. 224–5.
28 Derby MS, III, p. 825.
29 Thelwall to R. W. Elliston, 18 July 1816; Baker Library, Harvard Business School, Kress Collection, MS 330.
30 In *Ellipsis in English Literature: Signs of Omission* (Cambridge: Cambridge University Press, 2015), Anne Toner surveys these, and other, uses of ellipses, including their association with Lovelace in *Clarissa* (pp. 68–76) and with the elocution movement (pp. 78–82), as well as the 'reader's pleasure in completing libellous blanks in the periodical press' (p. 76).
31 Its verse form is Burnsian (adapting the 'standard Habbie' stanza), but its sensibility is all Byron. See *The Burns Encyclopedia*, www.robertburns.org/encyclopedia/StandardHabbie.22.shtml (accessed 28 September 2016).
32 *Monthly Magazine*, 60 (1 November 1825), 335. In 1825, Thelwall was the editor of this magazine.
33 Damian Walford Davies (in *Presences that Disturb*, p. 78) suggests that Thelwall constructed himself as a 'dark second self' of Wordsworth and Coleridge in his *Poems, Chiefly Written in Retirement*. On second-self images in Thelwall's work, see Judith Thompson, 'A Shadow in Profile: John Thelwall in the Lake District', in Richard Gravil (ed.), *Grasmere 2008: Selected Papers from the Wordsworth Summer Conference* (Tirril:

Humanities eBooks, 2008), pp. 175–212. For Thelwall's larger vision of reciprocity and correspondence, see *SPP*, p. 14, and Judith Thompson, *John Thelwall in the Wordsworth Circle: The Silenced Partner* (New York: Palgrave, 2012), especially pp. 15–17, 26–7, 125–60.

34 Thelwall to Dr Peter Crompton, 8 March 1798; Walford Davies, *Presences that Disturb*, p. 302.
35 Thelwall often ventriloquised and rewrote the poetry of others, including Collins, Wordsworth and Coleridge. On ventriloquism as an elocutionary technique, see Patricia Howell Michaelson, *Speaking Volumes: Women, Reading and Speech in the Age of Austen* (Stanford, CA: Stanford University Press, 2002), pp. 111–27, and Judith Thompson, 'Romantic Oratory', in David Duff (ed.), *The Oxford Handbook of British Romanticism* (London: Oxford University Press, 2018), p. 544.
36 On Algernon Sydney's feelings for his step-brother, and Weymouth Birkbeck's own implausibly gothic fate, see O'Boyle, 'A Son of John Thelwall'.
37 Algernon Sydney Thelwall, *Thoughts in Affliction* (London: Seeley and Burnside, 1831), p. 118.
38 *Ibid.*, pp. 117–22.
39 *Ibid.*, p. 119.
40 See Judith Thompson, '"And Bid the Mental Drama Rise Renew'd": Coleridge, Thelwall and "Visions of Philosophy"', *Coleridge Bulletin*, 44 (Winter 2014), 29–48.
41 Algernon Sydney Thelwall, *Thoughts in Affliction*, p. 119.
42 John Thelwall, *A Speech in Rhyme, Delivered at Westminster Forum ... on the Following Question, 'Is the assertion of the Marchioness de Lambert true, that Love Improves the Virtuous Soul?'* (London: Sammels and Ritchie, 1788).
43 *England Marriages 1538–1973*, Family Search database, https://familysearch.org/ark:/61903/1:1:NL35-45J (accessed 7 June 2018). Here again I have shared the puzzle and pleasure of counterfactual metafiction, leaving it to my reader to identify italicised allusions to poetry and fiction (those to Thelwall now made familiar from the body of the chapter). But I identify some of the allusions to historical fact surrounding St John the Baptist, Shoreditch (now generally called Hoxton), where the wedding of Ann Rowse and Cecil Thelwall Boyle took place in 1846. (No further information or indication of a possible connection to our Cecil Boyle Thelwall was available at time of composition.) According to its Wikipedia page, the church was built in 1826 from plans by Frances Edwards, the foremost pupil of John Soane, the architect who had left his mark on Thelwall's staircase at 57 Lincoln's Inn Fields. Its first vicar

was a recognised social reformer who founded a savings bank and a national school in an effort to address urban social deprivation. Mary Wollstonecraft was born in the parish; Newington Green, where she set up her school with her friend Fanny Blood, lies just to the north. My fantasy of a Boston marriage for widow Cecil is set within these coordinates of possibility.

Works cited

Primary texts (including MS sources)

Anon., 'A New Page in the History of Charles Dickens', *The Christian Union*, 31 (1885), 6–7

Anon., obituary for Susan Thelwall, *Morning Post*, 16 September 1816, p. 3

'Benedict' [John Thelwall], notice of his marriage, *Liverpool Mercury*, 27 June 1817, p. 6

Crabb Robinson, Henry, *Diary, Reminiscences and Correspondence of Henry Crabb Robinson*, ed. Thomas Sadler (London: Macmillan, 1872)

England Births and Christenings 1538–1975, Family Search database, www.familysearch.org

England Marriages 1538–1973, Family Search database, www.familysearch.org

Hazlitt, William, *A View of the English Stage; or, a Series of Dramatic Criticisms* (London: R. Stodart, 1818)

Thelwall, John, advertisement for his therapeutic institution, *Morning Chronicle*, 5 January 1813, p. 1

Thelwall, John, 'A Remembrance', *Monthly Magazine*, 60 (1 November 1825), 335

Thelwall, John, *A Speech in Rhyme, Delivered at Westminster Forum … on the Following Question, 'Is the assertion of the Marchioness de Lambert true, that Love Improves the Virtuous Soul?'* (London: Sammells and Ritchie 1788)

Thelwall, John, 'Derby manuscript', *Poems, Chiefly Suggested by the Scenery of Nature* (Derby Central Library, Local Studies MSS, 5868–70)

Thelwall, John, Letter to R. W. Elliston (18 July 1816), Baker Library, Harvard Business School, Kress Collection, MS 330

Thelwall, John, *Plan and Objects of Mr Thelwall's Institution* (London: J. M'Creery, 1813)

Thelwall, John, *Selected Poetry and Poetics*, ed. Judith Thompson (New York: Palgrave, 2015)

Thelwall, John, *The Daughter of Adoption*, ed. Michael Scrivener, Yasmin

Solomonescu and Judith Thompson (Peterborough, ON: Broadview Press, 2013)
Thelwall, John, *The Peripatetic*, ed. Judith Thompson (Detroit, MI: Wayne State University Press, 2001)
Thelwall, John, *The Poetical Recreations of the Champion* (London 1822)
Thelwall, Algernon Sydney, *Memorials and Testimonials* (London, 1858)
Thelwall, Algernon Sydney, *The Reading Desk and the Pulpit* (London: Wertheim, Macintosh and Hunt, 1861)
Thelwall, Algernon Sydney, *Thoughts in Affliction* (London: Seeley and Burnside, 1831)

Secondary texts

Burns Encyclopedia, The, www.robertburns.org/encyclopedia/Standard Habbie.22.shtml
Johnston, Kenneth R., *Unusual Suspects: Pitt's Reign of Alarm and the Lost Generation of the 1790s* (Oxford: Oxford University Press, 2013)
Michaelson, Patricia Howell, *Speaking Volumes: Women, Reading and Speech in the Age of Austen* (Stanford, CA: Stanford University Press, 2002)
O'Boyle, Patty, '"A Son of John Thelwall": Weymouth Birkbeck Thelwall's Romantic Inheritance', www.rc.umd.edu/praxis/thelwall/HTML/praxis.2011.oboyle.html
Scrivener, Michael, 'Frankenstein's Ghost Story: The Last Jacobin Novel', *Genre*, 19:3 (Fall 1986), 299–318
Scrivener, Michael, *Seditious Allegories: John Thelwall and Jacobin Writing* (University Park, PA: Penn State University Press, 2001)
Seaton, Beverly, *The Language of Flowers: A History* (Charlottesville, VA: University of Virginia Press, 1995)
Solomonescu, Yasmin, *John Thelwall and the Materialist Imagination* (New York: Palgrave, 2014)
Thompson, Judith, '"And Bid the Mental Drama Rise Renew'd": Coleridge, Thelwall and "Visions of Philosophy"', *Coleridge Bulletin*, 44 (Winter 2014), 29–48
Thompson, Judith, 'A Shadow in Profile: John Thelwall in the Lake District', in Richard Gravil (ed.), *Grasmere 2008: Selected Papers from the Wordsworth Summer Conference* (Tirril: Humanities eBooks, 2008), pp. 175–212
Thompson, Judith, 'Citizen Juan Thelwall: In the Footsteps of a Free-Range Radical', *Studies in Romanticism*, 48:1 (Spring 2009), 67–100
Thompson, Judith, *John Thelwall in the Wordsworth Circle: The Silenced Partner* (New York: Palgrave, 2012)
Thompson, Judith, 'Romantic Oratory', in David Duff (ed.), *The Oxford*

Handbook of British Romanticism (London: Oxford University Press, 2018), pp. 529–46

Tomalin, Claire, *The Invisible Woman: The Story of Nelly Ternan and Charles Dickens* (London: Penguin, 2002)

Toner, Anne, *Ellipsis in English Literature: Signs of Omission* (Cambridge: Cambridge University Press, 2015)

Walford Davies, Damian, *Presences that Disturb: Models of Romantic Identity in the Literature and Culture of the 1790s* (Cardiff: University of Wales Press, 2002)

Weinreb, Ben, Christopher Hibbert, Julia Keay and John Keay (eds), *The London Encyclopedia*, 3rd rev. edn (London: Macmillan, 2008)

8

Counterfactual speculations in late Romanticism: Scott, Banim, Galt and Mitford

Angela Esterhammer

Counterfactualism takes on a variety of forms in the literature of the 1820s – the decade in which the concept of the factual itself emerged.[1] In the prose genres that increasingly dominated the literary marketplace, 'fact' in the form of history, documentary and life-writing confronts that which counters or mediates fact: fantasy, fakery, imagined history, pure speculation. Indeed, the term *speculation* is especially prevalent in this era and often stands in for what would later be termed *counterfactual*. 'Speculation' appears in the opening sentence of Isaac D'Israeli's 'Of a History of Events Which Have Not Happened', an essay that could be considered the first explicit discussion of counterfactual historiography. It remains central to this sub-genre a century later, as shown by J. C. Squire's introduction to *If It Had Happened Otherwise: Lapses Into Imaginary History* (1931), a now-classic collection of essays in alternate history, where he describes the contents of the volume as 'speculations by curious minds as to the differences that would have been made had certain events "taken another turn"'.[2]

This chapter considers several varieties of counterfactualism that appear *avant la lettre* in literary and paraliterary texts published almost simultaneously in 1824, one of them being Isaac D'Israeli's essay. The 'what if' approach to history-writing proposed by D'Israeli is put into practice in the historical novel *Redgauntlet*, Walter Scott's most blatant experiment with counterfactual narrative. John Banim achieves a revisionary perspective on history and a critical intervention into contemporary society by directing speculative fantasy toward the future in his collection of essays entitled *Revelations of the Dead-Alive*. Two other productions of the literary climate of 1824, *The Bachelor's Wife* by John Galt and Mary Russell Mitford's *Our Village*, broach the counterfactual through their experimentation with hybrid genres. Both these texts explicitly claim a documentary perspective, yet both incorporate elements of idyllic fantasy that run counter to the purely factual.

Reading these texts against the background of the mid-1820s, an era characterised by rampant speculation on financial markets and lively competition within the literary marketplace, is itself an exercise in speculative literary history. It tests the premise that during the 1820s – thanks in part to the prominence of periodical journalism with its mode of writing 'to the moment' – there is an unusually close connection between material conditions, socio-economic behaviour, public discourse and literary representation. In all these spheres, speculation operates as a mode of behaviour that incorporates observable or factual components into hypothetical or fictional structures. In the economic sphere, for instance, these structures include financial markets and valuations driven by speculation on material resources that are always vulnerable to contingencies of timing, accident and unpredictable shifts of public opinion. Speculation, contingency, accident and shifts of perspective also determine the direction of history-writing and indeed of history itself, according to Isaac D'Israeli's 'Of a History of Events Which Have Not Happened', which appeared in the second series of his *Curiosities of Literature* in 1824. The deliberate paradox of his title, which defies the conventional definition of history as events that *have* happened, is nicely echoed in D'Israeli's self-referential opening sentence:

> Such a title might serve for a work of not incurious nor unphilosophical speculation, which might enlarge our general views of human affairs, and assist our comprehension of those events which are enrolled on the registers of history.[3]

The conditional mood ('might serve') and the double negatives ('not incurious nor unphilosophical') imitate on the level of grammar what counterfactual history does semantically: it posits events under certain conditions, naming but simultaneously negating them, thereby maintaining a rhetorical and cognitive distinction between the plane of 'events which are enrolled on the registers of history' and that of imagined alternatives.

D'Israeli's examples of counterfactual historiography range from ancient to modern, from Livy's history of Rome (what if Alexander the

Great had invaded Italy?) to William Roscoe's biography of Lorenzo de' Medici (what if Lorenzo had not died when he did?). Events are identified that might have had a momentous effect on the religious and political history of Europe (what if Charles II had won the Battle of Worcester? what if Charles Martel had not won the Battle of Tours in 732? what if Mary Queen of Scots had ascended the English throne?). Only a fraction of his examples, though, are precisely concerned with 'events which have not happened'. Rather, D'Israeli accurately summarises at the end of his essay the varieties of historiographical speculation he has discussed: 'Thus important events have been nearly occurring, which, however, did not take place; and others have happened which may be traced to accident, and to the character of an individual.'[4]

As much as his essay is about counterfactual alternatives, it is also about contingencies: he analyses why events *did* take place by tracing them to accident or individual character, to tiny coincidences, near misses, lucky or unlucky timing and unpredictable emotional reactions. This last category includes world-changing events that result from a chance remark and its effect on the disposition of an individual. D'Israeli quotes a historian who attributed the Protestant Reformation to the 'injurious and threatening words' used by the apostolic legate Cardinal San Sisto, which elicited a strong reaction from Martin Luther owing to his unusual sensitivity to insult.[5] D'Israeli's observations about the history-making role of 'accident' and 'the character of an individual' resemble the Romantic-era speculations of Heinrich von Kleist in his 1805 essay 'On the Gradual Completion of Thoughts while Speaking' ('Über die Allmähliche Verfertigung der Gedanken beim Reden'), in which he cites historical examples when analysing the relationship between cognition and utterance. As his most resonant example of the way in which thoughts are formulated in the process of speaking, Kleist considers Mirabeau's pronouncement in the National Assembly on 23 June 1789, when he refused to follow the king's order to dismiss the Assembly and instead suddenly proclaimed the authority of the Deputies as representatives of the nation. Kleist suggests that Mirabeau had no idea where his utterance was going when he got up to speak; while articulating his thoughts in the charged public atmosphere of the National Assembly, however, he reacted emotionally to the unthinking gestures of the Master of Ceremonies who challenged him. 'Perhaps it was in this manner finally the twitch of an upper lip, or an ambiguous toying with a cuff, that effected the toppling of the order of things in France', Kleist concludes.[6] With his rhetorical-cognitive approach, Kleist arrives at the same insight that D'Israeli reached by thinking through the 'what if' mode of historiography. Revealing how little it would have taken for events to have happened otherwise leads to a realisation of how little it took for them to have happened the way they actually did.

Damian Walford Davies has suggested that this widespread interest in contingency predisposed writers of the Romantic era to counterfactual history: 'That aspect of the Romantic aesthetic that valorizes the contingent and possible over the rigidly determinist is always attuned to alternative histories and realities.'[7] Walford Davies highlights the decade of the 1790s, with its historical upheavals, as an era that made thinkers especially aware of the conditional, and the example from Kleist illustrates a further way in which writers looked to recent revolutionary events when analysing historical contingency. Arguably, though, speculation about contingency grew even more acute a generation later, during the 1820s. Prose genres that were popular during this decade – including the historical novel, silver-fork fiction and late-Romantic Gothic – revel in detail and accident, both in the sense of mishap and of chance or coincidence. Other aspects of history-making and history-writing that D'Israeli highlights, such as subjective perspective and individual disposition, also come to the fore in paraliterary genres like periodical journalism and personal essays. I follow D'Israeli's lead in considering several examples and variations of the counterfactual by discussing four texts that combine, in different ways, the factual with that which counters or mediates fact. Unlike D'Israeli's examples from the *longue durée* of European history, these texts all date from the same moment in 1824. Together, they point to a crux in the history of factual and counterfactual writing that coincides – *not* by accident – with a heightened awareness of speculation and its role in driving economic behaviour, including the economy of the literary marketplace.

It is at this moment, ten years after Walter Scott's initial success with the historical novel *Waverley*, that the genre he popularised takes a distinct counterfactual turn. In 1824, Scott – still nominally hidden behind the pseudonym 'the Author of Waverley' – published *Redgauntlet*, a tale that repeats the basic plot established by *Waverley* in which a young Englishman becomes involved with Scottish rebels supporting the Stuart claim to the British throne. But while previous Waverley novels involved their heroes in the actual Jacobite rebellions of 1715 and 1745, *Redgauntlet* swerves from the course of eighteenth-century history by postulating a third attempted uprising in the summer of 1765, along with the fictitious return of the ageing Young Pretender, Charles Edward Stuart, from exile on the Continent. Scott's other novels typically place fictional characters in historical settings; *Redgauntlet*, while implicitly claiming the same degree of authenticity, places historical figures on an alternate plane of reality. Speculation operates on multiple levels of the narrative; as Scott speculates about what might have happened had the adventurous spirit of the Pretender and his Jacobite followers survived after 1745, he represents the Jacobite cause itself as a speculation, a high-risk enterprise founded on hope and belief rather than on actually existing conditions. The would-be rebellion led by Hugh Redgauntlet, a Stuart sympathiser who spends his life 'altogether engaged in political speculations and intrigues', turns out to be nothing more than a 'bubble' that inflates and soon dissolves.[8] Like other speculators, Redgauntlet goes beyond empirical evidence into the realm of self-delusion when he ignores the fact that history has moved on and there is no widespread infrastructure of Stuart sympathy left to build on in the Scottish borders. At the end of Scott's novel, the treasonous project of Charles Edward Stuart and his loyal lieutenant Redgauntlet fizzles out when an emissary from King George arrives on the scene and restores order by telling everyone to go quietly back home. Narratively, the failure of the rebellion before it really gets underway allows the counterfactual plotline to rejoin the trajectory of actual Scottish history under a Hanoverian monarchy and a Whig government. To put Scott's alternate-history narrative in the context of D'Israeli's essay, the conclusion to be drawn from this pseudo-historical speculation on an 'event which has not happened' is that a return by Charles Edward Stuart to lead a third uprising would not have changed a thing.

Before closing the book on the Redgauntlet saga, Scott reinforces the text's ironic claim to historical accuracy by appending a 'Conclusion' in the form of a letter by the researcher Dr Dryasdust to the 'Author of Waverley' in which Dryasdust summarises the subsequent history of the main characters and details his documentary sources: newspapers, family archives, eyewitnesses. Such paratextual devices and 'authenticity effects', as Ian Duncan calls them, are standard fare in Scott's novels, as are imaginary events within real historical settings.[9] But *Redgauntlet* is distinctive for its more blatant conflation of historical fact with fantasy and for its metafictional reflections on speculative storytelling. The plot has fictional characters interact on the same plane with historical figures, and at its centre is a counterfactual life of Charles Edward Stuart. In the introduction he wrote for the Magnum Opus edition of *Redgauntlet* in 1832 (dated, interestingly, 1 April), Scott describes the decline of Jacobite sympathy in Britain and the personal deterioration of the exiled

Pretender so as to make clear that even the aborted rebellion that takes place in the novel could not have taken place in reality. Instead, the Jacobite cause is 'a theme … for fictitious composition, founded upon real or probable incident', and the author admits that when reflecting on eighteenth-century history for the purposes of a novel he was induced to 'alter its purport considerably, as it passed through his hands'.[10]

The degree and nature of this alteration might have been less clear to readers when *Redgauntlet* first appeared without an introduction in 1824, since it looked very like the history-based Waverley novels that preceded it, with the attribution 'by the Author of "Waverley"' on the title page lending it the same degree of credibility. But if the 1824 text does not make the counterfactual nature of the plot explicit, it instead signals in more subtle ways that storytelling is a speculative activity. Early in the novel there is a veiled reference to what the novelist himself is doing when one character accuses another of 'making histories out of nothing', just like a child blowing 'bubbles'.[11] As several critics have noted, reflection on storytelling is unusually prominent in this novel; James Kerr describes it as a form of metafiction in which Scott foregrounds the perspectivism and storytelling techniques that make up historical narrative.[12] Fiona Robertson, too, reads *Redgauntlet* as a 'story about telling stories', and Kathryn Sutherland writes that the novel's '"true centre" turns out to be storytelling itself'.[13] Thus, while Scott's 'what if' narrative makes the historical point that the outcome of the Stuart claim could not have been otherwise, given the political and social conditions of Britain and the personal disposition of Charles Edward, it also affirms the centrality of counterfactual speculation to the historical novel and to storytelling in general.

The Irish writer John Banim, who was influenced and encouraged by Scott, inverts the historical novel in a different way in his satirical *Revelations of the Dead-Alive*, which appeared at nearly the same time as *Redgauntlet*. Banim's anonymously published work juxtaposes contemporary science with revisionary history and futuristic speculation in a starkly original synthesis that is nevertheless thoroughly interwoven with its mid-1820s context. While *Revelations* is essentially a volume of satirical essays on contemporary British culture, Banim begins with recent medical literature as the basis for his premise that he can achieve a 'dead-alive' state and travel into the future while in that condition. With accurate and verifiable references to texts by early-nineteenth-century physicians John Cheyne (1777–1836) and John Reid (1776–1822), Banim cites cases of people who were physically dead and then returned to life.[14] After quoting a salient case study from Dr Cheyne, a physician active in Edinburgh and Dublin, Banim makes the leap from science to fantasy by purporting to be a close friend and relative of Cheyne's patient, a man who counterfeited death for a long period of time before coming to life again: 'My relative, whose pretensions have been fully established in the quotation, derived his talent from his father, who had it from his uncle, and it has been as regularly transmitted to me.'[15] He also lays claim to a hereditary gift for prophecy and finds that the two in combination allow him to enter a dead-alive state and travel a year into the future for every day he continues in that state.

At this point he makes it his mission to develop the ability to remain dead-alive as long as physically possible by researching how other creatures – including boa constrictors and the Otomac people of South America – manage to survive without food for long periods. Having travelled to the Otomac territory, tied himself to the boughs of a tree and trained himself to remain dead-alive for over 198 days, the narrator is able to travel that many years into the future. He relates his adventures in the England of 2023, where he converses with writers, artists and scientists and learns how his own century's history has been recorded. In 'Chapter the Last', he wakes to find himself still in the tree among a crowd of large monkeys; after staying with the Otomac people for several more days, he sets sail for England and arrives back on the precisely documented date of 18 December 1823.

In some ways, John Banim presents his experience as a prophetic vision resembling that of John of Patmos, as suggested by rhetorical echoes of the Book of Revelation in his opening chapter. But he also insists that his journey into the future is an experiential reality. He describes his dead-alive state in medical and material detail and claims to have had concrete, not just visionary, experiences in the year 2023; among other things, he marries and leaves an unborn child behind (or ahead?) in the future. Banim's volume of essays thus takes on a novelistic dimension and becomes a science-fiction story about time travel. Like Mary Shelley's *The Last Man* (1826), this genre allows Banim to speculate about material conditions and scientific inventions that don't yet exist. In Banim's twenty-first-century England, the post office has just begun to use horseless carriages or 'self-impelling coaches' and machinery has 'put an end to human labour'.[16] Mr Angle, 'one of the most eminent experimentalists' of the future, tells the author about his further 'speculations' for automata or 'automeda' that do everything from fighting battles to writing periodical reviews; a 'balloon-ship' that takes thirteen months to make a trip to the moon has been able to establish a British colony there to which 'cargoes of speculators' have emigrated.[17] Banim thus interweaves pointed critique of everyday realities – the predictable, unthinking quality of Romantic-era periodical reviews that might as well have been composed by machines, for instance – with futuristic speculation.

While the alternate reality of this text is located in the future, it also participates in counterfactual historiography since it (re)writes nineteenth-century history from the vantage point of an imagined future. This retrospective viewpoint overturns the values and even the facts of Banim's contemporary world. In *Revelations*, Thomas Campbell is revealed to have written the Waverley novels and 'Tommy Moore' succeeds Robert Southey as poet laureate. As the narrator discovers by reading a history book in the British Museum in 2023, while Britain was helping Spain fight for independence during the 1830s, Czar Alexander of Russia stormed Britain; Napoleon, who was 'still alive and doing well', helped the British unite and drive the Russians out, after which he settled on a farm in Yorkshire.[18] Banim uses the imagined perspective of 2023 to intervene in his own era's historiographical controversies. He engages in a passionate campaign to rehabilitate the character of Mary Queen of Scots and condemn the actions of Elizabeth I, taking up the efforts of historians John Whitaker (1735–1808) and George Chalmers (1742–1825), in books published in 1787 and 1818 respectively, to clear away 'the rotting heap of slander, under which the poor Mary lay … entombed'.[19] While Banim's own historiographical argumentation is interpretative and subjective, he lays claim to a more authoritative viewpoint thanks to his purported ability to converse with citizens of the twenty-first century. He affirms that by 2023, history will have decided in Mary's favour and Elizabeth I will have been branded a 'hypocritical and blasphemous' tyrant.[20] Like D'Israeli's essay on 'Events Which Have Not Happened', *Revelations* reveals the extent to which historical 'facts' depend on public acceptance of one perspective over another; thanks to his purported time-travelling ability, Banim claims to have advance knowledge of which version of history will win out. With his quirky hybrid of fact and speculative fantasy, he inverts Scott's genre of the historical novel by attempting to write a history of the future. In this multi-perspectival text, then, a counterfactual premise about the present – that time travel in a dead-alive state is physically possible – provides the basis for counterfactual speculation about the future, which becomes the vantage point for writing counterfactual history.

Contemporaneous with *Revelations of the Dead-Alive*, and just as ephemeral, is John Galt's *The Bachelor's Wife; A Selection of Curious and*

Interesting Extracts, with Cursory Observations, which critiques other aspects of 1820s culture – in particular, its publishing practices and reading habits. Galt, a prolific writer of fiction, drama and poetry and of factual genres such as biography, geography and political economy, was thoroughly familiar with the literary marketplace of London as well as that of his native Scotland. An entrepreneur in business ventures and a self-described speculator on the literary market, he seized opportunities to publish in emerging genres and creative formats. During the early 1820s, Galt's fiction rose to popularity on the basis of several novels published by William Blackwood's firm, some of them having first appeared in instalments in *Blackwood's Edinburgh Magazine* alongside Galt's non-fictional journalism. *The Bachelor's Wife* may be read against the background of Galt's experience with the rapidly evolving periodical market. The work is a speculative publishing venture in a hybrid genre – a compilation of extracts from prose and poetry, fiction and non-fiction, English literature and literature in translation, many of them gleaned from periodicals including the *Edinburgh Review* and the *Quarterly Review*. Its avowed purpose, according to Galt's preface, is to offer entertainment and useful knowledge to male and female readers in a manner that is accessible, popular, democratic and more time-efficient than reading the lengthy originals from which the extracts are taken.

Galt draws on several forms of publication and reading that were popular during the 1820s: the private pastime of collecting extracts in albums and scrapbooks, periodicals that reprinted excerpts from other publications (such as the annual compilation entitled *The Spirit of the Public Journals*), and miscellanies of eclectic knowledge (of which D'Israeli's *Curiosities of Literature* is a leading example). What makes *The Bachelor's Wife* distinctive and opens it to the counterfactual, however, is an elaborate editorial fiction. All the extracts are introduced by what Galt calls 'colloquies' between a newlywed couple, 'the Bachelor' (who is also called 'our old chum Benedict') and his 'faultless … ever-placent, ever-pleasant companion, Egeria'.[21] These colloquies add an element of dramatic performance to the anthology since the excerpts are assumed to be read aloud, usually by Egeria to Benedict; the miscellany is a record of their reading performances, their discussions of each excerpt and their spousal relationship. Yet this marriage, like the character of Egeria, is counterfactual, for the oxymoronic 'Bachelor's Wife' does not and cannot exist. Playing on the idiomatic phrase 'bachelor's wife' for 'the ideal wife of which a bachelor theorizes or dreams', Galt underlines her non-existence by naming her 'Egeria' after the idyllic nymph supposed to have had a relationship with King Numa in Roman mythology (as he reminds readers with an epigraph from Byron's *Childe Harold's Pilgrimage*).[22] A mythical construct made up of a palimpsest of texts, this 'airy-handed lady' is no more than a 'beautiful thought'.[23]

The Bachelor's Wife derives all possible benefit from Egeria's counterfactual status. As an imaginary being, she represents not only the ideal female companion, being an excellent housekeeper and an intelligent conversationalist without any hint of bluestocking pedantry, but also the ideal editor. Conversationally at least, she is the dominant partner in this counterfactual marriage. Her colloquies with her husband display her superior knowledge of contemporary journalism, belles-lettres, travel writing, religious history and military strategy; her judgement is more reliable than Benedict's, and she wins all their debates. Sometimes she even pre-empts possible objections and takes over both sides of the argument ('But ... perhaps you will say that ...'), offering a knock-down illustration of her point and leaving Benedict able only to respond, in the manner of Socrates' interlocutors, with 'Let me hear it.'[24] Because Egeria has no material or legal existence, she can voice daring opinions and forthright literary judgements without fear of reprisal. When she takes strong positions – expressing anti-Catholic sentiments, likening Muhammad to Luther as a religious reformer, severely criticising Kant or exposing Milton's plagiarisms from Hesiod – her counterfactual status couches her opinions in a different register, like alternate history that maintains the distinction between what is real and what is only postulated as a thought-experiment. Egeria also has the enviable ability to keep a virtual library in her head; knowing immediately which passage in a book or journal is germane to the topic under discussion, she is able to lay her 'airy' hand on the desired volume in no time at all.

Paradoxically, while the extracts included in the miscellany are heavily mediated by the commentary of Egeria and Benedict, Egeria's nonexistence also counters the mediating role of the editor with a fiction of transparency and objectivity. Often *The Bachelor's Wife* represents the selection process as random, as if the best extracts were somehow choosing themselves. Egeria opens volume 22 of the *Quarterly Review* 'at haphazard', leafs through books that 'happened to be lying on the table', and reads manuscripts that she finds scattered about their home.[25] Thanks to the fiction of the transparent Egeria and these happened-on manuscripts, Galt is able to include a substantial amount of his own writing among the extracts from other authors while distancing himself from authorial and editorial roles. As Egeria finds these stray manuscripts of poetry and prose, penned by a friend whom Benedict coyly refuses to name (since they are really Galt's), she decides which of them are worth reading out and commenting on, and thus which gain entry into the miscellany.

But if *The Bachelor's Wife* insists on the non-existence of the bachelor's wife, it just as emphatically reinforces her existence as an actual woman by providing a superfluity of material detail and domestic allusion. Imitating a novel of manners, the colloquies place Egeria and Benedict in everyday situations and conversations characteristic of a newly married couple. Benedict is a struggling young lawyer and 'the perfect Egeria' is a model of femininity that female readers are encouraged, in conduct-book style, to emulate, especially by the practice of copying poetry into their albums as a way of 'polishing their minds'.[26] The couple's colloquies are triggered by quotidian encounters with objects and material texts: Egeria brings up a topic she happened to be reading about in the morning paper; she picks up a volume of Ben Jonson after tea and commands Benedict to listen to a passage she wishes to read aloud; 'having no other household care' one morning, she begins a conversation while absent-mindedly reading the spines of books on the shelves.[27] The couple look together at engravings of Henning's casts of Athenian marbles in the British Museum, contemplate a tour to Scotland and argue about the merits of Shakespeare after returning from a production of *Hamlet*.

Other conversational triggers take the materiality and ephemerality of periodical literature to a humorous extreme, as when Egeria orders Benedict to fetch a copy of *The Wandering Jew* (a book published anonymously by Galt himself in 1820) that she knows to be behind his wig-box, or becomes absorbed in the content of some old magazine pages that she is using as curl-papers for her hair. According to the mixed reviews that Galt's book received, contemporary readers were nonplussed at the conflation of materiality and ideality in the frame narrative. The *European Magazine* found the extracts to be 'excellent' but the framing narrative 'in the very worst taste', especially the idea of having the Bachelor return to his 'etherial nymph' from the tavern, 'befumed with tobacco and exhaling narcotics!!!'.[28] Yet the insistence on quotidian detail juxtaposed with the denial of physical reality seems characteristic of the counterfactual mode of the 1820s; Galt's vividly described yet 'airy-handed' 'bachelor's wife' corresponds in this sense to the 'dead-alive' visit to the future that Banim depicts as both bodily experience and prophetic vision.

The name of Benedict's and Egeria's residence is 'Paper Buildings' – an actual barristers' residence in London, but also a double-entendre implying that they inhabit print culture itself, and that their colloquies may be interpreted figuratively as allegories of editing and reading. It is tempting to take these staged colloquies as models for the way actual readers should respond to the miscellany by reading it aloud and discussing it with spouses and friends. Such a move would connect Galt's perspective to other strategies deployed by 1820s periodical writers such as Hazlitt, Hunt and Lamb that attempt to (re-)create intimacy with readers in an age when periodicals had increasingly distant and anonymous reading audiences.[29] But this interpretation is undercut by the counterfactual status of the Bachelor's Wife. If Egeria is a transparent fantasy, the colloquies in *The Bachelor's Wife* can be nothing but idealisations of the hours that a lonely barrister spends in Paper Buildings surrounded by his books and journals. The narrative about a bachelor and his counterfactual wife thus functions in Galt's miscellany as an ironic commentary on contemporary print culture and reading habits. In contrast to the predominantly masculine environment of the periodicals for which Galt wrote during the 1820s – an environment memorably depicted in the 'Noctes Ambrosianae' segments in *Blackwood's Edinburgh Magazine* as the homosocial conviviality of Ambrose's Tavern – Galt evokes a domestic context where the wife is the dominant intellect, yet her existence is denied even as it is brought into being. The way in which extracts are chosen for the anthology, partly by fortunate happenstance and partly thanks to Egeria's idealised overview of the best passages relevant to everyday middle-class life, presents an alternative to the more politicised and heavy-handed editorial practices of late-Romantic periodicals. As a representation of reading habits, finally, the colloquies between Egeria and Benedict evoke a sociable, discursive context for the reception of literature that, somewhat poignantly, dissolves with the realisation that the bachelor's wife is a creature of the imagination.

Mary Russell Mitford – like Galt, a market-dependent writer heavily involved with periodical publishing – offers a different allegory of the reading process in *Our Village: Sketches of Rural Character and Scenery*. Poet, playwright, essayist and editor, Mitford made her name primarily with *Our Village*, a volume of interlinked prose pieces that debuted in 1824 and generated four sequels over the period 1826–32. Despite her popularity throughout the nineteenth century, Mitford was forgotten by twentieth-century criticism except as the founder of the minor genre of the Victorian idyll. In recent years, critics have begun to locate her in the context of dynamic forces that include urbanisation and migration, changes in land use and labour practices, publishing and marketing trends, literary networks and the new media of the mid-nineteenth century.[30] In addition, she merits consideration as a contributor to nineteenth-century counterfactual writing because of the subtle but influential way she blends documentation with idealisation by merging literal walks through the countryside of Berkshire with the experience of reading.

Writing of herself in the third person in a brief preface to the 1824 edition of *Our Village*, Mitford lays claim to eyewitness accuracy: 'Her descriptions have always been written on the spot and at the moment, and in nearly every case with the closest and most resolute fidelity to the place and the people.'[31] But the long opening paragraph of *Our Village* tells a different story by overlaying local geography with literary history and contemporary reading habits:

> Of all situations for a constant residence, that which appears to me most delightful is a little village far in the country ... Even in books I like a confined locality, and so do the critics when they talk of the unities. Nothing is so tiresome as to be whirled half over Europe at the chariot-wheels of a hero, to go to sleep at Vienna and awaken at Madrid; it produces a real fatigue, a weariness of spirit. On the other hand, nothing is so delightful as to sit down in a country village in one of Miss Austen's delicious novels, quite sure before we leave it to become intimate with every spot and every person it contains; or to ramble with Mr. White over his own parish of Selborne, and form a friendship with the fields and coppices, as well as with the birds, mice, and squirrels, who inhabit them; or to sail with Robinson Crusoe to his island, and live there with him and his goats and his man Friday – how much we dread any new comers, any fresh importation of savage or sailor! ... or to be shipwrecked with Ferdinand on that other lovelier island – the island of Prospero, and Miranda, and Caliban, and Ariel, and nobody else, none of Dryden's exotic inventions; – that is best of all. And a small neighbourhood is as good in sober waking reality as in poetry or prose; a village neighbourhood, such as this Berkshire hamlet in which I write, a long, straggling, winding street at the bottom of a fine eminence, with a road through it ... Will you walk with me through our village, courteous reader?[32]

Mitford locates herself and *Our Village* in a web of literary affiliations that blend the intensely local with the fantastically exotic. She approaches the 'little village' posited in her opening sentence by way of a mental voyage through popular fiction, the writings of her literary hero Austen and the pioneering naturalist Gilbert White, Defoe's *Robinson Crusoe* and Shakespeare's *The Tempest*. When she returns to her own 'village neighbourhood' after this excursus, it comes into view not as the factual place that it is, but as one example among many possibles: '*such as* this Berkshire hamlet'. Ironically, the imagined spaces of literature set the standard by which 'sober waking reality' gets measured; in this context, Mitford's real village neighbourhood appears 'as good' as in books. When the deictics at the end of the first paragraph fuse the reading and the writing self, 'this Berkshire hamlet in which I write' becomes a space both geographical and textual. The two-page paragraph with which *Our Village* opens *nearly* turns the actual into the counterfactual. Although Mitford returns to her actual village at the end, a trace of the counterfactual remains and makes *Our Village* (as she puts it in the introduction to the fifth and last volume of 1832) 'the history, half real, and half imaginary, of a half imaginary and half real little spot on the sunny side of Berkshire'.[33]

With this opening paragraph and with *Our Village* in general, Mitford stakes out a counter-position relative to the currently fashionable genre of travel writing. She lays claim to an alternative form of travel opposed to the rapid changes of exotic location that featured prominently in contemporary fiction, poetry (Byron's, for instance) and literary magazines, including *The Lady's Magazine* where some of Mitford's sketches first appeared before being collected in book form. By contrast, Mitford invites her 'courteous reader' on a short, slow pedestrian tour uphill along the main street of her village and back again, pointing out each dwelling and describing its inhabitants. Throughout *Our Village*, however, Mitford's dedication to documenting the material details of physical space contends with a nostalgic, idealising perspective. This double vision manifests itself in representations of space that are literal and symbolic at once, and in a sustained parallel between the physical activity of walking and the cognitive activity of reading.

Mitford's village, located on the turnpike road leading south from Reading to Basingstoke, is called Three Mile Cross – a name that risks exposing it as nothing but a distance marker, an intersection that forms an X on the landscape at a determinable distance from the town of Reading. While Mitford's initial tour takes the reader in a geographical straight line along the through road, Franco Moretti has shown in his analysis of the spatial patterns of *Our Village* that the volume symbolically organises space into what he terms 'a little solar system' of 'concentric rings' as Mitford describes people, places and events within the village and at distances of one to three kilometres around it.[34] Moretti suggests that in doing so she counters the linear orientation of the road that runs through Three Mile Cross as well as the linear temporality of 'progress', symbolically reversing the effect of Romantic-era land enclosure that imposed linear patterns on the previously circular arrangement of unenclosed parishes.

In the arrangement of the twenty-four sketches that make up *Our Village*, Mitford also imposes a temporal circularity: seven of them are identically titled 'Walks in the Country', and these walks, dispersed more or less regularly throughout the volume, lead the reader through the cycle of the seasons. Orientating the volume around the seven 'walks' reaffirms the analogy between walking and reading introduced in the opening paragraph of *Our Village*. Both activities involve an appropriation of geographical or literary space by the individual subject who puts her own patterns on a given environment by making choices among fixed parameters: turnpikes, paths and gates on the one hand; texts, allusions and commonplaces on the other. Mitford anticipates Michel de Certeau's parallel between reading and walking as subversive activities of appropriation by the subject who challenges an imposed system. For de Certeau, 'Readers are travellers; they move across lands belonging to someone else, like nomads poaching their way across fields they did not write.'[35] With her choices of direction and perspective, Mitford provokes reflection on the givenness of the physical environment and of literary history, on details and contingencies but for which she might have taken a different turn.

Mitford's may be a 'soft' – even 'pedestrian' – version of counterfactualism in which 'the closest and most resolute fidelity' of observation that she claims in her preface is coloured by subjective choices and layers of texts. But alongside the contemporaneous works of Galt, Banim and Scott, her popular and influential sketches show how forms of writing that purport to be intensely factual incorporate counterfactual elements, thereby revealing how the factual as well as the counterfactual depends on perspectives and contingencies. By including explicitly counterfactual components – a historical event that never happened, a 'dead-alive' narrator, a 'bachelor's wife' whose epithet simultaneously affirms and denies her existence, a 'half imaginary and half real' village – these writers challenge readers to reflect on what constitutes accuracy and authenticity.

Further variations on counterfactual speculation, still from the year 1824, could be multiplied, such as Theodore Hook's popular *Sayings and Doings: A Series of Sketches from Life*. Hook's anecdotes of fashionable life are more obviously ironic than Mitford's rural sketches, but he too claims that they are based on accurate observation of the quotidian: 'I have watched the world, and I have set down all that I have seen.'[36] Like

Mitford, Hook uses a quasi-documentary style in which his characters seem to be subjects of sociological observation and often real people whom he knows personally, but he undercuts facticity by simultaneously satirising them and typecasting them in formulaic plots. Another mode of counterfactual history appears in Walter Savage Landor's *Imaginary Conversations*, where he stages meetings and dialogues between famous historical figures that never occurred in reality. Last but not least, James Hogg's *Private Memoirs and Confessions of a Justified Sinner* juxtaposes irreconcilable perspectives on the same events by different narrators and goes to extremes in claiming to authenticate fantastic events by citing public records, eyewitness experience, handwritten testimony and a previously published article by Hogg in *Blackwood's Edinburgh Magazine*.

Like all of the texts discussed in this chapter, Hogg's *Private Memoirs* introduces elements of speculative fantasy into genres that supposedly foreground history, documentation and accurate observation. Scott's *Redgauntlet* offers alternate history within the frame of the historical novel; Banim critiques the journalism and historiography of the 1820s by means of an imagined sojourn in the 2020s; and Galt and Mitford employ elements of the counterfactual to comment on contemporary habits of producing and consuming periodicals and books. Blending the Romantics' commitment to the liberty of the imagination and their interest in contingency with new practices of observation, documentation and journalism, late-Romantic varieties of the counterfactual thus reflect critically on the new media environment of the 1820s.

Notes

1 *Oxford English Dictionary* ('factual', definition A.1) cites, as its earliest example, Coleridge's *Marginalia* (1820–32).
2 J. C. Squire (ed.), *If It Had Happened Otherwise: Lapses into Imaginary History* (1931; London: Sidgwick & Jackson, 1972), p. viii.
3 Isaac D'Israeli, *Curiosities of Literature* (Second Series), 2nd rev. edn, 3 vols (London: John Murray, 1824), I, p. 99.
4 *Ibid.*, p. 119.
5 *Ibid.*, p. 108.
6 Heinrich von Kleist, *Sämtliche Werke und Briefe*, ed. Helmut Sembdner, 7th rev. edn, 2 vols (München: Hanser, 1984), II, p. 321; my translation.
7 Damian Walford Davies, 'Introduction: Reflections on an Orthodoxy', in Damian Walford Davies (ed.), *Romanticism, History, Historicism: Essays on an Orthodoxy* (New York: Routledge, 2009), p. 10.

8   Walter Scott, *Redgauntlet*, ed. Kathryn Sutherland (Oxford: Oxford University Press, 2011), pp. 401, 331.
9   Ian Duncan, 'Authenticity Effects: The Work of Fiction in Romantic Scotland', *South Atlantic Quarterly*, 102:1 (Winter 2003), 93–116.
10 Scott, *Redgauntlet*, pp. 3, 11.
11 *Ibid.*, p. 46.
12 See James Kerr, *Fiction Against History: Scott as Storyteller* (Cambridge: Cambridge University Press, 1989), pp. 102–23.
13 Fiona Robertson, *Legitimate Histories: Scott, Gothic, and the Authorities of Fiction* (Oxford: Oxford University Press, 1994), pp. 249, 254; Scott, *Redgauntlet*, p. xv.
14 John Banim, *Revelations of the Dead-Alive* (London: Simpkin and Marshall, 1824), pp. 1–3. Cf. 'The Inquirer. No. XIII', *Edinburgh Medical and Surgical Journal*, 4 (1808), 197–8, and John Reid, *Essays on Hypochondriacal and Other Nervous Affections* (Philadelphia, PA: M. Carey & Son, 1817), pp. 11–13.
15 Banim, *Revelations*, p. 4.
16 *Ibid.*, p. 343.
17 *Ibid.*, pp. 342, 346–7, 367, 370.
18 *Ibid.*, p. 296.
19 *Ibid.*, p. 301.
20 *Ibid.*, p. 304.
21 John Galt, *The Bachelor's Wife; A Selection of Curious and Interesting Extracts, with Cursory Observations* (Edinburgh: Oliver & Boyd, 1824), pp. iv, 1–2.
22 *Oxford English Dictionary*, 'bachelor', definition 4b.
23 Galt, *The Bachelor's Wife*, pp. 14, 1.
24 *Ibid.*, pp. 13, 14.
25 *Ibid.*, pp. 66, 114.
26 *Ibid.*, p. 397.
27 *Ibid.*, p. 67.
28 *European Magazine*, 85 (April 1824), 351.
29 See David G. Stewart, 'Charles Lamb's "Distant Correspondents": Speech, Writing and Readers in Regency Magazine Writing', *Keats-Shelley Journal*, 57 (2008), 96–7.
30 See Deidre Lynch, 'Homes and Haunts: Austen's and Mitford's English Idylls', *PMLA*, 115:5 (October 2000), 1103–8; Franco Moretti, *Graphs, Maps, Trees: Abstract Models for a Literary History* (London: Verso, 2005); Kevin A. Morrison, 'Foregrounding Nationalism: Mary Russell Mitford's *Our Village* and the Effects of Publication Context', *European Romantic Review*, 19:3 (July 2008), 275–87; and Katie Halsey, '"Tell Me

of Some Bookings": Mary Russell Mitford's Female Literary Networks', *Women's Writing*, 18:1 (February 2011), 121–36.
31 Mary Russell Mitford, *Our Village: Sketches of Rural Character and Scenery*, 5 vols (London: G. and W. B. Whittaker, 1824–32), I, p. v.
32 *Ibid.*, I, pp. 1–3.
33 *Ibid.*, V, p. 3.
34 Moretti, *Graphs, Maps, Trees*, p. 80.
35 Michel de Certeau, *The Practice of Everyday Life*, trans. Steven Rendall (Berkeley, CA: University of California Press, 1984), p. 174.
36 Theodore Hook, *Sayings and Doings: A Series of Sketches from Life*, 2nd edn, 3 vols (London: Colburn, 1824), I, p. iv.

Works cited

Primary texts

Anon., review of John Galt's *The Bachelor's Wife*, *European Magazine*, 85 (April 1824), 351

Anon., 'The Inquirer. No. XIII', *Edinburgh Medical and Surgical Journal*, 4 (1808), 197–8

[Banim, John], *Revelations of the Dead-Alive* (London: Simpkin and Marshall, 1824)

Chalmers, George, *The Life of Mary, Queen of Scots*, 2 vols (London: John Murray, 1818)

D'Israeli, Isaac, *Curiosities of Literature* (Second Series), 2nd rev. edn, 3 vols (London: John Murray, 1824)

Galt, John, *The Bachelor's Wife; A Selection of Curious and Interesting Extracts, with Cursory Observations* (Edinburgh: Oliver & Boyd, 1824)

Hook, Theodore, *Sayings and Doings: A Series of Sketches from Life*, 2nd edn, 3 vols (London: Colburn, 1824)

Kleist, Heinrich von, *Sämtliche Werke und Briefe*, ed. Helmut Sembdner, 7th rev. edn, 2 vols (München: Hanser, 1984)

Mitford, Mary Russell, *Our Village: Sketches of Rural Character and Scenery*, 5 vols (London: G. and W. B. Whittaker, 1824–32)

Reid, John, *Essays on Hypochondriacal and Other Nervous Affections* (Philadelphia, PA: M. Carey & Son, 1817)

Scott, Walter, *Redgauntlet*, ed. Kathryn Sutherland (Oxford: Oxford University Press, 2011)

Whitaker, John, *Mary Queen of Scots Vindicated*, 3 vols (London: John Murray, 1787)

Secondary texts

de Certeau, Michel, *The Practice of Everyday Life*, trans. Steven Rendall (Berkeley, CA: University of California Press, 1984)

Duncan, Ian, 'Authenticity Effects: The Work of Fiction in Romantic Scotland', *South Atlantic Quarterly*, 102:1 (Winter 2003), 93–116

Halsey, Katie, '"Tell Me of Some Booklings": Mary Russell Mitford's Female Literary Networks', *Women's Writing*, 18:1 (February 2011), 121–36

Kerr, James, *Fiction Against History: Scott as Storyteller* (Cambridge: Cambridge University Press, 1989)

Lynch, Deidre, 'Homes and Haunts: Austen's and Mitford's English Idylls', *PMLA*, 115:5 (October 2000), 1103–8

Moretti, Franco, *Graphs, Maps, Trees: Abstract Models for a Literary History* (London: Verso, 2005)

Morrison, Kevin A., 'Foregrounding Nationalism: Mary Russell Mitford's *Our Village* and the Effects of Publication Context', *European Romantic Review*, 19:3 (July 2008), 275–87

Robertson, Fiona, *Legitimate Histories: Scott, Gothic, and the Authorities of Fiction* (Oxford: Oxford University Press, 1994)

Squire, J. C. (ed.), *If It Had Happened Otherwise: Lapses into Imaginary History* (London: Sidgwick & Jackson, 1972 [1931])

Stewart, David G., 'Charles Lamb's "Distant Correspondents": Speech, Writing and Readers in Regency Magazine Writing', *Keats-Shelley Journal*, 57 (2008), 89–107

Walford Davies, Damian, 'Introduction: Reflections on an Orthodoxy', in Damian Walford Davies (ed.), *Romanticism, History, Historicism: Essays on an Orthodoxy* (New York: Routledge, 2009), 1–13

9

Piratical counterfactual, piratical counterfictional: from Misson to melodrama

Manushag N. Powell

The principal contention of this chapter is that literature about piracy in the eighteenth- and nineteenth-century British tradition has a marked dependency on both counterfactual and counterfictional experimentation. Eighteenth-century pirate history-writing liked to speculate about pirate colonies and utopias; the specific case of the speculative pirate paradise summons up a counterculture ideal of freedom that resonates well with yearnings for *liberté*, *égalité* and *fraternité*. Further, we can trace a direct line from the speculative tendencies of early-eighteenth-century pirate literature to the inflections made to these pirate histories in their later-stage incarnations.

One of the most widespread and colourful elements of the popular Romantic-period stage was the pirate drama (a 2015 catalogue finds at least 120 of them staged between 1789 and 1850).[1] That pirates held significant appeal for late-eighteenth- and nineteenth-century audiences is not surprising: they represented rebellion, class warfare, the troubles of empire and the sort of magnetic, misanthropic antiheroes often termed Byronic. I suggest that the figure of the pirate should also hold significant appeal for readers interested in counterfactual speculation given that an examination of foundational texts reveals that the genre of counterfactual fiction was available in popular anglophone writing well before its rapid expansion in the nineteenth century. It is surely no coincidence that the early nineteenth century, which nurtured an aesthetics of boundary-pushing, witnessed a major increase in both counterfactual fiction and pirate fictions.

While reprints and revisions of pirate histories were unflaggingly popular from the first decades of the eighteenth century onwards, between the seventeenth-century romance and the nineteenth-century inventions of Byron and Walter Scott there was a general absence of tales whose main characters were fictional pirates (apart from certain exceptions such as Defoe's *Captain Singleton* (1720)). My suggestion is that a gradual shift from pirate counterfactual to pirate counterfictional explains this generic transformation. Indeed, it is not far wrong to consider nearly all latter-day literary pirates as 'counterfictions' or deliberate revisions of established literary and historical worlds – consider J. M. Barrie's Captain Hook, who is meant to have served with Blackbeard (real) and who frightened Captain Flint (fictional).[2]

Counterfactual histories can be distinguished from other forms of speculation such as alternative or secret histories by their commitment to an 'explicit or implicit past-tense, hypothetical, conditional conjecture' that is widely accepted as divergent from historical fact, and which then remains fairly focused on the implications of the hypothetical divergence.[3] Before they could be fictionalised or counterfictionalised, historical pirates were adapted and counterfactualised; however, as was typical of history-writing in the period, this process always included an element of fictional invention as the blank spaces in their autobiographies were filled in and the dimmer elements of their personae made more brilliant. Pirate lore itself – particularly the melodramatic form that dominated in the nineteenth century and which remains very much in circulation today – is energised by a tradition of counterfactual thinking. Ultimately, using pirates both real and imagined as the case in point, this chapter claims that by the eighteenth century, counterfactual writing was already in place and ready to bequeath to nineteenth-century audiences a genre of pirate literature that would satisfy their appetites.

On 9 April 1798, the Royal Circus Theatre hosted the premiere of John Cartwright Cross's *Black Beard; Or, The Captive Princess*, a spectacular pantomime opera with music by James Sanderson that proved an immediate hit, running through July and spreading quickly to the provinces until it became unquestionably the most famous pirate melodrama of its day. It was still being adapted and staged successfully in the 1850s.[4] From the start, the play glories in its pirate clichés, opening with a cheerful buccaneer chorus about the joys of life at sea with plentiful 'jolly, jolly grog'. Its plot, which centres on the capture by Blackbeard of the Grand Mughal Aurengzeb's ship and the travails of Princess Ismene, imprisoned by the lustful Blackbeard who carries her to his treasure-laden fortress in Madagascar, deliberately capitalises on the vogue for oriental stage themes (an example being George Colman's popular afterpiece, *Blue-Beard*, which in 1798 transformed the French fairy tale into a story about lustful Turks). Plot twists allow for compelling tropes such as layered racial politics, cross-dressing, wife murder, ghosts and sword fights aplenty. The play eventually ends, as one might suppose, with a sea battle, fiery explosions, 'British Valour and Humanity conspicuously triumphant', all true lovers reunited and Blackbeard vanquished by the hero, Lieutenant Maynard.[5] Cross's *Black Beard* is valued today as a paradigmatic example of the popularity and characteristics of musical stage productions at the turn of the nineteenth century, but critical discussions have not attended to the fact that *Black Beard* is a counterfiction: the deeds it describes concerning the kidnapped princess have an archival basis (different from a 'factual' basis, note), but they were actions originally attributed to a different pirate – the Red Sea Man John Avery, not Blackbeard the Caribbean marauder. Such interpenetration of histories and fictions is a feature of nineteenth-century British pirate drama.

'Blackbeard', the nickname of Edward Thatch or Teach, was a historical figure, and Maynard was the name of his vanquisher, but he was a West Indian rover with no base in Madagascar, nor did he ever molest a Mughal princess. If he was haunted by a wife's vengeful ghost, no documentary evidence survives. To spice up his show with the oriental exotic, Cross deviated from history and seems to have borrowed heavily from the plot of Charles Johnson's *The Successful Pyrate* (1712), a tragicomic account (whose flexible morality distressed critics such as John Dennis) of the exploits of Captain Avery, who had been the most famous English pirate pre-Blackbeard. Cross's reframing of Teach in Avery's mould catalysed an extensive tradition of the lustful stage pirate and captive maiden that was replicated over and over in the early nineteenth century. The twist is that, while Avery was both real and remarkable, and his renowned assault on Aurengzeb's pilgrim fleet in 1696 was well-documented, his most famous action – marrying the princess he found on board the *Ganj-i-sawai* and, with her, founding a dynasty in his piratical colony on Madagascar – never happened. The *Ganj-i-sawai* held no princess, and Avery's actual fate is unknown; he escaped capture and vanished, untraced by any historian, making his story a rich source for counterfactual conjecture. Thus he and his fabled princess were immortalised in periodicals, histories, fictions, poetry and on stage – which is how the imagined deed of founding a half-Mughal pirate dynasty came to be available for reassignment to Blackbeard.

Cross's play was the most popular source for pirate yarns for two decades until the appearance of Sir Walter Scott's Captain Cleveland (who was brought to life in three competing stage versions within less than a month of the publication of Scott's novel *The Pirate* in December 1821) and Byron's Conrad (his poem the *Corsair* was staged in at least five different adaptations before mid-century).[6] It is telling that the dashing, romantic qualities of Cross's Averian Blackbeard are picked up in Cleveland and that Cleveland in turn crossed so quickly to the theatre. Cross hardly invented the idea of the lovelorn pirate king that helped make his opera so successful. The fact that he was inspired to appropriate that fictional plot element from one pirate history in the service of another reveals the close relationship between pirate narratives and counterfactual experimentation.

That is, Cross's play is not inventive, quite, but rather highly speculative, not only asking what if Blackbeard had been more like Avery, but also, crucially, building on previous widespread speculation that Avery had planned a Roman-style future for himself, complete with bride-theft and a growing empire. Blackbeard, meanwhile, was a popular name, in large part owing to his sensational treatment as a highly theatrical, lascivious devil figure in *A General History of the Robberies and Murders of the Most Notorious Pyrates* (1724–28), which was in the nineteenth century (and remains) the single most important source text for anglophone pirate stories. In the *General History*, Blackbeard was more than a raider who harried the Carolina coastline: he was a monster who made his ship a living, smoking hell, shot underlings at random and placed twists of flaming hemp under his hat during raids for maximum enemy intimidation. After fictionalising the lives of both Blackbeard and Avery, the *General History* introduces a romance concerning a liberty-loving French pirate named Captain Misson, who was tangentially linked to Avery but whose ideals were shockingly (for the time and place) republican. As the self-styled anarchist intellectual Peter Lamborn Wilson exclaims, the section devoted to Misson reads 'like pages out of Rousseau – or Byron! (neither of whom were yet born)' thanks to its riffs on justice and equality for all.[7] Misson's idealistic, bifurcated narrative feels markedly out of place in the *General History*, whose values, for the most part, are those of law and order.

Within Misson's story, the *General History* experiments with a number of modes, including history and romance, whose demarcation was seldom very clear in the long eighteenth century. More radically, however, it combines those modes in an unusual, highly speculative fashion, presenting a philosophical romance interwoven with the historical record in order first to present and then to reject the possibility of a radical republican empire. This is more than just an interesting quirk of composition. It is profound experimentation, an extremely early and atypical example of the counterfactual mode. Further, through Misson, the *General History* shrewdly formalises what has always been constitutive in pirate legends, namely that since such stories require transgression outside the bounds of law, culture and nation, they are also fundamentally receptive to the conflation of fiction and history. The tendency in later pirate writing is towards what are called 'upward counterfactuals' or retellings that make imagined piracy more palatable than it really was – more thoughtful, chivalric, ideologically pure; less violent, acquisitive and threatening, less implicated in uglier crimes like the slave trade.[8] This is not an impulse limited to the literary realm, either; historians too often want piracy generally, and Misson in particular, to be representative of an organised anti-capitalist counterculture that never really materialised in a consistent form.[9] All pirate legends run contrary to facts in fairly predictable directions, but the *General History*'s use of Misson is a sophisticated attempt to replace a flawed legend (Avery's) with what is supposed to be an upwardly counterfactual version. This is what makes rewritings such as the one represented by Cross's *Black Beard* possible; likewise, this is what allows later authors like Scott and Byron to sentimentalise their pirates so unashamedly. Maritime musicals were politically freighted phenomena. When Cross's Captain Blackbeard sings that a pirate enjoys 'A heart of oak, he steers it in all weathers', he assimilates the British pirate and the British tar by referencing David Garrick's song, 'Heart of Oak' (from *Harlequin's Invasion*, 1760), the pantomime number that became the official song of the Royal Navy.[10] The question raised time and again at such moments is whether a sailor is at heart an upwardly counterfactual pirate (and a pirate a downwardly counterfactual sailor).

In a curious coincidence, counterfactual speculation has become part of the critical apparatus around the *General History* itself in recent years since its authorship invites as much speculation as some of the famous figures it profiles. The work advertises itself as authored by 'Captain Charles Johnson', likely a pseudonym for a London-based writer-publisher; Daniel Defoe and Nathaniel Mist have been suggested as the true creator. This chapter chooses to dwell in uncertainty by taking 'Johnson' as the author.[11] Regardless of the pen behind it, much of the *General History* is historically accurate, and yet it is also an unreliable text for historians, riddled with literary flights and inscrutable political agendas. The text's considerable literary merits have rarely been interrogated since the rejection of its attribution to Defoe. Indeed, given the now widespread assumption that Defoe is not the author, scholars find themselves speculatively evaluating the text through a counterfactual lens as they negotiate the claims of prior scholarship: *if* Defoe had authored the text, what might that mean?[12]

But from its beginnings, the *General History* can be seen to wrestle with a desire to speculate on other paths for its pirates. One of its major throughlines – a strong interest in Madagascar and the pirates who settled there – is bound up with a clear desire to damage the fame of the man who was, in the late seventeenth and early eighteenth centuries, the most famous pirate of them all: 'Bold' Captain John Avery, also known as Benjamin Bridgeman and Henry Every (most likely his legal name). The *General History* stakes its claim to authority over other pirate histories by purporting to reveal unknown 'facts' (really fictions and speculations) about Avery and his men. In trying to account for, and repurpose, the popularity of Avery (who, we recall, was later to become the basis for Cross's Blackbeard owing to his crucial centrality to pirate writing), the *General History* starts down the path of counter-writing.

The conceptual stakes are high, given that one aim of the *General History* is to analyse what it means for a nation of pirates, as England was often called, to engage with a real pirate nation. In each of what we might call its inaugurating chapters – the Preface and Introduction, the first chapter of Volume I, and (added in 1728) the first chapter of Volume II – the *General History* makes a point of carefully weighing up the possibility of a pirate nation. Johnson's first counterfactual speculation is in the introductory pages, which reflect on Ancient Rome (here a parallel to England) as a nation both of, and dogged by, pirates: what if, Johnson wonders, Pompey's fleet had failed to quash a pirate threat, and what will become of Britain if she fails to deal with the pirates harassing her interests in Caribbean waters? The second counterfactual experiment – which is far more sustained – appears in Johnson's chapter 1, a heavily revisionist representation of the life and fate of Captain Avery and his men, who were commonly rumoured to be living as kings on the island of Madagascar. This chapter draws attention to itself as diverging from the rest of the volume in both mode and matter. Most of the narrative of the *General History*, especially Volume I, is more or less historical and contemporary with its publication, and yet 'Captain Avery and His Crew' had not been heard from in nearly thirty years. Johnson's version of the Avery legend is not a faithful history but an attempt to push back against the tradition that had sprung up around Avery's name, which included a mighty, prosperous Madagascan pirate utopia. Johnson reduces Avery and his band to penurious exiles, suggesting to the reader that Johnson is in possession of secret information not known to other historians, and claiming ownership of the most glamorous pirate legend then extant. He is, he says, 'rejecting the idle Stories which were made of [Avery's] fantastic Greatness', but he is at the same time indulging in fabrication of his own.[13]

Though the captain himself had not been sighted since 1696, Avery's band lived on in speculative fictions and were depicted as merry outlaw imperialists in texts such as the 1709 *Life of Avery* by the pseudonymous Adrian van Broeck, which was substantially plagiarised (with a few interesting additions) from a narrative entitled 'Some Memoirs Concerning that Famous Pyrate Capt. Avery' that appeared in the November 1708 issue of the *Monthly Miscellany, or, Memoirs for the Curious*.[14] With the notable exception of the British East India Company, the English public was inclined to view Avery as a seafaring champion of the downtrodden, representing a powerful fantasy of riches and freedom for the lowly labourer. Such was the appeal of the Avery myth that the existence of his Madagascan utopia was commonly accepted as true, and accounts of travellers coming across Avery's abandoned stronghold persisted for many decades (while there was actually a small pirate settlement on Madagascar, Avery did not live there, and he certainly did not build any fort or raise an army). For example, as late as 1737 the sailor Clement Downing reported meeting Avery's son Tom, a handsome mixed-race man in the employ of John Plantain, a pirate and trader in Madagascar who was supposed to be renovating Avery's abandoned fortress in order to set up yet another pirate empire that never materialised.[15] In other words, a counterfactual proposition – what if Avery had a Malagasy settlement? – was commonly accepted as a factual basis for later accounts. This matters because of the thematic speculation such accounts always bring about, as they ask readers and audiences to grapple with what, if any, difference there would be between a British empire and an empire founded by pirates – a question that grew increasingly pointed and urgent in the nineteenth century.

Johnson, for one, finds such a connection between pirates and nascent empires compelling and worrisome in equal measure. The *General History*'s version of Avery dies penniless in Ireland, but not content with that disgrace, his chapter takes pains to depict his band as unhappy, threadbare exiles. Johnson initially describes the pirates as increasing their numbers by intermarrying with the natives of Madagascar, taking slaves, setting up plantations and generally behaving wretchedly to the indigenous population; profiled here is a society with the potential for growth, but also a debased and debasing one, since 'Tyrant like they lived, fearing and feared by all' (*General History*, p. 61). But this, Johnson reveals, is all a myth. When the pirate hunter Woodes Rogers comes upon them, he finds the petty pirate princes in a bestial state: 'I cannot say they were ragged since they had no Cloaths ... being overgrown with Beard, and Hair upon their Bodies' (*General History*, p. 61).[16] Savage pariah-figures, they offer no real threat to a well-armed, civilised Englishman, nor do they hold any deep appeal for the reader. The only fantasy element at work is the ease with which a handful of disorderly pirates are able to subdue all the Malagasy natives; in reality, of course, the power balance worked in the opposite direction, and the pirates who did live on Madagascar had to do so largely on the terms of non-European peoples – the feared spectacle at which Rogers's description seems to hint.

It would be fairly simple to read this version of the pirates as satirically dystopian if Johnson were to stop here. This is a fairly simple downward counterfactual concerning Avery's fate, mingled with some probabilistic speculation about the welfare of his men; its purpose is to educate the reader out of romantic notions of pirate treasure or pirate empires. However, Volume II opens with a seemingly disjunctive yarn about a beautiful, upright and egalitarian (and doomed) pirate republic. This is the thought experiment Johnson spins out in the first chapter of this second volume, 'Of Captain Misson', and extends later in the chapter 'Of Captain Tew'. To be clear: Misson is fictional; Tew is not; their meeting makes Misson's story the *General History*'s clearest example of counterfactual writing since it interweaves a point-of-divergence pirate colony and well-documented pirate history, then uses the latter to assure us that the former was only ever speculation. The flirtation with republicanism in Misson's story is firmly stamped out in Tew's. Further, the counterfactual tale of Misson and Tew underscores the *General History*'s need to *keep re-writing* the Avery myth – a need that, as we see in Cross's example, persisted even when Avery's name was no longer famous.

Captain Misson's story is presented as a translation of a French text, and it is certainly plausible that it is based on a French novel as yet unrecovered by scholars. In Volume I, Johnson had reimagined Avery, depicting a criminal who had really led a group of sailors in successful rebellion against wage slavery as a craven opportunist with no principles and little intelligence. Johnson's purpose is to decouple the name Avery from the trope of the piratical freedom fighter, preserving the concept and its fascinating possibilities while pushing it more firmly into the realm of fiction. The opening chapter of Volume II replaces Avery with the aggrandised and – crucially – obviously fictional figure of Misson. Johnson's Misson begins his career in mutiny and ends with a failed attempt to establish a Madagascan dynasty; unlike Avery, he bases his career on revolutionary principles of liberty that would feel less out of place in 1789 than in the 1720s.[17] While purporting to offer histories, Johnson effectively introduces his readers to a text in which they must learn to interpret the factual, the fictional and finally the counterfactual with respect to pirate writing. The *General History* is fascinated by its own subject, but also recognises pirates as a threat to the social and economic orders; it is therefore undesirable for the reader to be allowed to admire real pirates too much. The best-natured pirate, Misson, is marked as counterfactual as a sort of moral indicator to the reader.

This is why Misson is not allowed to stand on his own as an independent or self-contained fiction. Johnson tempers the subversive power of Misson by intertwining his imaginary destiny with that of a historical pirate, Thomas Tew, who at one point had actually sailed with Avery. Ultimately, Johnson kills off both men – the invented and the real – simultaneously rejecting the dangerous example of successful rebellion that Avery represents in all his incarnations in their collectively failed potential. According to Catherine Gallagher, counterfactual writing in the eighteenth century was mostly concerned with religious debates and 'critical military histories', not with fictions that set out to question political ideologies and social mores (these would come later, in the nineteenth century).[18] Most eighteenth-century counterfactuals made use of the idea of many possible worlds, a notion compatible with religious debate. In the *General History*, Johnson – strikingly – is not engaging in religious, existential or military hypothesising; multiple worlds are nowhere invoked. In contrast to what we are told to expect as typical counterfactual writing of the period, he creates a point of divergence wherein a Madagascan pirate colony is founded by a good man without reference to military innovation or overt act of Providence. Both Misson's ideals and the structure of the narrative are atypical enough of its cultural moment to seem more at home half a century or more later. Throughout the *General History*, Johnson struggles to thread the needle in embracing the popularity of a subject originating in mutiny and criminality; as a coping strategy, he invents or stumbles into the counterfactual mode.

Perhaps the counterfactual mode is especially prone to usher in discontent, regardless of time and place, or perhaps thematic discontent leads to counterfactual thinking. As Damian Walford Davies has remarked, 'That aspect of the Romantic aesthetic that valorises the contingent and the possible over the rigidly determinist is always attuned to alternative histories and realities'; this would seem to be true, also, of a curious yearning in Johnson's work.[19] In the counterfactual story of the Madagascan colony founded on liberal principles, Misson, a younger son (of course), but a promising naval officer, falls in with an eloquent, if lamentably deistic, priest, Caraccioli, who convinces Misson that reason is divine, and that he has the right to 'lawfully make War on all the World, since it wou'd deprive him of that Liberty to which he had a Right by the Laws of Nature' (*General History*, p. 391). Misson assembles his men and announces he wants 'a Life of Liberty'; if they choose (as they do) to invest him with authority, he will wield it only for their good.

The most interesting aspect of Misson's thirst for liberty is his hatred of slavery. He cannot abide it, and – though the narrative was composed half a century before the Mansfield Judgement clarified the position of slaves under British law – he frees all the male slaves he encounters. When Misson's crew encounters a slaver, the captain tells his men, in terms that presage the rhetoric of later abolitionists, 'that the Trading for [*sic*] those of our own Species, cou'd never be agreeable to the Eyes of divine Justice ... no Man had Power of the Liberty of another', and further, that he will never assert 'his own Liberty, to enslave others' (*General History*, p. 403). This contrarian tendency of Misson's is strongly linked both to his political radicalism and to counterfactual history: pirates on the whole (and within the *General History*) were frequent participants in the slave trade, but here we have one who is an avowed abolitionist. Nonetheless, noble as he seems, he has no way to finance his freedom-fighting except by stealing from others at sea, claiming, with flawed logic, that this is not piracy but 'Self-Preservation' (*General History*, p. 394). Eventually, Misson and his men end up near Madagascar, first landing on the island of Johanna, then deciding to found a colony on the north-west coast of the main island. He calls it Libertalia, 'and gave the Name of *Liberi* to his People, desiring [that] in that [new name] might be drown'd the distinguish'd Names of *French, English, Dutch, Africans*, &c.' (*General History*, p. 417). Here, with the birth of a new nation and new nationality, the story suddenly breaks off, to be taken up a few chapters later in Captain Tew's history.

At this point, it is worth briefly taking stock, in literary-historical

Piratical counterfactual, piratical counterfictional

perspective, of these complex, hybrid layers of history, speculation and invention. In Cross's 1798 *Black Beard*, a fictionalised story about a real pirate that had become so popular it was indistinguishable from history for the general public is reassigned to a different historical pirate, Blackbeard, thus creating a pirate counterfiction. (Necessarily, the Romantic-period audience may also have regarded that counterfiction as a counterfactual, since they are likely to have firmly associated the romantic details of Cross's play with the life of Avery.) I am suggesting that the grounds for such creative experimentation were laid much earlier in the century by two elements: a popular obsession with the idea, never realised, of a powerful piratical colony in Madagascar led by exiled English nationals who might still be nudged to feel some latent loyalty to the nation of their birth, and the fact that the tremendously influential *General History* engaged that obsession by means of carefully crafted counterfactual writing, as we will further witness when Misson's story is swallowed up by Tew's.

Misson's chapter thus concludes with the founding of Libertalia. We do not discover the final fate of that colony until we encounter Captain Thomas Tew, who, like Avery, but unlike Misson, was emphatically real and very well known. In fact, he was the first pirate to become famous for his success in sailing the deep-sea seasonal route known as the Pirate Round, which stretched from the western Atlantic all the way to the Red Sea. Tew's famous theft of a spectacular sum – around £100,000 – in 1693 was probably the inspiration for Avery's decision to become a Red Sea Man himself.[20] The legendary version of Avery might even be read as a grander, what-if version of Tew; meanwhile, later historians retold and sometimes still retell Tew's fatal encounter with the unhistorical Misson as though it were simple fact. Tew, the 'Rhode Island Rover', had been hailed as a hero by the people of Newport and by the governor of New York, Benjamin Fletcher, whose wife and daughters Tew helped dress in stolen finery, but he never achieved the status of Avery. Captain Tew's adventures in the *General History* begin accurately. Johnson recounts how he was sent out as a privateer to attack a French trading settlement in Africa; reasoning that following orders would only endanger his life without making him rich, he decided to become a pirate instead. As Johnson must have known (given the other details he includes), Tew met his fate in 1695; having him survive for additional adventures is counterfactual. Further, when he has Tew meet Misson, Johnson deploys the latter to present an alternative version of the Avery myth: that is, Misson is an upwardly fictional revision of a previous fiction – a counterfiction. Or, to put it otherwise: Tew counterfactually encounters a counterfictional pirate. Johnson breaks up the historical pairing of Tew and Avery in favour of a far more imaginative one when he has Tew visit Captain Misson's utopian colony, though this is a trip not only to no place, but also to no time, since Misson's story takes place at least a decade after the death of the historical Tew.

It is through yoking Misson to Tew that Johnson is able to move Misson's story from the fantastical to the counterfactual, for Tew's presence restores the original timeline, however paradoxically. Tew befriends and admires Misson and joins his naval company, but their partnership is short-lived, since one night, 'without the least Provocation given ... the Natives came down upon [the Liberi] in two great Bodies, and made a great Slaughter, without distinction of Age or Sex' (*General History*, p. 437). The survivors take to the sea, but 'the unhappy Misson's Sloop went down' in a storm 'within a Musquet Shot of Captain Tew, who could give him no Assistance' (*General History*, p. 438). Misson's radical experiment is, in short, wiped from the Earth as though it never existed – and indeed, unlike Avery and Tew, it really never existed. Tew is saddened, but can take no positive action to try to alter things either for Misson or himself. Johnson knew that after their first successful voyage in the *Amity*, Tew and sixty of his men, emboldened by a privateer's commission from New York, joined Avery's squadron in 1695 to stalk the pilgrim fleet in the Indian Ocean, and that Tew died on that journey.[21] Placing Tew as doomed witness between the reader and Misson may contain and reduce the broader impact of Misson's radical ideas, but the gict is ambivalent at best.

Christopher Hill suggests that reading Misson's story as a direct political critique of radical democracy is difficult, since the narrative could, but does not, show Libertalia collapsing because of the problems inherent in its governmental system.[22] Generically speaking, this is to be expected: as one critic has noted, 'Counterfactuals often accentuate personal factors (human agency) instead of, in particular, structures.'[23] Also attuned to the *General History*'s apparent discomfort with the pirate utopia, Lincoln Faller posits that Johnson merges Misson's story with Tew's because the narrator has no idea where to go with Misson's revolutionary ideas, but 'knows how to end Tew's story and the story of the English pirates'.[24] One might suggest that, for Johnson, the foreclosure allowed by the hypothetical nature of strict counterfactual writing is a way out of a problem he has created by being too imaginative, too open to possibilities beyond the world he knows. That is, the counterfactual mode rescues him from the moral temptations of historical fantasy.

Piratical counterfactual, piratical counterfictional

On the factual side of Tew's narrative, interestingly, the historical record itself grows fuzzy. According to Joel Baer, Tew's *Amity* missed the battle with the Indian pilgrim ships *Fath Mahmamadi* and *Ganj-i-sawai* that would launch Avery into pirate lore, and Tew died around this time.[25] But according to other reports, including the one in the *General History*, Tew was fatally shot during the voyage; his men were forced to make their profitless way home or onwards (which at least some of them did by stealing the slaver *Charming Mary* and cruising the Indian Ocean).[26] In Johnson's version, while engaging the ship, 'a Shot carry'd away the Rim of Tew's Belly, who held his Bowels with his Hands some small Space; when he dropp'd, it struck such a Terror in his Men, that they suffered themselves to be taken' (*General History*, p. 439).

However he met his end in 1695, meet it he did, and Tew's second Red Sea voyage was a failure without a satisfying historical explanation; in this sense it is tonally relatable to Avery's end, which has never been discovered. As he had done with Avery, Johnson actually gives Tew a more concrete fate than the extant record provides.[27] Given the way he revises the Avery legend to imagine the famous pirate in effect dying penniless in a ditch, it seems reasonable to conclude that Johnson viewed Avery's fame and public acclaim with no very friendly eye. In connecting the virtuous and moderate Tew to Misson rather than to Avery, he may have meant further to marginalise the latter. The larger point, however, is that he built into the very structure of the *General History* a mechanism through which pirate stories could be used to revise each other, and in which important plot events could reappear and be assigned to new figures as his aesthetic or moral requirements demanded.

Historians often opt for a decorous silence around the problem presented by the unruly republican fantasy that Captain Misson's divided narrative creates in an otherwise fairly factual collection. Literary scholars display only marginally more ease with the subject, usually circling around its links to Defoe (who did not write it) and literary depictions of Africa. Marcus Rediker calls Libertalia 'a version of Hydrarchy' – his term for the special tradition of oppositional living that he detects in working-class maritime life.[28] While accepting Misson's story as fiction, Rediker, expanding on Christopher Hill's work, contends it is a 'fictive expression' of a historical phenomenon (that is, hydrarchical ideals).[29] Misson's radical stance on slavery does not exactly tally with the historical record, given the (at best) 'ambiguous' relation between white and black pirates, and the former's participation in the slave trade. The idea that pirates entered a life of crime not from economic motivation but

263

because of idealism or social activism is hard to accept, particularly since the literary location of most of these utopias – Madagascar – was already fully populated by multiple vibrant, hierarchical societies whose existence had to be elided in order to sustain the fiction that pirates might found new nations there based on experimental principles of government.[30] I am inclined to agree more with Faller's instinct that the *General History*'s abrupt attempts to contain Misson and his radical free thinking shows Johnson being of two minds about his own narrative creation.[31] My reading is that instead of positioning Misson's story as a stand-alone fictional interlude, Johnson makes his arc a counterfactual aside within Thomas Tew's otherwise historical narrative in order to de-radicalise the threat Misson's mission might have posed. Attaching Misson to Tew emphasises that the thought experiment behind Libertalia's government is ultimately rejected by a historical impulse on the part of Johnson.

Both volumes of the *General History* use allohistorical writing in their first chapters, describing the failure of different Madagascar-based piratopias that never were. In Avery's case, it is not the pirate himself who is counterfactual, but his settlement, his Madagascar stronghold. Johnson can be seen compulsively to rewrite the demise of Avery perhaps as a basic reaffirmation of the need for strong, reliable government, particularly at the dawn of the age of empire. And yet, if that is his purpose, he fails. His counterfactual writing is seized on by historians as historical and by literary authors as imaginative prompts. Libertalia has persisted as a rumoured utopia for centuries, persuading scholars such as Don Carlos Seitz, Chris Land, Christopher Hill and Marcus Rediker to entertain the reality of radical pirate principles more seriously than they ought to. Johnson also failed, at least in part, to quash Avery's fictionality, since his fabled exploits are now typically assigned to Blackbeard or other fictional pirates in fiction and film – a pattern Johnson himself arguably pioneered by apportioning some of Avery's history to Misson and Tew. In mixing history and counterfactual propositions, Johnson opens the way to counterfictions like Cross's and ultimately guarantees that the myth of the pirate nation will be available to, and perpetually mutable in the hands of, later writers.

Counterfactual writing is not a new genre, although its popularity in fiction is fairly modern. I am attempting to be provocative by using the term here, for although the concept of counterfactual thinking and writing has generated excitement in nineteenth-century studies, its place, if any, in the eighteenth century remains mostly unexplored. Among the treatments of eighteenth-century counterfactualism that exist, none accounts for the kind of writing in which Johnson is engaged. We recall Catherine Gallagher's definition: 'Historical counterfactuals are past-tense hypothetical conditional conjectures'; we know Avery and Tew were real; we know Misson was not.[32] What Johnson is asking is: what would have happened if a real freedom fighter, which Avery was not, actually did try to found a kingdom of justice in Madagascar – how would good men have felt, and how might history have changed? Paradoxically, the text laments, through Misson, that Avery's empire of liberty was never, and never could be, real; it does so in the form of a political parable that opens the gate for authors like John Cartwright Cross at the end of the 1790s to repurpose a notorious villain as a swashbuckler – with accompanying princess. Cross's Blackbeard is no idealist, but he is magnetic in his approach to villainy, fearless in the face of storms, fire, gunfire and all else that pirate flesh is heir to. While he is eventually subdued by more conventionally moral heroes (the romantic lead, Abdallah, and the heroic Maynard), he loses none of his fascination in the process. The counterfictional speculation – what if the Avery story of a princess in Madagascar had belonged to Blackbeard, a man notorious for fearing nothing – is undercut when the historical figure of Maynard enters the scene to give Blackbeard the death that the historical narrative demands, and yet (as with Johnson's deployment of Misson), unruly fictive speculations possess an imaginative excess that cannot be fully contained.

Calling something counterfactual usually assumes that readers recognise the point at which the narrative deviates from known history, and where it returns. In the case of Cross's *Black Beard*, Maynard was famous as the slayer of Blackbeard; the audience would likely have recognised him as authentically historical while rejecting such interpolations as the ghost of his wife Orra as fantastical. With Johnson, things are less clear. I have already indicated that many readers seem to have mistaken Misson as historical; however, it is a fair assumption that Johnson expected his readers to know Misson's narrative was a fiction, even if they had bought into the Avery myth. The text offers a number of genre signals more likely to tip off, rather than trick, a reasonably engaged reader. As the first sentence of Volume II explains, 'by a very great Accident, we have got into our Hands a *French* Manuscript, in which [Misson] himself gives a Detail of his Actions' (*General History*, p. 383); the idea of a found or translated text, particularly in French, that has come to light almost miraculously in a 'very great Accident' is a common trope for framing English romances and tales of fantastic voyages. Such a preface is more likely to reveal than deceive. Misson's narrative is very different from everything around it, detailing as it does a highly educated main character born into an 'ancient Family' and entertaining both a level of biographical detail and moral elevation not found elsewhere in the *General History*. Further, Misson's is not a sordid tale of criminality either fated or chosen; rather, his decision to become a pirate is the result of a principled, idealistic stance. No one else in the *General History*, not even Captain England or Mary Read – historical figures for whom the narrator voices some sympathy – are nearly so unambiguously or consistently ethical.

Johnson's interposition of Tew is not even the first historical detail of Misson's counterfactual tale. Early on, Johnson troubles the generic waters in the naval battle that gains Misson his first command. He summons here the story of the *Winchelsea*, an English ship destroyed in a hurricane near Antigua in 1707. In Johnson's work, we are informed that attributing the wreck to a storm is a mistake, for in truth it was taken by Misson's ship and accidentally blown up during the battle. 'None ever knew before this Manuscript fell into my Hands how the *Winchelsea* was lost', Johnson claims (*General History*, p. 390). There is no chance that Johnson is merely confused; he knows enough of the histories of Avery and Tew to be certain that the real Tew exited the historical record in 1695, but his pirates' relative chronologies do not add up. The mismatched timescales underscore how popular pirate writing is from the beginning a melange of history and invention, with layered fictions present even in the foundational texts so that any creative literary ventures that take their inspiration from the *General History* directly or indirectly are almost by default counterfictions.

John Richetti nicely terms Misson's tale 'a deliberately constructed counter-myth, a fable which exploits to the full the ideological implications of the pirate legend while purging it of its grosser aspects of violence'.[33] As Richetti implies, Misson is not only a pirate but also a counter-pirate, a point Johnson underlines through simple colour symbolism. When Misson's boatswain wants to fly the black flag, Caraccioli instead talks the crew into raising 'a white Ensign, with Liberty painted in the Fly' and with the motto 'For God and Liberty' as a sign of their 'Uprightness and Resolution' (*General History*, p. 393). Reading Misson's narrative as a self-aware exercise in counterfactual thinking, then, moves us crucially closer to understanding the popularisation that the figure of the pirate experienced especially in the nineteenth century – the age not of Avery, but of Cleveland, Conrad and Long John Silver. Stevenson's Silver, who, like Barrie's Captain Hook, claimed to have known Blackbeard, hops about with a waggish, dynamic swagger more likely to be found on the stage than on the quarterdeck. Scott's Clement Cleveland was roughly based on the real pirate John Gow, about whom both Johnson and Defoe had written; Byron's Conrad emerged from the complex phenomenon of pirates in the Greek archipelago who resisted Ottoman rule but who were also known to attack European targets from time to time. Both Cleveland and Conrad, like Cross's Blackbeard, were brought low when they fell in love ill-advisedly: Cleveland loses all effectiveness as a pirate in trying to woo the idealistic Minna Troil; Conrad betrays his men and his wife in his confusion over what to make of the homicide Gulnare, who murdered her captor to free him; and Blackbeard is undone by the captive princess Ismene's various avengers.

One of the hallmarks of nineteenth-century pirate yarns is the incompatibility of affairs piratical with affairs of the heart; nineteenth-century literary pirates are not good at family.[34] The fictional Misson also has this flaw. A major element of the nineteenth-century reimagining of literary pirates is the introduction of a woman problem: Conrad, Cleveland and Cross's Blackbeard are, as noted, all brought low by lusting after the wrong lady. As a mark of his relevance to the development of the genre in the nineteenth century, Misson – atypically for the pirates of the *General History* – introduces a serious fracture into his empire's ideals in his treatment of his new nation's wives. Misson's radical notion of liberty and equality may cross racial and national lines, but not gender roles. Although he has a willing wife, a Johanna queen, most of his men lack female companionship, and resent it. A single page after heroically freeing an entire slaver's worth of Africans, Misson leads his men in taking an Indian ship from which they keep '100 Girls, from 12 to 18 Years old'. The girls clearly do not wish to go, and their 'Lamentations' disturb Misson, but he defers to his men. In what is probably not a coincidence, both the 1708 and the 1709 versions of the *Life of Captain Avery* had given Avery's fabled colony the same challenge of a scarcity of women; Avery solved the problem simply by buying women from local tribes. Johnson omits the problem of a wife shortage from his chapter on Avery but includes it, along with some measure of acknowledgement of the women's traumatised subjectivity, in his portrait of Misson. Libertalia decides that it needs a government and forms one that appears strikingly egalitarian at first glance: 'the ablest among them, without Distinction of Nation or Colour' are chosen as governors (*General History*, p. 432). But the captive women are neither consulted nor chosen to govern. This is not merely the lamentable misogyny of a bygone age: Misson's inability to maintain his ideals while securing the human capital he needs to perpetuate the next generation of his empire is a crucial node where the fantasy stutters, reminding us that the radical experiment of Libertalia runs contrary to historical fact. Romantic pirate dramas pick this up and amplify it, transforming their pirates from anarchic thieves to compelling swashbucklers, but also compulsively including love interests to bring down their too-attractive villains.

When Cross's show helped make new pirate writings popular again, the pirate authors who followed him remained alive to the dramatic underpinnings of their subject. There is always something performative and theatrical about pirates, even when rendered in prose. A particularly apt example is the strolling actor-turned-rover who features in Scott's *The Pirate* as Captain Cleveland's loyal right-hand man. Again, the genetics of the righteous pirate of the nineteenth century appear in Johnson's counterfactual flights a century earlier: under his white flag, Misson – a pirate who thought he was better than his kind – appears in more ways proleptically akin to Byron's idealistic and doomed Conrad than to Johnson's notoriously cruel Blackbeard or his cunning Avery.

Inevitably, the role played by women both on stage and in histories in as thoroughly masculine an enterprise as piracy is challenging. Orra and Ismene are the women who bring down Blackbeard, but a prominent sub-plot in Cross's *Black Beard* features a third woman, the chaste she-pirate Nancy, who has come to sea to remain at the side of, and fight for, her beloved Willy. In her valour, monogamy and trousers, Nancy (also called Ann) is a variation on – one might say, a counterfictional version of – the duo Mary Read and Anne Bonny, whose historical lives had already been fictionalised in the pages of the *General History*. These were real, rather small-time she-pirates whom the *General History* had immortalised in highly sensational accounts that included invented cross-dressing childhoods and numerous sexual liaisons. As reimagined by Cross, Nancy, who is much more sexually demure than the *General History*'s versions of Read and Bonny, helps deliver her beloved from the career into which he has been forced, and the two retire from the roving life to be married.

In earlier eighteenth-century versions of Avery, the Captain's rape or courtship (depending on the version) of a princess is a sign of his triumph; it is with the Mughal's fabled daughter that he might have founded his counterfactual empire. Johnson's decision to excise the princess completely from his version of Avery's narrative is extremely unusual, and clearly shows the downward nature of his revision of the fictional narrative that had glorified Avery. Meanwhile, further to blacken the character of Blackbeard, Johnson represents him as a lustful monster, an abusive polygamist with some fourteen wives. In general, then, Johnson is careful to avoid representations of positive heterosexual relationships among pirates. Cross modifies Johnson's apparent discomfort with the idea of pirate sex into a central point, making heterosexual bonds the downfall of pirate might. Willy is saved from piracy by a woman, while Blackbeard brings about his own doom by angering women to whom he is sexually attached: his unlawful attention to Ismene causes his wife, Orra, to betray him and her ghost to haunt him, distracting him at a crucial moment while Ismene's lover leads the vengeful Maynard to hunt him down. Historically, women were involved mostly on the margins of piratical networks; counterfictional pirate writing in the nineteenth century, however, gives them the prominent place they lacked on the factual deck.

The history of *Black Beard* and the what-if speculation of its source, which Johnson indulged throughout the structure of the *General History*, show the fruitful flexibility of counterfactualism, not least because it opens the door to a seemingly *verboten* discussion of pirate sex. Pirate lore in the Romantic period is strongly anchored by the Golden Age of piracy in the late seventeenth and early eighteenth centuries (roughly 1650–1730) as re-told by the *General History*, and yet at the same time (as with Johnson's counterfactual experimentation with Misson), it is adrift in atemporal seas. The voyages that Stevenson's Silver undertook with Blackbeard and Captain England – and Barrie's Hook with Silver and Captain Morgan – are made possible, even anticipated, when Johnson decides to have Captain Tew leave Avery (with whom he really did consort) for Captain Misson (with whom pirates could sail only in dreams). In Cross's *Black Beard*, while we might be tempted to dismiss his singing pirates as entertaining frippery, it would be wrong to miss the complicated textual ancestry on which those repurposed figures drew as they strode the stage in rhodomontade splendour. Cross's source material includes the legend built up around Captain Avery, whose fanciful Madagascan empire Johnson had first cried down in Volume I of the *General History*, and then revisited and purified via Captain Misson in Volume II.

The romance and arguably romantic land of Libertalia has certainly lived on in pirate lore. In the 1952 Errol Flynn film, *Against All Flags*, for example, there is a pirate community in Madagascar called Libertalia; the film appropriately has strong affinities with Cross's *Black Beard* melodrama, though a version of the pirate captain Roc Brasiliano (1630–c.1671) replaces Blackbeard as the dynamic antagonist. The film features a captured Mughal ship and a princess who falls in love with the pirate who, like Byron's Conrad, gallantly rescues her from its flames. In a literary example, William S. Burroughs concludes his Red Night Trilogy with *Cities of the Red Night* (1981), an interesting nonlinear novel whose plot concerns the pirate community Libertalia that Johnson invented for Misson. Burroughs evidently mistook (or in any case, treats) the Misson narrative as historical fact; his premise is to ask: what if Misson had survived, and with him Libertalia as a place in which men could live by his articles of radical freedom?[35] *Cities of the Red Night* is thus a compelling example of a counterfiction that thinks itself counterfactual, opining in its prefatory materials that 'Had Captain Mission [*sic*] lived long enough to set an example for others to follow, mankind might have stepped free', but the chance 'to live where you want, with companions of your choosing, under laws to which you agree, died in the eighteenth century with Captain Mission.'[36] Audiences for pirate lore of all kinds are remarkably willing to balance a fascination with the 'real' history of piracy with a love of those fantasy versions of pirates who never sailed, but could have: the Misson who wasn't, but who redeemed the greedier side of Tew from Avery's influence; the Blackbeard torn by softer passions; and the 'Nancy' version of Mary Read who evaded capture and lived happily ever after, disappearing safely into the waters of time. The 'what if?' questions that seem radical and daring intellectual acts for contemporary critics were the core enabling aesthetic of such tales.

Notes

1 See Frederick Burwick and Manushag N. Powell, *British Pirates in Print and Performance* (New York: Palgrave, 2015), pp. 161–6.
2 See Richard Saint-Gelais, 'How to Do Things with Worlds: From Counterfactuality to Counterfictionality', in Dorothee Birke, Michael Butter and Tilmann Köppe (eds), *Counterfactual Thinking–Counterfactual Writing* (Berlin: De Gruyter, 2011), p. 251. Saint-Gelais uses a narrower definition of counterfiction than Matt Hills, on whose work he builds, choosing to focus on those texts that 'modify the diegesis of a former fictional narrative' rather than those that offer a creative modification of a pre-existing fictional world. That is, for Saint-Gelais, a counterfiction changes a particular detail of a previous fiction but also retains many basic plot parameters, rather than launching something effectively new

into a familiar setting (pp. 243–4). My contention is that both definitions of the term apply to my treatment.

3   Catherine Gallagher, *Telling It Like It Wasn't: The Counterfactual Imagination in History and Fiction* (Chicago: University of Chicago Press, 2018), pp. 2–3.

4   See Burwick and Powell, *British Pirates*, pp. 39–42.

5   John Cartwright Cross and James Sanderson, *The Songs, Duets, Glees, Chorusses, &c. In the Popular Grand Spectacle of Music, Dance, and Action, called, Black Beard; Or, The Captive Princess: As Performed Upwards of 100 Nights, at the Royal Circus, Last Season; and Revived with New Songs, Scenery, Dresses, &c. on Wednesday, May 15, 1799* (London: T. Burton, 1799), p. 6.

6   See Burwick and Powell, *British Pirates*, pp. 73, 59–72.

7   Peter Lamborn Wilson, *Pirate Utopias: Moorish Corsairs and European Renegadoes*, 2nd edn (Brooklyn, NY: Autonomedia, 2003), p. 196.

8   The 'upward counterfactual' is a concept commonly found in psychological examinations of counterfactual thinking. See for example Keith D. Markman, Igor Gavanski, Steven J. Sherman and Matthew N. McMullin, 'The Mental Simulation of Better and Worse Possible Worlds', *Journal of Experimental Psychology*, 29:1 (January 1993), 87–109.

9   Referring to historians such as Marcus Rediker, Christopher Hill and Chris Land, Peter Earle warns: 'Historians of piracy are well aware that Captain Misson is fictional and that Libertalia never existed, but many tend to be radically minded or romantic writers who would like their pirates to be as Captain Misson's were'; Peter Earle, *The Pirate Wars* (New York: St Martin's Press, 2003), p. 130.

10 Cross and Sanderson, *The Songs, Duets, Glees, Chorusses*, p. 11.

11 John Robert Moore attributed the *General History* to Defoe in *Defoe in the Pillory and Other Studies* (1939); Furbank and Owens reject the attribution in *The Canonisation of Daniel Defoe* (1988) and in *Defoe De-Attributions* (1994). Arne Bialuschewski makes the case for Mist in 'Daniel Defoe, Nathaniel Mist, and the *General History of the Pyrates*', *Papers of the Bibliographical Society of America*, 98:1 (March 2004), 21–38.

12 Christopher Hill takes the *General History* to be the work of Defoe even while recognising that Misson's radical division of property is not in keeping with that author's general ethos. See Christopher Hill, 'Radical Pirates?', in *The Collected Essays of Christopher Hill*, 3 vols (Amherst, MA: University of Massachusetts Press, 1986), III, p. 179. He reconciles this apparent contradiction by making Defoe into an interviewer of pirates who is 'reproducing the substance of what he had been told'; 'Some

pirates must have seen themselves as egalitarian avengers', he claims (p. 165). However, he later undermines this assumption by positing that, while a few political radicals, dissenters and would-be patriots may have transitioned into buccaneering, 'most men had no choice' (p. 174). Real piracy, unlike Misson's, was the lesser of two evils, not, generally speaking, a bold stand for freedom.

13 Charles Johnson, *A General History of the Pyrates*, ed. Manuel Schonhorn (Mineola, NY: Dover, 1999), p. 57. Subsequent references refer to this edition and appear in the body of the text.

14 For a discussion of the sources, see Burwick and Powell, *British Pirates*, pp. 28–30.

15 See Clement Downing, *A Compendious History of the Indian Wars; With an Account of the Rise, Progress, Strength, and Forces of Angria the Pyrate* (London: T. Cooper, 1737), p. 118.

16 In 1713, Rogers ventured to Madagascar to reconnoitre the state of the pirates living there, and actually ventured to propose (unsuccessfully) that they be pardoned and used as the basis for a British colony in those parts; see Colin Woodard, *The Republic of Pirates* (New York: Harcourt, 2007), p. 117. The description quoted here and attributed to Rogers appears only in the *General History*, and may be Johnson's invention.

17 There does not appear to have been any eighteenth-century pirate of note named Misson. Benerson Little suggests the character might be named for the fictional travelogue of Jacques Massé (by Simon Tyssot de Patot) or the famed French travel writer François Maximilien Misson, perhaps in combination with the English pirate William Mason; Benerson Little, *Pirate Hunting: The Fight against Pirates, Privateers, and Sea Raiders from Antiquity to the Present* (Dulles, VA: Potomac, 2010), pp. 167–8; 'A Further Note on Captain Misson's Name', www.ben ersonlittle.com/_i__center_pirate_hunting___br__the_fight_against_ pirates__privateers__and_sea_r_71424.htm (accessed 14 May 2018).

18 See Catherine Gallagher, 'What Would Napoleon Do?: Historical, Fictional, and Counterfactual Characters', *New Literary History*, 42:2 (Spring 2011), 323.

19 Damian Walford Davies, 'Introduction: Reflections on an Orthodoxy', in Damian Walford Davies (ed.), *Romanticism, History, Historicism: Essays on Orthodoxy* (New York: Routledge, 2009), p. 10.

20 See Joel Baer, *Pirates of the British Isles* (Stroud: Tempus, 2005), p. 94 and David F. Marley, *Pirates of the Americas, Volume II: 1686–1725* (Santa Barbara, CA: ABC-CLIO, 2010), p. 785. It is not completely clear what Tew did to gain this immense booty, but certainly he did not, as his privateer's commission directed, restrict himself to attack-

ing French slavers. Further confusing matters, Marley reports that Tew 'touched at the open pirate port known as Libertatia [*sic*]' on his way home. 'Libertatia' (Libertalia) is of course a fiction; Marley is not the only historian to make such an error.

21 Tew's commission authorised him to attack only French Canadians. See Jan Rogoziński, *Honor Among Thieves: Captain Kidd, Henry Every, and the Pirate Democracy in the Indian Ocean* (Mechanicsburg, PA: Stackpole Books, 2000), p. 73.
22 Hill, 'Radical Pirates?', p. 164.
23 Georg Christophe Berger Waldenegg, 'What-If? Counterfactuality and History', in Birke, Butter and Köppe (eds), *Counterfactual Thinking–Counterfactual Writing*, p. 145.
24 Lincoln Faller, 'Captain Misson's Failed Utopia, Crusoe's Failed Colony: Race and Identity in New, Not Quite Imaginable Worlds', *The Eighteenth Century: Theory and Interpretation*, 43:1 (Spring 2002), 6. Faller also points out the careful contrast between Mison's well-organised, consensually but strictly governed utopia and the English pirate expatriate community visited by Tew, which is lawless and far less communitarian.
25 Baer, *Pirates of the British Isles*, pp. 99–100.
26 Rogoziński, *Honor Among Thieves*, p. 75. Rogoziński later seems to contradict himself, stating (p. 85) that the *Amity* was too slow to join the fight. No explanation of Tew's demise is offered.
27 Captain Kidd, who was an incompetent pirate hunter before himself turning pirate, was initially commissioned to hunt down Tew, although Tew was almost certainly already dead.
28 Marcus Rediker, 'Hydrarchy and Libertalia: The Utopian Dimensions of Atlantic Piracy in the Early Eighteenth Century', in David J. Starkey, E. S. van Eyck van Heslinga and J. A. de Moor (eds), *Pirates and Privateers: New Perspectives on the War on Trade in the Eighteenth and Nineteenth Centuries* (Exeter: University of Exeter Press, 1997), p. 30.
29 *Ibid.*, p. 31.
30 Without mistaking the account of Misson for a factual one, Chris Land (whose essay leans rather heavily on Rediker) still sees its inclusion in Johnson's *General History* as clear evidence that 'pirates were perceived as politically dissident, revolutionary figures'. See Chris Land, 'Flying the Black Flag: Revolt, Revolution, and the Social Organization of Piracy in the "Golden Age"', *Management & Organizational History*, 2:2 (May 2007), 180. More problematically, Land concludes that Misson's absurdly utopian behaviour (which we should note, as most historians do not, extended pointedly to all except women) has a basis in reality

(p. 182). Land ultimately understands Misson's as a failed revolution, one that offers no real alternatives to the status quo.
31 Faller, 'Captain Misson's Failed Utopia', p. 5.
32 Gallagher, 'What Would Napoleon Do?', 322. For Gallagher, fiction writers are conscious of 'shifting referential gears' when they blend historical and more purely fictional characters in their narratives; counterfactual and fictional characters are not perfect equivalents, nor, importantly, are they meant to be, and only a few fictions are also counterfactual.
33 John Richetti, *Popular Fiction Before Richardson: Narrative Patterns, 1700–1739* (Oxford: Clarendon Press, 1992), p. 70.
34 See Burwick and Powell, *British Pirates*, p. 118.
35 In his preface, Burroughs cites not Johnson but Don Carlo Seitz's *Under the Black Flag: Exploits of the Most Notorious Pirates* (New York: Dial Press, 1925) – a text that extracts, revises and plagiarises liberally from the *General History*; see William S. Burroughs, *Cities of the Red Night* (New York: Viking, 1981), p. xi.
36 Burroughs, *Cities of the Red Night*, pp. xiv–xv. Burroughs returned to his counterfictional Misson in *Ghost of Chance* (New York: Whitney Museum of American Art, 1991).

Works cited

Primary texts

Anon., 'Some Memoirs Concerning that Famous Pyrate Capt. Avery, with Remarks on St Laurence, Otherwise Called Madagascar, and the Neighbouring Islands on which He Now Resides,' *Monthly Miscellany, or, Memoirs for the Curious*, 10 (November 1708), 344–53

Cross, John Cartwright and James Sanderson, *The Songs, Duets, Glees, Chorusses, &c. In the Popular Grand Spectacle of Music, Dance, and Action, called, Black Beard; Or, The Captive Princess: As Performed Upwards of 100 Nights, at the Royal Circus, Last Season; and Revived with New Songs, Scenery, Dresses, &c. on Wednesday, May 15, 1799* (London: T. Burton, 1799)

Downing, Clement, *A Compendious History of the Indian Wars; With an Account of the Rise, Progress, Strength, and Forces of Angria the Pyrate* (London: T. Cooper, 1737)

Johnson, Charles, *A General History of the Pyrates*, ed. Manuel Schonhorn (Mineola, NY: Dover, 1999)

Marley, David F., *Pirates of the Americas, Volume II: 1686–1725* (Santa Barbara, CA: ABC-CLIO, 2010) van Broeck, Adrian, *The Life and Adventures of Captain John Avery, the Famous English Pirate (Rais'd from a Cabbin-Boy, to a King), Now in Possession of Madagascar: and Faithfully Extracted from His Journal* (London: J. Baker, 1709)

Secondary texts

Baer, Joel, *Pirates of the British Isles* (Stroud: Tempus, 2005)
Bialuschewski, Arne, 'Daniel Defoe, Nathaniel Mist, and the *General History of the Pyrates*', *Papers of the Bibliographical Society of America*, 98:1 (March 2004), 21–38
Burroughs, William S., *Cities of the Red Night* (New York: Viking, 1981)
Burroughs, William S., *Ghost of Chance* (New York: Whitney Museum of American Art, 1991)
Burwick, Frederick and Manushag N. Powell, *British Pirates in Print and Performance* (New York: Palgrave, 2015)
Earle, Peter, *The Pirate Wars* (New York: St Martin's Press, 2003)
Faller, Lincoln, 'Captain Misson's Failed Utopia, Crusoe's Failed Colony: Race and Identity in New, Not Quite Imaginable Worlds', *The Eighteenth Century: Theory and Interpretation*, 43:1 (Spring 2002), 1–17
Furbank, P. N. and W. R. Owens, *Defoe De-Attributions: A Critique of J. R. Moore's Checklist* (London: The Hambledon Press, 1994)
Furbank, P. N. and W. R. Owens, *The Canonisation of Daniel Defoe* (New Haven, CT: Yale University Press, 1988)
Gallagher, Catherine, *Telling It Like It Wasn't: The Counterfactual Imagination in History and Fiction* (Chicago: University of Chicago Press, 2018)
Gallagher, Catherine, 'What Would Napoleon Do?: Historical, Fictional, and Counterfactual Characters', *New Literary History*, 42:2 (Spring 2011), 315–36
Hill, Christopher, 'Radical Pirates?', in *The Collected Essays of Christopher Hill*, 3 vols (Amherst, MA: University of Massachusetts Press, 1986), III, pp. 160–87
Land, Chris, 'Flying the Black Flag: Revolt, Revolution, and the Social Organization of Piracy in the "Golden Age"', *Management & Organizational History*, 2:2 (May 2007), 169–92
Little, Benerson, 'A Further Note on Captain Misson's Name', www.benersonlittle.com/_i__center_pirate_hunting___br__the_fight_against_pirates__privateers__and_sea_r_71424.htm
Little, Benerson, *Pirate Hunting: The Fight against Pirates, Privateers, and Sea Raiders from Antiquity to the Present* (Dulles, VA: Potomac, 2010)
Markman, Keith D., Igor Gavanski, Steven J. Sherman and Matthew

N. McMullin, 'The Mental Simulation of Better and Worse Possible Worlds', *Journal of Experimental Psychology*, 29.1 (January 1993), 87–109

Moore, John Robert, *Defoe in the Pillory and Other Studies* (Bloomington, IN: Indiana University Press, 1939)

Rediker, Marcus, 'Hydrarchy and Libertalia: The Utopian Dimensions of Atlantic Piracy in the Early Eighteenth Century', in David J. Starkey, E. S. van Eyck van Heslinga and J. A. de Moor (eds), *Pirates and Privateers: New Perspectives on the War on Trade in the Eighteenth and Nineteenth Centuries* (Exeter: University of Exeter Press, 1997), pp. 29–46

Richetti, John, *Popular Fiction Before Richardson: Narrative Patterns, 1700–1739* (Oxford: Clarendon Press, 1992)

Rogoziński, Jan, *Honor Among Thieves: Captain Kidd, Henry Every, and the Pirate Democracy in the Indian Ocean* (Mechanicsburg, PA: Stackpole Books, 2000)

Saint-Gelais, Richard, 'How to Do Things with Worlds: From Counterfactuality to Counterfictionality', in Dorothee Birke, Michael Butter and Tilmann Köppe (eds), *Counterfactual Thinking–Counterfactual Writing* (Berlin: de Gruyter, 2011), pp. 240–52

Seitz, Don Carlo, *Under the Black Flag: Exploits of the Most Notorious Pirates* (New York: The Dial Press, 1925)

Waldenegg, Georg Christophe Berger, 'What-If? Counterfactuality and History', in Dorothee Birke, Michael Butter and Tilmann Köppe (eds), *Counterfactual Thinking–Counterfactual Writing* (Berlin: de Gruyter, 2011), pp. 130–49

Walford Davies, Damian, 'Introduction: Reflections on an Orthodoxy', in Damian Walford Davies (ed.), *Romanticism, History, Historicism: Essays on Orthodoxy* (New York: Routledge, 2009), pp. 1–13

Wilson, Peter Lamborn, *Pirate Utopias: Moorish Corsairs and European Renegadoes*, 2nd edn (Brooklyn, NY: Autonomedia, 2003)

Woodard, Colin, *The Republic of Pirates: Being the True Surprising Story of the Caribbean Pirates and the Man Who Brought Them Down* (New York: Harcourt, 2007)

10

Romanticism and the (counterfactual) Chinese awakening

Peter J. Kitson

China and Romantic orientalism

Today, 'Romantic Orientalism' is an established and vibrant sub-field of postcolonial Romantic Studies, with major new interventions appearing with great frequency. The focus of this critical endeavour, following Edward Said, has primarily been on the 'Near East', the Levant and India. This is because – as Said argued – British and French colonial policy in the eighteenth and nineteenth centuries was largely preoccupied with these geopolitical areas.[1] Knowledge of these territories was essential to establishing western hegemony there. The key objects of European orientalist knowledge were the Islamic and Hindu religions and the Persian, Arabic and Sanskrit languages. British, French and American involvement with China, Japan and other southeast Asian states is generally regarded as a later, mid- to late-nineteenth-century manifestation of this preoccupation. British and European knowledge of the Far East was limited by the exclusiveness of China and Japan, which managed to resist European encroachment at least until the 1840s and 1850s. The establishment of a professional body of work, with the institutions and scholarly infrastructure to support it – the discipline and politico-cultural project that became 'sinology' – was thus a comparatively belated enterprise in the orientalist field.

A number of studies have recently appeared on the British cultural response to China in the period.[2] China in the eighteenth century was possessed of enormous prestige; its military and political success was spectacular. Its exports of tea, porcelain and silks were in great demand in Britain, and Chinese-inspired designs in the form of the European craze for chinoiserie were highly sought after. China was a 'world power', and its role in the global economy of the eighteenth century was substantial. World systems theorists such as André Gunder Frank have postulated the existence of a global network of trade in the eighteenth century dominated by China and India – a network to which Britain, and northern Europe more widely, were latecomers. Frank claimed that from around 1500, China and India functioned as the core of a single, global world economy with a worldwide division of labour and multilateral trade. From the seventeenth century onward, European desire for superior Asian products created an expanding global trade whose net balance was easily in China's favour.[3] It has been calculated that China's GDP as late as 1820 was around 29 per cent of global production and much larger than that of all Europe – including industrial Britain – combined. Chinese economic strength was fully understood by Europeans. The Jesuit historian of China, Jean-Baptiste Du Halde, judged that in 1735 trade within China was vastly greater than that of Europe as a whole, and Adam Smith declared in *The Wealth of Nations* (1776) that China was 'a country richer than any part of Europe'.[4] Certainly, China's prosperity was legendary, leading Robert Markley to describe its enormous riches and revenues as representing to the eighteenth-century European imagination 'a kind of socioeconomic sublime'.[5] With this vast economic strength came a powerful cultural cachet that fuelled the enormous and increasing consumer demand for Asian products in the West.

The foundation of the eighteenth-century Canton trade was the exchange of Chinese tea for South American silver, acquired from Europeans.[6] All the world's tea exports came from China; it was not until 1839 that the very first Indian tea was sold on the British market.[7] In the eyes of many, the China trade was 'the most important in the world'.[8] British consumers desired many Chinese products – silks, porcelain and lacquerware; but it was the newly fashionable beverage of tea they craved most avidly, the consumption of which grew exponentially in the eighteenth and early nineteenth centuries. It is well known that the East India Company's response to this trade imbalance from the 1820s was to produce larger volumes of the opium grown at Patna in Bengal. This opium was auctioned off to private or 'country' traders who transported it to China where it was smuggled into the country. As the Chinese had forbidden the trade, the Company did not engage in selling their opium directly. Opium thus became firmly enmeshed in British commercial and colonial policy in the Romantic period; in effect, it funded British rule in India. This expedient would exacerbate a series of events that would lead to the conflict known as the Opium Wars.[9]

Given the crucial economic significance for the British of the tea trade with China and their desire for Chinese products, it is surprising that the *topos* of China itself does not feature more prominently in the literature and culture of the Romantic period – as for instance, India does. It is also puzzling that there was so much less engagement with the Chinese language and with Chinese literature and thought, especially in comparison to that shown in the case of Indian and Persian literature. Sir William Jones's famous translations from Sanskrit and Persian were celebrated throughout Europe and were highly influential texts for the Romantic poets, notably Coleridge and Shelley. China, however, did not make the same kind of cultural impression and did not attract the kinds of cultural engagement that one might have predicted. This chapter explores the vexed relation of Romantic-period writing and China by developing an imagined, counterfactual account of what might have been had China, as both a *topos* and culture, become one of the dominant strands – as it may well have – of Romantic Orientalism, in addition to India, Arabia and the Levant.

The Eighteenth-century discovery of China: (counterfactual) Percy, Walpole and Jones

In many ways, our assumptions about British responses to China and its impact on British culture have been influenced by the decline of China after the First (1839–42) and Second (1856–60) Opium Wars. The massive decline in the prestige of the Qing empire in the nineteenth century and its collapse in the early twentieth century have unfairly coloured the impression we have of the dynasty and its cultural achievements in the context of the seemingly irresistible rise of a modern, technologically superior British empire. However, in mid-eighteenth-century Britain, the fashion for all things Chinese was at its height. Chinoiserie, or the 'Chinese taste', was seemingly ubiquitous.[10] Increasingly, British consumers drank Chinese tea (still very much a luxury) in Chinese porcelain or inferior British and European copies, enhanced by intricate chinoiserie designs. The parks and gardens of the British aristocracy were landscaped according to the 'Anglo-Chinese' taste of natural wildness.[11] Middle-class Britons decorated their houses with Chinese furniture and Chinese wallpapers. Sir William Chambers published dissertations on the beauties of Chinese gardens and Chinese architecture; as architect to the future George III, he famously added a nine-storey pagoda to the royal gardens at Kew.

As David Porter argues, it was ultimately the long-standing prestige of imperial China – founded on an ancient pedigree that validated Chinese culture as against parvenu European empires such as Britain's – that occasioned this admiration and, perhaps, cultural anxiety. Voltaire famously praised the contemporary Qing empire as a rational and enlightened despotism, with the Kangxi emperor as a model ruler, presiding over a meritocratic bureaucracy staffed by Confucian scholars who earned their employment through a process of competitive examination. Catholic missionaries (largely Jesuit) to China extolled the virtues of a well-ordered, ancient and thus legitimate Confucian civilisation that could provide a model for Europe. They hinted that Confucianism concealed within its thought an ancient, original monotheism that had been lost to the Judaeo-Christian world after the catastrophe of the Flood and that the Chinese language, with its ideogrammatic forms, might be related to the primal Adamic language that existed before Babel and might even reveal traces of a prelapsarian natural correspondence between word and thing before they were irreparably sundered by the Fall.[12]

In the literary culture of the mid-to-late eighteenth century, it really did seem as if there might be a Chinese moment inspired by all these influences. Certainly there were signs that China was about to take off in a major way for British culture. David Garrick, for example, brought the spectacular French entertainment *Les Fêtes Chinoise* (translated as *The Chinese Festival*) to the London stage in 1755. In 1759, one of the most popular dramas of its day, Arthur Murphy's *The Orphan of China*, also with Garrick in the lead role, was staged to full houses at Drury Lane and frequently performed thereafter in Britain and North America. Murphy's drama was the product of a complex process of adaptation deriving from a thirteenth-century Yuan period song-drama, *Zhaoshi guer* (The Orphan of the House of Zhao).[13] The play's Preface, composed by the laureate, William Whitehead, makes the point rather bluntly in the form of an extraordinary rejection of ancient classical civilisation in favour of Confucian China: 'Enough of Greece and Rome. The exhausted store / Of either nation now can charm no more.' China will now provide 'fresh virtues' and 'bring / Confucius' morals to Britannia's ears'.[14] Murphy's China drama was extremely popular, one reviewer commenting that 'every one has, by this time, seen or read, and must have applauded it'; it presented an exotic spectacle with chinoiserie-inspired costumes and settings combined with severe Confucian moralism.[15]

It was against this background that the 32-year-old Thomas Percy, hoping to capitalise on this defining cultural moment, began his early, ambitious Chinese project. In 1761, he published *Hau Kiou Choaan; or, the Pleasing History* (1761), an edition of the first Chinese novel to be translated into English, the *Haoqiu zhuan* (1683?), which was followed by his scholarly compendium, *Miscellaneous Pieces Relating to the Chinese* (1762), containing essays by himself and others (including Samuel Johnson) on aspects of Chinese philosophy, literature (especially poetry) and language, as well as translations of Chinese poetry and drama. Responding to the great popularity of Chinese-inspired design, Percy seems to have calculated that Chinese literary and cultural texts would sell well at this critical moment and make a significant impact on British tastes. The edition of the Chinese novel contained extensive annotation describing and explaining Chinese beliefs and customs. Percy's work thus provided a body of learning and a sourcebook of ideas and images that would establish Chinese literary forms as potential models for British artists.

Percy is much better known for his recovery of the British ballad and romance tradition – widely regarded as a forerunner of what we know as 'Romanticism'. A number of scholars, however, have argued for the importance of Percy's 'Chinese project'. By studying Chinese literature, language and thought, Percy first encountered a cultural heritage that enabled his 'theorization of a non-classical, alternative English antiquity'.[16] Percy was attracted to Chinese thought and writing as an expression of an ancient and primary cultural moment. He may also have identified parallels between his role as a literary editor and man of letters dependent on patronage and that of the Confucian scholar in the service of an imperial polity. Paradoxically, perhaps, Percy's early engagement with Chinese literature, language and philosophy would occasion a crucial turn, by him and his admirers, to the medievalism of the Walpoleian gothic and the northern antiquarian ballad tradition. Early Chinese literature thus provided a model for Percy to consider Britain's own past and literary heritage.

Recent commentators contend that it was the commercial and intellectual failure of this Chinese project that encouraged Percy to move from the eastern and oriental to embrace the northern and medieval English ballad tradition. Yet there were continuities between these projects. With its stress on the ancient and established literary and philosophical canon, the China editorial work provided Percy with a prior literary model for the recovery of the romance tradition in the late eighteenth century and for what we have come to recognise as the Romanticism of Wordsworth and Coleridge, as articulated by the *Lyrical Ballads* of 1798 (for many, the ur-text of the 'movement'). Ultimately, however, Percy (and the Romantic tradition) came to reject the highly civilised and cultured forms of Chinese literature and Confucian philosophy for the ruder, less polished, and thus more authentic, ancient English ballads.

This chapter, however, tacks a different course. In counterfactual mode, it asks what shape Romanticism would have taken in Britain if Percy's edition of the Chinese novel *Hau Kiou Choaan*, with its Confucian moralistic romance, and his two-volume collection of scholarly essays about, and translations of, Chinese poetry, *Miscellaneous Pieces Relating to the Chinese*, had become the major commercial success he hoped for, establishing themselves as key literary models for contemporary British writers. Had Percy's work on Chinese language and culture, and his novel with its Confucian scholar and chaste female, its mandarins and bonzes (Buddhist priests), proved successful, in what ways might the main currents of British Romantic writing have been diverted from the channels in which they were actually to flow? Might these writings have catalysed a departure from the more frivolous expressions of French rococo-inflected chinoiserie and prompted a desire to comprehend what was thought of in the period as 'the Chinese mind'?

Commentators from A. O. Lovejoy to David Porter have firmly established the crucial link between chinoiserie and the gothic in the public mind in the 1740s and 1750. However, while chinoiserie declined as a fashion, the gothic, from its inception in Horace Walpole's *The Castle of Otranto* (1764), established itself as a popular and resilient literary genre both during and after the Romantic period.[17] Walpole – a noted early enthusiast for China – became a determined opponent of chinoiserie in his latter years, preferring, with Percy, the gothic mode that claimed a nativist medieval and national origin. Although Walpole is firmly associated with the gothic novel and the revival of European and British medievalism in the mid-to-late eighteenth century, he showed a strong interest in chinoiserie in his earlier years. He encountered China in the pages of Du Halde's influential *Description de l'Empire de la Chine* (1735; translated into English in rival editions of 1736 and 1738) – a work that made a great impression on him while an undergraduate at Cambridge. At one stage he even planned a Chinese house for Strawberry Hill.[18]

Walpole was fully aware of contemporary fashions in architecture, writing in 1750 that 'temples, bridges, etc. are generally Gothic or Chinese and give a whimsical air of novelty that is pleasing'.[19] Criticising the inappropriateness of the Palladian style for domestic buildings for failing to allow 'variety' or 'charming irregularities', Walpole asserted that

Romanticism and the Chinese awakening

he was 'almost as fond of the *Sharawaggi*, or Chinese want of symmetry, in buildings, as in grounds or gardens'.[20] Lovejoy and Porter have argued that Walpole's dismissal of chinoiserie in the 1740s was motivated by a growing patriotic preference for a nativist English medieval tradition. This led Walpole to claim that the real beauties and strengths manifest in chinoiserie were in fact of English rather than Chinese origin: our 'Chinese ornaments are not only of our own manufacture, like our French silks and our French wines, but, what has seldom been attributed to the English, of our own invention'.[21]

The question that arises, therefore, is: why did the mid-eighteenth-century interest in Chinese language, literature, philosophy and material artefacts prove to be something of a cultural dead end in the Romantic period? Was this historically inevitable, or could there have been a sustained Romantic engagement with Chinese culture as there was with Indian and Islamic culture? Was there something about Romanticism that was inimical to China? In a revolutionary age, the negative example of China as an ancient and established despotism certainly took hold. Whereas Voltaire admired the enlightened despotism of the Chinese empire, democrats and republicans (with whom Romanticism is frequently associated) increasingly regarded the empire as an ossified oriental tyranny. Confucianism as a social philosophy stressed the importance of obedience to the state and, within the family, filial obedience to the father as head of the household. The view of eighteenth-century Qing China was predominantly a construction of the Jesuits – a religious order that esteemed hierarchy and authority. The oft-noticed relationship between Romanticism and Protestantism, together with the Rousseauvian stress on individual feeling and the individual's unmediated personal relationship with the divine or noumenal, also cut across the Chinese valorisation of the individual's subservience to the imperial state. Similarly, the Romantic concern with the importance of the organic nation state that we see in Herder, Burke, Wordsworth, Coleridge and others was at odds with the multi-ethnic imperial polity of the Qing empire. However, many of these objections also applied to Hindu and Islamic cultures (with all their alleged oriental despotism), for which Romantic writers had an exotic fascination.

Even in Walpole's medievalist *Castle of Otranto*, there is a sustained fascination with the oriental – in this case, the crusades of the eleventh century. In 1785, as one of his *Hieroglyphic Tales*, Walpole penned 'Mi-Li' – a short piece that draws on his earlier fascination with chinoiserie. What might have happened if Walpole had not relinquished his early Chinese obsession? Strawberry Hill might have been designed as an elaborate chinoiserie folly, complete with dragons, bells, pagodas and Chinese temples, infusing the established 'Chinese taste' with enhanced life and new vigour. And so a counterfactual scenario can now be outlined. Fascinated by all things Chinese, Walpole enthusiastically reads Percy's *Hau Kiou Choaan* and his *Miscellaneous Pieces* and is inspired by them to write his new form of novel, *The House of Zamti* in 1764 – a heady mixture of romance, orientalism and chinoiserie, combined with unmistakable Shakespearean overtones.

Initially, the novel is claimed as a genuine translation from a thirteenth-century Chinese manuscript by a Spanish Jesuit missionary, Onuphrio Muralto, who travelled to Peking in the seventeenth century. This translation (it is claimed) was later found among the papers of an East India Company captain returned from Canton (Guangzhou). In the second edition of the novel, Walpole acknowledges the work as his own creation. The novel deploys the setting of thirteenth-century China under the Yuan dynasty as a way of exploring the displaced politics of legitimacy in mid-eighteenth-century Britain. The shrewder of Walpole's contemporaries saw through the novel's chinoiserie trappings and recognised it as a commentary on the current disputes between Whig and Tory in the wake of the 1688 settlement. The novel's protagonist, Zamti (a name taken from Arthur Murphy's drama of 1759, *The Orphan of China*), faces a tragic choice between his loyalty to the Song dynasty and his accommodation with the new invading Mongol dynasty with its charismatic emperor, Kubla Khan.

Appearing just after Oliver Goldsmith's *The Citizen of the World* (1762) with its Chinese Confucian narrator, Lien Chi Altangi, Walpole's tale establishes the new genre of the China novel. Influenced by Walpole's example, William Beckford in 1786 publishes an even more exotic chinoiserie fantasy, *Wanli* (loosely inspired by the downfall of the last Ming emperor), replete with necromancy, the supernatural and a pervasive and perverse hedonism. The novel's main character is a decadent and effete Chinese despot given to sensual excess. Among the novel's other characters are Wanli's mother, the dowager Empress Lu, a hyper-masculine creation delighting in sorcery and destruction, and possibly a fictionalised version of Beckford's own mother. The novel also features Wei-wei, a pederastic eunuch who runs the imperial household. Beckford cleverly uses seventeenth-century Ming China as a backdrop to explore eighteenth-century issues relating to gender and masculinity, as well as his own psychopathology. The novel proves extremely popular, especially admired by Lord Byron, who later pens his own fashionable Chinese tale, *The Fan-kwai; Or, the Foreign Devil*, in 1814. Combining psychological verisimilitude with exotic Chinese settings, Byron's new genre of the Chinese narrative verse romance firmly establishes itself as a paradigmatic mode within eighteenth- and early-nineteenth-century Britain. Its hybrid origin means that it is frequently entwined with other forms, notably the less influential but still significant medievalism or historical 'gothic' of Clara Reeve and others. Many authors adapt the form, including the Irish poet Thomas Moore in his narrative poem *Lady Wang* (1817), in which he uses the historical narrative of the Manchu invasion and occupation of Ming China in 1644 as a device to comment on the English oppression of his native Ireland. The 'China novel', as it comes to be known, persists throughout the period with a number of notable contributions, including Matthew Lewis's full-blooded shocker, *The Bonze* (1796), and Ann Radcliffe's corresponding psychological terror, *The Cantonese* (1797), in which the grisly superstitions of Chinese Buddhism are deployed to shore up a modern British Protestant understanding of the self.

Had literary figures of the cultural influence and prestige of Walpole, Radcliffe and Byron and their followers adopted Chinese *topoi* for their works instead of the gothicism and orientalism they actually deployed, the landscape of Romantic Orientalism and thus of Romanticism in general would have been very different. This chapter takes historical and literary-historical events and develops them as a counterfactual imaginary in an attempt to explore a different trajectory for Romanticism. Marshalling actual personalities from the period, their literary and scholarly activities and comments they did make about China and the Chinese, I imagine a related but alternative path, both as a way of encouraging the reader to reflect on the nature of the choices writers made and to highlight the problematic 'absent presence' of Qing China in British culture during the period of the tea and opium trade up to the First Opium War in 1839. Instead of Sir William Jones heralding an orientalist renaissance premised on a discovery of Sanskrit and Hindu mythology, I posit that his genuine ambition to master the Chinese language and translate the Chinese 'classics' was actually fulfilled – with significant cultural consequences.[22]

In my counterfactual imaginary, the understanding of Chinese literature and thought was greatly enhanced by the first wave of 'Romantic Sinology'. The first truly great British sinologist, Sir William Jones, mastered written Chinese, among some twenty other languages. Based in

Bengal where he served as a judge of the Supreme Court, Jones founded the Asiatic Society in 1784, one of the major aims of which was to study the written and spoken forms of the Chinese language. Jones had already been instructed in the basics of the language by the celebrated Chinese visitor to London, 'Whang Atong' (Huang Yadong), before he departed for India.[23] Whang returned to Canton in 1778 but remained in contact with Jones through their mutual friend, the British 'sing-song' (or musical clock) merchant, John Henry Cox, and in 1784 Jones renewed his friendship with Whang. Eager to assist his British friend, Whang supplied Jones with valuable Chinese texts, notably the Confucian Canon of the Four Books (*Sishu*) and the Five Classics (*Wujing*) as well as Zang Maoxun's landmark compilation of Yuan dynasty song drama, *Yuanren baizhong qu* (One Hundred Yuan Plays; 1615–16).

For Jones, the Chinese language was 'so ancient and so wonderfully composed', its literature abounding in 'useful as well as agreeable books'.[24] After studying it intensively, he became convinced that Chinese, not Sanskrit, was the closest relative then known to an original metalanguage. With extensive sponsorship from the East India Company, which was anxious to develop its knowledge base about China to facilitate its extensive tea trade, Jones was able to bring a team of Chinese scholars and literati from Canton to aid him with his translations. His team quickly produced workable, if rudimentary, Chinese/English dictionaries and grammars, followed by his monumental translation of the Qing legal code in 1787, the *Ta Tsing Leu Lee*.[25] The latter had a profound impact in changing prevailing (mis)understandings of oriental despotism as promulgated by Montesquieu, and it provided the Company with a tool to aid its negotiations with the Chinese. For the first time, Britons could see that the Qing empire was actually governed not by despotic whim but according to a rational and equitable system of punishments – in Jones's formulation, a precious knowledge 'drawn from the fountainhead of the wisest *Asiatick* nation'.[26] The understanding created by Jones's legal work greatly facilitated British and Chinese encounters at Canton, significantly easing intercultural tensions. Recovering from a serious illness in 1794, Jones produced the first English translations of Confucius's sayings, the *Lunyu* (Analects) and his tract on education, the *Daxue* (Great Learning).[27] Even more influential than these, however, were his literary translations, which included versions of Chinese drama, notably *Han Koong Tsew; or the Sorrows of Han* (1785) – his beautiful version of Ma Zhiyuan's *Hangong qiu*; and *Huielau ji* (The Chalk Circle), from Li Qianfu's *Hui lan ji* (later adapted by Berthold Brecht as *The Caucasian Chalk Circle*).²⁸ But, above all, it was his translations of Cao Xueqin's contemporary Chinese novel, *Hong lou meng* (as *The Dream of Red Mansions; or Story of the Stone*) and of the *Shijing* (Classic of Poetry), containing 300 short poems (odes), that made the greatest impact.²⁹ Notably, in places where he sensed the poems' condensed style might render them 'obscure' for a British audience, Jones imported the Miltonic sublime into his translations, stating at the same time that 'many think that even this obscurity is sublime and venerable, like that of ancient cloysters and temples, "*shedding*", as MILTON expresses it, a "*dim religious light*"'.³⁰ Jones's eighteenth-century diction and manner, however, somewhat obscured the moral point of the odes. Nevertheless, these translations formed an influential model for European writing. Alongside Percy's landmark translation of the *Haoqiu zhuan*, Jones's monumental translation of the *Shijing* provided important inspiration for the Romantic writers that were to follow.

Romantic China and the (counterfactual) Chinese awakening

To return, however, to the (literary) history we've inherited: Romantic-period writers did not commonly engage with China as a *topos*. There are, it is true, substantial and still unexplored writings about China in the period, many deriving from or relating to the first two Royal British embassies to Beijing – those of Macartney in 1793 and Amherst in 1816. There are also a number of popular dramas and pantomimes exploiting Chinese subjects, though fewer than one might expect given the interest in China inspired by the Macartney and Amherst embassies and the inclusion of Chinese characters and narratives (such as 'Aladdin') in *The Thousand and One Nights* and its various imitators.³¹

There may, of course, be many texts that have not yet attracted our attention in the still neglected field of Romantic-period Sino-British cultural relations; however, the absence of a major literary treatment of an explicitly Chinese subject by one of the canonical Romantic poets, novelists or essayists raises questions. The only exceptions are Coleridge's 'Kubla Khan', Lamb's rather whimsical essays 'Old China' and 'A Dissertation Upon Roast Pig' and, of course, Thomas De Quincey's *Confessions of an English Opium-Eater* (1821). All these texts, it might be argued, engage with 'China' in one form or another, but they do so in puzzlingly oblique ways. Coleridge's poem references the thirteenth-century Mongol Chinese emperor, Kubla Khan, and his pleasure gardens and dome, but does so within a vast geographical sweep, which also takes Abyssinia within its purview. De Quincey similarly uses a generalised orientalist gothic mode to articulate his opium nightmares, and his later essays on the opium wars display a characteristically bellicose Victorian view of the celestial empire. Lamb's brief essays approach the subject by way of chinoiserie porcelain or cumbersome fable.[32]

There are more occasional pieces by Robert Southey, Leigh Hunt and Walter Savage Landor about China and chinoiserie, but there is no substantial piece to rival Southey's highly influential verse narratives concerning India, South America and Arabia, or Byron's and Moore's enormously popular oriental tales. In making such a statement, I am perhaps guilty of privileging a much-extended yet still largely traditional literary canon over discursive prose and popular drama. A number of theatrical works such as Andrew Cherry's musical drama, *The Travellers, or Music's Fascination* (1806), and popular harlequinades such as *Harlequin Quixote; or, The Magic Arm* (1797) were produced, and yet Chinese *topoi* could have featured much more prominently on the stage than they did. Certainly, there is no drama in the Romantic period to match Arthur Murphy's (thoughtful and serious) tragedy, *The Orphan of China* – which continued to be performed in the Romantic period.

Further, there are very few extended discussions of China and matters Chinese outside diplomatic and missionary writing. For instance, the intellectual philhellenism and classicist bias of both Keats and Shelley seem to have prevented their embracing China in an imaginative way. Keats wrote extremely suggestively but briefly in one of his letters about how 'Agriculture is the tamer of men; the steam from the earth is like drinking their mother's milk – it enervates their natures. This appears a great cause of the imbecility of the Chinese'; Percy Shelley referred to the 'stagnant and miserable state of social institution' possessed by nineteenth-century China and Japan in the Preface to his oriental drama, *Hellas*.[33] Coleridge, in *Biographia Literaria*, also wrote of 'the immense empire of China improgressive for thirty centuries'.[34] These references remain curt, undeveloped and reductively stereotypical. There is, of course, the powerful eruption of China in Book VIII of *The Prelude*, where Wordsworth deploys the emperor's imperial garden as an antithesis to the communal and environmental relations of the English Lakes, based on John Barrow's account of the Macartney embassy.[35] This would seem to argue that Chinese subjects might well have been addressed in Romantic-period writing far more broadly.

A youthful Robert Southey, for instance, had planned to create a series of texts based on non-Christian religions, as outlined in his well-known letter to Anna Seward. His design – having treated 'the Mahommedan [religion] in *Thalaba*, and the Hindoo in this present poem [*The Curse of Kehama*]' – was to write a poem using 'every poetic faith that has ever been established ... the Persian, the Runic, the Keltic, the Greek, the Jewish, the Roman Catholick and the Japanese'.[36] Absent from the list is any reference to the religions of China, about which he knew a great deal more. The unexpected inclusion of Japan and the exclusion of China are puzzling and seem to argue for some form of psychological denial or evasion on Southey's part.[37]

This is all the stranger since China was part of the experience of so many whose lives were caught up in the global flows of trade. As well as enthusiastically consuming products of Chinese origin such as tea, porcelain and silks, many were involved in the China trade more directly, or had family, friends or acquaintances who were. Canton (Guangzhou) was a city encountered by Britons in the service of the East India Company or the Royal Navy. Jane Austen's brother, Frank, served in the Navy and acted as an agent for the Company as captain of the *St Albans* in 1809–10 at Canton.[38] Both Charles Lamb and Thomas Love Peacock were employees of the Company, and Lamb's friend and correspondent, Thomas Manning, travelled to Canton in 1807, becoming the first Briton to visit the Tibetan capital, Lhasa, in 1811. Manning accompanied Amherst's embassy to China in 1816–17 as an interpreter, though he left no account of his experiences. It is well known that William and Dorothy Wordsworth's elder cousin, and then their elder brother (both named John), traded at Canton. Thomas De Quincey's son, Horace, died aged 22 of a fever contracted during the Opium Wars with China in 1842. In the summer of 1819, Keats toyed briefly with the idea of becoming a surgeon on an Indiaman, writing to Dilke in June: 'I have my choice of three things – or at least two – South America or Surgeon to an I[n]diaman – which last I think will be my fate.'[39] It was a possibility Percy Shelley also considered. How would their literary careers have been shaped had they actually taken up this option? Entering the Company's service had potentially lucrative consequences for ambitious young men; this was the path, for instance, taken at the age of 18 by William Jardine, founder of the opium-trading firm, Jardine Matheson, in 1802.[40]

In my counterfactual narrative of Romantic cultural relations with China, in which Chinese subjects and tastes assume a greater degree of cultural hegemony, the literary landscape would have been very different. Informed by the new Romantic Sinology of Thomas Percy and

William Jones, the Macartney embassy to China of 1793 – while not an unqualified success – nevertheless came to be regarded as important in developing relations between the two empires.[41] While the historical embassy had to rely on the linguistic skills of Chinese Catholic converts who did not speak English and who communicated with the British in Latin, our counterfactual embassy included, as interpreters, several of Jones's students in Calcutta who had mastered spoken and written Chinese. We know that Macartney's actual embassy foundered on a series of cultural misunderstandings. One of the main ones related to the Qing ceremonial of the *ketou* – three prostrations accompanied by nine knockings of the forehead. Another concerned the exchange of gifts. It is generally thought that the British unwittingly presented the emperor with culturally inappropriate gifts that appeared boastful to the Qing court. In my counterfactual scenario, however, Macartney – informed by the new understanding of Qing guest ritual and advised by expert linguists who understood something of Mandarin Chinese and the symbolism of Qing manners – would have comfortably performed the imperial kowtow. With cultural understanding improved, at least on the British side, tensions over trade and access to Chinese markets in the early nineteenth century might have relaxed, resulting in better relations between the two empires.

Inspired by translations of Chinese literature by Percy and Jones, the Romantic medievalism and Romantic philhellenism with which we are familiar might have been less culturally pervasive, and the development of the organic nationalism we associate with Romantic thinking mitigated by a more cosmopolitan and global cultural outlook. Robert Southey, who read Percy's edition of the *Hau Kiou Choaan*, instead of turning his attention to Islam to compose *Thalaba the Destroyer* from 1798 onwards, might instead have penned an epic verse narrative about a young iconoclastic Confucian scholar waging war against what he perceived as the grisly superstitions and mendacious priesthood of popular Chinese Buddhism – a faith resembling contemporary Catholicism in his Protestant imagination. This work, entitled *Tieh-chung-u the Destroyer* (1801), while not a popular success, nevertheless inspired later writers such as Shelley to take up the subject of China in their work.

Southey's extensive research for *Tieh-chung-u* in the writings of the Jesuit historians of China, combined with the researches of Percy and Jones and sympathetic accounts of Chinese languages, customs and religions resulting from the Macartney embassy, were undertaken with Coleridge. The latter's Chinese dream poem, 'Kubla Khan', symbolically explored the dichotomy between Kubla's spiritual Tibetan Buddhist beliefs and the Confucian rationalism of the Song empire – a conflict of world views that Coleridge related to his own intellectual concerns. It subsequently became an ambition of Coleridge's to visit China, and when the opportunity arose in 1803–4, he enthusiastically grasped it.[42] Coleridge believed that his medical condition, brought on by his growing addiction to laudanum, would be improved by residing in a warmer climate such as that of South China. Sailing with Captain John Wordsworth on the *Earl of Abergavenny*, Coleridge arrived at Canton in 1804; he worked there for the East India Company as a senior 'writer', or clerk, occupying his spare time learning Mandarin and translating works of Chinese literature and philosophy. In *Biographia Literaria*, he paid fulsome tribute to the impact on his work of Chinese philosophers such as Confucius, Mencius and Laozi. In Confucianism, Coleridge found an echo of his earlier Unitarian religious and political dissent with its emphasis on the virtues of an active and ethical life, which he had explored in his Bristol lectures of 1795 and in politically attuned poems such as 'Reflections on Having Left a Place of Retirement'. At the same time, Confucianism's socially conservative and patriarchal elements also chimed with his growing tendencies to orthodoxy after 1805, though Coleridge never admired the reluctance of Confucius to engage in religious speculation. In the conflict between Confucian ethical activism and the Daoist renunciation of the material world, Coleridge also glimpsed a familiar repetition of his own inner conflict between civic activism and Romantic pantheism and solipsism. In the Daoist hypothesis of the 'Way' – which he interpreted as an active power infusing the natural world – Coleridge found another confirmation of his intuitive recognition of an active and creative principle similar to his early conception of the 'Plastic and vast ... intellectual breeze' of 'The Aeolian Harp'.

China also featured prominently in the (counterfactual) Romantic-period novel. Notably, Jane Austen, whose brother Frank had visited Canton and the South China coast, was led to satirise Romantic chinoiserie in her work. In *Mansfield Park* (1814), Fanny Price is discovered reading what is usually identified as Lord Macartney's 'Journal of the Embassy', published in the second volume of John Barrow's *Some Account of the Public Life of the Earl of Macartney* (1807). Edmund may jest that Fanny is 'taking a trip into China', and asks '[h]ow does Lord Macartney go on?'; for Fanny, however, China comes to represent a moral counterpoise to the goings-on at the park.[43] In particular, readers of the novel were most impressed by the set piece description of the Bertrams' visit to Mr Rushworth's estate at Sotherton with its chinoiserie-style improvements featuring Chinese pagodas and tea houses as well as a Chinese drawing room, complete with an extensive porcelain collection. Sotherton has been landscaped as an Anglo-Chinese garden inculcating the principles of artificial wildness advocated by William Chambers. It is against this backdrop that the enthusiastic sinophile, Henry Crawford, toys with the affections of Maria and Julia Bertram while Fanny Price looks on distrustfully. For the conservative-minded Austen, an immersion in the enormously popular 'Chinese taste' was a hallmark of lax morality. Notably, many of her less praiseworthy male characters – Messrs Willoughby, Wickham, William Walter Elliot, Elton and Collins – are all pronounced sinophiles. Elsewhere in *Mansfield Park*, Fanny's brother William returns to Portsmouth to regale her with stories of his service in the East India Company as he shuttled between Calcutta and Canton. Suspicious of the continuing fashion for chinoiserie-inspired novelty, Fanny finds a serious moral counterpoise in Edmund Bertram's enormous admiration for Confucian thought.

Given the mid-eighteenth-century interest in matters Chinese and the importance of trade with the Qing empire, it is conceivable that British Romanticism might have moved in a different trajectory, inspired by the Chinese researches of Percy, Walpole and Jones. It is also plausible that, as a result, China would have achieved a more substantive place in British literary history and culture. The status of Chinese thought and culture would, of course, have remained ambivalent. The sinophobia of those like Thomas De Quincey would no doubt have remained a strong element in British cultural life, but its place may have been much more contested. Adopting a counterfactual mode may help us explore the reasons why it seems that China was so unapproachable for the Romantics, and why – when it *was* negotiated – it was from an oblique or whimsical direction, as in Lamb's 'Old China' essay, or from a highly personalised perspective, as in De Quincey's *Confessions*. My counterfactual discussion of a Chinese-dominated version of what Raymond Schwab has termed 'the Oriental Renaissance' prompts a debate about the reasons why British Romantic writers, who knew much about China and whose friends and family were so often heavily involved in China trade, evaded it.

In *The Chinese Taste*, David Porter argues that there is a pervasive 'instrumental amnesia' to British writing about China in the eighteenth century that deliberately occludes 'rival claimants to exemplarity' and the memory of 'a more truly cosmopolitan early modern past'.[44] For example, a trope of the actual literary response to China, witnessed in the work of

Romanticism and the Chinese awakening

Joanna Baillie, Robert Southey, Leigh Hunt and Charles Lamb, is that all that Britons know about China is gleaned from the distorted and exaggerated visual representations appearing on teacups and porcelain ware. Yet a substantial archive about China already existed, formed from two hundred years of sophisticated Jesuit scholarship in several well-known English translations. In addition, the Macartney and Amherst embassies generated numerous new 'first-hand' accounts. Missionaries and traders were now resident in China, and they sent back narratives of their experiences of the country and translations of its literature and philosophy. Yet Britons persisted in reading China through an older, chinoiserie-inspired aesthetic, with Leigh Hunt, for example, decrying 'Chinese deformities' and monstrosities in his essay on the newly designed Grand Saloon of Drury Lane Theatre as late as 1817.[45]

The reasons why many such writers had a tendency to evade, repress or forget China are complex and not reducible to easy summary. Porter's helpful notion of 'instrumental amnesia' suggests that Britons were led to efface their Chinese imperial rival since so much of their own culture was actually influenced or inspired by Chinese examples. The construction of 'Englishness' that emerges from this encounter with China 'is neither pure nor hybrid in any straightforward sense, but rather is constituted paradoxically through a simultaneous appropriation of and denial of "Chineseness" and an instrumental amnesia with respect to some of the decidedly non-English origins of British aesthetic culture'.[46] Situating the work of earlier writers – Swift, Milton and Defoe – in the context of an economic analysis of Far-East trade and its effects on Britain, Robert Markley has argued that Britons, faced with the economic power of China and the superiority of its products, adopted a series of compensatory strategies to obviate such anxieties.[47]

The question this chapter raises is this: what if this denial of 'Chineseness' – which critics such as Porter have claimed to be at the heart of modern constructions of the British national self – were itself denied? What if the impetus to engage with Chinese models and explore Chinese languages, thought and philosophy that seemed to be growing from the mid-eighteenth century had developed beyond the pioneering works of Percy and Walpole to result in a fully fledged cultural movement that had as its basis a more inclusive, cosmopolitan grounding? Surveying the cultural landscape of the period, this possibility does not seem to be quite as unlikely as the later history of the century suggests. The counterfactual possibilities outlined in this chapter are not as remote or inconceivable as they may at first seem. A Romantic-period literary culture engaged with

Chinese models would certainly have complicated our established binaries of Romantic Orientalism and may have led to more sophisticated understandings of the British self. A more sympathetic engagement with Chinese culture might also have had more material consequences. Support for military engagements with China in the 1840s, in the wake of Commissioner Lin's 1839 seizure of the opium of British, American and Parsee merchants at Canton the previous year, was never homogenous or unquestioned at home. Whether cultural understanding and engagement might have mitigated the tensions and conflicts at Canton relating to the opium trade, or whether the global historical forces of colonialism and free trade would have continued in their historical trajectories are questions worth asking. China-centred historical studies have tended to explain the Qing empire's long economic, political and military demise in the nineteenth century and its eventual collapse in the twentieth primarily as a result of internal pressures that led to a weakening of its ability to handle western nations intent on opening its territory to free trade. Thus the discovery and greater appreciation of Chinese culture, literature and thought in the late eighteenth and early nineteenth centuries may have changed far more than the shape of Romantic literary history.

Notes

1 See Edward W. Said, *Orientalism* (London: Routledge, 1978), pp. 1–48.
2 See David Porter, *The Chinese Taste in Eighteenth-century England* (Cambridge: Cambridge University Press, 2010); Elizabeth Hope Chang, *Britain's Chinese Eye: Literature, Empire and Aesthetics in Nineteenth-century Britain* (Stanford, CA: Stanford University Press, 2010); Peter J. Kitson, *Forging Romantic China: Sino-British Cultural Exchange, 1760–1840* (Cambridge: Cambridge University Press, 2013); Eugenia Zuroski Jenkins, *A Taste for China: English Subjectivity and the Prehistory of Orientalism* (Oxford: Oxford University Press, 2013); Ross G. Forman, *China and the Victorian Imagination: Empires Entwined* (Cambridge: Cambridge University Press, 2013); Peter J. Kitson and Robert Markley (eds), *Writing China: Essays on the Amherst Embassy and Sino-British Cultural Relations* (Cambridge: D. S. Brewer, 2016).
3 See André Gunder Frank, *ReOrient: Global Economy in the Asian Age* (Berkeley, CA: University of California Press, 1988), pp. 52–3.
4 Adam Smith, *An Inquiry into the Nature and Causes of the Wealth of*

Nations, ed. R. H. Campbell and A. S. Skinner, 2 vols (Oxford: Oxford University Press, 1972), II, p. 202.
5 See Robert Markley, *The Far East and the English Imagination, 1600–1730* (Cambridge: Cambridge University Press, 2006), pp. 75, 110.
6 See John L. Cranmer-Byng and John E. Wills Jr, 'Trade and Diplomacy with Maritime Europe, 1644–*c*.1800', in John E. Wills Jr (ed.), *China and Maritime Europe, 1500–1800: Trade, Settlement, Diplomacy, and Missions* (Cambridge: Cambridge University Press, 2011), p. 183.
7 See William Harrison Ukers, *All About Tea*, 2 vols (New York: Tea and Coffee Trade Journals, 1935), I, p. 130.
8 Frederick Wakeman, 'The Canton Trade and the Opium War', in John K. Fairbank (ed.), *The Cambridge History of China, Volume 10: Late Ch'ing, 1800–1911, Part 1* (Cambridge: Cambridge University Press, 1978), p. 173.
9 See Julia Lovell, *The Opium War: Drugs, Dreams and the Making of China* (London: Picador, 2011), pp. 17–38.
10 See Porter, *The Chinese Taste* and Stacey Sloboda, *Chinoiserie: Commerce and Critical Ornament in Eighteenth-century Britain* (Manchester: Manchester University Press, 2014).
11 See Kitson, *Forging Romantic China*, pp. 182–209.
12 See David Porter, *Ideographia: The Chinese Cipher in Early Modern Europe* (Stanford, CA: Stanford University Press, 2001), pp. 15–77.
13 See Kitson, *Forging Romantic China*, pp. 216–21.
14 Arthur Murphy, *The Orphan of China: A Tragedy* (London: P. Vaillant, 1759), p. i.
15 See Kitson, *Forging Romantic China*, p. 220.
16 See Porter, *The Chinese Taste*, pp. 154–83; Eun Kyung Min, 'Thomas Percy's *Chinese Miscellanies* and the *Reliques of Ancient English Poetry* (1765)', *Eighteenth-century Studies*, 43:3 (Spring 2010), 307–24; James Watt, 'Thomas Percy, China, and the Gothic', *The Eighteenth Century: Theory and Interpretation*, 48:2 (Summer 2007), 95–109; Kitson, *Forging Romantic China*, pp. 26–44.
17 See A. O. Lovejoy, *Essays in the History of Ideas* (New York: George Braziller, 1955), pp. 99–135 and Porter, *The Chinese Taste*, pp. 115–30.
18 See Timothy Mowl, *Horace Walpole: The Great Outsider* (London: John Murray, 1996), pp. 118, 12 and Porter, *The Chinese Taste*, pp. 115–30.
19 Quoted in Porter, *The Chinese Taste*, p. 121.
20 *Ibid.*; letter to Horace Mann, 25 February 1750.
21 *The World*, 22 March 1753, p. 72.
22 See Kitson, *Forging Romantic China*, pp. 45–59 for Jones's interest in China and the scholarly activities he undertook.

23 See Peter J. Kitson, '"The Kindness of My Friends in England": Chinese Visitors to Britain in the Late Eighteenth and Early Nineteenth Centuries and Discourses of Friendship and Estrangement', *European Romantic Review* 27:1 (January 2016), 55–70.
24 The quotation is taken from Jones's 'On the Second Book of the Chinese' (1790) in *The Works of Sir William Jones*, 2 vols (London: G. G. and J. Robinson and R. H. Evans, 1799), I, pp. 366–7.
25 The Qing legal code was not translated until 1811, by George Thomas Staunton.
26 Jones, *Works*, I, p. 366.
27 Jones died in Calcutta on 27 April 1794 at the age of 47. His early death tragically curtailed his Asian studies. It is likely that, had he lived longer, Jones would have turned his scholarly attentions to the Chinese language and the Confucian translations that he aspired to master.
28 This was translated by John Francis Davis in 1829.
29 Composed by Cao Xueqin in the mid-eighteenth century, the novel is also known as *Dream of the Red Chamber*. It is regarded as one of China's four great classical novels and the apogee of Chinese literature. The first attempt to translate the novel into English was made in 1812 by the first British Protestant missionary to China and sinologist, Robert Morrison (1782–1834), who rendered part of the fourth chapter of the novel, intending to include it in the second (unpublished) volume of his 1812 book, *Horae Sinicae*. The first abridged translation had to wait until 1929 for publication. Had the novel – longer than Tolstoy's *War and Peace* – been fully translated into English during the Romantic period (as I imagine above), its cultural impact would surely have been enormous.
30 Jones, *Works*, I, p. 370.
31 See Kitson, *Forging Romantic China*, pp. 210–40.
32 See *ibid.* and Karen Fang, *Romantic Writing and the Empire of Signs: Periodical Culture and Post-Napoleonic Authorship* (Charlottesville, VA: University of Virginia Press, 2010), pp. 60–4.
33 Keats to John Taylor, 5 September 1819, in Hyder E. Rollins (ed.), *The Letters of John Keats*, 2 vols (Cambridge MA: Harvard University Press, 1958), II, p. 156; Donald H. Reiman and Neil Fraistat (eds), *Shelley's Poetry and Prose* (New York: W. W. Norton, 2002), p. 156.
34 S. T. Coleridge, *Biographia Literaria*, ed. James Engell, 2 vols (Princeton, NJ: Princeton University Press, 1983), II, p. 137.
35 See Kitson, *Forging Romantic China*, pp. 182–209 and Chang, *Britain's Chinese Eye*, pp. 37–54.
36 Kenneth Curry (ed.), *New Letters of Robert Southey*, 2 vols (New York: Columbia University Press, 1965), I, p. 146.

37 See Kitson, *Forging Romantic China*, pp. 163–6.
38 See David Nokes, *Jane Austen: A Life* (London: Fourth Estate, 1997), pp. 371–2; J. H. Hubback and Edith C. Hubback, *Jane Austen's Sailor Brothers: Being the Adventures of Sir Francis Austen, G.C.B., Admiral of the Fleet and Rear-Admiral Charles Austen* (London: John Lane, 1906).
39 Rollins (ed.), *The Letters of John Keats*, II, p. 114.
40 See Richard J. Grace, *Opium and Empire: The Lives and Careers of William Jardine and James Matheson* (Montreal, QC: McGill-Queen's University Press, 2014).
41 For the embassy, see James L. Hevia, *Cherishing Men From Afar: Qing Guest Ritual and the Macartney Embassy* (Durham, NC: Duke University Press, 1995).
42 This offer to sail to Canton was actually made by John Wordsworth, but Coleridge went to Malta instead; see Kitson, *Forging Romantic China*, pp. 187, 190.
43 Jane Austen, *Mansfield Park*, ed. Jane Stabler (Oxford: Oxford University Press, 2003), p. 123.
44 Porter, *The Chinese Taste*, pp. 1–13.
45 See Lawrence Huston Houtchens and Carolyn Washburn Houtchens (eds), *Leigh Hunt's Dramatic Criticism, 1808–1831* (New York: Columbia University Press, 1949), pp. 154–5; Kitson, *Forging Romantic China*, pp. 178–81.
46 Porter, *The Chinese Taste*, p. 10.
47 See Markley, *The Far East*, pp. 1–30.

Works cited

Primary texts

Austen, Jane, *Mansfield Park*, ed. Jane Stabler (Oxford: Oxford University Press, 2003)

Coleridge, Samuel Taylor, *Biographia Literaria*, ed. James Engell, 2 vols (Princeton, NJ: Princeton University Press, 1983)

Curry, Kenneth (ed.), *New Letters of Robert Southey*, 2 vols (New York: Columbia University Press, 1965)

Houtchens, Lawrence Huston and Carolyn Washburn Houtchens (eds), *Leigh Hunt's Dramatic Criticism, 1808–1831* (New York: Columbia University Press, 1949)

Jones, William, 'On the Second Book of the Chinese', in *The Works of Sir William Jones*, 2 vols (London: G. G. and J. Robinson and R. H. Evans, 1799)

Murphy, Arthur, *The Orphan of China: A Tragedy* (London: P. Vaillant, 1759)
Percy, Thomas (ed.), *Hau Kiou Choaan; or, the Pleasing History: A Translation from the Chinese Language*, 4 vols (London: R. and J. Dodsley, 1761)
Percy, Thomas (ed.), *Miscellaneous Pieces Relating to the Chinese*, 2 vols (London: R. and J. Dodsley, 1762)
Reiman, Donald H. and Neil Fraistat (eds), *Shelley's Poetry and Prose* (New York: W. W. Norton, 2002)
Rollins, Hyder E. (ed.), *The Letters of John Keats*, 2 vols (Cambridge MA: Harvard University Press, 1958)
Smith, Adam, *An Inquiry into the Nature and Causes of the Wealth of Nations*, ed. R. H. Campbell and A. S. Skinner, 2 vols (Oxford: Oxford University Press, 1972)
Walpole, Horace, 'To Mr Fitz-Adam', *The World*, 22 March 1753, pp. 67–72

Secondary texts

Chang, Elizabeth Hope, *Britain's Chinese Eye: Literature, Empire and Aesthetics in Nineteenth-century Britain* (Stanford, CA: Stanford University Press, 2010)
Cranmer-Byng, J. L. and John E. Wills, Jr, 'Trade and Diplomacy with Maritime Europe, 1644–c.1800', in John E. Wills, Jr (ed.), *China and Maritime Europe, 1500–1800: Trade, Settlement, Diplomacy, and Missions* (Cambridge: Cambridge University Press, 2011), pp. 183–254.
Fang, Karen, *Romantic Writing and the Empire of Signs: Periodical Culture and Post-Napoleonic Authorship* (Charlottesville, VA: University of Virginia Press, 2010)
Forman, Ross G., *China and the Victorian Imagination: Empires Entwined* (Cambridge: Cambridge University Press, 2013)
Frank, André Gunder, *ReOrient: Global Economy in the Asian Age* (Berkeley, CA: University of California Press, 1988)
Grace, Richard J., *Opium and Empire: the Lives and Careers of William Jardine and James Matheson* (Montreal, QC: McGill-Queen's University Press, 2014)
Hevia, James L., *Cherishing Men From Afar: Qing Guest Ritual and the Macartney Embassy* (Durham, NC: Duke University Press, 1995)
Hubback, J. H. and Edith C. Hubback, *Jane Austen's Sailor Brothers: Being the Adventures of Sir Francis Austen, G.C.B., Admiral of the Fleet and Rear-Admiral Charles Austen* (London: John Lane, 1906)
Kitson, Peter J., *Forging Romantic China: Sino-British Cultural Exchange, 1760–1840* (Cambridge: Cambridge University Press, 2013)

Kitson, Peter J., '"The Kindness of My Friends in England": Chinese Visitors to Britain in the Late Eighteenth and Early Nineteenth Centuries and Discourses of Friendship and Estrangement', *European Romantic Review*, 27:1 (January 2016), 55–70

Kitson, Peter J. and Robert Markley (eds), *Writing China: Essays on the Amherst Embassy and Sino-British Cultural Relations* (Cambridge: D. S. Brewer, 2016)

Lovejoy, A. O., *Essays in the History of Ideas* (New York: George Braziller, 1955)

Lovell, Julia, *The Opium War: Drugs, Dreams and the Making of China* (London: Picador, 2011)

Markley, Robert, *The Far East and the English Imagination, 1600–1730* (Cambridge: Cambridge University Press, 2006)

Min, Eun Kyung, 'Thomas Percy's *Chinese Miscellanies* and the *Reliques of Ancient English Poetry* (1765)', *Eighteenth-century Studies*, 43:3 (Spring 2010), 307–24

Mowl, Timothy, *Horace Walpole: The Great Outsider* (London: John Murray, 1996)

Nokes, David, *Jane Austen: A Life* (London: Fourth Estate, 1997)

Porter, David, *Ideographia: The Chinese Cipher in Early Modern Europe* (Stanford, CA: Stanford University Press, 2001)

Porter, David, *The Chinese Taste in Eighteenth-century England* (Cambridge: Cambridge University Press, 2010)

Said, Edward W., *Orientalism* (London: Routledge, 1978)

Sloboda, Stacey, *Chinoiserie: Commerce and Critical Ornament in Eighteenth-century Britain* (Manchester: Manchester University Press, 2014)

Ukers, William Harrison, *All About Tea*, 2 vols (New York: Tea and Coffee Trade Journals, 1935)

Wakeman, Frederick, 'The Canton Trade and the Opium War', in J. K. Fairbank (ed.), *The Cambridge History of China, Volume 10: Late Ch'ing, 1800–1911, Part 1* (Cambridge: Cambridge University Press, 1978) pp. 163–212

Watt, James, 'Thomas Percy, China, and the Gothic', *The Eighteenth Century: Theory and Interpretation*, 48:2 (Summer 2007), 95–109

Zuroski Jenkins, Eugenia, *A Taste for China: English Subjectivity and the Prehistory of Orientalism* (Oxford: Oxford University Press, 2013)

11

Counterfactual and future Romanticisms: the academy and the canon

Edward Larrissy

Romanticism, ideology and the counterfactual

Counterfactual histories are heuristic constructions: they are made in order to reveal and explore the road not taken, the possibility whose potential was thwarted by a chain of events of different origin or temper. They thus share characteristics with those alternative histories that were beloved of postmodernist fiction-writers and theorists. Yet the motives that prompted the latter were subtly different from those that animate the constructor of a counterfactual history, who not only finds inspiration in the construction – for there is creativity in the endeavour – but also seeks to lay bare the omissions or blindness of a dominant ideology or aesthetic preference. Yet such phrases mask complexity. We know that Coleridge and Southey did not really go to live in America and establish a Pantisocratic community on the banks of the Susquehanna, as Paul Muldoon fancies they did in his long poem *Madoc* (1990). The complexity arises from the danger of over-confidence about what might constitute the factual in a general sense – the way things are or were; and it is presumably because of the general inferences that might be drawn from them that such constructions claim value. To take a pertinent and well-known example: was the 'Romantic Period' either 'Romantic' or a period?

For many years, readers and university students were encouraged to forget the ascendancy, as poets, of Thomas Campbell, Samuel Rogers, Thomas Moore and Felicia Hemans and to relegate the poetry of Burns and Clare and the novels of Walter Scott to a kind of respectable second division. The Romantic credentials of some of the poets here are not especially strong: Rogers' *The Pleasures of Memory* (1792), for instance, is a poem squarely in the neoclassical couplet tradition, as are some of Thomas Moore's satires. These writers were replaced with the so-called Big Six poets (including Blake, who in fact joined the canon quite late). If the counterfactual historian undertakes, as a first step, to characterise the facts of a particular time, how easy is it to ascertain, through the long and distorted perspectives of subsequent history, that this characterisation is well-founded? After so much has happened through the rediscovery of lost elements of the Romantic period, the point hardly needs labouring. Nevertheless, I hope at least to suggest that our own period is hard to pin down, and in ways that reflect on its attempts to characterise the past.

I begin by constructing a canon for the 'Romantic period' that is very close to what exists already. I conceive of it as a core course in the academy, since the closest one can approach the idea of a canon in our own day – when extended reading in the Romantic period is not a popular pastime – is through what schools and departments deem necessary for their students to know and understand. In brief, I assume that the academy constructs the canonical literature of the past, and I build on this point in the next section.

By definition, neither the selection of texts in the curriculum, nor the way in which they are discussed, offers a linear route back to what happens in the research of scholars; rather, it constitutes a kind of averaging out, where not only research findings, but also the values espoused by humanities scholars, are exemplified and distilled, in submission to the discipline of offering the student a representative and interconnected list. In constructing this canon, then, I am not denying the multiplicity of activities going on under the title of 'research into Romantic-period literature'. Nor am I attempting to show that areas of research unrepresented in my list would not bear fruit in some real future. Nevertheless, the averaging out to which I refer reflects a notable fact about current research in general: if one attends a conference on British Romanticism, the amount of time devoted to the old canon of great Romantic poets is vastly reduced compared with that allotted to work on writers representing a kind of reordering of the period that has been going on for some years.

What will constitute the counterfactual in this construction? My answer to this is founded on a fundamental point: our period is, on the whole, inimical to canons and the ideal of constructing a canon. There is an element of paradox here, since the interests, political and ethical, that have transformed the study of Romanticism since the 1980s – within a broadly historicist understanding of what makes for good scholarship – are not and cannot be pluralist in the sense of being unreflectively permissive about what is worth studying and why. But this is not to say that they are theoretically pondered in any systematic way. The revulsion from the theoretical excesses of the 1970s and 1980s has, on the whole, encouraged an empirical methodology, even though the choice of research object or question may palpably derive from value-laden presuppositions about what it is valuable to study. In this connection, it is interesting to consider the approach taken by Jerome J. McGann, in *The Romantic Ideology* (1983), both because of the role of theory in this work, and because of his encouragement of a historicist approach that would be alive to the aesthetic, or at least to some aspects of the aesthetic.

The Romantic Ideology derived substantial impetus from Marxist theory – from the Frankfurt School, and from the work of Pierre Macherey and Terry Eagleton.[1] This is especially evident in its approbation of the idea that art 'establishes myth and illusion as *visible objects*'.[2] Where McGann differs from Macherey is in his insistence that art does not, by its special nature, transcend the realm of ideology and false appearances. Effectively insisting that art and literature speak to us out of their historical conditions, rather than being objects of aesthetic or theoretical contemplation, McGann puts them unambiguously within the realm of ideology, and convicts the Romantic Ideology of various forms of mystification. While his insistence on this point has merit since it demands that we attend fully to what the text is communicating, it too readily relegates the historical understanding of form – one of the most fruitful aspects of classical Marxist aesthetics – and helps to usher in a period where thematic criticism and the explication of content and context are dominant even in cases that cry out for responsiveness to form. As Damian Walford Davies observes, '"Context" in New Historicist analysis has often appeared so "determining" that the literary work achieves no life independent of "history"'.[3] However, my counterfactual history does not reveal a world in which this flaw is addressed or overcome. Rather, it focuses on the absence of a developed world view to support the values that animate contemporary research of this kind.

In the debate to which McGann refers – about the way ideology is reflected in the literary work – it is in reality Macherey who offers an updated version of Marxist orthodoxy. If Marx and Lukács found that Balzac was objectively a progressive writer (as they did), this was by no means because of his overt ideological tenets, which were conservative and royalist.[4] It was rather because of the formal work performed by the text beyond the intentions of the author. What Macherey did was to take the idea of blindness implicit in accounts such as these, which see literature as making statements beyond the conscious intention of its authors, and develop it in the light of Althusser's Lacan-influenced account of ideology. Jameson's *The Political Unconscious* (1981) proclaims in its title the Freudian inflection of these ideas, and references Macherey, Althusser and Lacan.[5] But to repeat: McGann's method ends up being far more common-sense than this in its direct reading of ideology conceived of as stated in the text, and this straightforwardness has characterised much of historicist scholarship relating to the Romantic period. His *The Poetics of Sensibility: A Revolution in Literary Style* (1996) is an attempt – only partially successful – to redress the balance in favour of stylistic analysis (discussed later in this chapter). There have been exceptions, of course, particularly in the earlier years of the New Historicisms: the 'deconstructive materialism' of Marjorie Levinson or Alan Liu, for example.[6] These days, however, many scholars might offer the jibe that this phrase is an oxymoron. Perhaps they would have a point, since Liu, pondering the fundamentals of his method, concludes that 'No one can know the differential relation between history and literature, or any other register of mind, with full certainty. This is why, after all, I say "I believe". I treat not of certainty but of credibility.'[7] In the introduction to my edited collection, *Romanticism and Postmodernism* (1999), I refer to this inability to entertain certainty about the relationship between literature and history as resulting in a kind of 'bleak hand-wringing' in the face of fundamental methodological questions.[8]

The broadly left-liberal assumptions of recent research have prompted the rediscovery and revaluation of literature about the colonies and colonisation; of neglected women's writing; and of the literary cultures of Scotland, Wales and Ireland. They have led to the explication of representations of gender; to a new appreciation of the radical years of Wordsworth and Coleridge and the early socialist songbooks of Shelley; to the regular appearance of John Clare on the book list; and to the study of groups meeting beyond the confines of the polite salon. Impatience with the bardic pretensions and aesthetic legacy of High Romantic poetry has led to a new recognition of the number of significant poets who did not operate by lights we would now call Romantic, and has encouraged the regular inclusion of prose fiction (not just Austen) on Romantic-period courses. This left-liberal tendency that has guided the choice of object has little to do with theoretical Marxism, or any other theory of totalising tendency. Not that this is an unprincipled position; it rests on the contemporary suspicion of totalising intellectual systems in general. A question worth asking, though, is whether or not that suspicion is itself fully theorised.

But there is a second reason why a new canon is hard to imagine in the world of current fact, and that is because many departments are unwilling to renounce the preponderant selection of the Romantic writers that held sway throughout most of the twentieth century. What if one were to seek a new canon for the curriculum by giving primacy to those texts that exhibited or made creative use of the themes that animate contemporary investigation, while sternly avoiding the tendency to say that Wordsworth must be liberally represented and other texts must often give way? I shall act, for the moment, in this spirit. However, a modifying assumption is at work in my construction, and it is a practical one: pressure on time and space will lead to an emphasis on texts where more than one of the desired themes can be exhibited at once. But this requirement can assume the aspect of opportunity in allowing for those fruitful juxtapositions beloved of the module designer, since the themes, to qualify as themes, need more than one text to illustrate them. So, in sum, I assume that the academy will agree to forging a canon, and that it will happily renounce the tacit or explicit requirement to represent the image of Romanticism that prevailed through much of the twentieth century. But as for the content of this canon, it consists of a promotion of writers who already offer substance to conferences and option modules, so my model is an emphatic underlining of current trends.

The academy, the core course and the canon

In what follows, I postulate a new canon for 'British Romanticism' based on the fact that in our day the 'canonical' literature of past periods is a selection made by the academy. Indeed, this fact should be more clearly recognised as the 'factual' in the present cultural universe (to re-emphasise my earlier point about the difficulty of recognising what is actually the case). The logical development of this assumption leads to the conclusion that any new canon will manifest itself not as an option module in the academy, but as a core course. In order to reach my counterfactual core course, I have accepted tendencies in the selection of texts that are already strongly at work. I have then introduced as a modifying factor the kind of pressure that often drives the creation of courses, where there is never sufficient time to do everything – a situation that results in a text being privileged if it allows for the simultaneous discussion and exemplification of a range of themes. I also assume that the deviser of this course will want to compare and contrast texts that exhibit similar themes or styles. And a fundamental assumption is that the 'academy' is an international entity and that its priorities are not just shaped by American and Indian academics, for instance, but are strongly driven by them.

'British Romanticism' in the counterfactual core course is conceived in archipelagic terms. Writing from all of the 'four nations' is represented. A greater emphasis on Welsh, or Scottish, or English regional writing might be more profoundly counterfactual than what I suggest. Irish writing has become something of a 'global brand' because of Ireland's early rebellion against the British empire, and because of the prestige enjoyed by twentieth-century Irish literature. For this reason I give it a slight privilege – one that would probably not, in the end, endure in either the real or the counterfactual universes. The emphasis on women's writing is maintained and furthered: Wollstonecraft and Austen figure alongside each other. Working-class writing figures in the list. Writing about the colonial world is always present, which means India, but also America, reflecting the continued strength of humanities departments in American universities, and their interests. The strong presence of gothic tropes and imagery in contemporary popular – and indeed 'high' – culture supports not only the regular appearance of 'the Gothic' in the study of Romanticism, but also a regular emphasis on such tropes and imagery among authors by no means solely associated with it (Blake, Wordsworth, Percy Shelley). The growing dominance of science in the academy, as well as a continued promotion of interdisciplinarity in all subject areas, leads to the taken-for-granted presence of texts under the heading of 'Literature and Science'. Alongside this, there is a Romantic Ecology section that includes the 'One Life' poetry of Wordsworth and Coleridge, and alongside Clare, the work of Robert Bloomfield, represented by *The Farmer's Boy* (1800) and *Nature's Music* (1800). More generally, there is some attempt to maintain the New Historicist aim of representing the self-understanding of the period by including texts that were famous in their own day but which have until recently been neglected.

So far, so relatively simple. But, as I have already asserted, the pressure on time and space in the curriculum leads to an emphasis on texts in which more than one of the above themes are exhibited. A good example is Thomas Moore's *Lalla Rookh* (1817), which obviously petitions for inclusion as one of the most widely read poems of the nineteenth century. It makes the grade for two other substantial and instructively overlapping reasons: it is centred on representations of the 'Orient' and it is a major work by an Irish author. Furthermore, its representation of the 'Orient' is a displaced representation of Ireland and of Irish problems. Thus, not only can the module deviser include a text that was neglected in the twentieth century; they can also cover at least two desirable topics for the price of one – one of them ('Irish Orientalism') permitting the development of a discussion about Ireland and postcolonialism.[9] For as I have already pointed out, the curriculum is organised around themes that allow for the study of several texts alongside each other, and, where possible, for overlap or connection among the themes they exhibit.

Under the heading of Irish Writing, similar considerations to those that favour *Lalla Rookh* lead to the inclusion of Sydney Owenson's (Lady Morgan's) *The Missionary: An Indian Tale* (1811), which can figure also in the category of women's writing and writing about India. The missionary of the title is a Franciscan friar who comes from an aristocratic Portuguese family; he is admired for his virtuous combination of passion and humility and for his eloquent and forceful preaching. He becomes fascinated by the beautiful Luxima, High Priestess and consecrated vestal of Brahma. This is an encounter steeped in the traditional gendering of East and West: 'she like the East, lovely and luxuriant; he, like the West, lofty and commanding'.[10] However, despite this fall from grace, the missionary is said to be confident in his access to 'immutable truth'.[11] Ireland is covertly identified with the Orient, and while there was an element of disabling stereotype in identifying both Ireland and the Orient with the 'feminine', Owenson does manage to insinuate the weakness of a certain kind of post-Enlightenment rationality and natural religion when confronted with ancient traditions and their passionate adherents, and makes this topic overlap with a critique of the arrogant presumption of patriarchal authority.

Examples of writing about America are not that abundant, but Thomas Campbell's *Gertrude of Wyoming: A Pennsylvanian Tale* (1809) will appear on the reading list – a poem that was very popular in the nineteenth century, especially with American readers, for its sympathy with the American revolutionary cause. Conveniently, Campbell is a Scottish poet and can thus also figure in the archipelagic section of the course. The political import of this poem can be used to supplement discussions of political tendencies in Britain. Campbell's Whig politics render him sympathetic to American republicanism, though they also make him conscious of the blight of slavery, as is very evident from his biting lyric,

Counterfactual and future Romanticisms

'To the United States of North America'. *Gertrude of Wyoming* offers an allegorical resolution of the tension between loyalism and republicanism. A notorious massacre in 1778 in Pennsylvania's Wyoming Valley saw 300 partisans of the American revolutionary cause slaughtered by loyalists and their Iroquois allies. But Campbell stresses the ties of kinship and affection that bind all the settlers to their distant origins in Britain (not surprisingly, the virtues of Scottish as well as English settlers are lauded). And despite the fact that the loyalists bore the chief responsibility for the massacre, Campbell lays the blame on a native American chief.

Alongside this poem, the lecturer will present some of Thomas Moore's writings deriving from his American journey (Moore was moved by the beauty and sublimity of the American and Canadian landscapes through which he passed). 'A Canadian Boat Song' was a staple in North American anthologies well into the twentieth century. However, satirical epistles in his *Epistles, Odes and Other Poems* (1806) surprisingly reveal the scorn this lifelong Whig felt for Jeffersonian republicanism. He found its adherents uncultivated and hypocritical, and the hypocrisy, as he saw it, was epitomised in Jefferson himself keeping a black slave as a mistress. In America, this castigator of British policy in Ireland felt that he had more in common with the conservative Federalists who espoused closer links with Canada and Britain. The ambivalent political postures assumed by these two poets in this context can be linked to a discussion of attitudes to the French Revolution in Britain.

Moore will be a major beneficiary of the rationale behind the new canon. If the literature of Romantic Ireland is to be represented, then *Irish Melodies* must feature; their fusion of sentiment and patriotism – rightly understood – is vulnerable to charges of mellifluous meaninglessness only for those who have not read Moore with due attention to the political use to which he puts the poetry of sentiment. Indeed, *Irish Melodies* represents the other, more suggestive, side of a poet who was also – and simultaneously – a great satirical poet. Jane Moore offers a justly admiring account of his Juvenalian satires, *Corruption* and *Intolerance* (both 1808) and *The Sceptic* (1809). Her summing up at the end of a discussion of the latter can serve to indicate the flavour of all three: 'the whole resounds with anti-British and anti-Tory feeling ... as Moore once more condemns Castlereagh and his Tory comrades for travestying the rights of man, a point of particular relevance to Ireland'.[12] Moore also takes his place in an account of the development of Celticism, alongside Felicia Hemans's *A Selection of Welsh Melodies* (1822).

The part of the course devoted to science and literature will include

Humphry Davy's prose description of his visit to Tintern Abbey alongside Wordsworth's poem, scientific extracts from Coleridge's Notebooks, specimens of the influence of scientific speculation on Percy Shelley's imagery and a consideration of the scientific background to *Frankenstein*.[13] The latter also figures as 'gothic', alongside Hogg's *The Private Memoirs and Confessions of a Justified Sinner* (1824), present also as an example of Scottish literature. Under that heading, Scott has to be present both as novelist and poet. And the move away from the stylistic preferences of the 'Romantic Revolution' will be confirmed by a section devoted to 'The Poetics of Sensibility'. But under this rubric, writers such as Charlotte Smith, Mary Robinson and Felicia Hemans have already joined the canon, and the new core course simply confirms their presence. This is appropriate confirmation that my core course assumes that the interests and ethical preoccupations compelling the choice of texts remain similar to what they are at the moment, but without the requirement to include all or much of the 'Big Six'. Moore, Campbell, Hemans, Smith, Robinson, Owenson, Wollstonecraft, Austen, Mary Shelley: these are the dominant names, with the themes and styles they exhibit seen in relation to works by Clare, Wordsworth, Southey, Bloomfield, Scott, Hogg and Burns, which are studied in less detail.

Creative writing and the counterfactual canon

But – to ask a slightly different question – will something like this model come to pass, since it relates to future facts rather than an alternative contemporary history? This is unlikely. Tempting though it may be to invoke the agency of fashion in support of that estimate, or the tendency of one age to question the assumptions of the preceding one, it is not necessary to be so vague. A future idea of Romanticism is much more likely, in the real world, to follow a path one could almost think of as opposite to the one I have just outlined. In other words, what follows – my second canon, so to speak – constitutes something more like a forecast than a counterfactual history. There is a specific fact about English Literature departments that will impel the curriculum in a new direction: namely, the proliferation of creative writing courses. These have now become so widespread that they will drive further and consequent developments. The imperative to devise strategies that emphasise the character and interconnectedness of a department's research, and of the 'learning experience' of its students, has led to the appearance of mission statements that claim as an advantage the synergy of 'the creative' and 'the critical'.

This will become the standard account of the way creative and scholarly modules coexist. But in order for it to be convincing, there will have to be common ground between them. This common ground will centre on stylistic motifs and desiderata; on the experience of writing; and more generally on the broad category of 'personal experience'. It will be of no avail to complain that 'personal experience' is a social construct (a nostrum that is in any case questionable in its stronger versions), for the high value accorded to it in popular discourse has inflected the way in which creative writing is taught. At the same time, it is within this context that a formally conscious alternative will be offered to New Historicism's privileging of context.

One of the most widely distributed creative writing textbooks, Janet Burroway's *Writing Fiction* (1994, and many subsequent editions), was something of a pioneer among such publications. From its pages we learn that 'Not all experience reveals, but all revelation comes through experience.'[14] In Kim Addonizio's and Dorianne Laux's *The Poet's Companion: A Guide to the Pleasures of Writing Poetry* (1997), we are informed that poems 'use language to tell the truth, to accurately portray someone's experience or vision'.[15] In a book first published in 2006, we discover early on that a fundamental requirement is 'Writing what you know': 'Writing is a process of becoming aware, of opening the senses to ways of grasping the world, ways that may previously have been blocked.'[16] In Britain, Ted Hughes's *Poetry in the Making* (1967) is still used on creative writing courses, and to study it is to realise how strongly its view of poetic language may actually have influenced the use of metaphor and simile by poets. Making comparisons, Hughes tells us, forces you 'to look more closely, and to think, and make distinctions, and be surprised at what you find ... How is a dragonfly like a helicopter?'[17] Of course, it is easy to criticise such an emphasis on experience being the direct way to truth or reality. The difference in the assumptions made by the writers quoted here is itself telling – Burroway talks about revelation, while Hughes is concerned with the direct transcription of sense-data. There is no agreement as to the nature of reality. Nevertheless, the fact that the appeal to experience is common currency in the discussion of composition, both inside and outside the creative writing class, is an indication of its power as a prompt to endeavour.

Creative writing courses, plus the common-sense insistence on personal experience, mean that a book list different from the counterfactual one I have been describing is likely to come into existence. There will be an emphasis on writing as a topic within Romanticism. Grist to this mill will be Blake's poems introductory respectively to *Innocence* and *Experience*, with their figuring of composition as the work either of the inspired 'Piper' or the reflective 'Bard'; Byron's foregrounding of the writing process in *Don Juan*; and Keats's *Letters* with their metacritical excavations of the process of thinking and writing. The value accorded to personal experience will re-establish the merits of Wordsworth's and Coleridge's version of the great Romantic structure of decline and rebirth of imaginative powers in the individual. We will be back within the Romantic Ideology, but the emphasis on writing will allow the lecturer to maintain a distance between the idea of the recovery of inspiration and the larger metaphysical claims in which Coleridge, above all, attempted to involve it. 'Personal experience' will also bring to the fore Hazlitt's *Liber Amoris: Or, The New Pygmalion* (1823). Wider considerations flow from the emphasis on contemporary experience. Thus the urban context of much modern writing will encourage the reliable appearance of Blake's 'London' alongside the London passages of Wordsworth's *Prelude*. The ecological section will remain, as will the gothic and the literature of science, since these reflect the interests of readers. However, the Poetics of Sensibility will be relegated to the sidelines, as will the poetry of Campbell and Moore.

This last will be the change of great note. Poetic diction, however fortified with wit and subtle thought, cannot survive as a mainstream object of study in a context where the student is being encouraged to find inspiration in the past for contemporary writing, or points of comparison with it, and the overt language of sensibility or sentiment will become taboo. Therefore many of the poets who have been subject to upward valuation by historicist criticism will be quietly sidelined. In *The Poetics of Sensibility* (1996), McGann traces with great delicacy the clever working out by the Della Cruscans of personification and simile as an enactment of imaginative thought. But he proceeds:

> To Wordsworth ... these literalists of the imagination were deplorable not for having failed in their art, but for having proposed such an artistic procedure in the first place. It was, in a word, insincere: a game of words rather than a true expression of true feeling. The language of poetry is not to be measured by a norm of artifice but by what Wordsworth calls the 'real language of men'.[18]

Indeed, there is a Wordsworth problem for most of the poets of sensibility whose merits McGann promotes, since Wordsworth's critique of poetic diction and conventional personification has prevailed in the practice of writing. As McGann notes, Ann Yearsley 'accepts as an aesthetic given all those stylistic devices that Wordsworth would repudiate as mannered, false, and artistically dead'.[19] Admittedly, if the Romantic poets followed Wordsworth's lead, it may sometimes have been only in order to give poetic diction and personification a more lively form, as in the case of Keats. But there is no doubt that the taste for the poetic diction developed in the eighteenth century gradually faded in the nineteenth century, and that by the modern period it was incapable of being resurrected. As McGann states in the introduction to *The Poetics of Sensibility*: 'the twentieth-century critique of the sentimental tradition focused on poetry. The scholastic success of this critique not only disappeared a large corpus of vital and important poetry, it obscured the conventions that supported such poetry.'[20] McGann claims to concentrate on matters of style in this book, and to find that the 'poetics of sensibility' were revolutionary in their dramatising of feeling and their assumption of the inextricability of body and mind. He does indeed read closely, but tends to take the revolutionary wish for the deed: his analysis still tends towards the thematic, and he himself admits that, as far as strictly rhetorical and figurative devices are concerned, there are vital continuities with the age of Pope.[21] Further, McGann's understandable impatience with Wordsworth's concept of the 'real language of men' leads him to ignore another revolutionary aspect of the new type of writing practised by Wordsworth and Coleridge: its radical embrace of verisimilitude in representing experience and objects, which is what one might call the referential aspect of the revolution in diction. Geoffrey Thurley puts this well in referring to the 'Rise of Object-Dominance' in the Romantic period:

> From this time onwards, things – phenomena, objects – begin to exist in their own right and for their own sake. The poet's concern is still with meaning, we note, not with natural history. But in order to gain meaning – to be poetic – the poet now requires the thing to be itself, not the emblem of some anterior world-view, and this ... marks off his [*sic*] work from that of earlier poets.[22]

One might quibble with this, at least to the extent of saying that the poet requires the thing to appear to be itself *and* have some ulterior (or anterior) motive. But as far as the stylistic requirement for direct presentation is concerned, the point is well made. It may be illustrated by reference to contemporary painting and the works of Constable and Turner. The poetry of sensibility and sentiment does not work with these desiderata; neither does the neoclassical tradition of personification.

It is instructive to recall that there has been one valuable attempt to reintroduce poetic diction to modern poetry – that mounted by Donald Davie, the self-proclaimed 'pasticheur of late-Augustan styles'.[23] He offered a critical apologia and theory in his *Purity of Diction in English Verse* (1952), most notably a highly illuminating and useful account of the intellectual subtlety with which eighteenth-century personification might be handled.[24] This was a guide to his own early practice, though the strenuousness with which he adopted this aesthetic, and the complexity with which he imbued it, tends towards the Empsonian. Empson was much admired by other Movement poets, but although Davie's book is often referred to as a Movement manifesto, there is scant evidence of late-Augustan styles in the work of other Movement poets such as Philip Larkin or Kingsley Amis. As for Davie, this lifelong advocate of the merits of Ezra Pound seems often now to be regarded, at best, as a minor poet who was ruined by the academy, and his mature work – indebted to Pasternak and Lowell – is by many forgotten or disregarded. A similar fate awaits anyone foolhardy enough to try to make a living poetic style out of the materials on offer from Charlotte Smith, Ann Yearsley or Mary Robinson, or indeed from Moore or Campbell.

It is vital to realise that this question is not merely one of stylistic preference in isolation. This is not a case – if ever there were such – where contemporary readers can or should be lectured by historicist scholars about their reading habits. The contemporary writer lives in a society where it is unacceptable to resurrect a style and a series of conventions redolent of ancient literary elites, however progressive some of them may have been in their own day. Another way of putting this is to say that, if Romantic-period writing is still to offer models, however transformed and renewed, it will have to be Blake, Wordsworth, Coleridge, Clare and Mary Shelley who do so. Half a century ago, Dylan Thomas was still able to fashion something new out of his reading of Blake and Wordsworth, and it is not unthinkable that another poet might do something comparable. Certainly, Blake has continued to inspire writers of both poetry and prose fiction – Angela Carter and Iain Sinclair, for instance. Wordsworth and Clare are vital presences in the work of Seamus Heaney.

The new book list bears a strong resemblance to the traditional twentieth-century one. And it will be provided with theoretical underpinnings, but not those deriving from High Romantic aesthetics (our age is averse to the shadow of the sacred that hangs over them). Nor will there be a return to the painstaking deconstruction of High Romantic themes. Rather, the new theorising will derive partly from a revolt against historicism and partly from the imperative to show that Romantic-period writing provides models that are still relevant for the representation of personal experience. The theory will be a revival of existentialism. While it will take its point of departure from the content of Kierkegaard's criticism of Hegel's system, it will defer to the force of Adorno's critique and the relevance of the deconstructionist critique of phenomenology to its own assumptions. This is no easy matter, since Adorno's insistence on the unavoidable immanence of cultural mediation is hard to assimilate to the primacy of Being in existential thought. Further (and this is a serious consideration), an age that is in any case so sceptical of systems, and so aware of their provisionality, will not be able confidently to adopt Adorno's insistence on reason. Its point of departure will have to be an insistence on the radical perception motivating the development of existential philosophy: that no system of thought can represent Being. Conscious of the potential weakness of lauding the authenticity of writers fortunate enough to be insulated from the full effects of exploitation and inequality, the politically and ethically responsible philosophy of Sartre will offer a vocabulary of understanding. Indeed, the reawakening of interest in an ethics of responsibility to which the contemporary discussion of Levinas bears witness will also favour Sartre. I have already begun to outline the two main influences on this future reading list: the representation of writing and the representation of the renewal of the self. The theoretical trend I have predicted offers a third, overlapping, strand: texts in which existentialist insights or themes are arguably prefigured or emerging. This means that Blake's Spectre, slave to inauthentic labours, will appear on the scene.[25] Keats's focus on the moment of the perception of Beauty, also. And Carlyle's *Sartor Resartus* will round off the course.

Two contrary states of the contemporary reader

I have described the elements of two book lists that could be caricatured as contraries to each other if one were to consider the prejudices and thinking that inform them. The first does not quite exist. The second might be struggling to be born. In reality, my counterfactual book list, and my possible future one, are two contemporary tendencies, and the only argument I would make is that each has a strong probability of becoming more salient. The reason for putting it no more strongly is this: the strongest counterfactual element behind my first book list, and the most improbable in my second, is simply the erection of a canon, for our age is addicted to pluralism and averse to grand narratives. I have already referred to the lack of a strong theoretical framework for the prejudices informing the current choice of research objects. It is this very suspicion of system out of which, ironically, an existentialist tendency might emerge. But as for a new canon, it will have to await some new revelation, as Yeats might have said, where the word will no longer suggest a kind of literary authoritarianism. Needless to say, such a revelation will arrive alongside new social relations that lie beyond our event horizon.

Notes

1 Jerome J. McGann, *The Romantic Ideology: A Critical Investigation* (Chicago: University of Chicago Press, 1983), pp. 153–9.
2 *Ibid.*, p. 156.
3 Damian Walford Davies, 'Introduction: Reflections on an Orthodoxy', in Damian Walford Davies (ed.), *Romanticism, History, Historicism: Essays on an Orthodoxy* (New York: Routledge, 2009), p. 5.
4 See Sandy Petrey, 'The Reality of Representation: Between Marx and Balzac', *Critical Inquiry*, 14:3 (Spring 1988), 448–68; George Lukács, *Studies in European Realism: A Sociological Survey of the Writings of Balzac, Stendhal, Zola, Tolstoy, Gorki and Others*, trans. Edith Bone (London: Merlin Press, 1950).
5 See Fredric Jameson, *The Political Unconscious: Narrative as a Socially Symbolic Act* (Ithaca, NY: Cornell University Press, 1982); p. 95 for Macherey, and *passim* for Lacan and Althusser.
6 The phrase is coined by Levinson; Marjorie Levinson, *Wordsworth's Great Period Poems: Four Essays* (Cambridge: Cambridge University Press, 1986), p. 10. It is adopted by Liu to characterise his own method: Alan Liu, *Wordsworth: The Sense of History* (Stanford, CA: Stanford University Press, 1989), p. 39.
7 Liu, *Wordsworth*, p. 501.
8 Edward Larrissy, 'Introduction', in Edward Larrissy (ed.), *Romanticism and Postmodernism* (Cambridge: Cambridge University Press, 1999), p. 6.
9 See Joseph Lennon, *Irish Orientalism: A Literary and Intellectual History* (Syracuse, NY: Syracuse University Press, 2004).
10 Sydney Owenson, *The Missionary: An Indian Tale*, ed. Julia M. Wright (Peterborough, ON: Broadview Press, 2002), p. 109.
11 *Ibid.*
12 Jane Moore, 'Thomas Moore as Irish Satirist', in David Duff and

Catherine Jones (eds), *Scotland, Ireland, and the Romantic Aesthetic* (Lewisburg, PA: Bucknell University Press, 2007), p. 154.
13 For Davy's note on his visit to Tintern Abbey, see John Ayrton Paris, *The Life of Sir Humphry Davy, Bart., LL.D*, 2 vols (London: Henry Colburn and Richard Bentley, 1831), I, pp. 108–11.
14 Janet Burroway, *Writing Fiction: A Guide to Narrative Craft*, 4th edn (London: HarperCollins, 1996), p. 295. The book is currently in its ninth edition (2014).
15 Kim Addonizio and Dorianne Laux, *The Poet's Companion: A Guide to the Pleasures of Writing* (New York: W. W. Norton, 1997), p. 65.
16 Derek Neale, 'Writing What You Know', in Linda Anderson (ed.), *Creative Writing: A Workbook with Readings* (London: Routledge, 2006), p. 45.
17 Ted Hughes (ed.), *Poetry in the Making: An Anthology of Poems and Programmes from 'Listening and Writing'* (London: Faber, 1967), p. 44.
18 Jerome J. McGann, *The Poetics of Sensibility: A Revolution in Literary Style* (Oxford: Clarendon Press, 1996), p. 87.
19 *Ibid.*, p. 57.
20 *Ibid.*, p. 1.
21 *Ibid.*, p. 16.
22 Geoffrey Thurley, *The Romantic Predicament* (London: Macmillan, 1983), pp. 56–7.
23 Donald Davie, 'Homage to William Cowper', *Collected Poems*, ed. Neil Powell (Manchester: Carcanet, 2002), p. 8.
24 Donald Davie, *Purity of Diction in English Verse* (London: Chatto & Windus, 1952), pp. 38–40.
25 See Lorraine Clark, *Blake, Kierkegaard, and the Spectre of Dialectic* (Cambridge: Cambridge University Press, 1991).

Works cited

Primary texts

Davie, Donald, *Collected Poems*, ed. Neil Powell (Manchester: Carcanet, 2002)
Owenson, Sydney, *The Missionary: An Indian Tale*, ed. Julia M. Wright (Peterborough, ON: Broadview Press, 2002)
Paris, John Ayrton, *The Life of Sir Humphry Davy, Bart., LLD*, 2 vols (London: Henry Colburn and Richard Bentley, 1831)

Secondary texts

Addonizio, Kim and Dorianne Laux, *The Poet's Companion: A Guide to the Pleasures of Writing* (New York: W. W. Norton, 1997)
Burroway, Janet, *Writing Fiction: A Guide to Narrative Craft*, 4th edn (London: HarperCollins, 1996)
Clark, Lorraine, *Blake, Kierkegaard, and the Spectre of Dialectic* (Cambridge: Cambridge University Press, 1991)
Davie, Donald, *Purity of Diction in English Verse* (London: Chatto & Windus, 1952)
Hughes, Ted (ed.), *Poetry in the Making: An Anthology of Poems and Programmes from 'Listening and Writing'* (London: Faber, 1967)
Jameson, Fredric, *The Political Unconscious: Narrative as a Socially Symbolic Act* (Ithaca, NY: Cornell University Press, 1982)
Larrissy, Edward, 'Introduction', in Edward Larrissy (ed.), *Romanticism and Postmodernism* (Cambridge: Cambridge University Press, 1999), pp. 1–12
Lennon, Joseph, *Irish Orientalism: A Literary and Intellectual History* (Syracuse, NY: Syracuse University Press, 2004)
Levinson, Marjorie, *Wordsworth's Great Period Poems: Four Essays* (Cambridge: Cambridge University Press, 1986)
Liu, Alan, *Wordsworth: The Sense of History* (Stanford, CA: Stanford University Press, 1989)
Lukács, George, *Studies in European Realism: A Sociological Survey of the Writings of Balzac, Stendhal, Zola, Tolstoy, Gorki and Others*, trans. Edith Bone (London: Merlin Press, 1950)
McGann, Jerome J., *The Poetics of Sensibility: A Revolution in Literary Style* (Oxford: Clarendon Press, 1996)
McGann, Jerome J., *The Romantic Ideology: A Critical Investigation* (Chicago: University of Chicago Press, 1983)
Moore, Jane, 'Thomas Moore as Irish Satirist', in David Duff and Catherine Jones (eds), *Scotland, Ireland, and the Romantic Aesthetic* (Lewisburg, PA: Bucknell University Press, 2007), pp. 152–71
Neale, Derek, 'Writing What You Know', in Linda Anderson (ed.), *Creative Writing: A Workbook with Readings* (London: Routledge, 2006), pp. 44–55
Petrey, Sandy, 'The Reality of Representation: Between Marx and Balzac', *Critical Inquiry*, 14:3 (Spring 1988), 448–68
Thurley, Geoffrey, *The Romantic Predicament* (London: Macmillan, 1983)
Walford Davies, Damian, 'Introduction: Reflections on an Orthodoxy', in Damian Walford Davies (ed.), *Romanticism, History, Historicism: Essays on an Orthodoxy* (New York: Routledge, 2009), pp. 1–13

Index

Note: page numbers for illustrations are given in *italics*, and for notes in the format 239 n.31. Names of spurious or pseudonymous authors appear in inverted commas; counterfactual events or works are indicated with an asterisk.

absences 131, 204, 205, 215
adaptation 43, 62
adoption 211–13
Adorno, Theodor 313
allegory 209–10, 216, 220
allusions 202–3, 206, 207, 223–4
American literature 306–7
antiquarians 54–5, 83–4
archives 35–6, 92, 203, 204–5, 253, 293
art, visual 59, 178–80
'Ashburton, Charles Alfred' 64
attribution 73 n.26, 74 n.41, 86, 217–19, 255–6, 271 n.12
Austen, Jane 16, 40–1, 43, 64, 120, 244, 289, 291–2
authenticity 53–5, 68, 69, 81–2, 84, 88
authors
    and attribution 73 n.26, 74 n.41, 86, 221
    and identity 159–60
    spurious 62–6
    women 63–4, 69–70
authorship 73 n.26, 74 n.41, 86, 217–19, 255–6, 271 n.12
autobiography 58–9, 137, 140, 141, 144–5, 168, 209
    see also biography
Avery, Captain John 253, 254, 256–9, 261–2, 268–9

Banim, John 166, 232, 237–9
bardism 89, 90–1, 93–5
Barker, Mary 142–3
Baxter, John 61
Beckford, William, **Wanli* 284–5
Benjamin, Walter 1–2
biography 203–9, 220, 236–7, 254, 257
    see also autobiography
birth 155–6, 160–1, 171–2
'birthing phantoms' 184, *185*
Blackbeard (Edward Teach/Thatch) 252–4, 269
Blake, William 2–4, *3*, 11, 13, 25, 130, 160, 310, 312, 313
Bloomfield, Robert 305
bodies 172–3
Bowyer, Robert 59
Boyle, Henrietta Cecil *see* Thelwall, Cecil Boyle
Britain *see* Great Britain
Broadhead, Alex 13
Burns, Robert 14, 86, 215, 300
Burroway, Janet 309
Byron, George Gordon, Lord 14, 145–7
    Childe Harold's Pilgrimage 135
    The Corsair 254, 267, 268
    Don Juan 135, 138, 141, 144–6, 310
    *The Fan-Kwai 285
    Hours of Idleness 137
    and Wordsworth 129–41

Byron, George Gordon, Lord (*cont.*)
and Wordsworth (*cont.*)
  and *The Excursion* 143
  meeting with 141–2
  *and *The Prelude* 138–41, 145, 147–8
  reviews by, actual 135–6
  reviews by, counterfactual 130–1, 137–8, 143

'Camden, Theophilus' 60
'Campbell, J.C.' 66
Campbell, Thomas 306–7
canon 156–7, 300–15
  'British Romanticism' 304–8
  and creative writing 308–13
  formation 301–2
Cao Xueqin 287, 296 n.29
Carlyle, Thomas 313
censorship 60
Chatterton, Thomas ('Thomas Rowley') 81, 82–3, 86–8, 96–7
Cheyne, John 237–8
China 277–97
  cultural influence on Britain 279–80, 283, 289, 292–3
  and English literature 283–93
  literature 281–2, 285–7, 290–1
  politics 283, 286
  religion 290–1
  trade 278–9, 289
  translations (actual and counterfactual) 280–2, 284–6, 289–90
  writings about 287–9
Chinese language 280, 285–7
chinoiserie 279, 282–3, 284–5, 291–2
Christensen, Jerome 17–18
Clare, John 303, 312
Clarke, Hewson 60, 65
class 144, 149 n.16, 305
Cobbett, William 62
Coleridge, Samuel Taylor 144, 147, 209, 218, 223, 281, 300, 303, 305, 308, 310, 311, 312
  'The Aeolian Harp' 291
  Biographia Literaria 140, 288, 291
  *China, visits 290–1
  'Fears in Solitude' 15–16

'Kubla Khan' 287–8, 290–1
Lyrical Ballads, 43, 136, 281–2
'To William Wordsworth' 139
colonialism 55–7, 256–7, 260–1, 267, 305, 306, 307
contingency 1–25, 33–49
  and history 34–6, 46, 234
  and identity 36–8, 44
  and literary criticism 42–4
  and plot 40–1
  of scholarly practice 45
  and speculation 234–5
  and time 33, 34, 36–7
Coudray, Angélique du 184, *185*
counterfactuals, counterfactualism 1–25
  angel 1–5, *3*, 24–5
  downward 23, 255, 258, 268–9
  historiography 9–13, 233–5, 239
  and imagination 5–6, 25, 180–1
  miracle 156, 169, 177
  narratives, compensatory 6–7
  nexus event 5, 7, 156
  plausibility 10–11, 35, 87, 131
  in poetry 205, 211–23
  reasoning and methods 5–9, 13–15, 18
  Romantic 1–25, 33–6, 42, 44, 46, 142, 147, 205, 209, 223
  second- and third-order 7, 10, 21, 156
  upward 23, 255, 261, 271 n.8, 310
  see also contingency; history: counterfactual; speculation
counterfiction 41–2, 252, 253, 264–6, 270, 270 n.2
'Cowley, Charles Augustus' 63, 64
'Cowley, Charlotte' 63–4
Craik, G.L. 67
Cross, John Cartwright, *Black Beard* 252–4, 255, 266, 268, 269–70
Cruikshank, Isaac 178, *179*

daughters 205–6, 211–13
Davie, Donald 312
Davy, Sir Humphry 308
death 87, 97, 155–6, 173
Defoe, Daniel 255–6, 271 n.12

Index

Deleuze, Gilles 108, 111, 121
De Quincey, Thomas 130, 139, 140, 287–8, 289, 292
Dickens, Charles 206, 225 n.4
digressions 145, 146
D'Israeli, Isaac 232, 233–4
dissection 172–3, 183, 184
doubles 8, 111, 112, 123
Douthwaite, Julia V. 159
drama 251, 252–4, 280, 288
drugs 96–7, 278

England 55–68, 256, 293
entailment 2, 3, 7–8, 157, 187
epistemology 33, 34–5, 38–9
epistolary narrative 112, 114
existentialism 313

facts
  and biography 207–9
  and historical fiction 109–10, 115–16
  and historiography 163–4
  and history 52–3, 55, 67–8, 239
  and truth 109–10
fakes/fakery *see* forgery
fathers 205–6, 211–13, 215–19
feminism 107–8, 112, 113, 118–19, 120, 122, 158
Ferguson, Niall 10–11, 35
fiction
  and authenticity 69
  and biography 254
  counterfiction 41–2, 252, 253, 264–6, 270, 270 n.2
  gothic 69, 111, 168–70, 178, 282–3, 305
  historical 68–70, 107–24, 170, 235–7, 254–69
  and historiography 163–4
  and history 54, 68–70, 255
  metafiction 205, 207
  realist 39–40, 41–2, 114
folklore 54, 64, 266
forgery 55, 68, 81–102, 112, 120
  and attribution 86
  and authenticity 81–2
  Chatterton, Thomas 86–8
  and cultural history 82–8

detection/exposure of 83–4, 88, 90, 92, 94–5
  by emendation 89–90
  literary merit of 87–8
  Macpherson, James ('Ossian') 82–8
  and manuscripts 91–2
  power of 92–3
  techniques 90, 91–2
  Williams, Edward 88–95
forgetting 123
form 137, 217, 284–5, 302–3, 310–12
  poetic 83–4, 91, 137, 219–20
fragments 219–23
Fuseli, Henry 178–80, *180*

Gaelic language 83, 84
Gallagher, Catherine 5–6, 10, 13, 259, 265, 274 n.32
Galperin, William 16, 40, 41
Galt, John, *The Bachelor's Wife* 232–3, 239–43
gaps 204, 205, 215
gender
  and historiography 63–4, 69–70
  and history 63–4, 177
  and midwifery 178, *179*
  in pirate literature 267–9
  and reading 57, 63–4
  roles 122, 221, 240–1, 242
genre 233, 239–43, 254–5
ghosts 96–7, 162, 202–3, 206–7
Godwin, William 107, 124 n.3, 155–6, 159, 160, 171, 205, 211
  An Enquiry concerning Political Justice 164
  History of the Commonwealth of England 62
  Memoirs of the Author of A Vindication of the Rights of Woman 158, 175, 189 n.15
  'Of Choice in Reading' 119
  'Of History and Romance' 12, 68, 108–10, 117, 119, 163–4
  St Leon 108, 164, 165, 181
  Things as They Are; or, The Adventures of Caleb Williams 102 n.55, 157, 181
  Thoughts on Man, 110

Goldsmith, Oliver 61, 67, 284
gothic 69, 111, 168–70, 178, 282–3, 305
Great Britain
  and China 279–80, 283, 287, 289–93
  historiography 55–68
  imperialism 256–7, 260–1
  national identity 55–7, 256, 293
Guattari, Félix 111

Harman, Graham 42–3
Hawthorne, Nathaniel 13–14, 21
Hazlitt, William 243, 310
Hemans, Felicia 70, 300, 307, 308
historical fiction 68–70, 107–24, 170, 235–7
historicism 1–2, 4, 17, 88, 92, 163–4, 313
  New 9, 11–13, 14–15, 156–7, 303, 305, 309
historiography 2–5, *3*, 55–68, 163–4
  authenticity of 53–5
  counterfactual 9–11, 233–5, 239
  and gender 63–4, 69–70
  modern 54–5, 56, 58–9, 68
  and publishing industry 57–8
  and religion 61–2
history
  allohistory 5, 264
  alternate 5, 13, 14, 16, 20, 108, 236, 241, 247
  authenticity of 53–4, 68
  and contingency 34–6, 46, 234
  counterfactual
    affordances of 5, 35
    in criticism 13, 44–6
    and feminism 107–8
    and forgery 82–9
    and historical fiction 115–16
    literary 89, 252
    and Napoleonic wars 134, 148 n.1
  cultural 82–8, 129–30
  and facts 52–3, 55, 67–8, 239
  and fiction 54, 68–70, 107–24, 255
  and folklore/myth 54, 64
  and gender 63–4, 177
  literary 80–1, 89

  and memory 170–1
  modern 52–74
    definition 53–4
    and fiction 68–70
    and national identity 55–7
    and publishing 57–67
    unmodern 54–5
  pre-history 64
  readers of 56, 57, 63–4
  and truth 4–5, 164
Hogg, James 247, 308
Hook, Theodore 246–7
Huang Yadong ('Whang Atong') 286
Hughes, Ted 309
Hume, David 56–9, 60
Hume-Smollett, *History of England* 59–61, 65
Hunt, Leigh, 243, 288, 293
hypothesis 33, 41, 129–30, 144–5, 205

identity
  and authorship 159–60
  of characters 115–18
  and contingency 36–8, 44
  of literary texts 42
  and metonymy 211
  national
    British 256, 293
    and historiography 55–7
    Irish 165–7, 168, 170, 185–6
    Welsh 91, 92
  personal 68, 116
ideology 12–13, 17–18, 61–2, 110–11, 300, 302–3
illustration 58, 59, 62
imagination 5–6, 7–8, 10, 109, 265
imitation 218
imperialism 55–7, 256–7, 260–1, 267, 305, 306, 307
incest 212, 214–15
incomplete works 135, 145–7, 158
'incompossibles' 108–10
inconclusiveness 145–7, 158
Ireland 165–78, 183–7
Ireland, W.H. 55
Irish literature 84, 170, 171, 305–6, 307

Index

Jeffrey, Francis 143
'Johnson, Captain Charles', *A General History of [...] the most Notorious Pyrates* 254–69
Johnson, Charles 253
Jones, Owen 90
Jones, Sir William 285, 290, 292, 296 n.27
*Chinese translations 286–7

Kearsley, George 60
Keats, John 6, 14, 130, 132, 143–4, 288, 289, 310, 313
Kelly, John 61
King, George 168
King, Margaret (Lady Mount Cashell) 162, 165, 168, 177, 182
Kleist, Heinrich von 234–5

Lamb, Charles 130, 243, 289
  'A Dissertation upon Roast Pig' 287–8
  'Old China' 287–8, 292
Landor, Walter Savage 247, 288
Lebow, Richard Ned 10–11
Lee, Sophia, *The Recess* 107–26
  and 'facts' 115–16
  feminism 118–19
  narratology 108, 112, 113–14, 121–2
  and paradox 108–9
  plot 112–13, 114, 115–17
  and romance 107–10
Leland, Thomas 69, 74 n.41
Levine, Caroline 38–9
Lewis, Matthew, *The Bonze* 285
linearity 46, 109, 113–14, 121–3
'Lloyd, Thomas Augustus' 60, 62
Lockman, John 61

Macartney, George 287, 290, 291, 293
Macaulay, Catharine 63
Macaulay, Thomas 135
Macherey, Pierre 302–3
Macpherson, James ('Ossian') 55, 81, 82–8
Malham, John 65

Manning, Thomas 289
manuscripts 79–80, 86, 89–90, 91–2, 209, 213–14
maps 178
marketplace, literary 233, 235, 240, 283
marriage 208
materiality 43–4, 86–7
McGann, Jerome J. 302–3, 310–11
memory 123, 170–1
men
  fathers 205–6, 211–13, 215–19
  as midwives 172, 178, *179*, 182–3
  as readers 57
metafiction 205, 207
metonymy 211
midwifery 171–2, *179*, 182–3, 184, *185*, 186
Miller, Andrew 41–2
miscellanies 239–43
Mitchell, George Berkeley 60
Mitford, Mary Russell, *Our Village* 232–3, 243–6
modernity 53, 67–8, 69
monsters 160, 183
Moore, Thomas 305–6, 307
  *Lady Wang 285
'Morganwg, Iolo' *see* Williams, Edward
Morson, Gary Saul 8–9
mothers 160, 187–8
  childbirth 155–6, 160–1, 171–2, 184, *185*
  pregnancy *174*, 183, 184
'Mountague, William Henry' 62–3
Mount Cashell, Lady (Margaret King) *see* King, Margaret
multiverses 163, 165
mutability 36–7
myth 54, 64, 266

narratives, compensatory 6–7, 158, 161
narratology 108, 113–14, 121–2, 164, 170, 183–4
nationalism 92, 94
national literature 60, 169–70, 181
Nogaret, François-Félix 159
novels *see* fiction

objects 34–5, 42, 44, 311–12
obstetrics 155–6, 171–2, 182–3, 184, 186
ontology, object-oriented 42, 44
optative mode 16, 33, 41–2
oral literature 84
oratory 207, 220
ordinary, the 40–1, 243–8
Orientalism 277, 279, 285, 294, 306
'Ossian' *see* Macpherson, James
Owenson, Sydney (Lady Morgan) 169, 170, 306, 308

paradox 108–9, 116–17, 156, 237–8, 240, 243
parody 8–9
pastiche 61, 62, 64
perception 34, 39–40, 42–4, 114–15
Percy, Thomas 280–2, 283, 284, 292
periodisation, literary 45
Pfau, Thomas 15, 34–5
Phillips, Mark Salber 6–7
philosophy
   Confucianism 280, 282, 283, 286, 290–1
   existentialism 313
   object-oriented 34, 42, 44
Piozzi, Hester 62
piracy (in literature) 251–74
   Black Beard (Cross) 252–4, 255, 266, 268, 269–70
   counterfiction 264–6
   drama 251, 252–4
   A General History of [...] the most Notorious Pyrates ('Johnson') 254–69
   historical fiction 254–69
   legacy 269–70
   and women 267–9
plagiarism 61, 62, 64–5
plausibility 10–11, 87, 131
plot 40–1, 111, 114, 115, 120
poetic diction 310–12
poetry 309
   allegory 209–10, 216, 220
   autobiographical 140, 141, 209
   bardic 90–1
   biographical 220
   Chinese 287

   as counterfactual mode 205, 211–23
   forged *see* Chatterton, Thomas; Macpherson, James; Williams, Edward
   form 83–4, 91, 137, 219–20
   and landscape 85–6
   Movement poets 312
   and politics 132–5, 137–8
   religious 217–19
   unfinished 145–7
Poignand, Dr Louis 155–6, 160–1
politics
   authoritarian 283, 286
   democratic 283
   and poetry 132–5, 137–8
   radical 89, 259, 260, 264, 273 n.30, 291
   and religion 283
   republican 306–7
   speculation 236
Porter, Jane 69–70
possibilities 38, 40–1, 95, 108–10, 119–20, 156
postmodernism 300, 303
pregnancy *174*, 183, 184
printing 65, 67
prophecy 16–17, 237–9
psychogeography 178
publication 90, 131–6
   serial 56, 58, 61–5, 66–7
   subscription 64, 65
   see also editions; texts, literary
publishing industry 57–67

Radcliffe, Ann, *The Cantonese* 285
Rapin de Thoyras, Paul de 56, 61
Rapin-Tindal, *Histoire d'Angleterre* 56, 61
readers/reading 147, 243, 244, 245–6, 313–14
   active 156
   and gender 57, 63–4
   of historical novels 68–70
   of history 56, 57, 63–4
   mimetic 113, 119
realism 39–40, 41–2, 81, 113, 114, 116–17, 119
reality 39–40, 109

Index

reanimation 157–62, 178, 237–8
Reeve, Clara 68, 69
religion 60, 61–2, 98 n.20, 110, 208, 217–19, 283, 285
   Chinese 280, 290–1
   dissenting 89, 91, 291
Robinson, Mary 308, 312
Rogers, Samuel 141, 301
romance 64, 68–70, 108–9, 163–4, 254–5, 281–2
'Rowley, Thomas' see Chatterton, Thomas
'Russell, William Augustus' 64

Saint-Amour, Paul 45
satire 237–9
Scotland 83, 85–6
Scottish literature 82–8
Scott, Sir Walter 14, 70, 93, 170, 232, 235–7, 254, 267, 268, 300
sensibility 308, 310
serial publication 56, 58, 64–5, 66–7
series (Deleuzian) 109, 113–14, 121–3
sex 210, 212, 214–15, 267–8, 269
Shelley, Mary Wollstonecraft 156, 162, 308, 312
   Frankenstein 37–8, 43, 156, 157, 159, 160, 164, 177, 178, 205, 308
   The Last Man 70, 238
   Perkin Warbeck 70
   Valperga 70, 107, 110
Shelley, Percy Bysshe 36–7, 38, 39, 130, 144, 288, 289, 290, 308
sideshadowing 8–9, 15, 156
simulacra 109, 111–12
slavery 260, 263, 306–7
Smith, Charlotte 12, 308, 312
Smollett, Tobias 58, 59, 65
   see also Hume-Smollett
sons 215–19
Southey, Robert 62, 288–9
   Tieh-chung-u the Destroyer 290
speculation 6, 15–16, 33, 41–2, 129, 205, 232–49
   and contingency 234–5
   economic 233, 235
   and genre 239–43

   historiographic 234
   prophetic 237–9
   quasi-documentary 243–8
   and storytelling 236–7
'Spencer, George William' 64
Squire, J.C. 10, 232
Stevenson, Robert Louis 266–7, 269
storytelling 236–7
structure, literary 111, 114, 115, 120
subjectivity 57, 68, 69, 93, 115
sublime 36
suicide 87, 97, 161
surrogacy 211–13
'Sydney, Temple' 64

Tew, Captain Thomas 259, 261–3, 272 n.20, 273 n.21
texts 38, 42, 43–4, 84
   see also editions; forgery; manuscripts
Thelwall, Algernon Sydney 208, 216–19, 222
Thelwall, Cecil Boyle (Henrietta Cecil Boyle) 206, 207–8, 216, 222–3, 225 n.4
   and John Thelwall's writings 210, 211, 212–13, 214–15
   writings 203, 209, 219–21
Thelwall, John 144, 202–29
   'adoption' 212, 213
   allegory 209–10
   autobiographical writing 221–2
   biography 203–9
   'Cupid's Disguise' 213
   The Daughter of Adoption 211–13
   Derby manuscript 209, 213–17, 219–23, 226 n.17
   'The Oak and the Woodbine' 210
   Pandolia fragments 219–23
   Poems, Chiefly Written in Retirement 210, 227 n.33
   religious poems, attributed 217–19
   'A Remembrance' 215–17
   A Speech in Rhyme 220–1
   'Thoughts and Remembrances' 212–13, 214–15
   'The Woodbine' 210
Thelwall, Maria 210–12

Thelwall, Susannah (Susan/'Stella')
  207, 208, 214, 222
time 9, 36–7, 245–6
  contingent 33, 34
  linear 46, 109, 113–14, 121–3
  present 38, 93, 111
  time travel 237–9
Tindal, Nicholas 56, 61
  see also Rapin-Tindal
Tomlins, F.G. 66–7
transcendence 36, 38
translation 88, 281, 282, 284, 286–7
travel literature 185, 245
truth 40, 95, 164, 214–17
  post-truth 18, 95

uchronia 5
uncertainty 33
unreliability 204, 209

van Riemsdyk, Jan 173, *174*
ventriloquism 217–19, 220
visual art 59, 178–80

Wales 89–90, 91, 92
Walford Davies, Damian 227 n.33, 235, 260, 302
Walpole, Horace 69, 282–3, 292
  *The House of Zamti 284–5
Warton, Thomas 87–8
Watkins, John 60
Welsh literature 79–80, 82, 88–95
Wesley, John 61–2
Whitman, Walt 139–40, 150 n.28
Wilde, Oscar 34
Williams, Edward ('Iolo Morganwg') 81, 82, 88–97
Williams, Griffith John 89, 94
Wollstonecraft, Mary 155–96, 211
  and childbirth 171–2
  death 155–6, 157
  *L'Estrange 165–88, *166*
  influences on 178–80
  and Irish Rebellion 165–71, 175–7
  and obstetrics 171–5
  plot 181–8
  national identity 165–7, 168
  *reanimation 155–6, 157–62
  A Vindication of the Rights of Men 158
  A Vindication of the Rights of Woman 158, 172
  The Wrongs of Woman; or, Maria 113, 157, 158
women
  authors 63–4, 69–70, 305
  bodies of 172–3
  daughters 205–6, 211–13
  and historiography 63–4
  idealised 240–1, 242
  as midwives 172
  in pirate literature 267–9
  and scholarship 63–4, 240–2
  see also mothers; daughters
Wordsworth, William 129–47, 288, 305, 308, 310–11, 312
  and Byron 130–1, 138–42, 145, 147–8
  The Excursion 138, 140, 143, 144, 149 n.15
  Lyrical Ballads, 43, 136, 281–2
  Lines Addressed to a Noble Lord 142–3
  Poems, in Two Volumes 135–6
  The Prelude 130–48
    *Byron, influence on 138–41, 145, 147–8
    *Byron, reviewed by 130–1, 137–8
    composition 133–4
    and French Revolution 132–3
    inconclusiveness 145–7
    influence of 139–40
    publication 131–6
  The Recluse 129, 132

Yearsley, Ann 311, 312

Milton Keynes UK
Ingram Content Group UK Ltd.
UKHW021338190624
444448UK00016B/61